Handbook of
Biblical Criticism

Richard N. Soulen
R. Kendall Soulen

James Clarke & Co., Ltd
Cambridge

Published by
James Clarke Co., Ltd
P.O. Box 60
Cambridge
CB1 2NT
England

e-mail: **publishing@jamesclarke.co.uk**
website: **http://www.jamesclarke.co.uk**

ISBN 0 227 17038 5 hardback
ISBN 0 227 17037 7 paperback

British Library Cataloguing in Publication Data:
A catalogue record is available from the British Library.

First published 1977 by The Lutterworth Press
Reprinted 2002

To Margaret Ann and Allison

PREFACE TO THE
THIRD EDITION

The invitation from Westminster John Knox Press to prepare a third edition of the *Handbook* was a welcome surprise. For one thing, the second edition was in sore need of a thorough update after twenty years of use. More important for us, the invitation permitted the *Handbook* to become the joint project of a biblical scholar and a theologian (who also happen to be father and son). Richard N. Soulen is a New Testament scholar with a passionate interest in theology, and R. Kendall Soulen is a systematic theologian with a passionate interest in the Bible. Given the tumultuous scene of biblical scholarship today, we think the combination is a good one. When the second edition was prepared, modern biblical criticism still enjoyed a near monopoly of critical attention, and it was still possible to regard biblical studies as a field of mostly complementary and interrelated approaches to the biblical text. More recently, modern biblical criticism has had to make room for a variety of postmodern and postcritical perspectives, not to mention a renewed interest in precritical approaches to the Bible. The new situation, with its plurality of methods and interpretive communities, makes it more important than ever to understand the various approaches to the Bible in light of their methodological, philosophical, and theological presuppositions. We have written the third edition of the *Handbook* with that imperative in mind. Moreover, and without intruding on a fair representation of each of the definitions here given, we have attempted to suggest paths through the thicket of conflicting interpretations that are supportive of the Bible as an authority and source of life for the community of faith. In this regard, we are happy to acknowledge our own status as interest-filled interpreters of the current scene of biblical scholarship.

Acknowledgments are due and here gratefully given to the many whose assistance has made this *Handbook* possible. We are especially grateful to those persons who magnanimously laid aside their own work to correct drafts of articles and to offer suggestions (often quite extensive and detailed) about various portions of the manuscript: Stephen L. Cook, David Sandmel, Peter Pettit, Sharon Ringe, David Hopkins, Denise Dombkowski Hopkins, Bruce Birch, and Sibley Towner. In addition, a special word of thanks is due to Beth Ward, who devoted many hours of careful attention to proofreading the mansucript and to doing research and writing for several entries. We are also indebted to Michael Jones, who graciously consented to review several entries and to do research and writing for the entry on deconstruction. Finally, we wish to express our gratitude to Carey C. Newman of Westminster John Knox Press for suggesting the project to us, and to Dan Braden for seeing the project through to its completion. It has been a cherished collaboration. Needless to say, however much we are indebted to these people, we alone are responsible for any errors of fact or judgment in the articles themselves or in their selection.

PREFACE TO THE
SECOND EDITION

In the five brief intervening years since the first publication of the *Handbook,* the field of biblical criticism has undergone a change so radical as to be described by one noted New Testament scholar as nothing less than a second revolution, analogous to the introduction of the historical-critical method into biblical studies two centuries ago. This revolution, says J. D. Crossan, has transformed biblical studies from a single discipline to a field of disciplines, each with its own theoretical assumptions and methods so diverse and complex (even contradictory) that no one practitioner of biblical criticism can master them all.

This edition of the *Handbook* tries to bring the student up to date with these new developments. It does so by concentrating on fields of study rather than on a plethora of technical terms within these larger areas. Over forty new articles have been added, including Canonical Criticism, Semiology, Structure, Sociological Interpretation, Reception Theory, Rhetorical Analysis, Theological Interpretation, Biblical Theology (Movement), Linguistics, Topos, and so forth. Another forty have been either revised or expanded. Many readers have asked for suggested readings to augment definitions, so bibliographical data is now a part of all major articles. This should not only stimulate further research but also serve to call attention to glossaries and lexica dealing with the specialized terms that could not be included in this work.

These remarks would be incomplete without a word of thanks to the many whose assistance in so many diverse ways has made a revised edition possible. Above all, to Dr. Richard A. Ray, Director of John Knox Press, for his wise counsel and friendship over the years and for his kind support of this project from its inception, I wish to express my deep appreciation. Gratitude is also to be expressed to the Deutscher Akademischer Austauschdienst of the Federal Republic of Germany, to the Association of Theological Schools in the United States and Canada, the Andrew W. Mellon Foundation, and the Arthur Vining

Davis Foundation, whose research grants enabled me to spend the academic year, 1977–1978, on sabbatical leave at the University of Heidelberg, where work on this and other projects was carried out. The cordiality of the theological faculty there was beyond all expectation, and I remain indebted to them for their help in academic as well as human concerns. I wish especially to thank Dr. Christoph Burchard, Dr. Hartwig Thyen, Dr. Lothar Steiger, and Dr. Ekkardt Stegemann for their hospitality, as well as members of the Doktoranden-Kolloquim for inclusion into that spirited group. Dr. Wolfgang Stegemann, pastor of the Evangelische Landeskirche in Nussloch, Dr. Paul Phillippi of the theological faculty and his wife, and Frau Elka Kruger, Assistant Librarian in the Theologisches Seminar, through their generous self-giving, made the stay in Germany an exceedingly happy as well as rewarding year.

Suggestions for the revision have come from so many sources that I cannot begin to list names. Hopefully colleagues and students alike will see the fruit of their advice, although, regretfully, not every recommendation could be acted upon.

I cannot fail to express appreciation to the Spence Library staff once again, especially Mrs. Martha Aycock, Research Librarian, and her able assistant, Ms. Cecelia Clark. Mrs. Portia Williamson, M.Div. candidate at the School of Theology of Virginia Union University, and Ms. Virginia Glen-Calvert assisted in various stages of research and are also due my thanks, as is David Hagstrom, Th.D. candidate at Union Theological Seminary in Va., who graciously consented to write the article on Canonical Criticism, having just completed a Master's thesis on the subject, and Mrs. Louise English, who turns questionable manuscript into beautiful typescript with amazing dexterity. And of course the initial dedication is now more in order than ever before.

CONTENTS

Introduction   xi

Handbook of Technical Terms with Names,
    Tools, and Interpretive Approaches   1

Abbreviations in Textual Criticism
    (Plus Common Latin Words and Phrases)   211

Abbreviations of Selected Works   215

Major Reference Works Consulted   231

Diagram of Biblical Interpretation   235

INTRODUCTION

This book is for the beginning and intermediate student in the critical study of the Bible. It is not for advanced students in the field—though perhaps it is for scholars of religion whose specialty lies elsewhere, as well as for pastors and interested laypersons. The volume is designed to aid the student in two ways. First, it can be used as a *dictionary*, to be called on whenever a name, a term, or an abbreviation is met for the first time unidentified, unexplained, or without a clarifying illustration, or when its meaning is simply forgotten. Second, it can be used as a *guide* to gain an initial overview and orientation in the field of biblical criticism as a whole. By reading the major entries on Biblical Criticism, Hermeneutics, and Theological Interpretation and by making use of the Diagram of Biblical Interpretation at the back of the book, the reader can gain a sense for the history and development of modern biblical criticism and its relationship to pre- and postcritical forms of interpretation. The simple system of cross references using SMALL CAPITALS alerts the reader to terms that are discussed in greater depth elsewhere so that the reader can seek further information on a given topic according to interest or need.

The entries fall into the following general categories:

1. *Overviews:* Major entries on Biblical Criticism, Hermeneutics, and Theological Interpretation, plus the Diagram of Biblical Interpretation at the back of the book, provide overviews that assist the student in gaining a sense of "the forest" of biblical criticism, apart from which they are likely to soon feel hopelessly lost in "the trees." By moving back and forth between forest and trees, the student can begin to gain familiarity with the history and terrain of contemporary biblical studies.
2. *Methodologies and Interpretive Approaches:* Textual Criticism, Historical Criticism, Literary Criticism, Form Criticism, Tradition Criticism, Redaction Criticism, Rhetorical Criticism, Structuralism, Postcritical Biblical Interpretation, Afrocentric Biblical Interpretation, Ideological Criticism, Reader-Response Criticism,

Feminist Biblical Interpretation, Advocacy Criticism, and others. Along with the overviews listed previously, these articles on methodologies provide an organizing framework for the work as a whole and give it the stamp of a handbook.

3. *Technical Terms and Phrases* associated with the above methodologies. The selection of terms is of course incomplete. The *Handbook* focuses on terms of interest and importance to the beginning student and on terms most likely in need of clarification.

4. *Theological Terms.* A few terms not strictly within the terminology of biblical criticism are nevertheless so closely connected with it that their absence would be missed, for example, apocalyptic, eschatology, theophany, Tetragrammaton, *Historie/Geschichte*, and so on.

5. *Names.* Those listed are limited to scholars now deceased whose insights and labor are most frequently cited as constituting lasting contributions to the field of biblical criticism. For further information and for names not listed, the reader is directed to John H. Hayes (ed.), *Dictionary of Biblical Interpretation* (Nashville: Abingdon Press, 1999). The *DBI* is the most comprehensive biographical reference work in the field. Other major reference works are cited at the end of this volume.

6. *Research Tools and Texts.* The *Handbook* provides basic information and bibliographical references for a variety of research tools, primarily for study in English but also for beginning students in Hebrew and Greek. Consult the entries on Bibliography and Exegesis, and also Analytical Lexica, Commentary, Concordance, Synopsis, and so on.

7. *English Translations of the Bible.* A number of English translations and paraphrases of the Bible are discussed in order to aid the student in the selection of an appropriate one (or ones) for study purposes. These include the (New) King James Version, Revised Version, (New) American Standard Version, (New) Revised Standard Version, New English Bible/Revised English Bible, Today's English Version, New International Version, New American Bible, (New) Jerusalem Bible, Living Bible, and so on.

8. *Abbreviations.* Two lists are found at the end of this *Handbook:* (a) Latin abbreviations (and phrases) basic to textual criticism yet rarely translated as they appear in critical texts of the Old and New Testament and in such volumes as the *Synopsis Quattuor Evangeliorum.* (b) Abbreviations of periodicals, reference works, Bibles, and biblical books, often unidentified, as for example in periodical literature. Both lists of abbreviations, however, are of necessity limited. An exhaustive listing may be found in the *DBI* (see no. 5 above) and in *The SBL Handbook of Style: For Ancient Near Eastern, Biblical, and Early Christian Studies* (Peabody, Mass.: Hendrickson Publishers, 1999).

Finally, we have chosen to retain a few terms from previous editions of the *Handbook* that were once current but are now largely out of date (e.g., Radical Criticism), both because the terms still populate the pages of important works of years past, waiting to perplex the beginning student, and because their inclusion helps to document the changing landscape of biblical studies. As for the definitions themselves, our intent throughout has been to present complex issues as clearly and succinctly as possible without sacrificing accuracy and to provide suggestions for further study. The *Handbook* is a first reference not a final one.

The authors and publisher welcome suggestions and corrections from teachers and students that may be incorporated in any future editions of the *Handbook*.

Handbook of Technical Terms with Names, Tools, and Interpretive Approaches

Acrostic A series of lines or verses whose initial, final, or other identifiable letters form a word, a phrase, the initial letters of a phrase, or the alphabet. Acrostics in the Hebrew OT include in whole or part Pss 2; 9–10; 25; 34; 37; 111; 112; 119; 145; Prov 31:10–31 and Nah 1:2–10. In some instances the acrostic is formed on every other line; in other instances more than one line opens with the same letter; e.g., Ps 119 is formed of 176 lines, eight lines for each of the twenty-two letters of the alphabet. Unfortunately, acrostics are inevitably lost in translation.

Advocacy Criticism is an umbrella term used to refer to those approaches that are centrally concerned with interpreting scripture in light of the history, contemporary circumstances, and aspirations of a particular historically oppressed group, such as AFROCENTRIC, FEMINIST, MUJERISTA, POSTCOLONIAL, and WOMANIST BIBLICAL INTERPRETATION. Generally speaking, these approaches hold in common the view that all interpretation is conditioned by the social location of the interpreter and that the purpose of interpretation is to expose oppressive tendencies in the Bible and the history of its interpretation and, so far as this is deemed possible, to use the Bible as a resource to confront and change current structures of oppression, whether social, political, religious, or academic. Practitioners of advocacy criticism regard these approaches as less, not more, vulnerable to ideological distortion than other approaches because they explicitly identify their theoretical presuppositions and cultural interests and do not claim to provide a value-free, positivistic knowledge.

Afrocentric Biblical Interpretation, as a hermeneutical perspective, refers to an approach to scripture that seeks to recover the rightful place of Africa, its peoples, and its cultures within the biblical tradition itself, and to draw attention to and correct misrepresentations of that place that have accrued over the centuries in Western exegetical traditions. The term *Afrocentricity*, attributed to M. K. Asante (1987), attempts to encapsulate this intention.

The practitioners of Afrocentric biblical interpretation contend that European-dominated exegetical and representational traditions have slowly but decisively painted Africa and its inhabitants out of the biblical picture, from its maps to its murals to its movies. Afrocentric biblical interpretation has therefore called for a "corrective HISTORIOGRAPHY," one that restores to Africa in general and Black people in particular the significant roles they play in biblical history. For example, attention is drawn to the fact that Ethiopia is mentioned over forty times and Egypt over one hundred times in the OLD TESTAMENT alone; that color prejudice is absent from scripture—indeed, that the beloved of the Song of Songs is "black and beautiful" (1:5); and that if race is to be applied to the populations of the ancient Near East then, in modern parlance, they should be termed *Afro-Asiatic.* (It is noted that no less a personage than Moses is depicted as married to a Cushite [Num 12:1].) Through such observations as these Afrocentric biblical interpretation seeks to provide a contribution to mainstream biblical interpretation and not just an ethnocentric perspective. See M. K. Asante, *The Afrocentric Idea* (Philadelphia: Temple University Press, 1987); D. T. Adamo, *Africa and the Africans in the Old Testament* (San Francisco: International Scholars Publication, 1998). For biblical interpretation in the African American tradition, see C. H. Felder, ed., *Stony the Road We Trod: African American Biblical Interpretation* (Minneapolis: Fortress Press, 1991); Vincent L. Wimbush, ed., *African Americans and the Bible: Sacred Texts and Social Textures* (New York: Continuum, 2000).

Agrapha (sg.: agraphon) is a Greek term meaning literally "unwritten (SAYINGS)" and was first employed by the German scholar J. G. Koerner in 1776 to designate sayings attributed to Jesus but not found in the canonical GOSPELS. The agrapha are also occasionally referred to as the "unknown" or "lost" sayings of Jesus. Since it is known that Jesus' teachings were first passed down orally, it is presumed that certain of these escaped the knowledge of the EVANGELISTS and were subsequently lost except as they are alluded to or preserved by early Christian writers, e.g., by Paul in Rom 14:14. In 1889, Alfred (not Arnold) Resch claimed to have recovered a large number of these from Paul's writings (such as 1 Cor 2:9: "'What no eye has seen, nor ear heard, nor the

human heart conceived, what God has prepared for those who love him,'" NRSV), which purportedly derived from a precanonical Gospel (but cf. Isa 64:4). The second, 1906 edition of his work "used the term to refer to extracanonical scriptural fragments whether of the OT or NT" (*ABD*).

Current scholarship rejects Resch's loose definition and (when used) limits the term *agrapha* to sayings (not allusions) explicitly attributed to Jesus. Sayings with some possible claim to authenticity that are not in the Gospels can be found in (a) the NT (Acts 20:35 and 1 Thess 4:16f.); (b) ancient MSS of the NT (such as the addition to Luke 10:16 in Codex Koridethi or the substitute reading of CODEX BEZAE at Luke 6:5: "Man, if indeed you know what you are doing, you are blessed; but if you do not know, you are cursed and a transgressor of the LAW"); (c) the church fathers (such as Justin Martyr, Clement of Alexandria, ORIGEN, etc., who in the main do not record ORAL TRADITION but passages from noncanonical gospels); (d) the GOSPEL OF THOMAS, some of whose 114 sayings are also found in *Oxyrhynchus Papyrus* 654; and (e) *Oxyrhynchus Papyrus* 1, 655, and 840.

Recent studies dedicated to the quest of the historical Jesus have elevated noncanonical sayings of Jesus to new prominence, claiming for them an authenticity equal or superior to those of the Gospels. The claim is disputed. See William D. Stroker, *Extracanonical Sayings of Jesus: Texts, Translations and Notes* (Atlanta: Scholars Press, 1988); also R. W. Funk and R. W. Hoover, *The Five Gospels: The Search for the Authentic Words of Jesus* (New York: Macmillan, 1993).

Additional sayings attributed to Jesus can be found in the TALMUD (ʿ*Abodah Zarah* 16b 17a and *Šabbat* 116 a, b) and in Mohammedan writings and inscriptions. These sayings are generally deemed spurious. (See Joachim Jeremias, *The Unknown Sayings of Jesus* [London: SPCK, 1958].)

Aktionsart   (Ger: type or kind of action) is a German technical term employed by grammarians to characterize an aspect of Greek verbs and participles not present in like manner in English (or German), viz., the kind of action involved in the verb. Greek verbs have two kinds of action: punctiliar and linear (Moulton). Whereas in English the primary task of the verb is to tell the time of an action or event (past, present, or future), in Greek the *kind* of action (*aktionsart*), whether extended (linear) or momentary (punctiliar) in time, is primary. Although exceptions to this generalization are numerous, in the main the present stem of a Greek verb (from which the imperfect tense is formed) denotes an action or an event continuous in time and can be translated into English only with auxiliary words, e.g., "I am praying" (or "I was praying"). The aorist stem (from which the future, perfect, and pluperfect tenses are also formed) denotes an action or an event momentary (punctiliar) in time, though its effects may still continue (perfect) or have continued for some time in the past (pluperfect), e.g., "I prayed." The "interpretation of many NT passages depends not a little" on the *aktionsart* of the verb (C. F. D. Moule).

Aland, Kurt   (1915–1994). Born and educated in Berlin, Aland became a student of the famed church historian and NT textual critic, Hans Lietzmann, under whose tutelage he began a lifelong passion for the Greek text of the NT. A member of the Confessing Church during the Nazi period and a declared public enemy of the German Democratic Republic following the war, Aland escaped East Berlin in 1958, finding an appointment in church history and TEXTUAL CRITICISM on the theological faculty at Münster, West Germany, in 1959. At Münster, where he spent the rest of his life, he founded the Institute for NT Textual Criticism. He became the coeditor and later editor of Erwin and EBERHARD NESTLE'S *Novum Testamentum graece*, from the 22nd edition through the 27th. In the 1960s he joined the editorial committee of the *Greek New Testament*, sponsored by the American Bible Society. He avidly collected photographs of all the manuscripts of the NT produced in the first millennium and began their collocation for the *Editio Critica Maior*, which is still being published. See CRITICAL APPARATUS, CRITICAL TEXT.

Albright, William Foxwell   (1891–1971). Born in Coquimbo, Chile, the son of Methodist missionaries, Albright received his Ph.D. in Semitic Studies at Johns Hopkins University in 1916. He was first a research associate and then director of the American Schools of Oriental Research in Jerusalem (1920–29 and 1933–36), becoming W. W. Spence Professor of Semitic Languages at Johns Hopkins in 1929. An outstanding archaeologist and teacher, Albright was the leading OT scholar in the U.S. from 1930 to 1950 and the recipient of six honorary degrees from foreign universities, and twenty from institutions in the U.S.

Alexandria, School of   The School of Alexandria and the School of Antioch have found their way into the parlance of contemporary biblical interpretation as useful but potentially misleading metaphors for two contrasting approaches to the interpretation of scripture. These two approaches are commonly represented as the allegorical (Alexandrian) and the literal (Antiochene), the former emphasizing the deeper, spiritual sense of scripture, the latter emphasizing its literal or historical sense. Both representations of the two schools have some basis in history. As the two largest urban centers in 3rd-cent. Eastern Christendom, Alexandria in Egypt and Antioch in Syria came naturally to be the home of "schools" of biblical interpretation and theology. The Alexandrian School came into prominence in the early 3rd cent. through the work of Clement of Alexandria and ORIGEN, who made robust use of allegorical interpretation especially in their approach to the OT. The founding of the School of Antioch in the late 3rd cent. is traditionally though perhaps somewhat arbitrarily attributed to Lucian, who is better known for the RECENSION of the SEPTUAGINT that bears his name. The most prominent member of this school was Theodore of Mopsuestia (ca. 350–428), whose concern to defend the distinctiveness of the NT, as well as the plain sense of the OT, led him to reject the unrestricted application of allegorical interpretation to the OT in favor of a more limited approach that emphasized typological resemblance between certain OT events and their NT counterparts. Despite their genuine differences, the two schools probably have more in common with each other than either does with modern HISTORICAL CRITICISM, as indicated, for example, by their common commitment to the hermeneutical role of the RULE OF FAITH. For both schools, the literal and spiritual senses of scripture work together to form interlocking parts of a theologically interested and christologically centered approach to the canon. See Frances M. Young, *Biblical Exegesis and the Formation of Christian Culture* (Cambridge: Cambridge University Press, 1997).

Alexandrian Text   In NT TEXTUAL CRITICISM, Alexandrian text is one of the geographical place names given to MSS of the NT bearing the same textual characteristics and thought to come from a common ancestor originating in Alexandria, Egypt. It was also called the "Egyptian text" or, more commonly and preferably perhaps, the "Neutral Text" by F. J. A. HORT (1882) on the theory that it was an essentially pure representative of the NT autographs. The principal witness to the Neutral text is the 4th-cent. MS CODEX VATICANUS (B), whence the more recent designation "Beta." According to E. J. Epp (*JBL*, 93 [September 1974]: 386–414), the Neutral text type is one of only two distinct early text types (with the Western) and can be traced from (i.e., identified with) P[75], P[23], P[20], P[50], etc., to Codex B and to more recent witnesses,

such as Codex L (8th cent.), MSS 33 (9th cent.), 1739 (10th cent.), and 579 (13th cent.). Whether the Alexandrian text is closer to the original than the Western is still a matter of dispute. See BYZANTINE TEXT; WESTERN TEXT.

Allegory   (Gk: "saying something other than one seems to say"). In LITERARY CRITICISM the term *allegory* is used to denote both (1) an allegorical representation and (2) an allegorical interpretation. (1) By the former is meant the presentation of spiritual or moral truths in the guise of concrete images and events. A classic example is John Bunyan's *The Pilgrim's Progress*, which is a sustained allegory based on a Puritan understanding of sin and salvation. Here the series of characterizations and actions are ultimately governed not by the NARRATIVE's own surface logic but by the pattern of religious truths beyond the work that the narrative is made to illustrate. (2) An allegorical interpretation assumes that the text to be interpreted says or intends to say something more than and other than what its literal wording suggests—that it contains hidden within it a deeper, mystical sense not directly disclosed in the words themselves (cf. GUNKEL, *RGG*[1]). (*Note:* Just as the noun has both these meanings, so the verb "to allegorize" is both transitive ["to make or treat a thing as allegorical"] and intransitive ["to construct or utter allegories"] —OED.)

The term *allegory* first appears in the Hellenistic period, arising probably within Cynic-Stoic philosophy, where it refers to the attempt to find deeper meanings within the ancient Greek MYTHS in order to modernize and thus preserve them (see Plutarch, "How to Study Poetry," 11, 19e). In this sense, the practice of interpreting ancient texts and myths for their deeper meaning passed over into Hellenistic (esp. Alexandrian) Judaism (e.g., Aristobulus of Alexandria, 2nd cent. B.C.E.), PHILO and JOSEPHUS (1st cent. C. E.) and was adopted by Christian writers, esp. Matthew and

Paul. In Paul's LETTERS, the allegorical interpretation of OT themes is found in 1 Cor 5:6–8 (leaven); 9:8–10 (LAW); 10:1–11 (the exodus); and Gal 4:21–31 (Hagar and Sarah; see v. 24 where the word *allegory* is used). Some scholars find a kind of allegory already in the OT, e.g., Isa 5:1–6; Ps 80:8–16; Prov 5:15–23; Eccles 12:1–6.

According to Joachim Jeremias, there are no allegories among the authentic teachings of Jesus. In time, however, Jesus' PARABLES, removed from their setting in life, became obscure (see Mark 4:10–12) and were subjected to allegorizing tendencies. The attempt to reclaim the parables from obscurity by way of allegorical interpretation is apparent in the GOSPEL accounts: in some instances allegorical interpretations have been added, e.g., the interpretation of the sower (Mark 4:12–20 pars.), of the tares (Matt 13:36–43), and of the fishing net (Matt 13:49–50); in other instances allegorical elements themselves may have been added in order to adjust the original parable to the changed circumstances of the early Christian community (e.g., Matt 22:11–13; 24:43–44, 45–51; 25:12–30; Mark 2:19b–20; 13:33–37). Also, Mark 12:10–11 pars., which may be linked to Isa 5:1–6.

Allegorical interpretation flourished among the early church fathers, thanks in part to Philo's influence on the ALEXANDRIAN SCHOOL of interpretation (see the *Epistle of Barnabas*, Clement of Rome, ORIGEN, etc.). A classic example is Augustine's interpretation of the good Samaritan (*Quaestiones Evangeliorum*, 11, 19; abbreviated English trans., C. H. Dodd, *The Parables of the Kingdom* [London: Nisbet & Co., 1953; New York: Charles Scribner's Sons, 1961], 11). Since the Reformation, Protestant theologians in particular have frequently judged this tradition of allegorical interpretation quite harshly. They have drawn (some would say overdrawn) a distinction between allegorical and typological interpretation and argued that the former fails to preserve the narrative or historical integrity of the persons and events depicted in the OT (and the NT), and thereby effectively undercuts the reality of God's action in history. This negative evaluation of allegorical interpretation has been seconded almost without exception by modern BIBLICAL CRITICISM. However, in recent years, some interpreters have argued for a more sympathetic and nuanced understanding of aims of allegorical interpretation. See especially David Dawson, *Allegorical Readers and Cultural Revision in Ancient Alexandria* (Berkeley, Calif.: University of California Press, 1992). See TYPOLOGY; also FOURFOLD SENSE OF SCRIPTURE.

Alt, Albrecht (1883–1956). Professor of OT: *Privatdozent* in Greifswald (1909–12); professor in Basel (1914–20), Halle (1921), and Leipzig (1922–48). From 1921 to 1923, he was the Director of the Deutsches Evangelisches Institut für Altertumswissenschaft des Heiligen Landes in Jerusalem, and from 1925 to 1945, President of the Deutscher Verein zur Erforschung Palästinas (Society for Palestinian Research). Alt's extensive knowledge of the ancient Orient, its geography, history and the documents pertaining to it, caused his writings to exert a profound influence on OT studies in general and particularly on the formulation of a new understanding of the history of Israel. (See Alt, *Essays on OT History and Religion* [Oxford: Basil Blackwell, 1966].) See LAW.

Amanuensis (Lat: by hand). One who is hired to write from dictation, a scribe or secretary. The apostle Paul frequently used an amanuensis; see Rom 16:22; 1 Cor 16:21; Gal 6:11; Col 4:18; 2 Thess 3:17. In the HEBREW BIBLE, the most prominent amanuensis is Baruch, secretary to the prophet Jeremiah (see Jer 36:4).

Amarna Tablets were discovered by accident in 1887 at Tell el-Amarna situated on the Nile River in Egypt, halfway between Memphis and Thebes. Archaeological excavations (1890–91; 1907–14;

1920–37) unearthed the royal archives, bringing the total number of cuneiform tablets at the time to about 380. Most contain diplomatic correspondence written in Akkadian (also HITTITE and Canaanite) by vassal kings and governors in Palestine, Phoenicia, and southern Syria to Amenhotep IV (Akhenaton) and his father, Amenhotep III, during a short period of thirty years in the middle of the fourteenth cent. B.C.E. when Amarna was the capital of Akhenaton's empire. The texts portray the exercise of Egyptian sovereignty over Palestine and reveal much about the SOCIAL WORLD of the era. Scholars often employ these data in reconstructions of the biblical judges period. Of considerable interest and controversy is the reference in the texts to the 'Apiru, whom some identify as the biblical Hebrews. For texts in English, see W. L. Moran, *The Armana Letters* (Baltimore: Johns Hopkins University Press, 1992).

American Standard Version/New American Standard Version   NASV/ ASV are the common abbreviations for this 1901 American revision of the 1885 Revised Version (of the KING JAMES VERSION) prepared by British scholars for British audiences. The RV and ASV are extreme efforts at literal translation, the ASV incorporating decisions of the American delegation to the RV translation committee. Most notably, the ASV translated the Hebrew name YHWH with "Jehovah" instead of "Lord," as in KJV, RV, and in the New American Standard Bible (NASB), which is a revision (1963) of the ASV in the direction of "more current English IDIOM" (Preface). It remains the most literal of modern translations. See CONTEMPORARY ENGLISH VERSION; DOUAY; JERUSALEM BIBLE; LIVING BIBLE (PARAPHRASED); NEW AMERICAN BIBLE; NEW ENGLISH BIBLE; NEW INTERNATIONAL VERSION; NEW JEWISH VERSION; PARAPHRASE; REVISED STANDARD VERSION; TODAY'S ENGLISH VERSION; VERSION.

'Am Ha'arez   (Heb: lit., "the people of the land") is a Hebrew term of varied meaning depending on the period of its use. In preexilic Judah, the 'Am Ha'arez appear to have played a role in the political, social, and economic life of the nation just below that of the priests (Jer 1:18; 34:19; 37:2; 44:21, etc.), holding slaves (Jer 34) and being open to the charge of oppressing the poor (Ezek 22:29). In postexilic Judah, the term (frequently plural, so Ezra 10:2, 11; Neh 10:20–31) refers either to those who opposed the rebuilding of the Temple or to the people who had not been carried into exile (the exiles being called the "people of Judah," Ezra 4:4) and whose blood and religion had become mixed with foreign elements by the time the exiles returned. In the rabbinic literature the term is generally derogatory and designates those who are either ignorant of or indifferent to the LAW.

A minore ad majus   means "from the lesser to the greater"; it is the Latin equivalent to *Qal waḥōmer* (Heb), the first of HILLEL'S seven principal rules of interpretation; also translated "from the easy to the difficult." Where the rule is used the PROTASIS states, "If such be (true) . . ."; and the *apodosis* states: "then how much more (must it be true that). . . ." In the NT see Matt 7:11; 10:25b; 12:11f., pars.; also Rom 11:12, 15, 24; Heb 9:13f.; etc. (best observed in RSV). Noteworthy is Paul's use of the figure with reference to the sequence of death and resurrection, cf. Rom 11:15. See HERMENEUTICS.

Anacoluthon   is a grammatical non sequitur in which the structure of a sentence as initially conceived is not carried out; sometimes anacoluthon is due to popular IDIOM, sometimes to the author's losing his or her train of thought (e.g., Gal 2:4–6; 2 Thess 2:2; 1 Tim 1:3ff.).

Anagogy, Anagogic   (Gk: to lead). See *FOURFOLD SENSE OF SCRIPTURE, THE.*

Analogy   (Gk: proportion, correspondence; Rom 12:6). To "draw an analogy" is to make a comparison between the similar features or attributes of two otherwise dissimilar things, so that the unknown, or less well known, is clarified by the known. Strictly speaking, an analogy proposes a similarity of relationships between two things (concepts, entities, etc.): Paul refers to the soldier as one who does not serve at his own expense as an analogue to the apostle's right to recompense (1 Cor 9:7); he compares the meaninglessness of speaking in tongues with a war bugle that gives forth only an indistinct sound (1 Cor 14:6–8); and, in 15:18, he uses sleep as an analogue of death, since in both there is a cessation of activity and an attendant repose. As the last example suggests, it is not always possible to draw a clear distinction between analogy and other types of comparisons (PARABLES, ALLEGORIES, images, etc.), cf. 1 Thess 2:7; 5:1–11; Gal 3:15–18; 3:23–4:7; 4:19, etc. In theological analysis, analogy stands between univocity on the one hand and equivocity on the other (cf. Thomas Aquinas, *Summa Contra Gentiles* 1.32–34).

Analytical [Greek; Hebrew] Lexica are volumes containing all the words and inflected forms of the Hebrew/Aramaic OT and the Greek NT, arranged in alphabetical order, parsed and defined. They are useful in identifying the stem of irregular verbs. Such editions are currently published by the Zondervan Publishing House, Grand Rapids, Michigan (Greek, 1967; Hebrew and Chaldee, 1970; 1974[2]), and Baker Book House, Grand Rapids, Michigan (Greek, 1981). An analytical CONCORDANCE to the NRSV of the New Testament, edited by Richard E. Whitaker and John R. Kohlenberger III has been published by Wm. B. Eerdmans Publishing Co. (2000).

Anaphora (also epanaphora; Gk: to bring or relate back to). In grammar, anaphora denotes the use of a word as a grammatical substitute for a preceding word or group of words. In Acts the use of the article in "the Spirit" is anaphoric in that it denotes a specific spirit, viz., the Holy Spirit of Pentecost, e.g., Acts 2:4; 8:18; 10:44 (see BDF, para. 257).

In RHETORIC, anaphora denotes the repeated use of the initial word or words of two or more clauses, lines or STROPHES in a sequence, usually for poetic or rhetorical effect. The repetition of "How long?" in Ps 13 and "By faith" in Heb 11 are examples of anaphora; also, in Paul's LETTERS (though occasionally lost or altered in translation): 1 Cor 3:9; 10:21, 23; 2 Cor 7:2, 4; Gal 3:28; 4:4–5; 5:26; Phil 2:1; 3:6; 4:12, etc.; in Hellenistic rhetoric: Epictetus, *Diss.* 1.4.14; 5.7; 16.3; 28.28–30; 3.22.48, etc.

In ecclesiastical usage, anaphora, here meaning "offering," is the name of the central prayer in the Eucharistic liturgy. See EPIPHORA, SYMPLOCE.

ANET, ANEP Common abbreviation (acronym) for *Ancient Near Eastern Texts Relating to the Old Testament*, ed. James B. Pritchard (Princeton: Princeton University Press, 1969[3]), and by the same editor and press, *The Ancient Near East in Pictures Relating to the Old Testament* (1954). Selections from the two are available in a combined, supplemented VERSION in paperback (1971[5]). A standard tool for OT study, containing the texts in translation from RAS SHAMRA and AMARNA. *ANET* may now be supplemented by William W. Hallo and K. Lawson Younger, Jr., eds., *The Context of Scripture:* [vol. 1, of 3 proposed] *Canonical Compositions from the Biblical World* (Leiden: E. J. Brill, 1997).

Angelophany. See **Theophany.**

Annotated (Study) Bible is a Bible supplied with clarifying historical, literary, and theological notes in introductory sections or paragraphs and/or footnotes, with maps, charts, CONCORDANCE, cross references, etc. In each case the notations provided represent the opinion of the editor(s) and may reflect a given theological position: conservative, fundamentalist, Roman Catholic, liberal Protestant, Jewish, etc.

The New Oxford Annotated Bible with Apocrypha (expand. ed., Oxford: Oxford University Press, 1994) is based on the

NRSV, as is the *HarperCollins Study Bible* (1993), ed. Wayne Meeks and Jouette M. Bassler. In 1994, Oxford also published a study Bible based on the Revised English Version. Almost every recent VERSION of the Bible has been published with annotations for study purposes (NKJV, NLB, NIB, etc.), whereas the JERUSALEM BIBLE/NEW JERUSALEM BIBLE was originally so conceived, being heavily annotated from the beginning.

Antioch, School of.   See **Alexandria, School of.**

Antiphrasis   (Gk: to speak the opposite). The use of a word when its opposite is meant; hence, often ironic or sarcastic, e.g., 2 Cor 11:19; 12:11b, 13b, etc. See IRONY; MEIOSIS.

Antistrophe.   See **Epiphora.**

Antithetic Parallelism.   See **Parallelism.**

Aphorism   (Gk: a short, pithy sentence; a definition) is the name given to a principle or general truth expressed succinctly; syn.: adage or maxim. In the *Aphorisms* of Hippocrates (5th cent. B.C.E.) one finds "If a woman is pregnant with a male child she is of good complexion; if a female, of a bad complexion" (V, XLII)—later "an old wives' TALE." Webster defines *aphorism* as a "pithy EPIGRAM" requiring "some thought." The Epistle of James is frequently termed "aphoristic" because of its tendency to present religious instruction in the form of succinct moral truths. The book of Proverbs in the HB is largely aphoristic: "Better is dry morsel with quiet than a house full of feasting with strife" (17:1; NRSV). See *VOLKSSPRUCH.*

Apocalypse, The; The Little Apocalypse   The Apocalypse is a common name for the Revelation to John, the last book of the NT, and is also the Greek name and the opening word of the Greek text; the term in Greek means "revelation." "The

Little Apocalypse" refers to the 13th chapter of Mark and, to a lesser extent, its parallels in Matt and Luke, containing a vision of the destruction of Jerusalem and a prediction of the coming of the Son of Man. See APOCALYPTIC; ESCHATOLOGY.

Apocalyptic; Apocalyptic Literature   (fr. Gk: *apokalypsis:* disclosure, revelation). Apocalyptic is an adjective in use in BIBLICAL CRITICISM since the beginning of the 19th cent. that means of, relating to, or characteristic of apocalyptic literature. Apocalyptic literature designates those ancient visionary writings or parts of writings that, like the NT book from which the name is derived, the book of Revelation, purport to reveal the mystery of the end of the world (age) and of the glories of the world (age) to come. Used as a noun, apocalyptic refers to the religious phenomenon that comes to expression in apocalyptic literature and to the social and intellectual matrix from which this type of literature springs.

Apocalyptic is a religious phenomenon of the ancient Mediterranean and Near Eastern culture that flowered within Judaism and Christianity in the four centuries between 250 B.C.E. and 150 C.E. with roots extending back into the 5th and 6th centuries B.C.E. The two canonical exemplars of the genre, Daniel and the book of Revelation, stand respectively at the beginning and end of this period. Other passages of the OT and NT, however, are classed by some scholars as apocalyptic (or "protoapocalyptic") in outlook and style: Isa 24–27 (the "Isaiah Apocalypse"); 34; parts of 56–66; Joel 1–3; Zech 1–8; 9–11; 12–14; Ezek 38–39; Mark 13; Matt 24–25; Luke 21; 1 Thess 4–5; 2 Thess 2:1–12; and 1 Cor 15. Many of the PSEUDEPIGRAPHA and APOCRYPHA are also called Apocalypses. Though no complete agreement exists, those so designated usually include *Apoc. of Abraham; Apoc. of Baruch (II* or *Syriac Baruch); Apoc. of Esdras (IV Ezra 3–14); 1 Enoch 1–36; 3 Baruch; 2 Enoch; Jubilees 23;*

Testament of Abraham 10–15; *Testament of Levi* 2–5; the *Animal Apocalypse;* the *Apoc. of Weeks;* the *Heavenly Luminaries;* the *Similitudes of Enoch;* the *Apoc. of Zephaniah;* et al. Of these, the first four, plus the canonical apocalypses, are the most notable as a literary type. Apocalypse also characterizes the DSS, with apocalyptic features in almost all the documents, but particularly in the *War Scroll,* the *Description of the New Jerusalem,* and the *Thanksgiving Psalms.* Found among the DSS were previously known apocalypses: *Daniel, 1 Enoch,* and *Jubilees.*

The question remains: What is apocalyptic? Debate continues. It seems best to distinguish apocalyptic as a literary genre, a worldview, and a social phenomenon. In none of these aspects does apocalyptic exhibit invariably fixed ingredients. Rather, apocalyptic phenomena share family resemblances, i.e., overlapping and crisscrossing traits. In fluid and dynamic combination, several of the following traits are often involved: (1) a dualism between heavenly and earthly planes of existence and between the two opposing moral forces of good and evil; (2) depiction of a radical transformation of this world, lying in the immediate future (Dan 12:11–12; Rev 22:20; *2 Bar.* 85:10; *4 Ezra* 4:50); (3) cosmic catastrophes (war, fire, earthquake, famine, pestilence) preceding the end; (4) predetermined epochs of history leading up to the end; (5) a hierarchy of angels and demons mediating the events in this world and the one to come, victory being assured by the divine realm; (6) a righteous remnant (often including the resurrected righteous) that will enjoy the fruits of salvation in a heavenly Jerusalem on earth; and (7) belief that the actual establishment of the new age is effected through a messiah, or the Son of Man, or simply an angel. See Klaus Koch, *The Rediscovery of Apocalyptic* (London: SCM Press, 1972), also J. J. Collins, ed., *Apocalypse: The Morphology of a Genre* (*Semeia* 14; Missoula, Mont.: Scholars Press, 1979).

The origin of apocalyptic has been variously ascribed to Iranian religion, to Hel-

lenistic syncretism, and to experiences of alienation and "deprivation" within post-exilic prophetic and Levitical factions. A persistent tendency among scholars has been to emphasize the influence of eastern religion, particularly Zoroastrianism, in apocalyptic's origins. Norman Cohn revived this view in the mid-1990s in his book, *Cosmos, Chaos and the World to Come: The Ancient Roots of Apocalyptic Faith* (New Haven, Conn.: Yale University Press, 1993). Despite this view's persistence, a focus on Persian influence in apocalyptic's origins cannot account for early apocalyptic material, such as *3 Isaiah* and *Joel,* which arose within an authentically Israelite ideational and social matrix. Further, a Persian-influence approach to the origins of apocalyptic fails to account for the cross-cultural pervasiveness of apocalyptic beliefs. New social-scientific approaches to apocalyptic, making use of cross-cultural studies of "millennial" groups and movements around the globe, have led to a total reappraisal of the question of its origins. ("Millennialism" is the term that social scientists use to describe apocalyptic as a social phenomenon.) Apocalyptic worldviews have arisen at many times and in many cultural contexts not traceable to Zoroastrianism. Further, millennial groups are frequently not deprived, peripheral factions, as assumed, e.g., in Paul Hanson, *The Dawn of Apocalyptic* (Philadelphia: Fortress Press, 1975). Rather, an apocalyptic worldview can be focused under many social conditions, whenever a group's mythology is integrated and fused into future-oriented, linear-time thinking. See Stephen L. Cook, *Prophecy and Apocalypticism: The Postexilic Social Setting* (Minneapolis: Fortress Press, 1995).

Recently, particularly with the turn of the millennium, there has been increased interest in apocalyptic material and its ancient and contemporary functions. For a broad-ranging discussion of apocalyptic in Judaism, Christianity, and Islam, see *The Encyclopedia of Apocalypticism,* 3 vols., edited by J. J. Collins et al. (New York: Continuum, 1998). A focal point of critical NT scholarship is whether, or to what extent, Jesus was an apocalyptic prophet, and whether apocalyptic views world history with unrelieved pessimism—the kingdom of God being discontinuous rather than continuous with world time— and whether only a heaven can vindicate both the righteous and God. A. SCHWEITZER, in 1906, identified Jesus as a radical apocalypticist, a view given creative reinterpretation by the Existentialist RUDOLF BULTMANN and, in recent decades of Jesus research, hotly debated. The American "JESUS SEMINAR" downplays apocalyptic in the historical Jesus in favor of his role as a wisdom teacher. In Jewish tradition, however, apocalyptic contains many wisdom components, so the Seminar's assumption that wisdom and apocalyptic are antithetical is debatable. For a good review of the issues, see L. T. Johnson, *The Real Jesus: The Misguided Quest for the Historical Jesus and the Truth of the Traditional Gospels* (San Francisco: HarperSanFrancisco, 1996); N. T. Wright, *The New Testament and the People of God*, vol. 1 (Minneapolis: Fortress Press, 1992). See ESCHATOLOGY, QUEST OF THE HISTORICAL JESUS.

Apocalyptic Eschatology. See **Eschatology.**

Apocrypha, The (Gk: "hidden things"). The books and portions of books present in the LXX (or its Old Latin translation) and accepted by Hellenistic Judaism and by the EARLY CHURCH as sacred scripture but not found in the HEBREW BIBLES. In the domain of critical biblical studies, the term now preferred is "DEUTEROCANONICAL literature."

In preparing his edition of the Bible in Latin (see VULGATE), JEROME (ca. 400) chose to follow the Hebrew canon rather than the LXX, separating the additional writings found therein into a distinguishable corpus, which he then termed "apocrypha." These he also described as "ecclesiastical books" in contradistinction to the "canonical books" of the Hebrew OT.

Since Jerome, the theological and physical place of the Apocrypha in the Christian canon has continued to be a matter of dispute, with the Orthodox, the Roman Catholics, and the Protestants accepting differing solutions as indicated below.

The Apocrypha comprise the following:

(A) Tobit; Judith; Wisdom of Solomon; and Ecclesiasticus or the Wisdom of Jesus, the Son of Sirach—and of the Apocrypha these alone were accepted as canonical by the Eastern Church at the Synod of Jerusalem in 1672.

(B) Baruch; the Letter of Jeremiah (or Baruch, ch. 6; in the LXX these two writings appear as additions to the book of Jeremiah); the Prayer of Azariah and the Song of the Three Young Men (or Holy Children); the History of Susanna; and Bel and the Dragon (in the LXX these last three appear as additions to the book of Daniel; see that book in the JERUSALEM BIBLE, chs. 3:24–90; 13; and 14 respectively); and, 1 and 2 Maccabees—these writings, plus (A) above, were confirmed as canonical by the Council of Trent in 1548, though called "Deuterocanonical" because they do not appear in the Hebrew Bible.

(C) 1 Esdras (called Esdras A [Greek for Ezra] in the LXX and 3 Esdras in the Vulgate where Ezra and Nehemiah are called 1 & 2 Esdras), which contains portions of 2 Chron (Ezra and Nehemiah plus other material); 2 Esdras (called 4 Esdras in the Vulgate, also known as "The Ezra Apocalypse" [specif. chs. 3–14]; chs. 15–16, in some MSS called 5 Esdras, are a composite work, and do not appear in the LXX); and, the Prayer of Manasseh, a brief penitential prayer—these writings were not confirmed as canonical by the Council of Trent and consequently appear in Catholic Bibles in an appendix or not at all (so Jerusalem Bible).

In modern Protestant editions of the Apocrypha (NRSV, REB), all of the above (A–C) are included.

(D) In the LXX and in the Appendix to the Greek canon are Ps 151 and 3 and 4 Maccabees.

Modern translations of the Apocrypha/ Deuterocanonical books are found in complete editions of the NJB, NAB, REB, NRSV: individual books appear in the Anchor Bible COMMENTARY series. *The Parallel Apocrypha* with a number of recent translations and the text in Greek appeared in 1999. For a discussion of the theological issues raised by the Apocrypha as they relate to the Christian canon, see Brevard S. Childs, *Biblical Theology of the Old and New Testaments* (Minneapolis: Fortress Press, 1993), 63–69.

Apocryphal, NT   (Gk: adj., hidden; also called "NT Apocrypha" in contradistinction to the [OT] APOCRYPHA.) Non- or EXTRA-CANONICAL writings dating principally from the second to the sixth centuries, written in the form or carrying the name of GOSPELS, acts (histories), LETTERS, and APOC-ALYPSES, and purporting to tell of events, teachings, and prophecies (apocalypses) related to Jesus and the early apostles but not, apart from a relatively few instances, recorded in the canonical scriptures. Generally speaking, these writings are thought to contain little of historical value in terms of the subjects with which they deal (the birth of Mary, the childhood of Jesus, etc.), but they are of inestimable value in understanding the mind of both orthodox and heterodox Christianity of the early centuries. During the last two decades of the 20th cent., these writings received unparalleled attention, and continue to do so, as numbers of scholars turned their focus from questions of ecclesiastical concern, both historical and theological, to those of literary, social, and cultural interest. In this shift, noncanonical writings are deemed equal in importance to the canonical, the distinction being irrelevant to delineating the lines of development within both "orthodox" and

"heterodox" Christianity. The proper nomenclature for these writings, Jewish and Christian, is widely debated.

For the English texts of the following, see J. K. Elliott, *The Apocryphal New Testament: A Collection of Apocryphal Christian Literature in an English Translation Based on M. R. James* [*The Apocryphal New Testament*, 1924] (Oxford: Clarendon Press, 1994) and W. Schneemelcher, ed., *New Testament Apocrypha*, rev. ed., translated and edited by R. M. Wilson (Louisville, Ky.: Westminster/John Knox Press, 1991–1992). Also see J. K. Elliott, *The Apocryphal Jesus: Legends of the Early Church* (New York: Oxford University Press, 1996). The latter includes writings not listed below:

Gospels: Arabic Gospel of the Infancy; Armenian Gospel of the Infancy; Assumption of the Virgin; Gospel of Bartholomew; Book of the Resurrection of Christ by Bartholomew; Gospel of Basilides; Cerinthus; Gospel of the Ebionites; Gospel According to the Hebrews; Protevangelium of James; History of Joseph the Carpenter; Gospel of Marcion; Gospel of the Birth of Mary; Gospel of Philip; Gospel of Pseudo-Matthew; GOSPEL OF THOMAS.

Acts: Apostolic History of Pseudo-Abdias; Acts of Andrew; fragmentary *Acts of Andrew; Acts of Andrew and Matthias; Acts of Andrew and Paul; Acts of Barnabas; Ascent of James; Acts of James the Great; Acts of John; Acts of John (by Prochorus); Martyrdom of Matthew; Acts of Paul; Martyrdom of Paul; Acts of Peter; Acts of Peter and Andrew; Acts of Peter and Paul; Martyrdom of Peter and Paul; Acts of Philip; Acts of Pilate; Acts of Thaddaeus; Acts of Thomas.*

Epistles: Epistles of Christ and Abgar; Epistle of the Apostles; 3 Corinthians; Epistle to the Laodiceans; Epistle of Lentulus; Epistles of Paul and Seneca; Apocryphal Epistle of Titus.

Apocalypses: Apocalypse of James; Apocalypse of Paul; Apocalypse of Peter; Revelation of Stephen; Apocalypse of Thomas; Apocalypse of the Virgin.

Additional writings, known by little more than name, could be added, as well as literature commonly classed in other categories. See Abbreviations of Selected Works. Also see NAG HAMMADI CODICES; OXYRHYNCHUS PAPYRI; AGRAPHA; PSEUDE-PIGRAPHA.

Apodictic Law   In form-critical studies of the OT, apodictic law refers to unconditional (divine) LAW, e.g., the Ten Commandments. According to ALBRECHT ALT, who first used the term, apodictic law was singularly characteristic of Israelite religious law, in contrast to the secular, casuistic law of Canaan (see *Essays on Old Testament History and Religion* [Oxford: Basil Blackwell, 1966 (1934)], 81–132). According to Alt, apodictic law may open with (a) the second person, negative: "Thou shalt not . . ."; (b) a participle (lost in English translation): "Whoever strikes his father or mother shall be put to death" (Exod 21:15); or (c) a curse: "Cursed be he who removes his neighbor's landmark" (Deut. 27:15–26). In some instances, apodictic forms have been molded with casuistic ones (Exod 2 1:23–25), indicating (so Alt) the encounter of two cultural traditions. According to more recent opinion, apodictic law is not limited to Israel, or to its settlement period, or even just to religious law. That it is the primary characteristic of Israel's understanding of its covenantal relationship to God is also disputed (see Dennis J. McCarthy, *Old Testament Covenant: A Survey of Current Opinions* [Oxford: Basil Blackwell, 1972; Richmond: John Knox Press, 1972]). Its predominantly religious subject matter has caused some (Klaus Koch) to prefer not the word *law*, but *commandment* or *prohibition*. For further discussion, see Joseph Blenkinsopp, *The Pentateuch: An Introduction to the First Five Books of the Bible* (New York: Doubleday, 1992).

Apodosis.   See **Protasis**.

Apology   (an apologetic; Gk: a defense). In the NT the Greek noun and verbal forms of apology (*apologia*) appear frequently (e.g., Acts 22:1; 24:10; 25:8, 16; 26:1–2; 1 Cor 9:3; Phil 1:7, 16, etc.) in the sense of a verbal defense or explanation of one's conduct or opinions. Luke's presentation of the story of Paul and of the EARLY CHURCH in Acts is that of a defense or apology. According to H. D. Betz, Paul's defense of his apostleship and GOSPEL in 2 Cor 10–13 is an ironic parody (esp. 12:2–4, 7–10) of the rhetorical apology as found among Sophists and among Paul's opponents in Corinth, in that here Paul inverts characteristic self-acclaim by pointing to his human weaknesses and failure. See IRONY.

Apophthegm   (pl.: apophthegmata; also APOTHEGM[S]; Gk: "to utter forth"). "A terse pointed saying, embodying an important truth in a few words" (OED). *Note:* Although the longer spelling conforms to the Greek, being a TRANSLITERA-TION, in English the shorter is both older and easier to pronounce ('a–pe–them).

In form-critical studies, the classification apothegm has received no clear definition. According to MARTIN DIBELIUS, in ancient usage apothegm applied both to (a) SAYINGS introduced without a setting, and (b) answers of a specific nature set within concrete situations that are narrated either briefly or at length. (The latter [b] Dibelius viewed as a subcategory of apothegms called *CHRIAE*.) So defined, the term fits the material in the *Apophthegmata Patrum* (Migne, *Patrologia graeca*, 65, 71–440).

According to RUDOLF BULTMANN, apothegms are "sayings of Jesus set in a brief context"; so defined they correspond to (b) above, viz., Dibelius's *"Chriae."* However, since for Dibelius the synoptic *Chriae* arose out of the church's need for sermon illustrations, he chose the term PARADIGM for (b). Thus, the paradigms of Dibelius and the apothegms of Bultmann are basically the same. According to Bultmann, apothegms are not historical reports but idealized constructions designed to illustrate some principle which the EARLY CHURCH has traced back to Jesus. Bultmann categorized apothegms according to content: (a) conflict and didactic sayings (e.g.,

Mark 3:1–6, 22–30; 7:1–23; 10:7–22, 35–40; 12:13–17) and (b) biographical apothegms (e.g., Mark 1:16–20; Luke 9:57–62; 10:38–42, etc.). Bultmann found twenty-four in the first category, twenty in the second (which he thought arose as sermonic illustrations). See FORM CRITICISM.

Apostolic Fathers is the title given by general consent to those Christian authors of the 1st and 2nd cents. whose works, though ultimately deemed noncanonical, were often read and valued by the EARLY CHURCH. The term, first used in the 17th cent., designates no firm corpus, varying from eight to twelve in number, viz.: 1 *Clement* (ca. 95), 2 *Clement* (ca. 150), the *Epistle of Barnabas* (2nd cent.), *Epistle of Diognetus* (late 2nd or 3rd cent.), the (seven) *Epistles of Ignatius* (ca. 115), the *Epistle of Polycarp to the Philippians* (ca. 150), the *Shepherd of Hermas* (ca. 145), THE DIDACHE or the *Teaching of the Twelve Apostles* (late 1st or early 2nd cent.); the *Martyrdom of Ignatius* and the *Martyrdom of Clement* are sometimes included. (See *The Apostolic Fathers*, ed. R. M. Grant [New York: Thomas Nelson & Sons, 1965]); for a complete listing, see Abbreviations of Selected Works.

Apostolicon (Gk: pertaining to an apostle). This neuter substantive had several meanings among the early church fathers. It referred to (a) a quotation from the GOSPELS; (b) a quotation from Paul; (c) (plural) the epistles as part of the NT; (d) the corpus of epistles collected into a volume, being the name given to MARCION's corpus of Pauline LETTERS; and (e) a LECTIONARY reading from one of the NT epistles, in contradistinction to a reading from the Gospels, called an *evangelistarion.*

Apothegm. See **Apophthegm.**

Apparatus criticus. See *Critical Apparatus.*

Aquila (abbrev.: 'A). By tradition a pagan who converted first to Christianity and then to Judaism in the 2nd cent., Aquila is noted for his literalistic translation of the Hebrew OT into Greek (ca. C.E. 140), which was accepted as the official Greek Bible of the Jews until replaced by Arabic translations of the 7th cent. His translation appeared in ORIGEN's HEXAPLA and is extant only in fragments (PSALMS and Kings), in marginal READINGS in certain LXX MSS, and where quoted by the church fathers. Aquila's RECENSION of Ecclesiastes, however, appears in the LXX in place of the original Old Greek translation. See SYMMACHUS; THEODOTION.

Aramaic Bible, The. See **Targum.**

Aramaism. See **Semitism.**

Aretalogy (fr. Gk: *arete:* virtue) is a technical term used in contemporary criticism with three closely related but distinguishable meanings: (1) a collection of miracle stories, existing independently of hortatory or didactic material and essentially functioning for propaganda purposes; (2) a celebration of the virtues and/or deeds of a god; e.g., concerning the god Isis in Apuleius' *The Golden Ass* (XI 22, 6); (3) a celebrative biography of a religious hero or semidivine being (THEIOS ANER); e.g., Porphyry's *Life of Pythagoras,* PHILO's *Life of Moses,* and Philostratus' *Life of Apollonius of Tyana.*

An aretalogist is thus a kind of religious advocate or propagandist who, it is suggested, related evidence of the supernatural power of a god or divine person to gain devotion to his or her person and adherence to his or her teachings. The vision of the true apostle (or the true prophet: see the Elijah and Elisha cycles in the OT) as a divine person who performed miracles seems to underlie some of Paul's difficulty with the church at Corinth (see 2 Cor 10–13).

The critical question is whether or to what extent the NT GOSPELS belong to the "genre" of aretalogy or the above aretalogies to the "genre" of gospel.

The term *aretalogy* is frequently misspelled as *aretology* which, now archaic, referred to that part of moral philosophy dealing with virtue.

See Theodore Weeden, *Mark: Traditions in Conflict* (Philadelphia: Fortress Press, 1971); also D. L. Tiede, *The Charismatic Figure as Miracle Worker* (Missoula, Mont.: SBL Dissertation Series, 1972).

Argumentatio.   See **Rhetorical Analysis.**

Aristeas, Letter of   A GOSPEL-length, 2nd-cent.-B.C.E. work purporting to recount the events surrounding the translation of the Hebrew PENTATEUCH into Greek, probably in Alexandria at the close of the 3rd cent. B.C.E., by seventy[-two] Jewish scholars in seventy[-two] days, hence the name of the translation (the SEPTUAGINT) and its designator LXX (70). In addition to validating the authority of the Septuagint through miraculous signs, the "LETTER" is an encomium to the superiority of Judaism over neighboring religions. The text may be found in J. H. Charlesworth, ed., *The Old Testament Pseudepigrapha* (2 vols., Garden City, N.Y.: Doubleday, 1983–1985).

Arndt-Gingrich-Danker.   See **Bauer, Walter; Exegesis.**

Asian Biblical Interpretation,   as a geographical designation, attests to increasing interest in the globalization of biblical interpretation and theological education generally. The term does not denote any particular methodological focus of interpretation but encompasses all the interpretive concerns and interests presented in the *Handbook*. No effort is taken here to illustrate its diversity; it may be feminist, postcolonial, liberationist, ideological, ethnocentric, historical-critical, comparative, cross-cultural, etc. For a brief overview, see *DICTIONARY OF BIBLICAL INTERPRETATION*, also cited in Major Reference Works Consulted. The dominant and most accessible vehicles of Asian biblical interpretation have been regional, ecclesial, and

institutional publications, notably the following journals:

Regional: *Asia Journal of Theology* (1987–). Published by the Association for Theological Education in South East Asia, the North East Asia Association of Theological Schools, and the Board of Theological Education of the Senate of Serampore College, India. Its predecessors were the East Asia and the South East Asia journals of theology. Of broader interest are the *Journal of Asian Studies* and *Journal of Indian and Buddhist Studies*.

India: *Bangalore Theological Forum* (1968–); *Bible Bhashyam* (1975–), published by St. Thomas Apostolic Seminary; *Jeevadhara: A Journal of Christian Interpretation* (1971–); and *Vidyajyoti* (1938–), published by Catholic Press in India.

Indonesia: *Bina Darma* (1983–); *Orietasi Baru* (1986–).

Hong Kong: *Jian Dao: A Journal of Bible and Theology* (1994–), published by Alliance Bible Seminary.

Philippines: *Boletin Eclesiastico de Filipinas*, published by the University of Santo Tomas; *Diwa: Studies in Philosophy and Theology*, published by Christ the King Missionary Seminary.

Japan: *Annual of the Japanese Biblical Institute* (1975–), published by the Japan Biblical Institute.

Korea: *The Theological Thought*, publishes in the Korean language.

Assimilation   is the term in TEXTUAL CRITICISM for the most common of all errors in textual transmission: the replacement of the original READING of a passage by a reading that comes from another document; in the NT, the assimilated passage usually comes from another GOSPEL. However, the Lukan account of the institution of the Last Supper (Luke 22:19–20) as preserved by CODEX SINAITICUS and CODEX VATICANUS (cf. NRSV and KJV) has undoubtedly been assimilated to 1 Cor 11:23–25; CODEX BEZAE et al. do not contain vs. 22:19b–20 (so NRSV). Cf. also Luke's account of the baptism and of the Lord's Prayer in the above

MSS. In LINGUISTICS assimilation refers to the disappearance of consonants when two or more MORPHEMES are joined together, as in the "assimilation" of the *n* and the reduplication of the *l* in the word "illogical," formed of "in" = "not" + "logical." The phenomenon is frequent in the HEBREW BIBLE. See CONFLATION; GLOSS.

Assyriology, a term coined in the mid-nineteenth century, generally refers to the study of the ancient cultures of Mesopotamia (Iraq) that developed between the third millennium B.C.E. and the rise of conquering powers (viz., the Medes, the Persians, the Greeks, and finally the Iranians) in the last half of the first millennium B.C.E. These ancient Mesopotamian cultures, in a roughly successive order, are more specifically known as the Sumerians, Babylonians, Hurrians, Assyrians, and Chaldeans. The term *Sumerology* denotes study of the earliest of these civilizations located in the southern half of Iraq and known in classical times as Babylonia. Numerous parallels and points of contact have been noted between the texts of these ancient cultures and the HEBREW BIBLE, from the stories of Creation and the Flood to the dates of kings and their battles. Assyriology flourished between 1850 and 1950, following initial archaeological discoveries and before political conditions made further archaeological research difficult. See H. W. F. Saggs, *Assyriology and the Study of the Old Testament*, 1969; for a recent bibliography on Sumerology, including English titles, see W. H. Ph. Roemer, *Die Sumerologie: Einführung in die Forschung und Bibliographie in Auswahl*, 2nd ed. (Münster: Urgarit-Verlag, 1999).

ASV (NASB). See **American Standard Version.**

Asyndeton (pl.: asyndeta; Gk: not joined together) is a technical term in RHETORIC denoting the absence of particles or conjunctions ordinarily linking coordinate words or sentences. It is characteristic of Aramaic, and its presence in Mark and John has been used in an attempt to prove an Aramaic origin for these GOSPELS. The frequency of asyndeta in Greek papyri from the 1st cent. C.E. and in the writings of Epictetus shows this line of reasoning must be treated cautiously (see E. C. Colwell, *The Greek of the Fourth Gospel* [Chicago: University of Chicago Press, 1931]). In Matt's use of Mark, however, asyndeton is frequently eliminated by the insertion of a connective; cf. Mark 3:35; 5:39b; 10:27, 28, passim with Matt parallels.

Audience Criticism is concerned with understanding the original historical recipients of biblical texts. Although the concern of audience criticism has been a part of HISTORICAL CRITICISM from the beginning, it has more recently come to be distinguished as a distinct field of inquiry of its own. Audience criticism seeks to characterize the intended historical recipient (e.g., of a given prophetic ORACLE or NT LETTER) on the basis of clues within the text itself. As a historical discipline, audience criticism also makes use of any available extra-textual evidence in constructing the historical recipient. See J. A. Baird, *Audience Criticism and the Historical Jesus* (Philadelphia: Fortress Press, 1969); Susan M. Elliott, "Choose Your Mother, Choose Your Master: Galatians 4:21–5:1 in the Shadow of the Anatolian Mother of the Gods," *JBL* 118 (1999): 661–683. See RECEPTION THEORY.

Authenticity. See **Criteria of Authenticity.**

Autobiography In the OT, autobiography, as the memoirs of an official, first appears in the Persian period in the books of Ezra and Nehemiah. First person accounts are, however, much older, particularly as preserved in oral accounts of the dreams and visions of Israel's Patriarchs (Gen 37; 40; 41; Judg 7:13–14; 1 Kgs 3:4–15; 22:17–22) and PROPHETS (Amos 7:1–9; 8:1–3; 9:1–4; Jer 1; Isa 6; Ezek 1–2; Zech 1–8; Dan 7–12, etc.). In these accounts and others, poetic, prophetic, and allegorical features often override historical reminiscence in the service of religious interpretation.

In the NT, autobiography appears particularly in the LETTERS of Paul. These passages are classified by Beda Rigaux (*Letters of St. Paul* [Chicago: Franciscan Herald Press, 1968], 122–123) as (a) simple autobiography: 1 Cor 16:5–9; 2 Cor 7:5; Rom 1:11–14; Phil 1:12–26; (b) apostolic autobiography, dealing with Paul's pastoral role: 1 Thess 2:1–12, 18; 3:1–2, 6; 1 Cor 1:12–16; 2:1–5; 3:1–4, 9–13; 7:8; 11:23; 2 Cor 1:6–8, 10; Rom 15:17–21; Col 2:1–3; 4:7–9; 2 Thess 3:7–9; (c) apologetic and polemic autobiography: 1 Cor 9:1–27; 15:9; 2 Cor 10:1–12:21; Gal 1:11–2:14; (d) mystical autobiography: 2 Cor 12:1–10; Eph 3:1–13; and (e) a special "I" type of autobiography: Rom 7:14–25. Some scholars believe authentic autobiography is also to be found in the DEUTEROPAULINE Pastorals, e.g., 2 Tim 4:10–18. See also WE-SECTIONS.

Autograph   refers to the original copy of an author's work. In every instance, the autograph of the biblical books is lost; extant MSS of the Bible are only later, imperfect copies of the autograph. Some fragments of NT writings do fall within 100 years of the originals, and certain fragmentary MSS of the Jewish sectarian community of Qumran appear to be closer still to the autographs of some of the late books such as Daniel. See P; DEAD SEA SCROLLS; TEXTUAL CRITICISM.

Babylonian Talmud.   See **Talmud.**

Barth, Karl   (1886–1968). A native of Switzerland, Barth (pronounced Bart) studied theology in Germany, and after completing his studies became a pastor of the Reformed church in Geneva (1909–11) and Safenwil (Aargau, Switz., 1911–21). His *Commentary on the Epistle to the Romans* (*Der Römerbrief* 1919; 2nd ed. 1921; Eng: London: Oxford University Press, 1933) marks the chief watershed of 20th cent. Protestant theology and caused him to be called to a new chair in Reformed Theol-

ogy at Göttingen (1921). Prior to his expulsion from Germany by the Nazis in 1935, Barth also taught at Münster (1925–30), and Bonn (1930–35), and then became professor of theology at Basel where he taught until his retirement in 1962.

Barth has exercised a major though in part delayed influence on biblical interpretation in the 20th cent. Until fairly recently, he was generally ignored by hermeneutical discussion, partly because he discussed hermeneutical theory only on a piecemeal basis, and partly because his hermeneutical practice was so difficult to assimilate to prevailing standards, whether of the left or right. In more recent years, however, Barth has been hailed as the greatest practitioner of THEOLOGICAL INTERPRETATION in the 20th cent. and a forerunner of many significant developments in biblical interpretation (CANONICAL CRITICISM, NARRATIVE interpretation, POSTCRITICAL BIBLICAL INTERPRETATION, POSTMODERN BIBLICAL INTERPRETATION, etc.). Already in his *Commentary on Romans*, Barth read the Bible theologically but eschewed claims to a faultless biblical text; he accepted the legitimacy of HISTORICAL CRITICISM but not its claim to delimit the Bible's proper subject matter. In his 13-volume *Church Dogmatics* (1932–67; 9,000 pages), Barth gave his theological interpretation of the canon an ever-denser christological focus by attending in pioneering ways to the GOSPELS as narratives and by critically appropriating modes of precritical EXEGESIS (e.g., TYPOLOGY). In other respects, Barth's exegetical practice remained irreducibly pluralistic to the end. Barth's exegesis has provided inspiration for methodological proposals that explicitly engage contemporary hermeneutical discussion (e.g., HANS FREI, Brevard Childs), although arguably in ways that depart from Barth's own practice and intention. See George Hunsinger, "Beyond Literalism and Expressivism: Karl Barth's Hermeneutical Realism" in *Disruptive Grace* (Grand Rapids: Eerdmans, 2000); Mary Kathleen Cunningham, *What Is The-*

ological Exegesis? Interpretation and Use of Scripture in Karl Barth's Doctrine of Election (Valley Forge, Pa.: Trinity Press International 1995). See SACHEXEGESE.

Bath Qol (also *Bat Kol;* Heb: lit., "daughter of a voice") is the name given to a heavenly voice that revealed God's will to humankind. The term first appears in rabbinic tradition where it is asserted that the *Bath Qol* had been heard already in the patriarchal period concerning Tamar, and later Moses, Samuel, Solomon, David, etc. After the cessation of PROPHECY, the *Bath Qol* remained as the only means in rabbinic theology of God's direct communication with humankind. In the NT, a *Bath Qol* is heard at Jesus' baptism (Mark 1:11), transfiguration (9:7), and crucifixion (John 12:28), at Paul's conversion (Acts 9:4, etc.), and Peter's vision (10:13).

Bauer-Arndt-Gingrich. See **Bauer, Walter.**

Bauer, Walter (1877–1960). Taught NT studies in Marburg (1903–13), Breslau (1913–16), and Göttingen (1916–45) in Germany; noted principally for his Greek-German LEXICON of the NT, translated into English by W. F. Arndt and F. W. Gingrich. A second revised edition by F. W. Danker appeared in 1979 from the University of Chicago Press.

Baur, Ferdinand Christian (1792–1860). Professor of church history and dogmatics in Tübingen, Germany (1826–60), Baur was the leading figure of the Tübingen School, which is often said to have created the modern discipline of historical theology by its consistent application of principles of HISTORICAL CRITICISM to origins and development of the EARLY CHURCH. Baur's own critical research led to several profoundly influential (though still debated) hypotheses: (1) the opposition in the early church between a narrow and legalistic Jewish Christianity (led by Peter and James) and a universalistic and free Gentile Christianity (led by Paul); (2) the amelio-

rating tendencies of the Acts of the Apostles regarding the split between Peter and Paul, between TORAH-observant and Torah-free Christianity, and its secondary value as a historical source for the life and thought of Paul; (3) the secondary and late character of the Pastorals; (4) the historical value of the Synoptics over John. The frequent characterization of Baur as an uncritical Hegelian who applied the dialectic of thesis and antithesis to every problem in the history of primitive Christianity has been proved a misleading if not false generalization. (See P. C. Hodgson, *The Formation of Historical Theology: A Study of Ferdinand Christian Baur* [New York: Harper & Row, 1966].) Nevertheless, Baur's influential reconstruction of the history of the early church, and especially the largely negative role it assigns Judaism and Jewish Christianity, has come under increasingly severe criticism in recent decades. (See, e.g., Craig C. Hill, *Hellenists and Hebrews: Reappraising Division within the Earliest Church* [Minneapolis: Fortress Press, 1992].) What is perhaps Baur's most important work exists in English translation: *The Church History of the First Three Centuries,* vols. 1–2 (London: Williams & Norgate, 1878–79).

B.C.E.; C.E. Before the Common Era; the Common Era. Terms employed particularly by the academic community as non-theological equivalents of B.C. and A.D. (*Anno Domini;* Lat: "In the year of our Lord"). Religiously, the terms may be satisfactory to no one, since it is still the putative date of the birth of JESUS CHRIST that demarcates the eras.

Beatitudes. See **Blessings.**

Benedictus is the traditional name of Zechariah's HYMN of PROPHECY concerning John the Baptist, recorded in Luke 1:68–79, from the opening word of the Latin text: *"Benedictus Dominus Deus Israel"* ("Blessed be the Lord God of Israel . . ." NRSV). Also called the "Song of Zechariah." The language of the hymn is styled after the Greek OT (LXX) and hence offers one of the best examples of "SEPTUAGINTISM" in the NT. See *MAGNIFICAT; NUNC DIMITTIS.*

Ben Sira (The Wisdom of Jesus ben Sira, or Sirach; also Ecclesiasticus). See **Wisdom Literature.**

Bible, The. See **Canon.**

Biblical Criticism refers in the broadest sense to the use of rational judgment in understanding the Bible. So defined, biblical criticism is a part of all biblical interpretation. More narrowly, however, it refers to an approach to the study of scripture that is centrally concerned with searching for and applying neutral, i.e., scientific and nonsectarian, canons of judgment in its investigation of the biblical text. Biblical criticism in this sense denotes a distinguishable chapter in the history of biblical interpretation, one that is linked to the rise of modern culture in the West. It comprises a large number of distinguishable (often interrelated, sometimes antithetical) methodologies, approaches, and perspectives, the terminology and leading practitioners of which make up a substantial portion of this *Handbook.* Until the middle of the 20th cent., biblical criticism was essentially synonymous with HISTORICAL CRITICISM, which began to appear little more than two centuries ago; today that definition is too narrow. As the Diagram of Biblical Interpretation indicates (see page 235), biblical criticism now includes approaches that are not historical in the traditional sense but are designed to address other dimensions of the text (i.e., "the world of the text," "the world in front of the text"). Several of these approaches do not consider themselves to be methods in any precise sense, but rather to be perspectives that must be a part of any critical interpretation of scripture, e.g., FEMINIST BIBLICAL INTERPRETATION.

As a distinguishable movement in the history of interpretation, modern biblical criticism stands in a complex relationship of continuity and discontinuity with chronologically earlier and logically subsequent forms of biblical interpretation. Precritical biblical interpretation (biblical interpretation prior to ca. 1750) was not less rational than biblical criticism but was centrally concerned with the task of THEOLOGICAL INTERPRETATION rather than with the search for and application of neutral standards of judgment to the biblical text. POSTCRITICAL and POSTMODERN BIBLICAL INTERPRETATION question, though from different perspectives, the possibility and profitability of modern biblical criticism's characteristic approach to the Bible. These challenges to biblical criticism are discussed in detail elsewhere in the *Handbook.*

Ancient Roots of Biblical Criticism

If by biblical criticism we mean the use of rational judgment in interpreting sacred traditions, it is as old as scripture itself. Indeed, the Bible itself is the product of biblical criticism so defined: 1 and 2 Chronicles contain a critique of the interpretation of history found in 1 Kings–2 Samuel; Job presents a critique of the Deuteronomic view of history; both Matthew and Luke offer critiques of Mark's interpretation of the life and person of Jesus; and so on. In each case, biblical writers make critical judgments about prior tradition based on their understanding of the nature and will of God, and these judgments are subsequently embedded in biblical tradition itself. Viewed from this perspective, the great monuments of ancient biblical criticism are the canons of church and synagogue, since every point in the long process of canonical formation and delineation reflects critical judgments regarding what sacred scripture is and is not and how sacred scripture is to be received and transmitted (see CANONICAL CRITICISM). Obviously, biblical criticism in this ancient and encompassing sense is a thoroughly theological enterprise, since its procedures of rational judgment are inseparable from theological premises and goals.

The ancient antecedents of *modern* biblical criticism are perhaps most recognizable in three areas: the preparation of competing translations (see VERSION), concern for the original wording of the text (see TEXTUAL CRITICISM), and the formulation of explicit rules for appropriate and fruitful interpretation. The last of these three areas has been called HERMENEUTICS since the 17th cent., and the reader is referred to that entry for further discussion. The ancients were well aware that translation is inevitably interpretation (see the prologue to Ecclesiasticus in the APOCRYPHA). Notably the translators of the HB had to face this fact. The SEPTUAGINT (*siglum:* LXX), an early Greek version of the HB prepared for Hellenistic Jews ca. 250 B.C.E., reflects many complex interpretive decisions about the meaning of the Hebrew text (cf. its famous rendering of Exod 3:14, "I am the Existing One") and contains words and passages not found in Hebrew MSS. The EARLY CHURCH used the LXX and ultimately came to rely on its unique READINGS to support its christological interpretation of scripture. In response, rabbinic Judaism came to favor more literal Greek translations for their own Greek-speaking constituency (see AQUILA, SYMMACHUS, THEODOTION). The conflict spurred Christian concern for identifying the best or most authoritative text of the Bible, a task known today as textual criticism. ORIGEN (ca. 185–254) undertook a massive experiment in textual criticism in order to provide the church with a reliable basis for EXEGESIS (see *HEXAPLA*); for similar reasons, JEROME based his Latin translation of the OT in part on the HB, and not exclusively on Greek versions (see VULGATE). Jewish copyists exhibited an analogous concern

for the best text in the system of notation known as *Qere* (see KETHIB and QERE). Textual criticism underwent little further development until the Renaissance and Reformation (16th cent.) placed renewed emphasis on biblical languages and on the authority of scripture over subsequent tradition. By this time the printing press made possible a fixed authoritative biblical text (which for the Greek NT came to be called the *TEXTUS RECEPTUS*, 1550); it also made translation profitable.

Modern Biblical Criticism

As noted, biblical criticism in the narrower sense belongs to the story of the rise of modern culture in the West (ca. 1650–). Over several generations, the scholarly study of the Bible became ever more occupied with finding and using what were taken to be neutral (secular, this-worldly, nonsectarian, nontheological) criteria for understanding the Bible. This development was both parent of and child to the powerful forces of Enlightenment and secularization that transformed Western institutions and culture generally. A decisive factor was the desire to break ecclesiastical authority over religious, academic, and political spheres of life; notably, this emancipatory impulse often justified itself by appeal to the authority of the Bible's LITERAL SENSE, understood as the sense intended by the author in his original context. Another factor was the desire to reconstruct biblical history in conformity with the current understanding of reality, a desire made irrepressible by the palpable success of the natural sciences.

The rise of historical consciousness in the late 18th and 19th centuries brought a flood of philological, historical, and literary questions regarding the origin of the biblical texts: date, place, authorship, sources, and intention (HISTORICAL CRITICISM, LITERARY CRITICISM, SOURCE CRITICISM, *TENDENZ* CRITICISM). The mid-19th cent.

saw the birth of impressive and long-lasting hypotheses touching on the origins of both Testaments: the Documentary Hypothesis (see GRAF-WELLHAUSEN HYPOTHESIS) concerning the PENTATEUCH and the TWO SOURCE HYPOTHESIS concerning the Synoptic GOSPELS. Both hypotheses taught subsequent generations to view the Bible as a multilayered composite made up of separate, preexisting literary traditions. At the same time, confidence in the power of historical reconstruction led to a passionate and conflicted QUEST OF THE HISTORICAL JESUS, which some hoped would provide a new basis for modern faith grounded in historical research.

In the later 19th cent., political and economic developments enabled scholarly research in the Middle East, and the recovery of ancient biblical MSS revolutionized textual criticism and Bible translation. Archaeologists also discovered non-Israelite texts astonishingly similar in content to that of the Bible. This further transformed biblical studies and gave impetus to the rise of comparative religions (see RELIGIONS-GESCHICHTLICHE SCHULE). The new approach took no account of the ancient distinction between canonical and noncanonical literature and simply sought to understand the religion of Israel and its neighbors in the context of ancient Near Eastern cultures. Applied to Jesus, the new approach suggested the central figure of Christian faith was a Jewish APOCALYPTIC prophet who expected an imminent end of the world (J. WEISS; A. SCHWEITZER). The discovery ended (at least for a time) the hope that "the historical Jesus" would provide a clear foundation for modern faith and forced subsequent theologians and biblical scholars to wrestle centrally with the theme of ESCHATOLOGY. Incipient SOCIOLOGICAL and PSYCHOLOGICAL INTERPRETATION, appearing also in these later decades, offered new and, more often than not, transient views of Jesus and of the social dynamics of the early Christian movement.

The story of biblical criticism in the first half of the 20th cent. was shaped by two main factors and by their volatile interaction. One was the further refinement of historical approaches to the Bible. In the first decades of the 20th cent., FORM CRITICISM arose as literary critics turned from a focus on the individual creative genius, so prominent in 19th-cent. thought, to the spontaneous self-expression of common people, that is, from author to GENRE. The study of ORAL TRADITION, in the form of LEGENDS, HYMNS, songs, proverbs, PARABLES, etc., provided access to the time prior to the fixing of tradition in written form. In the 1930s, TRADITION CRITICISM or *Überlieferungsgeschichte* sought to amplify form criticism's interest in genre by analyzing how genres are transformed over time by the traditioning process. In the 1950s, REDACTION CRITICISM sought to counterbalance the tendency of form and source critics to dissolve the scripture into ever smaller preexisting units by emphasizing the literary integrity of the larger literary units that were the final products of tradition. NT redaction critics, for example, insisted that the Gospel writers were not mere compilers of tradition but genuine interpreters of it.

The other main factor shaping biblical criticism in the first half of the 20th cent. was an effort on the part of leading OT and NT scholars to reassert the Bible's theological and ecclesial relevance in the face of the political and human crises of the day. In the early 1920s, the theologian K. BARTH called for exegesis to accept the necessity of historical criticism but to go beyond it to deal with the Bible's material theological concerns (see SACHEXEGESE). Influenced by Barth and others, OT scholars such as W. EICHRODT and G. VON RAD contributed to a flowering of BIBLICAL THEOLOGY that uneasily straddled the concerns of dogmatics and historical criticism, while the NT scholar RUDOLF BULTMANN sought to uncover the message of the NT for the modern temperament by his program of DEMYTHOLOGIZATION. Bultmann's approach in particular set the agenda for a subsequent generation of leading NT scholars who sought to combine historical-critical studies with reflection on hermeneutics. Their efforts gave rise to movements such as the NEW HERMENEUTIC and the New Quest of the Historical Jesus, which dominated NT studies up until the end of the 1960s.

Around mid-century, too, the denominational complexion of modern biblical criticism began to change. Until then, it had been (apart from a few notable Jewish exceptions), an almost exclusively Protestant enterprise, though it had long split the Protestant world into camps on left and right. Conservative Protestant suspicion toward biblical criticism crystallized in the early 20th cent. in the American Fundamentalist movement, which affirms the Bible's inerrancy, i.e., its freedom from error of any kind, theological, historical, or scientific. Liberal Protestants responded with charges of BIBLICISM and BIBLIOLATRY. The Roman Catholic Church likewise remained officially opposed to biblical criticism until Pope Pius XII's encyclical *DIVINO AFFLANTE SPIRITU* (1943). Since then, Roman Catholics, and more recently, non-Fundamentalist evangelical, Orthodox, and Pentecostal Christians, as well as increasing numbers of Jews, have contributed to biblical criticism of both Testaments. The change is due both to shifting perceptions of biblical criticism in the respective religious communities and to the shifting reality of biblical criticism itself, which has become increasingly if fitfully aware that critical inquiry into the Bible is possible on the basis of premises other than those of liberal Protestantism.

After 1970, biblical criticism was marked by waning interest in the theological concerns of the WWII generation and by the rapid growth of Departments of Religion in colleges and state universities.

Biblical scholars began to apply new literary approaches to the text (STRUCTURALISM, RHETORICAL CRITICISM) that were less concerned with the biblical text's historical origins ("the world behind the text") than with the text as a self-contained unity whose elements are meaningful as they stand ("the world of the text"). These and other new approaches proliferated during the 1970s and '80s and their impact was so pervasive and radical that some compared their advent to the introduction of historical-critical methods two hundred years before. By 1990, biblical criticism had been transformed from a basically historical discipline consisting in interrelated methods to a field of disciplines with much more disparate and conflicting interests (see LINGUISTICS; RECEPTION THEORY; SEMIOLOGY; SOCIOLOGICAL INTERPRETATION, PSYCHOLOGICAL BIBLICAL INTERPRETATION; NARRATIVE CRITICISM).

During the same decades, a variety of factors contributed to an accelerating focus on the identity and aims of the interpreter and how these shape the act of interpretation. Partly this shift to "the world in front of the text" represents a radicalization of previous concerns (see HERMENEUTICAL CIRCLE). But a major new factor was the entry of women and ethnic minorities into a field once exclusively the domain of white men. Another factor was the globalization of professional biblical studies. A host of new approaches appeared that sought to emphasize the distinctive viewpoints of historically marginalized communities of interpretation (see FEMINIST, WOMANIST, POSTCOLONIAL, MUJERISTA BIBLICAL INTERPRETATION; ADVOCACY and IDEOLOGICAL CRITICISM). In some cases, representatives of these perspectives continue to assume the premises and goals of modern biblical criticism and seek only to provide a corrective that exhibits its latent biases and omissions. Other practitioners disavow modern biblical criticism's commitment to neutral norms of judgment and propose instead the ideal of the biblical critic as an interested advocate of justice grounded in a particular community's history of oppression or marginalization.

Postmodern and Postcritical Interpretation

Some of the developments already noted pose challenges to the modern PARADIGM of biblical criticism, and so it is not always desirable to distinguish sharply between them and other recent approaches that style themselves with the prefix "post-." Nevertheless, the 1990s saw growing interest in approaches to biblical interpretation that are avowedly concerned with radically challenging modern biblical criticism's key philosophical and theological premises. One such approach is postmodern biblical interpretation, which draws its primary inspiration from philosophical and literary movements such as DECONSTRUCTION. Postmodern biblical interpretation often (though not always) shares modern biblical criticism's suspicion of traditional Christian theology but not its confidence in reason as a source of neutral, universal standards for determining textual meaning. Postmodern biblical interpretation emphasizes the polyvalence and indeterminancy of textual meaning and the relativity of all norms of judgment (see INTERTEXTUALITY). It seeks to unmask the problematic character of all claims to universal knowledge (METANARRATIVE) and to foster heterogenous, local communities of interpretation. A rather different approach is POSTCRITICAL BIBLICAL INTERPRETATION, a development more indigenous to guilds of theology and biblical studies. Postcritical biblical interpretation shares postmodernism's suspicion of modern claims to neutral standards of reason but not its hostility toward theological interpretation. Drawing on precritical forms of exegesis it seeks to renew an avowedly theological approach to biblical interpretation that

serves contemporary communities of faith. Finally, it is important to note that many of the approaches and perspectives outlined in the previous paragraphs can be combined in a variety of ways.

Conclusion

As the 21st cent. begins, modern biblical criticism has lost some of the luster of inevitability and superiority that it once had. Biblical scholars are now more aware that the Bible can be interpreted rationally from a variety of perspectives. The goal of applying neutral criteria of judgment to the Bible has largely given way to the goal of becoming critically aware of the premises (methodological, philosophical, cultural, and theological) that the interpreter brings to the study of the text. In the new situation, biblical scholars are as likely to draw inspiration from precritical interpretation or from contemporary philosophical and social movements, not to mention from the church and synagogue, as from the inaugurating concerns of modern biblical criticism. Nevertheless, modern biblical criticism has already permanently altered the way people understand the Bible. Its leading practitioners in the 19th and 20th centuries have set standards of industry, acumen, and insight that remain pace-setting today. Above all, it continues to set an agenda for biblical interpretation that remains potent at the beginning of the new millenium: to let the text speak on its own terms. The future of its significant achievements will depend on whether and to what degree new approaches to the Bible are capacious enough to include the concerns of modern biblical criticism while doubtless going beyond them in other ways.

See the Diagram of Biblical Interpretation (p. 235); BIBLICAL THEOLOGY MOVEMENT. For keeping up with biblical studies in the U.S. and Canada, see COUNCIL ON THE

STUDY OF RELIGION; SOCIETY OF BIBLICAL LIT-
ERATURE; CATHOLIC BIBLICAL ASSOCIATION.

Biblical Cultural Criticism, though
still in its infancy, seeks to analyze the
influence of the Bible on the Western tradition, ancient and modern, and especially
its impact, whether as icon or commodity,
on contemporary culture. It also seeks to
illuminate how culture and sociohistorical
location influence the interpretation of the
Bible. British practitioners in the field trace
its roots back to British cultural studies of
the 1950s and 1960s and to the Center
for Contemporary Cultural Studies at the
University of Birmingham. Those origins,
originally Marxist in orientation, have
since been largely abandoned for theoretical positions more eclectic, interdiscipli-
nary, and international in scope. Outside
Britain, biblical cultural studies have
grown out of the general influence of postmodernism, the rise of perspectivalism,
and, especially in the United States, the
long-held academic interest in the Bible's
role in literature and the arts. As currently
practiced biblical cultural criticism may
also be characterized as IDEOLOGICAL CRITI-
CISM. Many essays in the field tend to be
suspicious of the religious appropriation of
the Bible and seek to unmask the political
agendas thought to be implicit in such
appropriation. Understandably, its scope is
essentially limitless and may appear in
conjunction with feminist interpretation,
POSTCOLONIAL BIBLICAL INTERPRETATION,
ideological criticism, et al. Since biblical
cultural criticism generally focuses on popular culture, it frequently tends to be pre-
occupied with themes chosen for their
shock value.

An introduction to biblical cultural
studies may be found in *Biblical
Studies/Cultural Studies. The Third Sheffield
Colloquium*, ed. J. Cheryl Exum and
Stephen D. Moore (JSOTSup 266; Sheffield:
Sheffield Academic Press, 1998). A journal
devoted to biblical cultural criticism is *Bib-
licon*, founded in 1997. See also Stephen D.
Moore ed., *In Search of the Present: The Bible*
through Cultural Studies (*Semeia*; Atlanta:
Scholars Press, 1998), particularly the clos-
ing essay by Alice Bach.

Biblical Theology moves "somewhere between the normative statements
of dogmatic theology and the descriptive
concerns of the history of religions" (Walter Brueggemann, John R. Donahue, S.J.,
"Series Forward" to *Overtures to Biblical
Theology*, 41 vols. [Philadelphia: Fortress
Press: 1977–]). The term may be used to
refer to works that undertake the purely
descriptive task of explaining what the
Bible, or some portion thereof (e.g., OT, NT,
DEUTERO-ISAIAH, Mark, etc.), says about
God and reality in relation to God
(humankind, Israel, CHRIST, the church,
etc.) as this was likely to have been understood within the texts' original historical,
cultural, literary, etc., settings. The term
may also be used to refer to works that
undertake the essentially prescriptive task
of interpreting what the biblical texts mean
on these same topics for contemporary
faith. The attempt to distinguish between
these two conceptions of the discipline is
itself a perennial theme of biblical theology. Simplifying greatly, one can say that
the first definition corresponds to the older
conception of biblical theology (ca.
1790–1930) and reflects the effort of biblical
scholars to establish the autonomy of their
field as a historical discipline independent
of the tutelage of dogmatics and church
teaching. The second definition was given
enormous impetus by German OT scholars
(1930–60) who wished to reassert the theological character of their discipline against
what they perceived to be a sterile and
ecclesially ineffective historicism (see RELI-
GIONSGESCHICHTLICHE SCHULE). Today many
works that bear the name "Biblical Theology" (or "Theology of the OT," "Theology
of the NT," etc.) avowedly embrace something of both concerns while hewing more
closely to either the descriptive or normative task. In contrast, works that exclusively embrace the historical, descriptive
task, while eschewing the prescriptive

altogether, often avoid the title biblical theology.

Strictly speaking, a biblical theology from a Christian perspective must address the entire Christian canon, OT and NT. Nevertheless, such works are rare because of the difficuly of attaining scholarly competence in both Testaments, though some authors span both Testaments by concentrating on a single central theme (see Samuel Terrien and P. D. Hanson following). More common are biblical theologies that attempt a comprehensive overview of either the OT or the NT. The contribution of Jewish scholars to biblical studies does not often take the form of a biblical theology of the HB (see Jon D. Levenson, "Why Jews Are Not Interested in Biblical Theology," in *Judaic Perspectives on Ancient Israel*, ed. J. Neusner et al. [Philadelphia: Fortress Press, 1987]).

Biblical Theology of the Christian Bible

Important representative works include the following: Friedrich Mildenberger, *Biblische Dogmatik: eine Biblische Theologie in dogmatischer Perspektive* (Stuttgart: Kohlhammer, 1991–93), is original and thought-provoking from the perspective of dogmatics; Brevard S. Childs, *Biblical Theology of the Old and New Testaments* (Minneapolis: Fortress Press, 1992), is a mature statement from a major proponent of a canonical approach; Samuel Terrien, *The Elusive Presence* (San Francisco: Harper & Row, 1978) presents the thesis that God's self-disclosure and self-concealment stand at the center of biblical faith in the OT and NT; and P. D. Hanson, *The People Called: The Growth of Community in the Bible* (San Francisco: Harper & Row, 1986), discusses the development of human community at the intersection of divine initiative and human response.

Biblical Theology of the Old Testament

Important representative works include the following: Rolf Rendtorff, *Theologie des Alten Testaments: ein kanonischer Entwurf*, vol. 1 (Neukirchen-Vluyn: Neukirchner Verlag, 1999)—biblical theology from the major German proponent of a canonical approach; Bernhard W. Anderson, *Contours of Old Testament Theology* (Minneapolis: Fortress Press, 1999)—A dean of OT studies summarizes major themes of a lifetime of research; Walter Brueggemann, *Theology of the Old Testament: Testimony, Dispute, Advocacy* (Minneapolis: Fortress Press, 1997), presents biblical theology as courtroom drama that engages ancient and contemporary challenges to Israel's God; CLAUS WESTERMANN, *Elements of Old Testament Theology* (Atlanta: John Knox Press, 1982; Ger: 1978), attends equally to God's dramatic acts of salvation and God's ongoing work in blessing.

Also see WALTHER ZIMMERLI, *Old Testament Theology in Outline*, trans. David E. Green (Atlanta: John Knox Press, 1978; Ger: 1972), which presents a biblical theology centered in YHWH's declaration, "I am the LORD your God!"; G. E. Wright, *God Who Acts: Biblical Theology as Recital* (London: SCM Press, 1952), is a manifesto of "the BIBLICAL THEOLOGY MOVEMENT"; GERHARD VON RAD, *Old Testament Theology*, 2 vols. (New York: Harper & Row, 1962–64; Ger: 1957–60) presents the historical development of Israel's testimony about YHWH; and W. EICHRODT, *Theology of the Old Testament*, 2 vols. (Philadelphia: Fortress Press, 1961–67; Ger; 3 vols.: 1933–39)—among the first and greatest biblical theologies of the 20th cent., it expounds covenant as the unifying center of Israel's faith.

Biblical Theology of the New Testament

Important representative works include the following: N. T. Wright, *Christian Origins and the Question of God,* 2 vols. (London: SPCK, 1992–)—the most ambitious current project in NT theology; Peter Stuhlmacher, *Biblische Theologie des Neuen Testaments,* vol. 1 (Göttingen: Vandenhoeck & Ruprecht, 1992)—a developmental approach that emphasizes continuity between Israel's scriptures and Christian proclamation; G. B. Caird, *New Testament Theology* (Oxford: Oxford University Press, 1994); Donald Guthrie, *New Testament Theology* (Downers Grove, Ill.: Intervarsity Press, 1981)—a systematic, conservative presentation of NT teaching.

Also see Joachim Jeremias, *New Testament Theology: The Preaching of Jesus,* trans. John Bowden (New York: Charles Scribner's Sons; London: SCM Press, 1971; Ger: 1971); R. BULTMANN, *The Theology of the New Testament,* 2 vols. (New York: Charles Scribner's Sons, 1951–55; Ger: 1948–53)—the major NT theology of the 20th cent.; and Oscar Cullmann, *Christ and Time* (Philadelphia: Westminster Press, 1964; Ger: 1946), which emphasizes the linear understanding of time in the biblical history of revelation.

Journals dedicated to the promotion and discussion of biblical theology include *Horizons in Biblical Theology* (Pittsburgh, Pa.: Pittsburgh Theological Seminary), and *Biblical Theology Bulletin* (Jamaica, N.Y.: St. John's University; South Orange, N.J.: Seton Hall University).

For overviews of the field, see James Barr, *The Concept of Biblical Theology: An Old Testament Perspective* (Philadelphia: Fortress Press, 1999); Francis Watson, *Text and Truth: Redefining Biblical Theology* (Grand Rapids: Eerdmans, 1997); A. K. M. Adam, *Making Sense of New Testament Theology: "Modern" Problems and Prospects* (Macon, Ga.: Mercer University Press, 1995); J. H. Hayes and F. Preussner, *Old Testament Theology: Its History and Development* (Atlanta: John Knox Press, 1985); Robert Morgan,*The Nature of New Testament Theology* (Naperville, Ill.: Allenson, 1973); Brevard S. Childs, *Biblical Theology in Crisis* (Philadelphia: Fortress Press,

1970). See BIBLICAL THEOLOGY MOVEMENT; HERMENEUTICS; THEOLOGICAL INTERPRETATION; WILLIAM WREDE.

Biblical Theology Movement, The
The biblical theology movement was "the intellectual side of a more general religious reaction" against "liberal theology and its use of the Bible" that flourished in America (in Great Britain and other parts of Europe in a less pronounced way) between 1945 and 1960. Proponents include G. Ernest Wright and H. H. Rowley in OT and Paul Minear in NT. According to J. Barr, it was characterized by the following features: (1) opposition to the influence of philosophy and philosophical theology, (2) opposition to the presumed systematizing tendency of dogmatic theology, (3) an emphasis on Hebrew thought in contradistinction to Greek thought, (4) an emphasis on the unity of the Bible, (5) an approach to biblical language that concentrated on word studies, (6) an emphasis on the distinctiveness of the Bible vis-à-vis its environment, (7) an emphasis on divine revelation in history, and (8) the interrelationship of biblical study and theological concern. (See *IDB,* suppl. vol. [5], ad hoc.) The biblical theology movement came under severe criticism in the 1960s for a variety of reasons, including its equivocal use of terms such as "history" and "revelation" and an overemphasis on history at the expense of nature and creation. The now classic study of the movement, its rise and fall in America, is Brevard S. Childs's study *Biblical Theology in Crisis* (Philadelphia: Westminster Press, 1970). See BIBLICAL THEOLOGY; THEOLOGICAL INTERPRETATION.

Biblicism refers pejoratively to the uncritical, literal interpretation of scripture, particularly to a method that fails to distinguish between the scriptures and that to which the scriptures bear witness. See BIBLIOLATRY; HISTORICAL-CRITICAL METHOD; *SACHEXEGESE; SACHKRITIK.*

Bibliography   A list of writings on a particular subject, often with annotations. There are numerous bibliographical tools for the study of the BIBLE and related subjects, some of which are noted elsewhere in this volume under specific subjects. The following general works may be consulted when seeking bibliographic information: (1) *Bibliographic Index: A Cumulative Bibliography of Bibliographies* (New York: The H. W. Wilson Co.). Published semiannually (April and August), the *BI* is a subject list of bibliographies published separately or appearing as parts of books, pamphlets, and periodicals when such lists contain fifty or more entries. Published annually since 1969. (2) *Elenchus Bibliographicus Biblicus*, published by the Pontifical Biblical Institute in Rome, 1920–68, as a part of the periodical *Biblica* and thereafter separately, is the most exhaustive biblical bibliography available; it includes listings of books, articles, and reviews dealing with both Testaments, and the intertestamental and patristic periods.

The best single-volume guide to the tools of biblical study, including bibliographies in the various areas of interest is Frederick W. Danker's *Multipurpose Tools for Bible Study*, revised and expanded edition (Minneapolis: Fortress Press, 1993).

Periodical bibliographic aids most helpful include the following: *Internationale Zeitschriftenschau für Bibelwissenschaft und Grenzgebiete* (from 1951; currently published by Patmos-Verlag, Düsseldorf). Although reviews are mainly in German, this aid to periodical literature can be used to locate articles in English on OT, NT, and related areas. The Society for the Study of the Old Testament publishes annually in JSOT annotated "Book Lists" that are occasionally published as separate volumes; extensive annotated book lists and reviews are also published by the SOCIETY OF BIBLICAL LITERATURE in *JBL*. Also helpful is W. E. Mills, *An Index to Periodical Literature on the Apostle Paul* (Leiden: Brill, 1993). *New Testament Abstracts* (from 1956; published by Weston College of the Holy Spirit, Weston, Mass.) includes abstracts in English of articles and reviews from over 250 periodicals from around the world; and, similar in format and content, *Old Testament Abstracts* (from 1978; published by the BIBLICAL ASSOCIATION; The Catholic University of America, Washington, D.C.). See EXEGESIS; DEAD SEA SCROLLS; NAG HAMMADI CODICES.

Bibliolatry   is a pejorative term connoting the idolization of the BIBLE in such a way as to make it, instead of God, the object of reverence. Coined by G. E. LESSING, German dramatist and theologian, in 1777 in his argument against the "bibliolatry" of J. M. Goeze, a Lutheran pastor in Hamburg. See BIBLICISM; HISTORICAL-CRITICAL METHOD.

Bicolon.   See **Colon.**

Bildhälfte   (Ger: lit., "picture half") is a German technical term sometimes used in the interpretation of the PARABLES of Jesus to refer to the imagery of the parable, in contrast to its subject matter, content, or "reality" part (*Sachhälfte*). The "point of comparison," or *tertium comparationis*, is that point in the parable where, as it is argued, the picture and the meaning come together and are one. Recent interpreters have rejected this analysis of parables, which limits the parable to a single point, as too rationalistic. (For the terms see Eta Linnemann, *Jesus of the Parables* [New York: Harper & Row, 1966]; published in Britain as *Parables of Jesus* [London: SPCK, 1966].) See METAPHOR.

Blessings   Broadly speaking, blessings are words uttered to evoke, create, or pronounce well-being, to extol or praise God for his providence, or to consecrate or make (someone or thing) holy. More specifically the term may refer to (a) the actual words of blessing, (b) the power inherent in the utterance to produce an effect, or (c) the effect engendered or intended (health, prosperity, success, etc.).

The word *blessing* is used to translate two Hebrew nouns, *Berakah* and *Ashere,* the latter more often designating the state of being blessed, i.e., "happy." In the LXX, these terms are translated by *eulogia* and *makarios* (in Latin, respectively *benedictio* and *beati*), which distinction is preserved in more recent English translations by the words "blessing" and "happy," as in the Beatitudes (Matt 5; see JB, TEV).

Biblical blessings have been categorized in a variety of ways; one proposal is according to the giver and receiver of blessing: (1) God giver—creature (usually human) receiver: Gen 1:22 (creation); 1:28; 5:2; 9:1; 12:2–3; 22:17 (patriarchs); Exod 20:24; Lev 26:3–13; Deut 28:1–14 (the people of Israel); Deut 7:13; 11:26–30; Judg 13:24; 2 Sam 6:11–12 (the faithful); also God blessing through his Elect or Anointed One: Gen 12:2–3; 39:5; Num 24:9; Isa 19:24; in NT, through JESUS CHRIST or an angel: Acts 3:26; cf. Rev 14:13; 16:15; 19:9; 20:6; 22:7, 14. (2) Creature giver—creature receiver: Gen 9:26–27; 27:23–29 (heirs); Exod 39:43; Lev 9:23; Deut 33 (leaders bless people); Num 6:23–27 (priests—though God blesses); 2 Sam 6:18 (king); 1 Kgs 8:66 (people bless king); as in rabbinic literature, children and disciples are blessed (Mark 10:16; Luke 24:50); Jesus commands disciples to bless those who curse (Luke 6:28; cf. Rom 12:14; 1 Cor 4:12; 1 Pet 3:9). (3) Creature giver—God receiver: Gen 14:20; 24:27; Exod 18:10; 1 Sam 25:32; Ps 28:6; 1 Chron 29:10–13 (here in the sense of praising God for what he has done); Mark 6:41; 8:7 (also for food); in the EUCHARIST God is praised for a past act by a petition for his continued blessing (Matt 26:27; Mark 14:22; 1 Cor 11:24—here praise is called a "thanksgiving"). Cf. also Rev 5:9–10, 13–14.

For blessings in Qumran or DEAD SEA SCROLLS, see 1QSb; 1QS 11:1–4; in the *GOSPEL OF THOMAS*, LOGION 69.

Blessings (benedictions) commonly used since the Late Middle Ages to conclude divine worship include Num 6:24–26 (Aaronic blessing); Rom 15:13; 16:25–27; 2 Cor 13:14; Heb 13:20–21; 1 Thess 3:11–13, 5:23; Jude 24–25; Eph 3:20; 6:23; Phlm 25. Discussion of blessing in recent decades has been shaped by CLAUS WESTERMANN's proposal that blessing and deliverance are two distinct forms of God's activity in the HB. Blessing concerns God's fructification of ordinary patterns of nature and human activity while deliverance concerns God's intervention in specific, usually dramatic events. See *Blessing in the Bible and the Life of the Church* (Philadelphia: Fortress Press, 1978; Ger: 1973). The theme is further developed in R. Kendall Soulen, *The God of Israel and Christian Theology* (Minneapolis: Fortress Press, 1996).

Bousset, Wilhelm (1865–1920). Born in Lübeck, Germany, Bousset taught NT theology at Göttingen and from 1916 at Giessen. Considered one of the founders of the *RELIGIONSGESCHICHTLICHE SCHULE* (Comparative Religions), a method that he applied to his study of the relationship of Hellenistic religions to early Christianity and Judaism, he is particularly noted for *Die Religion des Judentums im späthellenistischen Zeitalter* (1903; 1926[3] rev. Hugo Gressmann, 1966[4]); *Hauptprobleme der Gnosis* (1907; 1973); and *Kyrios Christos* (Ger: 1913; Eng: Nashville: Abingdon Press, 1970). Bousset was a major architect of the model of Christian development that emphasized changes in Christology undergone in the transition from a Jewish Palestinian to a gentile Hellenistic environment, which, it was supposed, favored very different conceptions of what might be expected in a savior. In more recent decades aspects of this model have been increasingly called into question by more precise knowledge of Palestinian Judaism itself; see Larry W. Hurtado, "New Testament Christology: A Critique of Bousset's Influence" *TS* 40 (1979): 306–317.

Brown, Raymond E. (1928–1998). Born in New York City, Brown was ordained a Roman Catholic priest in 1953, receiving degrees from Catholic University, the Gregorian University in Rome, and St. Mary's Seminary in Baltimore, and the Ph.D. in Semitic Languages from Johns Hopkins University in 1958. He began his teaching career at St. Mary's and later (1971) accepted a call from both Woodstock (1971–74) and Union Theological Seminary in N.Y. (1971–90). A visiting scholar at numerous institutions, he retired in 1990 from UTS as Auburn Distinguished Professor of Biblical Studies. Known for his "compulsive desire to leave no question unaddressed," Brown became the foremost Catholic biblical scholar in North America in the 20th cent. This recognition is attested by the fact that he was the first ever to serve as the president of the three leading scholarly societies in the area of biblical studies: the CATHOLIC BIBLICAL ASSOCIATION OF AMERICA (1971–72), the SOCIETY OF BIBLICAL LITERATURE (1976–77), and Studiorum Novi Testamenti Societas (1986–87). He was also elected a Corresponding Fellow of the British Academy and a member of the American Academy of Arts and Sciences. His scholarly work invariably spoke from faith to faith without sacrificing critical acumen; for this reason he was often looked on as a scholar of the church as well as the academy. A prolific scholar, some of his most noted works include *The Jerome Biblical Commentary* (1968; reissued revised in 1990), *The Gospel according to John* (2 vols., 1966/70), *The Birth of the Messiah* (1977), *The Death of the Messiah* (1994), *An Introduction to New Testament Christology* (1994), and *An Introduction to the New Testament* (1997).

Bultmann, Rudolf (1884–1976). A student of WILHELM BOUSSET, HERMANN GUNKEL, Wilhelm Herrmann, Adolf von Harnack, ADOLF JÜLICHER, and JOHANNES WEISS, and later a colleague of Martin Heidegger at Marburg, Bultmann taught NT in Marburg (1912–16), Breslau (1916–20), and Giessen (1920), and again in Marburg (1921) until his retirement in 1951.

Few names in 20th cent. NT criticism and theology equal that of Bultmann and none exceeds it. As one of the inaugurating volumes on FORM CRITICISM, his *History of the Synoptic Tradition* (1921) is still an indispensable tool of NT criticism. His debates with KARL BARTH during the formative period of dialectical theology (1919–33) helped shape the principal themes of Continental theology for more than a quarter century; his program of "DEMYTHOLOGIZATION," that is, the interpretation of the biblical worldview and its language by way of EXISTENTIALIST (Heideggerian) categories, was the dominant issue in biblical theology until the 1960s. The most readily accessible introduction to his theology remains his little book *Jesus Christ and Mythology* (New York: Charles Scribner's Sons, 1958); also see Walter Schmithals, *An Introduction to the Theology of Rudolf Bultmann* (London: SCM Press, 1967). See APOPHTHEGM; HERMENEUTICS; MYTH; *SACHEXEGESE; SACHKRITIK*.

Byzantine Text is the name in TEXTUAL CRITICISM given to that form of the Greek NT current in Constantinople (earlier Byzantium and now Istanbul), the capital of the Eastern Empire (330 C.E. to 1453 C.E.). This text type, which is found among the majority of extant MSS, became the basis of ERASMUS' Greek NT (1516) and later of the TEXTUS RECEPTUS, the primary Greek source consulted in the preparation of the KJV of the NT (1611). The antecedent of the Byzantine text may be the work of Lucian of Antioch (d. 321), whose edition of the biblical text JEROME (ca. 403) acknowledged as the "*koiné*" or "common and widespread" text, referring to it also as the "Lucianic" text. Also called Antiochene or Syrian, the Byzantine text is characterized by clarifying the harmonizing INTERPOLATIONS and a general smoothing of diction.

Major witnesses are codices Alexandrinus (A), Ephraemi (C), Washingtonianus (W), and the *Koiné* group (E.F.G.H., etc.) and most MINUSCULES. *Note:* In the OT, Lucian's RECENSION (LXX^L) is based on a revision of Old Greek MSS, called the Proto-Lucianic recension. See ALEXANDRIAN TEXT; CODEX; FAMILY; WESTERN TEXT.

Caesarean Text, The   In TEXTUAL CRITICISM, Caesarean text is one of the geographical place names by which MSS of the NT bearing similar textual characteristics are sometimes identified (along with Alexandrian, Western, and Byzantine). The theory of the Caesarean text as a distinct text type was proposed by B. H. STREETER (*The Four Gospels* [London: Macmillan & Co., 1924]); it is based on the knowledge that in the two halves of his COMMENTARY on John, ORIGEN quoted from different MSS of the NT, the former available while he was in Alexandria, the latter while in Caesarea. Streeter deduced from this that a distinct Caesarean text type existed that he identified with Codex Koridethi θ and two families of MINUSCULES (Families 1 and 13; see FAMILY). Recent text-critical studies seem to indicate, however, that the witnesses purportedly within the Caesarean text type do not represent a text type sufficiently distinct from the two major strains, the Alexandrian (Neutral) and the Western, to warrant a separate designation. (See E. C. Colwell, *Studies in Methodology in Textual Criticism of the New Testament* [Leiden: E. J. Brill, 1969].)

Canon   (adj.: canonical) is a TRANSLITERATION of the Greek word *kanon* meaning "measuring stick" and by extension "rule" or "standard." Applied to sacred literature, canon denotes a list or collection of authoritative books. Christianity and Judaism are characterized by the centrality and importance they accord to their canons of sacred scripture, which they regarded as inspired by God. The canons are familiarly known

as "the BIBLE" in both communities, although of course the two canons differ in part. The Jewish canon consists of thirty-nine books in three main divisions: LAW, PROPHETS, and WRITINGS (see TANAKH). The Christian canon always includes these thirty-nine books (although in different order) and a second collection of twenty-seven books commonly known as New Testament. In addition, the Eastern Orthodox and Roman Catholic churches reckon additional books to the first collection (see APOCRYPHA).

The beginning of the idea of a canon of sacred scripture is discernible in scripture itself; see the "canonical" FORMULAS in Deut 4:2; 12:32; Jer 26:2; Prov 30:6; Eccl 3:14; 2 Pet 3: 15–16; Rev 22:6–8, 18–19. On the history of the Christian canon, see L. M. McDonald, *The Formation of the Christian Biblical Canon* (Peabody, Mass.: Hendrickson, 1995); on the Jewish, see S. Leiman, *The Canonization of Hebrew Scripture: The Talmudic and Midrashic Evidence* (Hamden, Conn., 1976). See CANONICAL CRITICISM; HEBREW BIBLE; OLD TESTAMENT/NEW TESTAMENT; *SUI IPSIUS INTERPRES.*

Canonical Criticism   is used rather ambiguously to refer to a variety of interpretive approaches that share a common concern with regard to the nature, function, and authority of canon. It is particularly interested in the meaning of texts within their canonical context, first in the book in which they appear and then within the larger context of the BIBLE as authoritative scripture, i.e., canon.

James A. Sanders coined the term *canonical criticism* (*Torah and Canon* [Philadelphia: Fortress Press, 1972]) to denote a method of BIBLICAL CRITICISM that operates subsequent to form- and REDACTION CRITICISM, that seeks to determine the function of biblical texts in their historical contexts, and that investigates the nature of their authority. The essence of canonical criticism, as practiced by Sanders, lies in discerning the HERMENEUTICS by which the ancient traditions were adapted for use in new contexts. An illuminative question of this perspective asks why the TORAH ends with Deuteronomy and its emphasis on the LAW rather than with Joshua and its story of the fulfillment of the promise to Abraham in the conquest of the land. (See *Canon and Community: A Guide to Canonical Criticism* [Philadelphia: Fortress Press, 1984] and *From Sacred Story to Sacred Text* [Philadelphia: Fortress Press, 1987].)

The term *canonical criticism* is also frequently applied to the interpretive approach to scripture advocated by Brevard Childs (*Introduction to the Old Testament as Scripture* [Philadelphia: Fortress Press, 1979], *Old Testament Theology in a Canonical Context* [Fortress, 1985, 1994], *The New Testament as Canon: An Introduction* [Philadelphia: Fortress Press, 1994]), and *Biblical Theology of the Old and New Testaments: Theological Reflection on the Christian Bible* [Minneapolis: Fortress Press, 1992]). With Sanders, Childs shares a broad definition of canon, a concern for the theological significance of the biblical texts, and a concern for the function of the biblical texts within the communities of faith that preserved and treasured them. However, Childs himself disavows the term *canonical criticism* and speaks instead of "a canonical approach." Childs does not consider the canonical approach to be another biblical critical method such as FORM CRITICISM or RHETORICAL CRITICISM or the like. "Rather, the issue at stake in relation to the canon turns on establishing a stance from which the Bible can be read as sacred scripture" (*Introduction*, 82).

Contrary to Sanders, Childs does not seek to determine the hermeneutics employed in the canonical process. Rather, the stance developed by Childs focuses on the shape and function of the final canonical text. Childs carefully describes and analyzes the final received form of the OT books. His primary concern is not with any particular editorial layer but rather with the final resultant product. According to Childs this final shape is of special significance because (1) it alone displays the full history of revelation witnessed to by scripture; (2) in it the community has exercised its critical judgment on the received traditions and modified them accordingly; and (3) by showing how the texts were actualized by generations removed from the original event and composition of the writings, the canonical shape may provide a hermeneutical key as to how we may actualize the text in our day.

Sanders and Childs both operate with a definition of canon considerably more broad than that in common parlance. They argue that the notion of canon should be understood as including not only the final literary stage in the Bible's development but also that development process itself. Moreover, they suggest that such a broadening is not a novel suggestion but results from a critical reevaluation of Semler's narrowing of the concept—on which the 19th-cent. critical consensus was based.

Along with Childs and Sanders a number of other scholars have shown an interest in a new understanding of canon. Among the other studies that might be comprehended by the term *canonical criticism*, the following are of special note: Joseph Blenkinsopp, *Prophecy and Canon* (Notre Dame, Ind.: University of Notre Dame Press, 1977); George Coats and Burke Long, eds., *Canon and Authority* (Philadelphia: Fortress Press, 1977); Donn F. Morgan, *Between Text and Community: The "Writings" in Canonical Interpretation* (Minneapolis: Fortress Press, 1990); C. E. Braaten and Robert Jenson, eds., *Reclaiming the Bible for the Church* (Grand Rapids: Eerdmans, 1995); and Mary C. Callaway, "Canonical Criticism," in Steven L. McKenzie and Stephen R. Haynes, eds., *To Each Its Own Meaning* (Louisville, Ky.: Westminster John Knox Press, 1999).

Case, Shirley Jackson (1872–1947). Born in New Brunswick, Canada, Case studied at Acadia University (A.B., 1893; M.A., 1896), Yale Divinity School (B.D., 1904; Ph.D., 1906), and the University of Marburg (1910). He taught NT and EARLY CHURCH history at the University of Chicago Divinity School (1908–38), serving as dean from 1933 until his retirement (1938), thereafter becoming dean of the School of Religion, Lakeland, Florida. He was managing editor of the *American Journal of Theology* (1912–20) and editor of the *Journal of Religion* (1927–39) and *Religion in the Making* (1940–43). A student of Christian mysticism and millennialism and a supporter of the social gospel movement, he is best known in BIBLICAL CRITICISM for his book *Jesus: A New Biography* (Chicago: University of Chicago Press, 1927).

Casuistic Law   In OT FORM CRITICISM, the term *casuistic law* refers to a class of law that addresses itself to cases, in contrast to APODICTIC LAW, which is formulated in terms of absolute prohibitions and commandments. Casuistic law is characterized by an opening conditional clause (PROTASIS) that describes the case, beginning "If . . . ," followed by a statement of the penalty in the *apodosis* or main clause, "then he (or she) shall . . ."; e.g., Deut 22:23–29. According to ALBRECHT ALT (see APODICTIC LAW), casuistic law was the typical formulation of law in the ancient Near East generally. See *SÄTZE HEILIGEN RECHTES*.

Catalog of Vices.   See *Lästerkataloge.*

Catalog of Virtues.   See *Lästerkataloge.*

Catechesis, catechetic, catechetical   (fr. Gk: oral instruction). Oral instruction in matters of faith; or a book or collection of materials so used. According to FORM CRITICISM, catechetical needs were formative influences in shaping biblical material; this is particularly evident in Deuteronomy and the Deuteronomistic redactions of the OT and, more clearly still, in the structural patterns of the GOSPEL according to Matt in the NT. Materials from a Eucharistic catechesis for example may possibly be found, it is suggested, not only in the PERICOPE of the Last Supper (Matt 26:14–30) but also in the miracles of feeding (Matt 14:15–21; 15:32–38). See CREDO.

Catena   (pl.: catenae) is a technical term borrowed from Latin (meaning "chain") and connoting a connected series, whether of SAYINGS, quotations, liturgical FORMULAE, miracle stories, etc. A *catena* of scriptural citations appears in some NT writings, e.g., Heb 1:5–13. In TEXTUAL CRITICISM, as in Roman Catholic tradition, a *catena* is a series of quotations extracted from the writings of the church fathers (*catena Patrum*) and used as a COMMENTARY on a passage of scripture (see, e.g., Codex 747 in J. H. Greenlee, *Introduction to NT Textual Criticism* [Grand Rapids: Eerdmans, 1964], plate 6).

Catholic Biblical Association of America, The (CBA)   Founded in 1938, the CBA publishes the *Catholic Biblical Quarterly (CBQ); Old Testament Abstracts,* and the *CBQ Monograph Series;* Active and Associate Membership is open "to those who qualify as specialists in biblical studies." Address: The Catholic Biblical Association of America, The Catholic University, Washington, DC 20064. See COUNCIL ON THE STUDY OF RELIGION; SOCIETY OF BIBLICAL LITERATURE.

Catholic Epistles   consist of James, 1 and 2 Peter, 1, 2, and 3 John, and Jude; also called the "General Epistles," i.e., LETTERS treated as being addressed to the whole church. Sometimes referred to in German as "church epistles" (*Kirchenbriefe*); however, 1 Peter, and 2 and 3 John identify their intended recipients and cannot in the strict sense be considered "catholic," i.e., addressed to all Christians. The names of the epistles are derived from the (putative) authors, rather than from the recipients as in the case of the Pauline letters. The term dates from at least the 4th century C.E. See PASTORAL EPISTLES.

Catholicizing Tendency is a term used chiefly by Protestant scholars to refer to a movement thought to be already evident in the 1st century toward the institutionalization of Christian belief and practice, particularly with the waning of the expectation of the imminent return of CHRIST. In the NT, see Matt 16:19; 18:18; Eph 4; 1 Tim 3, etc., and the whole of Acts.

CBA (CBQ). See **Catholic Biblical Association of America, The.**

C.E. is an equivalent of A.D. and means "Common Era"; see B.C.E.

Cento (Lat: patched cloth; pl.: *centos*). In BIBLICAL CRITICISM, a *cento* is a patchwork of scriptural quotations (e.g., Rom 3:10b—18; 11:34–35; 1 Pet 2:6–8; Heb 1:5–13).

CEV. See **Contemporary English Version.**

Chenoboskion is the name of the site of the first Christian monastery, founded by Pachomius ca. 320 C.E. and located on the Nile River in Egypt, approximately forty miles northwest of Luxor near the modern town of Nag Hammadi. For reasons of historical interest primarily, the name Chenoboskion was attached to the

Coptic GNOSTIC MSS discovered near there in 1945–46; these MSS are now commonly referred to as the NAG HAMMADI CODICES.

Chiasmus (chiasm; also called chiastic or inverted PARALLELISM). A Latinized word based on the Greek letter χ (*Chi*) to symbolize the inverted sequence or crossover of parallel words or ideas in a bicolon (distich), sentence, or larger literary unit. Chiasmus appears for example in Mark 2:27: "The sabbath [a] was made for man [b], and not man [b'] for the sabbath [a']," taking the simple form: a b b' a'. A chiasmus that appears in the Greek or Hebrew is often lost in translation, appearing only as simple synonymous parallelism. Its preservation can also be confusing, as in Matt 7:6, which parallels in chiastic form "dogs" with "maul" and "swine" with "trample": "Do not give what is holy to dogs; and do not throw your pearls before swine, or they will trample them under foot and turn and maul you" (NRSV). In prophetic literature, Isa 6:10 is a chiasm of two tricola (tristichs):

A Make the mind of this people dull,
B and stop their ears,
C and shut their eyes,
C so that they may not look with their eyes,
B and listen with their ears,
A And comprehend with their minds,
     And turn and be healed. (NRSV)

Chiasm in prose literature is more difficult to identify, and its role in interpretation

Chaism in 1 Cor 5:2–6

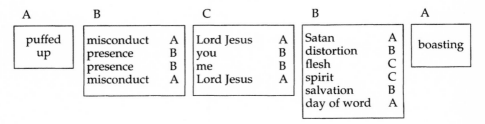

A	B		C		B		A
puffed up	misconduct presence presence misconduct	A B B A	Lord Jesus you me Lord Jesus	A B B A	Satan distortion flesh spirit salvation day of word	A B C C B A	boasting

more contested. John 6:36–40; Rom 2:7–10; 11:30–31; Matt 9:17; 1 Cor 7:3; 9:19–22; 11:8–12; Col 3:3–4, etc., are cited as examples, perhaps indicating an underlying Semitic influence on the writers. Nigel Turner (in *A Grammar of New Testament Greek*, vol. 3: *Syntax* [Edinburgh: T. & T. Clark, 1963]) suggests that 1 Cor 5:2–6 is chiasmus within chiasmus (see chart, p. 32).

For an overzealous but helpful analysis of chiasmus, see Nils W. Lund, *Chiasmus in the NT* (Chapel Hill: University of North Carolina Press, 1942). Such overzealousness is not uncommon in the alleged discovery of chiasm in scripture. See COLON.

Chria (pl.: *Chriae*; also Gk: *Chreia*; pl.: *-ai*) is a Greek technical term used in ancient RHETORIC to denote a literary form containing an EPIGRAM or "a sharp pointed saying of general significance, originating in a definite person and arising out of a definite situation" (DIBELIUS). In Hellenistic culture, *chriae* were told about and in honor of a famous man or simply as a means of preserving a humorous saying or incident concerning him. In his form critical studies, Dibelius distinguishes the *chria* from (a) the larger grouping of "Apophthegmata" by noting the former's connection with a particular situation, and from (b) the Gnome by its connection with a person (*From Tradition to Gospel* [London: Ivor Nicholson & Watson, Ltd., 1934; repr. James Clarke, 1971; New York: Charles Scribner's Sons, 1935], 152f.). Examples of *chriae* are to be found in Xenophon's *Memorabilia*, e.g., "On a man who was angry because his greeting was not returned: 'Ridiculous!' he [Socrates] exclaimed, 'You would not have been angry if you had met a man in worse health; and yet you are annoyed because you have come across someone with ruder manners!'" (III. xiii.).

According to Dibelius, literary tendencies within the EARLY CHURCH, particularly seen in Luke's GOSPEL, caused SAYINGS of Jesus to be adapted to the *chria* form, e.g., Luke 3:21–22; 8:21; 9:61–62; 11:27–28;

19:39–40, 45–46, etc. See APOPHTHEGM; PARADIGM.

Christ   (Gk: lit., "anointed one"). *Christos* approximates the Hebrew *mashîah* (messiah), meaning "Anointed One [of God]," viz., one invested by God with a unique status and mission. It was the central term used by Christians from a very early period to denote Jesus and his significance. The works of the NT use *christos* to refer generally to the coming "anointed one" of divine promise and to refer specifically to Jesus himself, affirmed to be this "Messiah." At points (as in Paul), the titular sense of the term recedes behind its use as a name, but even then does not entirely disappear (N. A. Dahl). According to Donald H. Juel, the NT's use of *Christos* appears highly singular when compared and contrasted with other manifestations of postbiblical Judaism. Ultimately, "Christ" in the NT receives its content not from a previously fixed concept of messiahship but rather from the person and work of Jesus himself.

See N. A. Dahl, *Jesus the Christ: The Historical Origins of Christological Doctrine* (Minneapolis: Fortress Press, 1991); Donald H. Juel, *Messianic Exegesis: Christological Interpretation of the Old Testament in Early Christianity* (Philadelphia: Fortress Press, 1992). See JESUS CHRIST; QUEST OF THE HISTORICAL JESUS.

Christophany,   meaning "an appearance, or manifestation, of CHRIST" was first used by D. F. STRAUSS (1836) of the appearances of the risen Jesus to the disciples and women (e.g., Matt 28:9–10, 16–17; Mark 16:9–10, 12, 14—the long ending; Luke 24:13ff., etc.). Other passages are variously described as Christophanies, such as the transfiguration (Mark 9:2ff. pars.) and Paul's confrontation on the road to Damascus (Acts 9:3–16, etc.). The common view of the EARLY CHURCH was that the OT theophanies were Christophanies. A modern rehabilitation of this view was attempted by Wilhelm Vischer (*Das Christuszeugnis des*

Alten Testaments, 2 vols.; Zurich, 1934–42), partly in order to underscore the indispensability of the OT for Christians at a time when this view was under sharp attack. See also Carey C. Newman, *Paul's Glory-Christology: Tradition and Rhetoric* (NovTSup 69; Leiden: Brill, 1996). See THEOPHANY.

Chronology The science that deals with measuring time and that assigns to events their proper dates. The authority recognized by the SOCIETY OF BIBLICAL LITERATURE for biblical chronology is *Civilizations of the Ancient Near East*, ed. Jack M. Sasson, 4 vols. (New York: Charles Scribner's Sons, 1995). See particularly vol. 2, part 5 ("History and Culture"). Also see Jack Finegan, *Handbook of Biblical Chronology*, rev. ed. (Peabody, Mass.: Hendrickson, 1998); J. Hughes, *Secrets of the Times: The Chronology of the Hebrew Bible* (JSOTSup 66; Sheffield Academic Press, 1990), and, for the NT, H. W. Hoehner, *Chronological Aspects of the Life of Christ* (Grand Rapids: Zondervan, 1997); Robert Jewett, *A Chronology of Paul's Life* (Philadelphia: Fortress Press, 1979); and Gerd Lüdemann, *Paul, Apostle to the Gentiles: Studies in Chronology* (Philadelphia: Fortress Press, 1984). See HISTORIOGRAPHY.

Coda, in LITERARY CRITICISM, is a term that refers to a concluding passage, often added by a REDACTOR, designed to bring a larger section or book(s) to a close by reiterating or summarizing its major themes. Second Sam 21–24 has been identified as a coda to the books of Samuel, 2 Kgs 11–12 to 1 and 2 Kings, Pss 146–150 to the book of PSALMS, Ruth 4:18–22 to Ruth, Deut 34 to the PENTATEUCH, Mal 4:5–6 to the prophetic books, et al. Recognition of structural elements, such as the coda, aids in the interpretation of texts.

Codex (pl.: codices). An ancient manuscript in book form, made of PAPYRUS or VELLUM. When the codex as an alternative to the scroll originated is uncertain. But its existence in the 2nd cent. C.E. is certain. Almost all extant early Christian manuscripts are in codex form, perhaps because it facilitated locating scriptural passages of interest and placing works in canonical order. (See Frederic G. Kenyon, *The Text of the Greek Bible*, 3rd rev. and aug. ed. by A. W. Adams [London: Duckworth Press, 1975]; also Eric G. Turner, *The Typology of the Early Codex* [Philadelphia: University of Pennsylvania Press, 1977]; and C. H. Roberts and T. C. Skeat, *The Birth of the Codex* [Oxford: Oxford University Press, 1983].)

Codex Alexandrinus (*siglum:* A) is a 5th-cent. MS of the Greek BIBLE, presently housed in the British Museum, earlier a gift from the Patriarch of Constantinople to James I (1603–25). The text type in the NT is both Byzantine (GOSPELS) and Alexandrian (Acts and Epistles). Of the NT, most of Matt is missing, as are John 6:50–8:52 and 2 Cor 4:13–12:6. The MS includes I and II Clement and contains, with P[47], one of the best texts of the book of Revelation. In the OT, the text is eclectic.

Codex Bezae Cantabrigiensis is a 5th-cent. Greco-Latin MS of the GOSPELS and Acts (*sigla:* D or D[ea] [Gk] and d [Lat]). It receives its name from Theodore Bezae and the University of Cambridge to which he presented it in 1581, having obtained the MS from St. Irenaeus' monastery in Lyons, France. Its origin is unknown but is probably Western Mediterranean. D is the principal representative of the WESTERN TEXT, which orders the Gospels: Matt, John, Luke, Mark. Though filled with innumerable orthographic and grammatical errors, the text, which is arranged colometrically, is of interest because of its omissions (called "Western non-INTERPOLATIONS" by WESTCOTT and HORT) in Luke and its additions in the book of Acts, which is 1/10th longer than the "Neutral" text (S, B, etc.). These apparent additions to the text of Acts are dominantly anti-Jewish in nature (see E. J. Epp, *The Theological Tendency of Codex Bezae Cantabrigiensis in Acts* [Cambridge:

Cambridge University Press, 1966]). The most famous addition to Luke follows 6:4: "On the same day he saw a man working on the Sabbath and he said to him, 'Man, if you know what you are doing, blessed are you; but if you do not know, you are accursed and a transgressor of the law.'"

Codex Ephraemi Rescriptus   (*siglum:* C). A PALIMPSEST CODEX of parts of the OT and NT dating from the 5th cent. The text, now in Paris, contains Alexandrian and Western READINGS, but also later readings of a Byzantine type, hence not of great significance for TEXTUAL CRITICISM.

Codex Sinaiticus   (*siglum:* א or S) is a 4th-cent. VELLUM MS of portions of the OT and the whole NT, discovered in 1859 by CONSTANTIN TISCHENDORF in the Orthodox monastery of St. Catherine at the foot of Mt. Sinai. Like CODEX VATICANUS, the text is Alexandrian. Absent from the text is the longer ending of Mark (16:9–19) and the *PERICOPE DE ADULTERA* (John 7:53–8:11). In order, the Pauline Epistles follow the GOSPELS (canonical order), then Hebrews, the PASTORAL EPISTLES, Acts, the CATHOLIC EPISTLES, and Revelation, followed by the *Epistle of Barnabas* and the *Shepherd of Hermas.*

Codex Vaticanus   (*siglum:* B) is a 4th-cent. VELLUM MS of the BIBLE, housed in the Vatican library since at least 1481. The text is Alexandrian (or Neutral) and, because of its antiquity, state of preservation, and text type, is extremely valuable as a textual source. The MS ends at Heb 9:14. The books missing in addition to Heb 9:15–13:25, are Philemon, the Pastorals, and Revelation. Also absent are the longer ending of Mark (16:9–19) and the *PERICOPE DE ADULTERA* (John 7:53–8:11). The CATHOLIC EPISTLES precede the LETTERS of Paul and follow the Acts of the Apostles.

Collate   (fr. a Latin verb meaning to compare). In TEXTUAL CRITICISM, collation refers to the critical comparison of ancient

handwritten exemplars of a given writing in order to ascertain textual differences with the aim of reconstructing the original text. Usually, MSS are collated against an accepted form of the text, such as the TEXTUS RECEPTUS of the Greek NT or a modern CRITICAL TEXT.

Colometric.   See **Colon.**

Colon   (pl.: cola). A single unit of poetry. The most commonly used technical term in the analysis of Hebrew poetry, colon refers to the most fundamental unit of Hebrew poetry. It occurs most frequently together with one or two other cola, creating the bicolon and tricolon respectvely. While older terminology has disappeared from contemporary scholarship (stich [or hemistich] = colon; distich [or stich] = bicolon, and tristich = tricolon), recent analysts have employed added additional terms: "line" and "verset" for colon and dyadic and triadic line for bi- and tricolon (Alter). Example:

Judges 15:16

"With the jawbone of   colon or verset
   a donkey
Have I mightily raged:
With the jawbone of a ⎫ bicolon or couplet or
   donkey   diadic line or
Have I slain a thousand⎬ linepair
   men"   ⎭

Ps 24:7

"Lift up your heads,   ⎫
   O gates:
And be lifted up, O   ⎬ tricolon or triadic
   ancient doors!   line
That the King of glory ⎭
   may come in."

In textual criticism, the term *colon* means a line containing a single clause, normally of at least nine syllables but not more than sixteen. Some ancient MSS of the NT are written colometrically, of which Codex

Bezae is the most famous; in them, each printed line is composed of one colon or clause. See M. P. O'Conner, *Hebrew Verse Structure* (Winona Lake, Ind.: Eisenbrauns, 1997); R. Alter, *Art of Biblical Poetry* (New York: Basic Books, 1985); D. Petersen and K. Richards, *Interpreting Hebrew Poetry* (Minneapolis: Fortress Press, 1992).

Colophon   (Gk: finishing touch) is the name given to an inscription at the end of a book; it may include the following, in whole or in part: the title or subject matter, the author, printer, date and place of publication; or it may contain simply a comment or warning by the author. In the OT a colophon can be found at the close of the HOLINESS CODE (Lev 26:46) and the second book of the PSALMS of David (Ps 72:20); also cf. Job 31:40; in the NT, Rev 22:18–19 may be so considered. According to B. H. STREETER, a common colophon on 11th- and 12th-cent. MINUSCULE MSS reads, "Copied and corrected from ancient exemplars from Jerusalem preserved on the Holy Mountain." See *ANET*, 424, 438.

Comedy   Although, as customarily understood, comedy appears nowhere in the Old or New Testaments as a literary genre, a medieval definition of *comedy* (and *tragedy*) has recently been revived in the context of PARABLE interpretation. In the Middle Ages *comedy* was defined as a movement from bad to good fortune, whereas *tragedy* embodied a reversal of fortune from good to bad. It is in this sense that Dante's *The Divine Comedy* is to be understood. For its application to the interpretation of parables see Dan O. Via's *The Parables* (Philadelphia: Fortress Press, 1967) and his *Kerygma and Comedy in the New Testament* (Philadelphia: Fortress Press, 1975). The term *comedy* has been applied to the BIBLE as a whole, the book of Revelation, as the last book, ending with a vision of the new Jerusalem where "mourning and crying and pain will be no more" (Rev 21:4c, NRSV).

Comma Johanneum.   See **Johannine Comma.**

Commentary   Although varied in form, content, and style, a commentary is a book that discusses the biblical text chapter by chapter and verse by verse, lifting up noteworthy phrases and words for clarification or comment. Much or even most of the work of figures such as ORIGEN, Luther, and Calvin took the form of commentaries, and the single most influential book in 20th-cent. theology was the 2nd edition of KARL BARTH's commentary on Romans (*The Epistle to the Romans* [Oxford: Oxford University Press, 1968; Ger: 1922]). Modern critical commentaries, in contrast to homiletical or devotional ones, deal with the text in terms of its linguistic, literary, historical, and religiocultural setting. Introductory articles often precede the commentary proper. Commentaries may appear as single volumes or in series.

The following are standard English commentaries of the BIBLE or of the NT alone. A number of the more important German commentaries are available through the *Old* and *NT Library* series (Westminster John Knox) and through *Hermeneia* (Fortress).

Anchor Bible, The (Garden City, N.Y.: Doubleday & Co., 1964–). Not strictly a commentary. Translation with extensive introduction and critical notes.

Abingdon New Testament Commentary (Nashville: Abingdon Press, 1996–). Compact critical commentary for theological students.

Ancient Christian Commentary on Scripture (Chicago: Fitzroy Dearborn Publishers, 1998–). Excerpts from early church fathers.

Berit Olam: Studies in Hebrew Narrative and Poetry (Collegeville, Minn.: Liturgical Press, 1996–). Technical.

The Broadman Bible Commentary (Nashville: Broadman Press, 1970–73). Evangelical. 13 vols.

Cambridge Bible Commentary: New English Bible (Cambridge: Cambridge University Press, 1963–). For lay readers by leading British and American scholars (paper).

Cambridge Greek Testament Commentary (Cambridge: Cambridge University Press, 1957). Prepared for British schools and colleges.

Clarendon Bible, The (Oxford: Clarendon Press, 1922–47 [incomplete]). Based on RV. Nontechnical.

Doubleday Bible Commentary (New York: Doubleday, 1998–). For laity.

The Eerdmans Critical Commentary (Grand Rapids: Eerdmans, 2000–). Prepared by "the foremost authorities in biblical scholarship worldwide." The commentary on 1 and 2 Timothy is 918 pages of detailed information; Philemon over 540. Includes extensive discussions of the SOCIAL WORLD of the text.

The Expositor's Bible Commentary with The New International Version of the Holy Bible (Grand Rapids: Zondervan, 1979–). Evangelical.

Harper's New Testament Commentaries (New York: Harper & Brothers, 1957–; same as Black's NTC). Requires some knowledge of Greek.

Hermeneia (Philadelphia: Fortress Press, 1971–). Based on Hebrew and Greek texts; for serious students. The series includes special studies and noncanonical works, such as the SERMON ON THE MOUNT, THE DIDACHE and the *Shepherd of Hermas*.

International Critical Commentary on the Holy Scriptures (New York: Charles Scribner's Sons, 1896–1937). Technical commentary; partly out of date.

International Theological Commentary (Grand Rapids: Eerdmans, 1983–). Less interested in descriptive historical approach than theological relevance for the life of the church.

Interpretation: A Bible Commentary for Teaching and Preaching (Louisville, Ky.: John Knox Press, 1982–).

Moffatt New Testament Commentary (London: Hodder & Stoughton, 1926–50). Nontechnical commentary by British scholars.

New International Biblical Commentary (Peabody, Mass.: Hendrickson, 1992–). Based on the NEW INTERNATIONAL VERSION of the Bible and designed for general readers.

The New Interpreter's Bible (Nashville: Abingdon Press, 1994–). Contains commentary and homiletical reflections in addition to general articles and introductions.

The New Testament in Context (Valley Forge, Pa.: Trinity Press International, 1994–).

Old Testament Library, The (Philadelphia: Westminster Press, 1961–). Contains commentaries and MONOGRAPHS. Scholarly. Languages generally not required.

Proclamation Commentaries. Rev. and enlarg. ed. (Minneapolis: Fortress Press, 1986–91). Especially designed for preachers but with high academic quality.

Sacra Pagina (Collegeville, Minn.: Liturgical Press, 1991–). Written by an international team of Roman Catholic scholars.

Westminster Bible Companion (Louisville, Ky.: Westminster John Knox Press, 1995–). Designed for the laity.

Recent one-volume commentaries include the following:

Interpreter's One-Volume Commentary (Nashville: Abingdon Press, 1971; London: William Collins Sons, 1972).

Jerome Biblical Commentary (Englewood Cliffs, N.J.: Prentice-Hall, 1969; London: Geoffrey Chapman, 1969). *The New Jerome Biblical Commentary* appeared in 1990; reprint, 1999.

A New Catholic Commentary on Holy Scripture (Camden, N.J.: Thomas Nelson & Sons, 1953; rev. 1969).

Searching the Scriptures: A Feminist Commentary, ed. Elisabeth Schüssler Fiorenza (New York: Crossroad, 1998). Book by book, rather than verse by verse.

United Bible Societies Handbook Series (New York: United Bible Societies, 1992–). Designed for Bible translators and not a commentary in the ordinary sense but immensely helpful. Published since 1960 on various topics related to translation.

The Women's Bible Commentary, ed. Carol A. Newsom and Sharon H. Ringe (Louisville, Ky.: Westminster/John Knox Press, 1992).

Composition Criticism   (Ger: KOMPO-SITIONSGESCHICHTE). Coined by Ernst Haenchen in the 1960s, the term refers to an analysis of the total effect of a redacted text, such as the GOSPELS and Acts, treating the composition as a whole, rather than concentrating only on the specific redactional elements within a text. The term has not been widely employed since its interests are often taken for granted as the goal of redaction-critical studies and, normally, of commentaries dealing with individual books of the Bible. However, see R. F. O'Toole, *The Unity of Luke's Theology: An Analysis of Luke-Acts* (Wilmington, Del.: Michael Glazier, 1984). See REDACTION CRITICISM; CANONICAL CRITICISM.

Conclusio.   See **Rhetorical Analysis.**

Concordance   A concordance is an alphabetical listing of all the principal words of a book, including a reference indicating the place where it occurs and usually some portion of the accompanying phrase. Concordances of scripture are numerous, varying in form, language, and comprehensiveness. In the original languages they are commonly known by the editor's (s') name, such as Davidson, or Mandelkern (Hebrew and Chaldee), Moulton and Geden (Greek NT), HATCH AND REDPATH (SEPTUAGINT), and Schmoller (*Handkonkordanz zum NT*). A new multivolume series of concordances of the scriptures, called *The Computer Bible* (*CB*), and of ancient texts pertinent to the study of scripture (called *The International Concordance Library* (*ICL*), is being published by Biblical Research Associates (Wooster, Ohio). The *CB* will include individual concordances devoted to a wide range of analytic data, including MORPHOLOGY, SYNTAX, style, linguistic phenomena, etc.; the *ICL* will include concordances of the APOSTOLIC FATHERS, PHILO OF ALEXANDRIA, the APOCRYPHAL NT, the DEAD SEA SCROLLS, et al. An exhaustive concordance to the Greek NT with word-statistical studies is being published by K. ALAND: *Vollständige Konkor-danz zum griechischen Neuen Testament* (Berlin/New York: Walter de Gruyter, 1975–).

English language concordances exist for the major English translations of the BIBLE. Standard ones include Cruden's (KJV, 1873); Strong's (KJV, reprint 1998); Young's (KJV, 1936); and Nelson's (RSV, 1957); less exhaustive concordances exist for NEB, JB, Moffatt's, etc. Two valuable concordances to the NT are the *Modern Concordance to the New Testament*, ed. Michael Darton (Garden City, N.Y.: Doubleday, 1977), which is designed for use with the JB, KJV, RSV, NAB, NEB, and LB(P); and Clinton Morrison, *An Analytical Concordance to the Revised Standard Version of the New Testament* (Philadelphia: Westminster Press, 1979). With the revision of these VERSIONS, new concordances have appeared: NRSV, prepared by Richard E. Whitaker and John R. Kohlenberger III (Grand Rapids: Eerdmans, 2000); Hebrew and English concordance to the Old Testament with the NIV (Grand Rapids: Zondervan, 1998); NKJV (Nashville: Thomas Nelson, 1992); NIV (Grand Rapids: Zondervan, 1990).

A concordance to the Dead Sea Scrolls has been edited by Karl Georg Kuhn: *Konkordanz zu den Qumrantexten* (Göttingen: Vandenhoeck & Ruprecht, 1960); also see *Graphic Concordance to the Dead Sea Scrolls*, by James H. Charlesworth et al. (Louisville, Ky.: Westminster/John Knox Press, 1991).

Note: Computer software for Bible study makes word searches fast and simple. For a recent guide see: Jeffry Hsu et al., *Computer Bible Study: Up-to-date Information on the Best Software and Techniques* (Dallas: Word Publications, 1993).

Conditio Jacobea (Lat: "the condition of James"), viz., "If the Lord wills." The term applies to Jas 4:15 but did not originate there (see also Acts 18:21; Rom 1:10; 1 Cor 4:19; 16:7; Heb 6:3; also cf. Phil 2:19, 24). This FORMULA is not found in OT or rabbinic writings although it abounded in the popular piety of the Greco-Roman culture and still survives in many languages: *deo volente* (Ital.), *Inshallah* (Arabic), etc. Its apotropaic (i.e., evil-averting) intention is evident by its setting in the so-called travelogue sections of Paul's LETTERS. An amusing and satirical parallel can be found in the *Alphabet of ben Sira*, an 11th-cent. Jewish writing; see STRACK-BILLERBECK, ad hoc.

Conflation, Conflate Reading In TEXTUAL CRITICISM, *conflation* is the term used to denote a scribal error or editorial change in which two VARIANT READINGS of a text are combined, forming a new reading not precisely identical with either of the two source readings. See ASSIMILATION; GLOSS; HAPLOGRAPHY; HOMOIOTELEUTON.

Congregational Rules, Church Rules. See *Gemeindeordnungen*.

Consistent Eschatology. See **Eschatology**.

Constructive Parallelism. See Synthetic Parallelism under **Parallelism**.

Contemporary English Version (The), commonly abbreviated CEV, was produced by the United Bible Societies (NT, 1991; OT, 1995) in response to the need to provide speakers of English as a second language with a more simplified VERSION of the Bible than then existed. Up to that time, *Good News for Modern Man* (TODAY'S ENGLISH VERSION of the Bible) had served that purpose. See DOUAY; JERUSALEM BIBLE; LIVING BIBLE (PARAPHRASED); NEW AMERICAN BIBLE; NEW ENGLISH BIBLE; NEW INTERNATIONAL VERSION; NEW JEWISH VERSION; KING JAMES VERSION; PARAPHRASE; REVISED STANDARD VERSION.

Corpus Hermeticum. See **Hermetic Literature.**

Council on the Study of Religion, The (CSR) The CSR "is a federation of learned societies in religion interested in developing greater coordination of the field as a whole. It seeks to initiate, coordi-

nate, and implement projects designed to strengthen and advance scholarship and teaching." The constituent members of the CSR are the American Academy of Religion, American Society of Christian Ethics, American Society of Missiology, American Theological Library Association, CATHOLIC BIBLICAL ASSOCIATION, Catholic Theological Society of America, College Theology Society, Religious Education Association, SOCIETY OF BIBLICAL LITERATURE, and Society for the Scientific Study of Religion. It publishes quarterly the *Bulletin* (announcing activities of member societies), *Religious Studies Review,* and TOIL (Teaching Opportunities Information Listing). CSR Executive Office address: Wilfrid Laurier University, Waterloo, Ontario, Canada N2L 3C5.

Covenant Form. See **Treaty Form.**

Covenant Lawsuit. See *Rib* **Pattern.**

Covenant Renewal Psalms. See **Psalms**.

Credo (Lat: I believe). A concise statement of faith that has its setting in the worship (cultic) life of the believing community. Examples in the OT are Deut 26:1–11; 6:20–24; 26:5–9; Josh 24:1–13; 14–25; etc. Creedal themes may appear in prayers, cult lyrics, or NARRATIVES, e.g., 1 Sam 12:8; Pss 78; 105; 135; 136. Here the major themes revolve around the exodus, the conquest of the Promised Land, and the Sinai Covenant. In the NT, christological FORMULAS and HYMNS constitute parallels to the OT credo. The scholar for whom the credo became an organizing principle for constructing the theology of the OT was GERHARD VON RAD. See esp. *Old Testament Theology 1: The Theology of Israel's Historical Traditions* (New York: Harper & Brothers, 1962). Whether a credo (as in Deuteronomy) is to be understood as precedent to its narrative elaboration, as von Rad thought, or a later "concentrated summary" of a preexisting narrative, as G. Fohrer argued, is disputed.

Criteria of Authenticity What in terms of subject matter has been called the "QUEST OF THE HISTORICAL JESUS" can in terms of methodology be called the quest of criteria of authenticity, that is, the quest for the conceptual means by which the (canonical and, in recent decades also, EXTRACANONICAL) SAYINGS tradition can be judged to go back either to the Jesus of history or to the EARLY CHURCH. Criteria adduced to determine authentic sayings of Jesus are known as criteria of authenticity. Although present in some form in the 19th cent. Quest, they were reformulated and sharpened by ERNST KÄSEMANN (1954) in what became known as the inaugural essay of "the New Quest of the Historical Jesus." In subsequent decades the criteria of authenticity, though variously nuanced, were generally recognized as three, best articulated by Norman Perrin and Reginald Fuller. With the beginning of the so-called "Third Quest" and its counterparts in the mid-1980s, the first criterion was either rejected or significantly revised because of its severe and limiting skepticism (see following). There is no effort here to note all the varied nomenclature assigned to the criteria by scholars, or the different nuances they entail.

1. The *criterion of dissimilarity* (so Perrin; Fuller: "distinctiveness"; also called "contradiction," "discontinuity," "originality," etc.): To be certain or reasonably certain of authenticity, a saying must be dissimilar to both Judaism and the teachings of the church. Although it is obviously possible and probable that Jesus incorporated Jewish thought into his own theology (e.g., Isa 61:1–2) or that the early church transformed authentic sayings into its own (e.g., Mark 8:34ff.), it is only where the tradition is dissimilar to both Judaism and the church that (relative) certainty can be assured. A LOGION that meets this criterion is embedded in the Beelzebul controversy (Luke 11:14–23): "But if it is by the finger of God that I cast out demons, then the kingdom of God has come upon you" (v. 20; Matt 12:28).

This admittedly minimalist criterion is now generally rejected as inadequate and perhaps tinged with anti-Judaism— but that is not a necessary conclusion. It is a question whether any highly influential historical figure could be understood on the basis of a standard requiring absolute historical discontinuity with past and future. The criterion also excluded from Jesus what is widely recognized as a leading characteristic of the early church, viz., APOCALYPTIC, whose relationship to the Jesus of history remains widely debated. Equally telling, the criterion of dissimilarity assumed that both 1st-cent. Judaism and the early church were single-faceted, monochromatic entities facilitating easy differentiation. They were not.

In place of this criterion alternatives are being proposed that are best captured by the suggested term "plausibility," that is, those sayings (and deeds) that (1) most plausibly fit the context of 1st-cent. Galilean Judaism yet are distinctive (*sic!*) enough to identify the novum within the Jesus of history, and (2) account for both his execution by Roman authorities and the rise of the early church. Within the latter (2), sayings (and deeds) that stand in the Jesus tradition yet are in conflict (*sic!*) with the interests of early Christian sources must be deemed most plausible (e.g., the cleansing of the Temple in Jerusalem). It has to be remembered, however, that within a range of possibilities there are likely to be several that are plausible. See Gerd Theissen/Dagmar Winter, *Criteria in Jesus Research: From Dissimilarity to Plausibility* (Leiderdorp, The Netherlands: Deo Publishing, 2000).

2. The *criterion of multiple attestation* (Perrin; Fuller: the "cross-section method"): Material whose theme is essentially duplicated elsewhere in the tradition in the same or additional forms, e.g., concern for the common people of the land, for the least, the lost and the last, is multiply attested in a variety of forms (LOGIA, PARABLES,

MAKARISMS [blessings], CHRIA, etc.) and is therefore likely to be authentic.

3. The *criterion of coherence* (Perrin; Fuller: "consistency"): To be considered authentic, any given saying must cohere with other established material in form and content. ALLEGORY does not cohere with the form of Jesus' parables and must be excluded or held in doubt from the "authentic sayings" (e.g., the allegory of the sower, Mark 4:1–9, pars., or at least its interpretation, Mark 4:13–20, pars.). Similarly, the spiritualization of Jesus' sayings, such as Matt's VERSION of the Beatitudes (5:3–6), are probably redactional elements. Criteria of authenticity can be applied as well to the deeds of Jesus; that he associated with tax collectors and sinners, aroused the antagonism of scribes and pharisees, practiced exorcism, etc., coheres with the sayings tradition. The danger of circular argument is of course apparent. (See Norman Perrin, *Rediscovering the Teachings of Jesus* [New York: Harper & Row, 1967; London: SCM Press, 1967], and Reginald Fuller, *A Critical Introduction to the New Testament* [London: Duckworth, 1966, 1974³].)

Note: The quest for criteria of authenticity serves as a useful reminder that the quest of the historical Jesus must always reveal as much (if not more) about the presuppositions of the historical inquirer as it does about the earthly Jesus and can never claim to present more than a hypothetical reconstruction. See APOCALYPTIC; ESCHATOLOGY; HISTORICAL-CRITICAL METHOD; JESUS CHRIST; JESUS SEMINAR; REDACTION CRITICISM.

Critical Apparatus   refers to the notes supplied primarily in Hebrew and Greek editions of the OT and NT that cite the MS sources and READINGS that either support or vary from the printed text; critical apparatuses are also found in certain study BIBLES such as the GOSPEL PARALLELS. A New Testament critical apparatus will include the following: PAPYRUS MANUSCRIPTS dating from the 2nd to 6th cents. (P¹, P², etc.); UNCIAL MSS from the 4th to 10th cents. (S, B,

C, D, etc.); MINUSCULE MSS from the 9th to 15th cents. (1, 13, 181, etc.); VERSIONS (Old Latin, Old Syriac, Coptic, etc.); church fathers (Clement, Justin, ORIGEN, etc.); and lectionaries. There are approximately 81 papyrus MSS, 266 uncials, 2,754 minuscules, and 2,135 lectionaries bearing witness to the NT text. The most exhaustive critical apparatus of the NT, called *Editio Critica Maior*, is a work in progress, the results of which are published in *Text und Textwert der griechischen Handschriften des Neuen Testaments* (Münster, 1997–). The ECM seeks to replace TISCHENDORF's *Editio Octava Critica Maior* (3 vols.; 1869), which is historic in the discipline for its scope of method and achievement. See ALAND, KURT; CRITICAL TEXT; PAPYRUS; LECTIONARY.

Critical Text   A critical text is a conjectural reconstruction of a document of which only divergent RECENSIONS are extant; it is therefore a hypothetical text usually based on the one or two best MSS available. A critical text is normally accompanied by a CRITICAL APPARATUS listing alternate readings. The most widely used critical text of the NT is the 27th edition of the NESTLE-ALAND *Novum Testamentum graece*, which is now identical to the 4th edition of the *Greek New Testament*, published by the American Bible Society. They differ in their critical apparatuses, the former prepared for students and theologians, the latter for translators. Prior to the last quarter of the 20th cent., the leading critical texts were those of TISCHENDORF (1869); WESTCOTT and HORT (1881); Nestle-Aland (*Novum Testamentum Graece* [New York: American Bible Society, 1898; 1963]); and *The Greek NT*, edited by Aland, Black, Metzger, Wikgren, and Martini (New York: American Bible Society, 1966, 1968²). Other critical texts are R. F. Weymouth (1886); BERNHARD WEISS (1894–1900); British and Foreign Bible Society (1904, based on Nestle's 4th ed.; 1958² ed. by G. D. Kilpatrick); Alexander Souter (1910, rev. 1947); H. J. Vogels (1920, 1950⁴); A. Merk (1933, 1965⁹); J. M. Bover (1943, 1968⁵).

Souter's edition reproduced the Greek text that lies behind the Revised Version (British) of 1881; originally prepared by E. Palmer, it is the closest to the TEXTUS RECEPTUS of any widely used Greek NT. The Greek NT of R. V. G. Tasker (1964) represents the text behind the NEW ENGLISH BIBLE (1961)—called an "anachronism" by Kurt Aland for its disregard of modern methods of textual criticism. See K. Aland and B. Aland, *The Text of the New Testament: An Introduction to the Critical Editions and to the Theory and Practice of Modern Textual Criticism* (Grand Rapids: Eerdmans,1995).

For the OT, throughout the 20th cent. various editions of R. KITTEL's *Biblia Hebraica* (1906) has served as the critical text of the HB, although never fully deemed satisfactory. The *Biblia Hebraica Stuttgartensia* (1967–77) and the planned *Biblia Hebraica Quinta* have been faulted for continuing to mix "textual facts and hypothetical emendation" (M. Goshen-Gottstein). A more consistent critical text, called the *Hebrew University Bible*, is being published in Jerusalem (Isaiah, 1995; Jeremiah, 1997). Critical editions of individual books of the SEPTUAGINT have been appearing over the past half-century in the Göttingen Septuaginta series (Germany), which is almost complete.

Cross-Cultural Biblical Interpretation refers to the conscious use of contemporary, culturally indigenous texts and concepts as hermeneutical keys in the interpretation of the BIBLE.

All interpretation of scripture is cross-cultural to the degree that the culture of the Bible is no longer identical with that of its interpreters. Were the cultures identical, cross-cultural biblical interpretation would not be necessary; were they totally different, interpretation would not be possible. Cross-cultural biblical interpretation approaches the resulting hermeneutical challenge by focusing on interpretive resources uniquely afforded by the interpreter's particular cultural location.This handbook describes, piecemeal and frag-

mentarily, how Western culture, in the persons of biblical scholars, has used Western thought forms and norms to make sense of the ancient world (or worlds) of the Bible. It has done so until recently (the term "postmodern" attempts to delineate the change) believing that its canons of judgment were neutral and universally valid, while being insufficiently aware of their cultural particularity and provisionality. Now it is more generally recognized that every interpreter is socially located within a culture, and that location shapes the perspective from which scriptures are interpreted and understood.

Cross-cultural biblical interpretation acknowledges this reality and intentionally employs culturally indigenous resources to shed light on biblical texts. The process itself is ancient. As the GOSPEL of John indicates, early Christians found Hellenistic thought forms valuable keys for interpreting the person and message of Jesus, just as PHILO, a Jew, was employing these same forms for interpreting the traditions of Judaism.

Since most BIBLICAL CRITICISM takes place in the Western world and employs Western critical perspectives, contemporary *cross-cultural biblical interpretation*, as a term, usually designates the work of non-Westerners (Asians, Africans, Indians, etc.) and their use of culturally indigenous texts (oral and written), customs, mores, rites, etc., in the interpretation of scripture. See Yeo Khiok-khng (K.K.), *What Has Jerusalem to Do with Beijing? Biblical Interpretation from a Chinese Perspective* (Harrisburg, Pa.: Trinity Press International, 1998).

Cryptogram (Gk: hidden writing). A cryptogram may be either a writing or a drawing that has a hidden or secret meaning. Cryptograms are particularly characteristic of APOCALYPTIC writings, and of oppressed communities generally, among which 1ST CENT. JUDAISM and early Christianity must be numbered. The epigraph of Daniel 5 ("Mene, Mene, Tekel, and Parsin") and the mark of the beast (666) in Rev 13:16–18 are cryptograms. The identifying cryptogram for the early Christian was a simple line drawing of a fish, which name in Greek (*Ichthus*) is an ACROSTIC for JESUS CHRIST, Son of God, Savior (see, e.g., the COLOPHON in the GOSPEL of the Egyptians, Nag Hammadi CODEX III.2 69, 14–15).

CSR. See **Council on the Study of Religion, The.**

Cult-Historical Method. See *KULTGESCHICHTLICHE SCHULE*

Cultural Criticism/Cultural Studies. See **Biblical Cultural Criticism.**

Cultural Translation. See **LB(P); LNT(P).**

Cursive. See **Minuscule.**

D: Deuteronomic Code is the name of the nucleus of laws (chs. 12–26) in the book of Deuteronomy; some scholars identify it with the book found in the Temple in 621 B.C.E. during the reign of Josiah (see 2 Kgs 22–23). See DE WETTE; LAW.

Damascus Document, The. See **Dead Sea Scrolls.**

Daughter Translation frequently refers to a translation of the LXX into another language, such as Latin, Ethiopic, Coptic, or Syriac; hence, a translation of a translation of the Hebrew scriptures, but it may properly be used of any such translation. See VERSION.

Dead Sea Scrolls (abbrev.: DSS). The name given to mainly parchment and PAPYRUS scrolls, written in Hebrew, Aramaic, and Greek, discovered in eleven caves along the northwestern coast of the Dead Sea between 1947 and 1956, generally dating from ca. 200 B.C.E. to 60 C.E. and assigned to an Essene community located about eight miles south of Jericho at the archaeological site known as KHIRBET QUMRAN. The community seems to have occupied the site from ca. 150 B.C.E. until its destruction by Roman armies under Vespasian in 68 C.E. during the First Jewish Revolt. The manuscripts discovered, in whole or in part, number more than 870, of which 220 have counterparts in the HB (with Deuteronomy, Isaiah, and PSALMS in leading numbers), and 650 are nonbiblical or sectarian (M. Abegg). Of the sectarian MSS, only seven different writings make up a full one-third of the total number. The term *DSS* is also used more broadly for texts found during the same and subsequent years at Masada, Nahal Hever, Wadi Murabba'ât, Nahel Se'elim, Khirbet Mird, and Nahal Mishmar, and, occasionally, includes texts from the Cairo Genizah. These MSS, broadly available to scholars only since 1991, are of inestimable value in understanding sectarian Judaism and Christianity of the 1st cent. and in gaining insights into the history of the transmission of the text of the HEBREW BIBLE, including the APOCRYPHA and PSEUDEPIGRAPHA, from the 3rd cent. B.C.E. to the 2nd cent. C.E. (when the Bar Kokhba finds from Wadi Murabba'ât and Nahal Hever are included). Scholars now have manuscripts of the Hebrew Bible 1,000 years older (i.e., closer to the original) than any Hebrew manuscript extant prior to the discovery of the DSS. Moreover, the texts of the Pseudepigrapha have reawakened interest in the history and form of Jewish religion and culture in the period just preceding the rise of rabbinic Judaism and the EARLY CHURCH.

In addition to the books of the HB (excepting Esther) and portions of the Apocrypha and Pseudepigrapha, the principal scrolls discovered (here listed with their present *sigla* followed by the older abbreviations) were the MANUAL OF DISCIPLINE (1QS = DSD), the *Rule of the Congregation* (1QSa), and the *Manual of Benedictions* (1QSb) (together constituting one scroll); *The War of the Sons of Light Against the Sons of Darkness* (1QM = DSW); Commentaries (*pesharim*) on portions of Habakkuk (1QpH = DSH), Nahum (4QpNah), Micah (1QpMi), also on small sections of Isaiah (4QpIsa^{a-d}), Psalm 37 (4QpPs37), Hosea (4QpHos) and Zephaniah (4QpZeph); the *Vision of the New*

Jerusalem (also called *The Temple Scroll,* since it describes the ideal temple; 11QT = 5QJN); the *Damascus Document* (closely related to 1QS, it was previously known from fragments found in a Cairo synagogue in 1896 and called the Zadokite Document; CD = CDC); the *Copper Scroll* (3QTreasure or 3Q15—thought to be unrelated to Qumran); the *Thanksgiving Psalms* (also known by the modern Hebrew term *Hodayot,* meaning thanksgiving; hence the *siglum* 1QH = DST); and, the *Genesis Apocryphon* (written in Aramaic; 1QapGen = DSL); the *Florilegia,* consisting of the *Eschatological Midrashim* (4QEschMidr), the *Patriarchal Blessings* (4QPBless), and the *Testimonia* (4QTestim), and "A Few Torah Topics" (11 QMMT), a letter that apparently relates to the separation of the Dead Sea Sectarians from the Jerusalem temple and priesthood.

Note: Each *siglum* above contains the number of the cave in which the scroll was found (1–11), the location of the cave (Qumran), and an initial(s) for the name of the document (p meaning PESHER or COMMENTARY); superscribed letters indicate the copy of the work at a given site (e.g., 4Qplsa^{a-d}). In some listings the *siglum* has prefixed to it an abbreviation of the material from which the text is made (papyrus [p, pap], copper [cu], ostracon [o, os, ostr], wood [lign], parchment [perg], or skin [no abb.]); and an appended abbreviation indicating the language in which the text is written (Hebrew, Aramaic, Arabic, Christian Palestinian Aramaic, Greek, Latin, or Nabatean). See F. Garcia Martinez, ed., *The Dead Sea Scrolls Translated: The Qumran Texts in English* (Leiden: E. J. Brill, 1996); also *The Dead Sea Scrolls Bible: The Oldest Known Bible,* translated by Martin Abegg Jr., Peter Flint, and Eugene Ulrich (San Francisco: HarperSanFrancisco, 1999); Peter W. Flint and James C. VanderKam, eds., *The Dead Sea Scrolls After Fifty Years: A Comprehensive Assessment,* 2 vols. (Leiden: E. J. Brill, 1998–99); and K. Stendahl, ed., *The Scrolls and the New Testament,* rev. ed., with an introduction by James Charlesworth (New York: Crossroad, 1992), and *Encyclopedia of the Dead Sea Scrolls,* 2 vols., eds. Lawrence H. Schiffman and James VanderKam, (New York: Oxford University Press, 2000). For a recent bibliography, see F. Garcia Martinez, *A Bibliography of the Finds in the Desert of Judah 1970–1995* (Leiden: E. J. Brill, 1996).

A CD-Rom edition is available: T. H. Lim et al., *The Dead Sea Reference Library,* vol. 1 (3 CDs) (Oxford and Leiden, 1997); also, a Penguin edition: G. Vermes, *The Complete Dead Sea Scrolls in English* (London: Penguin, 1998). For an exhaustive listing of DSS texts, see *The SBL Handbook of Style: For Ancient Near Eastern, Biblical, and Early Christian Studies,* ed. Patrick H. Alexander et al. (Peabody, Mass.: Hendrickson, 1999). See *DJD.*

Decalogue   (Gk: lit., "Ten Words") is the Greek (LXX) name for the "Ten Commandments" given according to tradition by God to Moses on Mt. Sinai; the term appears in Exod 34:28; Deut 4:13; 10:4; the commandments themselves in Exod 20 and Deut 5. A ritual Decalogue (expanded to thirteen) appears in Exod 34:11ff., the fragment of another in 23:14–19. A similar catalog of laws governing sexual relations (Lev 20:11–21; cf. 18:7–18) and social prohibitions in the form of curses (Deut 27:15–26) probably also numbered ten originally. See LAW.

Deconstruction is an approach to reading that is concerned with decentering or unmasking the problematic nature of centers in philosophical and theological texts. According to the main progenitor of Deconstruction, Jacques Derrida (b. 1930), Western thought is based on the idea of centers that provide a foundation for all meaning (an Origin, Truth, Ideal Form, Fixed Point, Immovable Mover, Essence, Presence, or God). For Derrida, the problem with centers is that they can perform their role only by marginalizing other reality. The Western longing for a center spawns binary opposites, one term of which is made central and the other marginal. In each case, the central term is conventionally assigned a positive or superior value while the marginal term is made to stand in a derivative, dependent, or supplementary relation to it. Derrida suggests that all of Western thought (and Christian thought not least of all) works in this way, generating binary pairs, assigning centrality to one member and banishing the other to the periphery.

As a strategy of reading, deconstruction seeks to expose and dismantle the hidden logic of centers, without, however, falling into a mere replication of their logic. A deconstructionist READING typically proceeds by drawing attention to the centrality of the central term. It then shows that the central term is unexpectedly dependent on the marginal term for its very definition. Deconstruction thus throws into question the priority of the central term and rescues the disfavored term from marginality. The goal of deconstruction is not simply to invert the original relation of the terms but to permit their interplay in the absence of a controlling center. The Western longing for meaning based on a stable center is exposed as a kind of bad faith that must make room for the free play of meaning without centers or guarantees. To express the latter notion Derrida invents a new French word, *différance*, that draws on the connotations of "to differ" and "to defer." *Différance* expresses the idea that meaning is not essential but relational, as STRUCTURALISM too had taught ("to differ"), but that it is also always indefinitely postponed, never completely captured, delimited, or defined by an utterance ("to defer").

Deconstruction has provoked lively interest and sharp denunciation among biblical scholars and theologians. Some charge quite plausibly that Derrida and others too quickly assimilate biblical and philosophical literature, that they fail to give "sufficient attention to an understanding of Judeo-Christian thought before it is synthesized with Greek and modern rationalisms; therefore, when these philosophers claim to have performed a de(con)struction of the whole of Western thought, their projects are severely limited by being blind to one of the most powerful influences on this thought" (Brian D. Ingraffia, *Postmodern Theory and Biblical Theology* [Cambridge: Cambridge University Press, 1995]). Others argue that deconstruction can help alert the reader to ways in which the biblical texts themselves are profoundly "de-centering" and subversive of binary oppositions. Two lucid works that introduce the reader to deconstruction and the study of the NT are Stephen D. Moore, *Poststructuralism and the New Testament* (Minneapolis: Fortress Press, 1994), and Patrick Chatelion Counet, *John, A Postmodern Gospel: Introduction to Deconstructive Exegesis Applied to the Fourth Gospel* (Leiden: E. J. Brill, 2000). See POSTMODERN BIBLICAL INTERPRETATION; INTERTEXTUALITY.

Deep Structure. See **Structure.**

Deeschatologize. See **Eschatologize.**

Deissmann, (Gustav) Adolf (1866–1937). Born in Langenscheid (Nassau), Germany, Deissmann taught NT in Marburg (1895–97), Heidelberg (1897–1908), and Berlin (1908–34). Deissmann's primary contribution to NT criticism derives from his study of newly discovered (1897–1904) Greek papyri, by which he proved the identity of biblical Greek with that commonly spoken (*Koiné*) in the 1st cent. His major works in English translation are *Light from the Ancient East* (New York: George H. Doran Co., 1910; rev., 1927) and *Paul* (Doran, 1926). See OXYRHYNCHUS PAPYRI.

Delay of the Parousia. See **Parousia.**

Demythologization (fr. Ger: *Entmythologisierung*). As a technical term in the biblical HERMENEUTICS of RUDOLF BULTMANN (1884–1976), demythologization refers to the interpretation of biblical MYTHS in terms of the understanding of existence that comes to expression in the imagery of the myths themselves. It does not refer to the elimination of myth but to its reinterpretation in EXISTENTIALIST terms. In this context, the term *myth* denotes imagery that speaks of the other world in terms of this world, the divine in terms of the human. To speak of God's transcendence in spatial terms as the One who dwells in heaven, or of universal sin in terms of Adam's Fall, are examples. Myths, says Bultmann, are true anthropologically, or existentially, not cosmologically; they are the objectification of human self-understanding not a scientific representation of external reality. The essay "New Testament and Mythology," 1941, which sparked almost two decades of debate, is found in *Kerygma and Myth*, H. W. Bartsch, ed., trans. R. H. Fuller (London: SPCK, 1954).

Deuterocanon (-ical)   is a Greek term meaning literally "second(ary) canon." As used by Roman Catholics since the Council of Trent (1545–63), Deuterocanonical designates books or parts of books not in the HEBREW BIBLE (the "proto" canon) but present in the Greek OT (LXX) and accepted as inspired both by early church fathers and the Council. In academic parlance the term *Deuterocanonical* is increasingly employed as more accurately describing the OT APOCRYPHA.

Used broadly, the term is applied to passages whose secondary character has been revealed by TEXTUAL CRITICISM, such as Mark 16:9–20; John 7:53–8:11; and 1 John 5:7 (KJV), all of which are absent from the oldest extant MSS of the NT. See CODEX SINAITICUS; CODEX VATICANUS.

Deuterograph   (Gk: second or secondary writing) is a term characterizing the relationship of certain OT writings to each other; e.g., 1 and 2 Chronicles are deuterographs of 1 Sam–2 Kings. In a sense Deuteronomy is a deuterograph of sections of Exod–Num; it often rewrites older laws in oratorical style, reinterpreting them in the process; e.g., cf. Deut 15:12–15 and Exod 21:2; Deut 19:1–13 and Exod 21:12–14; Deut 22:25–29 and Exod 22:16–17. Cf. also Deut 5 and Exod 20 (the Ten Commandments); Ps 14 and Ps 53; Ps 40:13–17 and Ps 70; Ps 57:7–11 plus 60:5–12 and Ps 108; Ps 18:2–50 and 2 Sam 22:2–51.

The word may be used to call attention to the repetitive nature of the subject matter of scripture; it may also be used in a noncritical way to hide the differences in perspective from which the common subject matter is viewed.

Deutero-Isaiah   (lit., Second Isaiah). The name commonly given to the author of Isa 40–55, written most likely during the period when the Jews were exiled in Babylon (586–538 B.C.E.); some scholars include chs. 56–66, but they are now more often dated later and called Third Isaiah or Trito-Isaiah.

Deuteronomist (-ic History)   is the name given to the author/compiler of the OT book of Deuteronomy and/or certain other portions of the OT that reflect the literary and theological characteristics of Deuteronomy, whether found in Gen–Josh, or Deut–2 Kgs, the latter called the "Deuteronomistic History" by the OT scholar, MARTIN NOTH.

Noth, in 1943, proposed that Deut–2 Kgs was a single work by a single author, written in Palestine during the exile from earlier oral and written traditions and expanded through secondary additions by later REDACTORS belonging to the Deuteronomistic School (see his *The Deuteronomistic History* [Sheffield: JSOT Press, 1980]). Noth's proposal of a Deuteronomistic History countered an older view that saw the Hexateuch (Gen–Judg 1) as a work augmented and redacted by the Deuteronomist. Noth denied any authorial relationship between Gen–Num and the Deuteronomistic History, even in those passages that Noth himself took to be secondary additions. Noth's hypothesis has been both rejected and vigorously defended (though rarely without qualification). The chief objections to his hypothesis are that it makes an artificial break between Gen–Num and Deut–2 Kgs, and that it oversimplifies the literary complexity of the latter.

To address this complexity scholars have proposed layers of redaction, making the final Deuteronomistic History the product of a circle or "school" of adherents. These layers of redaction are referred to as the work of the Deuteronomistic Historian (Dtr), a work that was then edited by a redactor interested in uniting it with the traditions of the PROPHETS (DtrP), which in turn was edited by a redactor for whom Israel's history was explicable only in terms of Israel's obedience to the LAW (DtrN). A continuing conundrum within the Deuteronomistic History is its intention, whether of censure or hope. Tracing these themes and accounting for them in the redactional evidence continues to occupy scholars. See A. D. H. Mayes, *The Story of Israel between Settlement and Exile: A Redactional Study of the Deuteronomistic History* (London: SCM Press, 1983); G. Knoppers and J. G. McConville, eds., *Recent Studies on the Deuteronomist History* (Sources for Biblical and Theological Study 8; Winona Lake, Ind.: Eisenbrauns Publishers, 2000).

Deuteropauline is a term applied to those writings in the NT that are explicitly attributed to Paul but are secondarily (deutero-) Pauline in content and were probably not written by him. Although no uniform agreement exists among scholars as to their number, those most often listed as deuteropauline are 2 Thess; Col; Eph; 1 and 2 Tim; and Titus. Also called sub-, post-, or pseudopauline.

De Wette, Wilhelm Martin Leberecht (1780–1849) was born in Weimar (Germany) and studied under J. J. GRIESBACH in Jena; in 1810, he joined FRIEDRICH SCHLEIER-MACHER at the newly founded theological faculty in Berlin, but was later removed at the urging of Pietists for his liberal theological and political views. In 1822, he became professor of ethics and practical theology at Basel; after F. C. BAUR, he was perhaps the leading historical theologian of his time. His earlier writings dealt primarily with OT and NT study; he was the first (1817) to argue persuasively that the Deuteronomic Code was the book found in the Temple in 621 B.C.E.

Diachronic; Synchronic (Gk: "through time"; "with time"). These two terms entered BIBLICAL CRITICISM from the linguistic theory of Ferdinand De Saussure (1857–1913). Saussure distinguished between the study of a language as a system that exists at a given point in time (synchronic analysis) and the study of changes in a language over time (diachronic analysis). For example, that the accent of a Greek word never falls behind the third syllable from the end (called the antepenult) relates to synchronic analysis; that over the centuries the final occlusives of Greek words gradually disappeared (*gunaik* becoming *gunai*) relates to diachronic analysis. (See F. De S., *Course in General Linguistics*, trans. Wade Baskin [Glasgow: Fontana/Collins, 1977]; first pub. 1916.) Saussure's followers (known as structuralists) have applied his distinction to the analysis of cultural and literary phenomena generally. Thus, a chronological study of the changing interpretation of Jesus' death in early Christianity is diachronic, a study of the relationship between death and resurrection in Paul's LETTERS, and a comparison between Paul and other Christian writers on the same topic, irrespective of CHRONOLOGY, is synchronic. (See Dan O. Via, Jr., *Kerygma and Comedy in the New Testament* [Philadelphia: Fortress Press, 1975].) Some methodologies of biblical criticism are thoroughly diachronic, e.g., TRADITION CRITICISM; others are thoroughly synchronic, e.g., STRUCTURALISM.

Diatessaron (Gk: through four). See **Tatian.**

Diatribe (Gk: DISCOURSE; short ethical treatise). In contemporary parlance a diatribe is a harangue, an abusively argumentative speech. In antiquity, as used by Zeno, Cleanthes, et al., it denoted a brief lecture on various ethical issues related to the public good: poverty, old age, banishment, apathy, freedom from affectation, etc. In this sense the diatribe appears about the 3rd cent. B.C.E., perhaps a kind of oral propaganda by which philosophical instruction of a popular character was propagated following the extension of Greek hegemony under Alexander the Great (see *RAC*).

According to H. I. Marrou, the diatribe, in literary-critical sense, is an imaginary or fictitious dialogue of moral PARAENESIS (e.g., Rom 12–15; Gal 5–6; Eph 4–6), characterized by (1) stereotyped address (e.g., Rom 2:1; 1 Cor 15:36); (2) rhetorical objections (e.g., Rom 9:19; 11:19; 2 Cor 10:10); (3) questions and answers in catechetical style (e.g., Rom 6:1, 15; Jas 2:18–22; 5:13); and (4) personified abstractions (e.g., Rom 10:6–8; 1 Cor 12:15–20). In terms of its formal STRUCTURE, the diatribe is characterized by (1) simple, PARATACTIC style (e.g., Rom 2:21–22; 13:7); (2) PARALLELISM and antithesis (e.g., Rom 12:4–15; 1 Cor 9:19–22; 2 Cor 4:8–11); (3) rich vocabulary, as in lists of vices and virtues (e.g., Rom 1:29–31; 1 Cor 6:9–10; 2 Cor 11:26–27); (4) imperatives or warnings (e.g., Rom 12:14–15; 1 Cor 11:6; Gal 5:12); (5) conversational tone, play on words, IRONY (e.g., Jas 2:2ff.; 1 Cor 4:8; Gal 5:12; Phil 3:19); (6) comparisons out of nature or life (e.g., 1 Cor 9:24–27; 2 Tim 2:4–6; Jas 3:3–6); (7) quotations from famous poets (e.g., 1 Cor 15:33—Menander; Titus 1:12—Epimenides; Acts 17:28—Aratus); (8) anecdotes, *bons mots*, historical examples (e.g., 1 Clem 55). (See *RAC* VI, 990–1009.)

Unfortunately, *diatribe* is sometimes used to translate the German term *Scheltrede*, which corresponds to the first definition listed and not to its literary and technical meaning.

Dibelius, Martin   (1883–1947). Born in Dresden, the son of a leading German pastor and church leader, Dibelius taught NT studies in Berlin (1910–15) and at Heidelberg (1915–47). Although best known for his pioneering work in FORM CRITICISM (1919), Dibelius wrote several commentaries on NT epistles, plus studies on the history of the EARLY CHURCH and on NT theology and ethics. He contributed significantly to the theological foundation of the ecumenical movement. See Martin Dibelius, *From Tradition to Gospel* (London: Ivor Nicholson & Watson, Ltd., 1934; repr. James Clarke, 1971; New York: Charles Scribner's Sons, 1935). See *CHRIA*; PARADIGM.

Dictionary of Biblical Interpretation (DBI),   edited by John H. Hayes (2 vols., Nashville: Abingdon Press, 1999), is a major resource for bibliographic information on hundreds of biblical scholars dating from the early Latin and Greek fathers to the present. It also contains sketches of the history of the interpretation of all the canonical and DEUTEROCANONICAL books, as well as brief articles on various hermeneutical perspectives and methodologies.

Didache; *The Didache*   (Gk: teaching; cf. English: didactic). A technical term for the didactic or instructional material of the EARLY CHURCH in contrast to KERYGMA or preaching; compare, for example, 1 Cor 7:1–40 (esp. v. 10 containing a teaching of Jesus) with the kerygmatic passage in Acts 2:22–24.

The Didache, or *Teaching of the Twelve Apostles*, is usually described as an early 2nd-cent. manual of church instruction, although its first section (chs. 1–6), known as "The Two Ways" (one of life and the other of death), may go back to a 1st-cent. Jewish document. These chapters, however, appear to be related in some way to the *Epistle of Barnabas*, a 2nd-cent. Christian writing, the direction of dependence being disputed. The second section (chs. 7–15) contains a series of instructions and admonitions on baptism, worship, the EUCHARIST, the treatment of apostles and PROPHETS, etc. The only extant Greek copy, dating from 1056 C.E. was discovered in 1875 by P. Bryennios in the library of the Jerusalem Monastery of the Holy Sepulchre in Constantinople. See Robert M. Grant, ed., *The Apostolic Fathers: A New Translation and Commentary*, Vol. 3: *Barabbas and the Didache* by Robert A. Kraft (New York/London: Thomas Nelson & Sons, 1965); also of interest, Walker J. Hazelden, *A Pre-Markian Dating for the* Didache: *Further Thoughts of a Liturgist* (Sheffield: Sheffield Academic Press, 1980).

Dilthey, Wilhelm (1833–1911). Born in Biebrich on the Rhein, the son of the court chaplain to the Duke of Nassau (Germany), Dilthey first studied theology and then philosophy and history with Leopold von Ranke in Berlin. He subsequently held professorships at Basel (1866), Kiel (1868), Breslau (1871), and Berlin (1882). Although few of his major works were ever completed (in Berlin, according to F. Rodi, he was known as "the man of Vol. I"), his influence on 20th-cent. thought was considerable. Called "the virtual creator of the philosophy of history in its present form" (*ODCC*) he extended the concept of HERMENEUTICS from the interpretation of difficult texts to the interpretation of all human acts and artifacts, and sought to describe the epistemological and cultural conditions that make such interpretation possible. A fundamental and enduring insight of Dilthey's is that while natural sciences seek to explain (*erklären*), the social, human, or interpretive sciences seek to understand (*verstehen*). He is also of interest to BIBLICAL CRITICISM and interpretation for his studies of SCHLEIERMACHER and Schleiermacher's hermeneutics, from which he derived much of the basic impetus and direction for his own work.

Discourse   In NT criticism particularly the term *discourse* is used to characterize in a formal way the distinction between the teachings of Jesus as found in the Synoptic GOSPELS and those in the Gospel of John. Whereas the former are short and pithy SAYINGS (e.g., Matt 5–7), the latter are extended elaborations (discourses) on major (Johannine) themes: light, life, truth, way, etc., all of which expound the mystery of Jesus and his relationship to God and to the believer (e.g., 3:1–21, 31–36; 4:4–42; 5:16–47; 6:25–71; 7:14–36; and 13:31–17:26).

Discourse Analysis.   See **Semiology.**

Dispositio.   See **Rhetorical Analysis.**

Dittography   (Gk: written twice). In TEXTUAL CRITICISM, *dittography* is the techni-

cal name for the scribal error in manuscript copying in which a letter, word, or line is mistakenly repeated; the opposite of HAPLOGRAPHY. In this context, a dittograph is an example of erroneous repetition.

Divino Afflante Spiritu, an encyclical letter issued by Pope Pius XII on September 30, 1943, inaugurated the modern period of Roman Catholic biblical studies. *Divino Afflante Spiritu* called for the study of scripture in its original languages (thereby supplanting the VULGATE in critical matters), for the use of the historical-critical method in establishing the LITERAL SENSE of the text (thereby reversing the church's historical stance concerning both the inerrancy of scripture and its preference for scripture's figurative meaning and dogmatic relevance) and for the study of scripture according to its literary forms (thereby advocating what Pope Benedict XV had condemned). The most recent comprehensive statement of principles of biblical interpretation in the Roman Catholic tradition is the 1993 document of the Pontifical Biblical Commission, "The Interpretation of the Bible in the Church" (*Origins: CNS Documentary Service*, vol. 23, no. 29). See Robert Bruce Robinson, *Roman Catholic Exegesis since* Divino Afflante Spiritu (Atlanta: Scholars Press, 1988).

DJD   Abbreviation for *Discoveries in the Judean Desert of Jordan*, a facsimile edition of the DEAD SEA SCROLLS published in Oxford at the Clarendon Press. They are the official editio princeps of the scrolls and have recently (1995) been digitalized and enhanced. The publication of *DJD* includes Vol. I: *Qumran Cave I* (1956: D. Barthélemy and J. T. Milik; text in French, introductory notes in French and English); Vol. II, 1 and 2: *Les grottes de Murabba'ât* (1961: P. Benoit, J. T. Milik, and R. de Vaux); Vol. III, 1 and 2: *Les 'Petites Grottes' de Qumran* [Caves 2–7 and 10] (1962: M. Baillet, J. T. Milik, and R. de Vaux); Vol. IV: *The Psalms Scroll of Qumran Cave 11* (1965: J. A. Sanders, text in En-glish); Vol. V: *Qumran Cave 4* (1968: John M.

Allegro; text in English); Vol. VI: *Qumrân Grotte 4, II: 1. Archéologie,* 2. Tefillin, Mezuzot et Targums (1977: R. de Vaux and J. T. Milik et al.; text mainly in French). The scrolls are available on microfiche: E. Tov, ed., *The Dead Sea Scrolls on Microfiche* (Leiden: Brill, 1993); and on CD: *The Dead Sea Scrolls on CD: The FARMS Electronic Database* (Provo, Utah: Foundation for Ancient Research and Mormon Studies, 1997). A complete listing of DJD publications may be found in *The SBL Handbook of Style* (Peabody, Mass.: Hendrickson Publishers, 1999), 178.

Documentary Hypothesis. See **Graf-Wellhausen Hypothesis.**

Dodd, Charles Harold (1884–1973). Professor of NT and later of BIBLICAL CRITICISM and EXEGESIS at Oxford (1915–30), Manchester (1930–35), and Cambridge (1935–49), England. Philosophically a Platonist, Dodd is noted with equal merit for his studies in the GOSPEL and LETTERS of John and Paul's letter to the Romans, and for *The Parables of the Kingdom* (London: Nisbet & Co., 1935) and *The Apostolic Preaching and Its Development* (Nisbet, 1936). Additional research in the area of NT backgrounds, in the study of scripture and in biblical theology made him unquestionably the leading British NT scholar of the 20th cent., a fact often noted by his peers who chose him to direct the translation of the NEW ENGLISH BIBLE. See ESCHATOLOGY; PARABLE.

Dominical Saying (fr. *Dominus.* Lat: Lord). A saying of Jesus.

Douay Bible is a common name for the first English Catholic VERSION of the BIBLE, with the NT published at Rheims (1582), the OT at Douay (1609–10). Based on the Latin VULGATE, it was revised by Bishop Richard Challones of London in 1750–63; by an American, Archbishop Kenrich, 1849–60; and again by the Confraternity of Christian Doctrine (NT), 1941. See CONTEMPORARY ENGLISH VERSION; JERUSALEM BIBLE; KING JAMES VERSION; LIVING BIBLE (PARAPHRASED); NEW AMERICAN BIBLE; NEW ENGLISH BIBLE; NEW INTERNATIONAL VERSION; NEW JEWISH VERSION; PARAPHRASE; REVISED STANDARD VERSION; TODAY'S ENGLISH VERSION.

Doublet As a technical term in LITERARY CRITICISM, doublet refers to a parallel NARRATIVE, PARABLE, saying, etc., which by ORAL TRADITION grew out of or alongside of an original narrative, parable, etc. For example, Matt 16:19b is undoubtedly a doublet of Matt 18:18; similarly, the two miracles of loaves and fishes (Mark 6:35–44 and 8:1–9) are probably two accounts of a single event or narrative. Alternatively, NT doublets have been accounted for by supposing that Jesus spoke or acted similarly in different contexts, giving rise to similar but independent traditions (cf. N.T. Wright, *Jesus and the Victory of God* [Minneapolis: Fortress Press, 1996]). In the OT, doublets (or three- and fourfold parallels) are evidence of multiple tradition; e.g., cf. Gen 12:10–13 and 20:1–18 with 26:6–11 (Sarah and Rebekah); Exod 20:1–17 with 34:10–28 (DECALOGUE); Exod 16 and 17:1–7 with Num 11:4–35 and 20:1–13 (wilderness miracles).

Double Tradition is a term employed to denote passages in the synoptic tradition common to Matt and Luke; it is used to avoid prejudging or implying the nature of its source or the order of dependence.

DSS (abbrev.). See **Dead Sea Scrolls.**

E: Elohist (fr. Heb: *Elohim:* God) is the accepted designation for one of the sources employed in the composition of the PENTATEUCH, derived from the source's preferred Hebrew name for the Deity, viz., Elohim, commonly translated "God." The provenance, date, and extent of the E document (or ORAL TRADITION), whose existence was first proposed by Jean Astruc in 1753, are much disputed. Of all the sources (traditionally: J, E, D, and P), its location in the Pentateuch is the most difficult to ascertain, which leads many scholars to view it as a REDACTOR's supplement to the older J source.

According to OTTO EISSFELDT, E views God as more remote and awesome than does J; its interpretation of the covenant is less materialistic and less nationalistic (see e.g., Exod 19:5–6 and Num 23:9, 21); and, most obviously, its terminology is different: God is called Elohim, not YHWH; the sacred mountain is called Mt. Horeb, not Sinai (Exod 3:12); Amorites, not Canaanites, inhabit the Promised Land (Gen 48:22; Exod 23:23; cf. Gen 12:6; 50:11), etc.

The opinion is generally held that E arose in the 9th or 8th cent. B.C.E. in northern Palestine (Ephraim) from traditions that were much older. According to MARTIN NOTH (1902–1968), the following passages (with minor refinements omitted) stem from the E tradition: Gen 15:1b, 3a, 5, 13–16 (16:9–10 redactional); 20:1b–18; 21:6, 8–34; 22:1–19; 28:11–12, 17–18, 20–22; 30:1–3, 6, 17–19, 22–23; 31:2, 4–16, 19b, 24–25a, 26, 28–29, 30b, 32–35, 36b–37, 41–45, 50, 53b—55; 32:1–2 (32:13b–21); 33:4–5, 8–11, 19–20; 35:1–5, 7–8, 14, 16–20; 37:3b, 22–24, 29–36; 40:2–23; 41:1–33, 34b, 35a, 36–40, 47–48, 50–54; 42:1a, 2–3, 6–7, 11b, 13–26, 28b—37; 45:2–3, 5b–15; 46:1–5a; 47:5b, 6a, 7–12; 48:1–2, 7–22; 50:10b–11, 15–26.

Exod 1:15–21; 3:4b, 6, 9–15; 4:17, 18, 20b; (chs. 7–10 in part); 13:17–19; 14:5a, 7, 11–12, 19a, 25a; 17:3; 18:1–27; 19:3a (3b–6*, 10–11a*, 14–15*), 16–17, 19; 20:1–22 (23:1–33* [special source]); 24:1–2, 3–8*, 9–11; 32:1b–4a, 21–24.

Num 20:14–18, 21; 21:21–35; 22:1a (redactional), 2–3a, 9–12, 20, 38, 41–23:27, 29–30. *Marks points where, according to Bernhard Anderson, many scholars deviate from Noth's analysis; passages in parenthesis are omitted by Noth. For bibliographic information, see J (YAHWIST). Also see GRUNDLAGE; P: PRIESTLY CODE.

Early Church (The)   is an ambiguous term that may be used to denote the church at its inception or through its development in the first five centuries. Less broad are the terms "primitive church" or "primitive Christianity," which are translations of the German terms Urkirche or URGEMEINDE, and Urchristentum (Ur- meaning original, primitive, ancient). These terms, also ambiguous, are used by some to denote Christianity prior to the rise of the institutionalized Catholic Church, whose incipient formation is found in the NT (Ger.: Frühkatholizismus: early or incipient Catholicism). This definition is based on the hypothesis that the earliest Christians anticipated the imminent return of CHRIST and that the institutionalization of Christianity was a product of the "Delay of the PAROUSIA" (i.e., since the Risen Lord had not returned, the church must act in his stead; see Matt 16:18–19). An imaginative effort to reconstruct the earliest beginnings of the church is found in John Dominic Crossan, The Birth of Christianity: Discovering What Happened in the Years Immediately after the Execution of Jesus (San Francisco: HarperSanFrancisco, 1998).

Ebla (Tablets/Texts)   Ancient name of the archaeological site known as Tell Mardikh, located between Hama and Aleppo in North Syria. In 1974/76, Italian archaeologists discovered the royal archives of Ebla, comprising several thousand cuneiform texts written in Sumerian (80%) and a previously unknown language called Paleo-canaanite or Eblaite (20%), the latter revealing many striking affinities with Hebrew. The tablets date from Ebla's empire years, ca. 2400–2250 B.C.E. (Early Bronze IV) or perhaps earlier (2600–2400 B.C.E.), and contain (1) economic-administrative texts, (2) lexical texts (onamastica), (3) historical and juridical texts, (4) literary and religious texts, and (5) syllabaries (the oldest in history). The texts are providing startling new chapters to our knowledge of the history and literature of the ancient Near East of the 3rd millennium B.C.E. Initial hopes for substantial new light on the HB have however subsequently diminished. See Paolo Matthiae, Ebla: An Empire

Rediscovered (Garden City, N.Y.: Doubleday, 1981); Giovanni Pettinato, *The Archives of Ebla: An Empire Inscribed in Clay* (Garden City, N.Y.: Doubleday, 1981); C. H. Gordon et al., eds., *Eblaitica: Essays on the Ebla Archives and Eblaite Language* (Winona Lake, Ind.: Eisenbrauns, 1987); and A. Archi, "Fifteen Years of Studies on Ebla," *Orientalistische Literaturzeitung* 88 (1998): 461–71.

Ecclesia   (ecclesiastical; ecclesiology) is the English TRANSLITERATION of the Greek word meaning "assembly," "meeting," or "gathering," which to Christians came to mean "a body (or the whole body) of believers in CHRIST," i.e., "a (or the) church." The latter term ("church") is thought to come from the Greek adjective *kuriakos*, meaning "belonging to the Lord." In time it took the place of ecclesia, which still appears in "ecclesiastical" (pertaining to the church), "ecclesiology" (the doctrine of the church), etc. For the use of ecclesia in the NT, see Kittel's *Bible Key Words*, vol. 1, trans. J. R. Coates (New York: Harper & Brothers, 1951), or *TDNT*.

Eichhorn, Albert   (1856–1926). Born near Lüneburg, Germany, Eichhorn was associate professor of church history in Halle (1886–1900) and Kiel (1901–13). Sometimes considered "the founder of the history-of-religions school" in Germany (H. J. Kraus) or at least one of its cofounders along with HERMANN GUNKEL, WILLIAM WREDE, and Hugo Gressmann, Eichhorn did not publish any single work of note primarily because of chronic poor health, but his influence was felt in articles and in discussions with the above named and others. See *RELIGIONSGESCHICHTE*.

Eichhorn, Johann Gottfried   (1752–1827), professor of Oriental languages in Jena (Germany) and professor of philosophy at Göttingen (1788–1827); introduced the concept of MYTH as used in classical philology to biblical studies; often called "the father of OT criticism" for establishing criteria for the discernment of divergent source materials in the OT, such as repetitions, duplicate stories, differences in style, characteristic phraseology and vocabulary, etc.

Eichrodt, Walter   (1890–1978). Born in Gernsbach in the southern German state of Baden, Eichrodt completed graduate degrees at Heidelberg and Erlangen and held various entry-level teaching positions at the latter from 1915 to 1922. The rest of his career was spent in Basel, Switzerland (1922–61), serving in his later years as rector of the university. In addition to his COMMENTARY on Ezekiel (Eng.: 1970) and his MONOGRAPH, *Man in the Old Testament* (Eng.: 1951), Eichrodt is noted for his multivolume *Old Testament Theology* (Ger.: 1933–39; Eng.: 1961–67). It is this work that revitalized OT theology as a theologically interested discipline after having been defined in exclusively historicist terms in the 19th cent. Whereas earlier studies saw Israel's religion in terms of developmentalism, Eichrodt emphasized the single idea of covenant as the unifying thread of Israel's faith, originating in the premonarchical period and continuing throughout the vicissitudes of its history. Using this single idea enabled Eichrodt to systematize the thought of the OT and connect it with that of the NT. For critical analysis, see D. G. Spriggs, *Two Old Testament Theologies: A Comparative Evaluation of the Contributions of Eichrodt and von Rad to Our Understanding of the Nature of Old Testament Theology* (Naperville, Ill.: A. R. Allenson, 1975); and Norman K. Gottwald, "Walter Eichrodt: Theology of the Old Testament," in R. B. Laurin (ed.), *Contemporary Old Testament Theologians* (Valley Forge, Pa.: Judson Press, 1970).

Eisegesis   (Gk: to lead, bring, or introduce into). In the interpretation of scripture, Eisegesis refers to the practice of reading into a text the meaning that one wants to get out of it. As such, the term is the opposite of EXEGESIS and is almost always used pejoratively.

Eissfeldt, Otto   (1887–1973). Born in Northeim, Germany, Eissfeldt studied OT with J. WELLHAUSEN, R. Smend, and H. GUNKEL; he taught OT in Berlin (1913–22) and in Halle (1922–57), becoming one of the most famous students of the Wellhausen-Gunkel school of OT criticism. His rejection of TRADITION HISTORY (*Traditionsgeschichte*) and his avoidance of any THEOLOGICAL INTERPRETATION of the OT (such as VON RAD's), plus his concentration on issues in comparative religions (*Religionsgeschichte*), led to the conservative appearance of his scholarship. A prolific writer, he edited the COMMENTARY series *Handbuch zum Alten Testament* (Tübingen: J. C. B. Mohr [Paul Siebeck], 1937–77) and Joseph Aistleitner's *Wörterbuch der ugaritischen Sprache* (Berlin: Akademie Verlag, 1963). His monumental *The Old Testament: An Introduction Including the Apocrypha and Pseudepigrapha* (Oxford: Basil Blackwell and New York: Harper & Row, 1965; Ger: 1934, 1964³) is called "the best of its kind." For a complete bibliography, see O. Eissfeldt, *Kleine Schriften*, vols. 5–6 (Tübingen: J. C. B. Mohr [Paul Siebeck], 1973, 1979).

Electronic Hermeneutics refers to an emerging discussion concerning the rise of the digital age and its impact on religious communities and on the nature, place, and meaning of sacred texts such as the Bible within these communities and within the culture at large. Cognizant of how epochal shifts in the technology of communication have transformed human culture (as exemplified by the successive inventions of writing, printing, and the predigital electronic media), scholars are now investigating how the transition from printed text to the digital, multisensate worlds of hypertexts, hypermedia, interactivity, and "virtual reality" will shape human experience and communication. Biblical scholars have been among the first to make use of computer technology and to reflect on how changes in communication technology affect beliefs and practices. See W. J. Ong, *Interfaces of the Word: Studies in the Evolution of Consciousness and Culture*

(Ithaca, N.Y.: Cornell University Press, 1977); R. Hodgson and P. A. Soukup, eds., *From One Medium to Another: Basic Issues for Communicating the Bible in New Media* (Kansas City, Mo.: Sheed & Ward, 1997).

Elohist.   See **E: Elohist.**

Endzeit   (Ger: end time). The eschaton or the end of the world and its attendant events. *Endzeit* is the temporal opposite of *Urzeit*, the time of the beginning and the primeval events accompanying it. See ESCHATOLOGY.

Enthronement Psalms.   See **Psalms.**

Entmythologisierung **(Ger).** See **Demythologization.**

Epanaphora.   See **Anaphora.**

Epigram   (adj.: epigrammatic). As made popular by 17th- and 18th-cent. epigrammatists, the epigram is a short poem (frequently an epitaph) stating concisely and often satirically or wittily a single thought or moral; today it may refer to any brief, pithy saying. Prophetic speech, Wisdom, and the SAYINGS of Jesus are in this broader sense epigrammatic: e.g., Amos 3:8: "The lion has roared; who will not fear? The Lord GOD has spoken; who can but prophesy?" (NRSV).

Epigraphy   (fr. Gk: inscription). That field of study concerned with the classification and interpretation of inscriptions. For biblical studies, the best collection of these texts is found in *ANET(P)*. For a popular history, see Maurice Pope, *The Story of Decipherment: From Egyptian Hieroglyphic to Linear B* (London: Thames & Hudson, 1975).

Epinicion   (pl.: epinicia; lit., "upon victory") is a Greek term denoting a song or ODE composed to celebrate a victory in war or in athletic competition. Judges 5 is an epinicion celebrating Deborah's victory over the Egyptian general Sisera in the plain of Jezreel ca. 1125 B.C.E.; see also Judges 15:16; 1 Sam 18:7b, etc.

Epiphany (Gk: manifestation; appearing). See **Theophany.**

Epiphora (also: epistrophe or antistrophe; Gk: repetition) denotes the repetition of a word or words at the end of two or more sequential verse lines, sentences, or STROPHES. Though often lost in translation, epiphora may be seen for example in the use of "Egypt" in Ezek 20:7–9, and in the use of "us" (the Hebrew pronominal suffix *nu)* in the chiastic structure of Ps 67, which is also an example of SYMPLOCE (the conjoining of ANAPHORA and epiphora). In Paul's LETTERS, epiphora is found at 1 Cor 7:12–13; 9:19–22; 12:4–6; 2 Cor 11:22, 27, etc. For examples in Hellenistic RHETORIC, see Epictetus 1.29.10; 2.19.24; 3.22.105; 4.1.102; 9.9. See CHIASMUS.

Epistle. See Letter.

Epithalamion (pl.: epithalamia) is Greek for nuptial and denotes a poem or song written to honor a bride or groom. In the OT, see Song of Songs 3:6–11 and 6:13–7:5; less certain are the royal PSALMS, Pss 2 and 45. It has been suggested that Ps 2 is an epithalamion ACROSTIC (in Hebrew): "To Alexander Janneus and his wife" (R. H. Pfeiffer). SIGMUND MOWINCKEL, however, designates this an Enthronement Psalm (*The Psalms in Israel's Worship* [New York: Abingdon Press, 1962; Oxford: Basil Blackwell, 1963], II, 61). See PSALMS.

Erasmus, Desiderius, von Rotterdam (1466/69–1536). Called "the most renowned scholar of his age" (*ODCC*), Erasmus is noted in BIBLICAL CRITICISM for his pioneering edition of the Greek NT (1516), which later became the basis of the *TEXTUS RECEPTUS.* His fame as a humanist scholar rests principally on his attacks against evils in the church and state of his day (*The Praise of Folly,* 1509; *Familiar Colloquies,* 1518). His humanist convictions, esp. his abhorrence of violence, led him to reject the Lutheran Reformation, perhaps never fully to understand it. They also led to his repudiation by the Roman Church and by Martin Luther, but likewise to the offer of patronage from the leading princes of his day (Henry VIII, Francis I, Archduke Ferdinand of Vienna), all of which he refused in favor of personal and intellectual freedom. This he found in Basel where he spent the last fifteen years of his life actively engaged in debate with Luther, publishing texts of the church fathers and writing religious tracts. See C. Augustijn, *Erasmus: His Life, Works, and Influence* (Toronto: Toronto University Press, 1991). See TEXTUAL CRITICISM.

Eschatologize;   Eschatologizing Tendency (fr. Gk: *eschaton:* last). Transitive verb: "To give an eschatological character to" (OED); correspondingly, to "deeschatologize" means "to remove eschatological character from" (a saying, PARABLE, etc.). In NT criticism what constitutes an eschatologizing or a deeschatologizing tendency depends on whether the message of Jesus and/or that of the EARLY CHURCH was itself eschatological, that is, whether it spoke of an imminent and radical transformation of the world by God. If the message of Jesus was noneschatological, as the 19th cent. thought and as has been proposed again by some scholars associated with the JESUS SEMINAR, then the primitive church "eschatologized" his message to conform to its expectation of his return. If, however, Jesus was an eschatologist (see, e.g., Mark 9:1; 13:26; 14:62 and passim) as most 20th-cent. scholarship tended to believe, then at numerous points and because of the delay of the coming of the kingdom and/or the delay of Jesus' return (PAROUSIA), many of the original SAYINGS and teachings of Jesus were gradually "deeschatologized." E.g., Luke deeschatologizes the teachings of John the Baptist (cf. 3:10–14 with 3:7–9 [Q]). Similarly, the purpose of 2 Thess seems to be to deeschatologize the message of 1 Thess, which fact is proffered as argument against its authenticity. See also 2 Pet 3:3–13 for its deeschatologizing tendency. The issue is and is likely to remain a matter of scholarly debate. See APOCALYPTIC; QUEST OF THE HISTORICAL JESUS.

Eschatology   (fr. Gk: *eschaton:* furthest, last, or final). The term *eschatology* was coined in the 19th cent. as the name for the part of dogmatic theology that treated "the doctrine of last things," viz., death, judgment, heaven, hell, and all attendant matters (the nature of resurrection, of the intermediate state of the dead, of Jesus' final coming, etc.). As a term in contemporary BIBLICAL CRITICISM, eschatology refers generally to God's future intervention to end the present course of events. This definition is subject to qualification depending on the part of biblical literature that is under discussion and the interpretive position that is adopted.

In OT criticism, eschatology is often applied quite broadly to refer to Israel's orientation toward the future as the arena where God will act decisively in accord with God's deity, promises, and commands. OT eschatology in this sense is fed by numerous strands of biblical tradition: God's promises to the ancestors (Gen 49:8–12; Deut 33:13–17; cf. Num 23:21, etc.); the prophetic "Day of the Lord" (Amos 5:18; Isa 2:12); cult traditions surrounding God's enthronement and kingship; traditions about David and Zion (2 Sam 7; Ps 132); warnings of divine judgment and the survival of a mere remnant (Isa 8:8; 37:31; Zeph 3:12; Jer 31:7; Ezek 20:33–44); and hopes of a perfected future (esp. Isa 40–66). Many of these themes coalesce in the notion of YHWH's divine kingship and rule, in the expectation that YHWH will come and establish his reign in Israel and among the nations and usher in an era of peace and well-being.

Some scholars draw a distinction between prophetic eschatology and APOCALYPTIC eschatology to differentiate between (a) expectations concerning the future found in the prophetic warnings/promises in the OT and (b) expectations concerning an imminent crisis characteristic of apocalyptic literature. Apocalyptic literature flourished in the SECOND TEMPLE and NT periods (200 B.C.E.–200 C.E.); its chief biblical examples are Daniel 7–12 and Revelation. Though prophetic eschatology and apocalyptic eschatology are continuous in many respects, their characteristic emphases differ. The PROPHETS addressed issues of status, relationships, prosperity, etc., within the present world, where God was at work guiding things toward fulfillment or consummation. In contrast, the apocalypticists warned of God's intervention from the beyond, in radical disjunction with history, to destroy and re-create the world. Prophetic eschatology announces God's activity within the arena of the present world; apocalyptic eschatology announces God's plans to interrupt and end history because it is heading in a direction contrary to God's will.

In NT criticism, the definition and role of eschatology in the teaching and expectation of Jesus have been of central importance since JOHANNES WEISS's *Jesus' Proclamation of the Kingdom of God* (1892) and ALBERT SCHWEITZER's *The Quest of the Historical Jesus* (1906). Schweitzer interpreted the eschatology of Jesus as radically discontinuous with the present: in an act of the near future, God would end the present evil age and replace it with his own divine rule. Schweitzer's opinion that Jesus could be understood only from a "consistently eschatological" point of view was countered by C. H. DODD's concept of "realized eschatology" (*The Parables of the Kingdom*, 1935), in which the rule of God is seen as efficaciously present in Jesus himself. The eternal is present in the now. A synthesis of these positions, which one might call "proleptic eschatology," understands the words and deeds of Jesus to represent God's rule, though its ultimate fulfillment is still to be realized. J. Jeremias developed perhaps the most adequate view of the NT's presentation of eschatology. This is the position that in Jesus we have "inaugurating eschatology" (from the German, *sich reali-sierende Eschatologie*), or eschatology in the process of being realized. It has become something of a consensus view and is frequently represented in many variations by the tags *already* and *not yet*, i.e., God's reign is *already* inaugurated in Jesus but *not yet* fully consummated.

Biblical eschatology has provided a decisive stimulus for Christian theology throughout the 20th cent., a trend that shows few signs of abating in the 21st. A list of theological movements decisively (though quite variously) shaped by biblical eschatology would include the social gospel, dialectical theology, the theology of hope, and liberation theology, among many others. At present it is fashionable, particularly among some participants in the JESUS SEMINAR, to depict Jesus in noneschatological dress, preferring instead a sage-like Jesus who preached a radical egalitarianism. In this view eschatological expectation belongs to the EARLY CHURCH and not to Jesus. Whatever the merits of this thesis, it seems safe to predict that eschatology, its relation to apocalypticism, and its role in the teachings of Jesus and in the life of the early church will remain a key theme in biblical studies in decades to come. See ESCHATOLOGIZE; EXISTENTIALIST; QUEST OF THE HISTORICAL JESUS.

Etiological Legends.   See Legend.

Etymology The nature and scope of etymology in the interpretation of scripture and in the study of language generally is widely debated, a fact hindering its precise definition. According to James Barr, it is necessary to distinguish between scholarly and popular etymology. In general terms, scholarly etymology contains three elements: (1) a historical perspective, that is, the tracing of the CHRONOLOGY of linguistic changes; (2) a classification of languages, showing cognate relationships, historical influences, etc.; and (3) an analysis of phonological correspondence between different languages or between

different stages of the same language. In practice, however, the term *etymology* has been used, appropriately, to designate one or more of the following linguistic operations: (a) the reconstruction of linguistic form and sense in a prehistoric (i.e., undocumented) protolanguage (e.g., proto-Semitic), (b) the tracing of forms and meanings within an observable historical development, (c) the identification and tracing of loan words from other languages, and (d) the analysis of words into component MORPHEMES (as frequently in this *Handbook*). Popular etymology as found in the OT and NT, but particularly in the TALMUD, is not etymology in the scholarly sense at all, but simply a play on word similarity, serving a poetic, humorous, or HAGGADIC function, e.g., see in Moses (Exod 2:10), Samuel (1 Sam 1:20), and cf. Peter (Matt 16:18). (See *Language and Meaning: Studies in Hebrew Language and Biblical Exegesis*, ed. James Barr et al. [*Oudtestamentische Studiën* 19; Leiden: E. J. Brill, 1947].)

Eucharist (Gk: thanksgiving) is the traditional name for the Lord's Supper (*DIDACHE* 9:1), probably based on CHRIST's having "given thanks" at its institution (1 Cor 11:24; Matt 26:26–28; Mark 14:22–24; Luke 22:17–20). The early significance of the eucharistic meal is indicated in Acts 2:42, 46; 20:7; its epiphanic character is suggested by its tie with the CHRISTOPHANY of the Emmaus road (Luke 24:30–35). It is suggested that the miracles of feeding (particularly in Matt, see chs. 14–15) are part of an early eucharistic catechesis. See APOSTOLIC FATHERS.

Evangelist In the broad sense of the term, an evangelist is anyone who is authorized to proclaim the GOSPEL of JESUS CHRIST; in its narrower usage within BIBLICAL CRITICISM, it refers to one or the other of the Gospel writers.

Evangelistarion.   See Apostolicon.

Example Story.   See Parable.

Exegesis; Exegetical Method; Exegetical Tools (Gk: explanation; interpretation; cf. [Greek] NT Luke 24:35; John 1:18; Acts 10:8; 15:12, 14, etc.). In the broadest sense, exegesis is the careful, methodologically self-aware study of a text undertaken in order to produce an accurate and useful interpretation thereof. More narrowly, the term *exegesis* is often used to denote the effort to establish the philological and historical sense of a biblical text (what it meant), in contrast to its applicative sense (what it means). Explication of a text that encompasses the latter concern is sometimes called EXPOSITION or interpretation rather than exegesis. Howeover, the definition of *exegesis* and its relation to exposition and interpretation is a matter of debate. In actual practice, the task of exegesis involves "examining a passage as carefully as possible from as many angles as possible" (Douglas Stuart), with the result that a sharp distinction between exegesis and exposition can be maintained only with a certain degree of artificiality.

The Diagram of Biblical Interpretation and its accompanying explanation located at the end of the *Handbook* (p. 235) is designed to give the reader a graphic representation of the different methods and interpretive approaches that biblical scholars have employed in approaching the task of exegesis.

The basic literary tools of exegesis, including the social context of the Bible, are fully discussed and evaluated by Frederick W. Danker, *Multipurpose Tools for Bible Study*, rev. and expanded edition (Minneapolis: Fortress Press, 1993).

For a detailed explanation of exegesis itself, of its standard methods and procedures, see Gordon D. Fee, *New Testament Exegesis: A Handbook for Students and Pastors*, 3rd ed. (Louisville, Ky.: Westminster John Knox Press, 2001); Douglas Stuart, *Old Testament Exegesis: A Handbook for Students and Pastors*, 3rd ed. (Louisville, Ky.: Westminster John Knox Press, 2001); and Odil Hannes Steck, *Old Testament Exegesis: A Guide to the Methodologies*, 2nd ed. (Atlanta: Scholars Press, 1998).

Existentialist/Existential (Interpretation) are English translations of two technical terms central to the biblical HERMENEUTICS of RUDOLF BULTMANN (1884–1976); in German they appear as *existential* and *existentiel* respectively, and are essentially derived from the German philosopher Martin Heidegger's terms *existenzial* and *existenziel*. The former refers to a formal, conceptual analysis of the permanent structures or possibilities of human existence and corresponds to the term *ontological* in philosophy. The latter term, *existential*, denotes a concrete decision regarding one's existence and corresponds to the term *ontic* in philosophy. According to Bultmann, philosophy talks in an ontological-existentialist way of the possibilities of human essence, while the NT and Christian theology speak in an ontic-existential way of the concrete *how* of human existence. However, Bultmann held, every ontic interpretation of human existence, including those of the NT and Christian theology, presupposes a generally hidden ground in ontology. Therefore, a proper exposition of the NT's understanding of the *how* of Christian life (e.g., faith, hope, and love) depends on a previous consideration of the ontological-existentialist structures of human being in general, which is to be accomplished with the aid of philosophy. Bultmann's method has been challenged on the grounds that NT writers portray not only the ontic-existential dimension of human existence but also the ontological-existentialist dimension as thoroughly determined by God, and hence as comprehensible only with reference to God. For this line of criticism, see Udo Schnelle, *The Human Condition: Anthropology in the Teachings of Jesus, Paul, and John* (Minneapolis: Fortress, 1996), chap. 1. For further discussion of Bultmann, see Walter Schmithals, *An Introduction to the Theology of Rudolf Bultmann*, trans. John Bowden [Minneapolis: Augsburg Publishing House, 1968], 677ff.). See also DEMYTHOLOGIZATION; ESCHATOLOGY.

Exordium.   See **Rhetorical Analysis.**

Exposition   (fr. Lat: *exponere:* to explain, to put forth). In biblical interpretation, exposition is sometimes distinguished from exegesis, usually for the sake of the latter which commonly denotes a special methodological approach to scripture. When so used, exposition is understood to follow after exegesis, building on it and elaborating the meaning of a text so as to show its contemporary relevance without falsifying its original sense as ascertained by exegesis. The standard illustration of the distinction between exegesis and exposition is to be found in *The Interpreter's Bible* (1st ed.), which assigns the two kinds of reflection to different authors. There is strong objection to this distinction on the grounds that an understanding of the original meaning of a text cannot be completely separated from an understanding of its contemporary significance, and vice versa. Perhaps for this reason the format was dropped from *The New Interpreter's Bible* (1994–). See EXEGESIS; HERMENEUTICS; *INTERPRETER'S BIBLE.*

External Parallelism.   See **Parallelism.**

Extracanonical   means "outside the canon," i.e., outside the BIBLE. (Because in Orthodox, Protestant, and Roman Catholic traditions the canon is not identical, differing with respect to the APOCRYPHA, some disagreement naturally arises concerning the employment of this term.) See CANON.

Family   is a technical term in TEXTUAL CRITICISM used to describe the lineal relationship that invariably exists between extant manuscripts of the BIBLE. Since every MS is a copy of a previously existing MS and, as the term suggests, is therefore related both to its predecessors and to all other MSS subsequently copied from it, determination of a family grouping is as important in fixing the value of a particular MS as is ascertaining its age. An MS from an early but inferior family is less important than a later MS from a good family in establishing the original reading of the text. Two of the better known family groupings of MINUSCULE MSS are "The Lake Group" (Family 1; *siglum:* λ) and "The Ferrar Group" (Family 13; *siglum:* φ). *Note:* The term *family* denotes a smaller and more closely related group of MSS than the more general term "text type."

Feminist   Biblical   Interpretation first arose as a concerted movement within American biblical scholarship in the 1960s, given impetus by the century-old feminist movement from which it received much of its initial theory and spirit, and by the civil rights movement, the rise of Black liberation theology, and the renewed and concurrent interest in biblical HERMENEUTICS. The aims of feminist biblical interpretation, consistent with those of feminism generally, are (1) to expose the patriarchal character of biblical literature, and where possible to recover women's insights, perspectives, and knowledge that have been marginalized or denied articulation; (2) to show how traditional forms of biblical interpretation are implicated in discrimination against women and how the resources of biblical interpretation may nevertheless be employed in the service of women and others; and (3) to secure for women the equal right of self-expression and self-determination within the domain of biblical scholarship, the academy, the church, and society generally. In short, feminist biblical interpretation seeks to give voice to what has been silenced or ignored and what is necessary for any complete understanding of God, scripture, and humankind.

Feminist biblical interpretation has roots that extend back into antiquity, the rediscovery of which has been part of its chosen task. Recognition, often tempered by trenchant criticism, is given to women who took to heart certain of the church's traditions, such as Paul's affirmation of oneness in CHRIST and the Reformation's doctrine of the priesthood of all believers, and coupled them to their own courage and spiritual insight. Among these are Anne Hutchinson (1591–1643), Mary Dyer (d. 1660), Susanna Wesley (1670–1742), Sojourner Truth (1779–1883), Antoinette Brown Blackwell (1825–1921), and Anna Cooper (1858–1964). Especially noteworthy for the history of feminist biblical interpretation is Elizabeth Cady Stanton (1815–1902), author of *The Woman's Bible* (1896–98), a COMMENTARY and fierce critique of those sections of scripture that bear particularly on women's status. Yet the study of these figures also illustrates why the feminist movement cannot be viewed as a monolithic development. It is acknowledged, with great discomfort, that some feminist leaders mirrored the prejudices of their age, including racism, anti-Judaism, elitism, etc. See G. Lerna, *The Creation of Feminist Consciousness from the Middle Ages to 1870* (*Women and History* 2, 1993), and M. J. Selvidge, *Notorious Voices: Feminist Biblical Interpretation, 1550–1920* (New York: Continuum, 1996).

Since its emergence as a major movement around 1970, feminist biblical interpretation has addressed both the Bible itself as the product of ancient cultures and the interpretation and use of the Bible today. In both cases, it has sought to critique depictions of God and humanity's relationship to God that are androcentric, i.e., that represent men as the prototypical humans and women as inferior and derivative beings (V. C. Phillips). For some, this critical task requires the rejection of BIBLICAL CRITICISM as it is perceived to be practiced in white-male-dominated professional academies, "with its processes of socialization, professionalization, and dedication to scientific disciplines" that are "inimical to the feminist project" (Mieke Bal). However, many other feminist biblical scholars emphasize the importance of historical study for recovering the scope and variety among women's lives in the ancient world and for casting new light on the biblical witnesses.

Since the widespread introduction of feminist studies into academic curricula during the 1980s, feminist biblical interpretation has become increasingly diverse, with texts and issues being addressed from many different ethnic perspectives, theological positions, religious traditions, ideological agendas, and methodological approaches. At one extreme are women who adamantly reject the very notion of feminism or at least question its suitability as a framework for women's future contributions to biblical studies. At the other are those who reject the Bible itself, the book that, "of all books, is the most dangerous one, the one that has been endowed with the power to kill" (Mieke Bal). In addition, there are liberal feminists, radical feminists, Marxist feminists, evangelical feminists, etc.; there are those who see males and females as essentially different, those who see them as sharing an essential human nature, and those who see gender differences as socially produced and culturally conditioned (*The Postmodern Bible*).

Among most feminist biblical interpreters, however, certain core principles provide a certain commonality amidst great differences in theory and approach. Chief among these is the rejection of androcentric viewpoints that represent men as prototypical and women as derivative. Also, practitioners are generally united by the conviction that both the scriptures themselves and their interpretation have been negatively affected by the systematic exclusion of female voices, and that women have both right and authority to correct these misrepresentations, misapprehensions, and errors.

The fundamental question faced by feminist interpreters of the Bible concerns the role and status of the Bible itself as a source and norm of faith. Should the Bible be viewed with suspicion as an oppressive product of a patriarchal culture or be recovered as a source of authority, empowerment, and belief? Most studies include something of both convictions and would agree with the contention that the Bible possesses a "multilayered, contradictory indeterminancy of meaning" that must be "searched" for relevant truth (Schüssler Fiorenza). Fundamental as well is the insight that the social location of the reader/interpreter, including gender, is an inescapable factor in all interpretation. Awareness of this contextual element in the hermeneutical enterprise has led to the particularization of feminist perspectives. The terms "WOMANIST BIBLICAL INTERPRETATION" and "MUJERISTA BIBLICAL INTERPRETATION" (to name just two), arising respectively among African American and Hispanic American feminists, attest to the conviction that, whatever commonality may exist among women generally, factors such as ethnic, racial, and social location require that the experiences and interpretations of distinctive groups be given separate voice. Some contend that race and class distinctions are more pervasive, delimiting, and powerful than gender, representing a blindspot in much feminist RHETORIC that stems from white, middle-class practitioners. The centrifical power of these distinctive concerns has led in recent years to the fracturing of the feminist movement, from its universalizing focus on gender to its reconfiguration in terms of local issues of ideology, domination, and liberation. (See AFROCENTRIC BIBLICAL INTERPRETATION; ASIAN BIBLICAL INTERPRETATION; POSTCOLONIAL BIBLICAL INTERPRETATION.)

Historians of feminist biblical interpretation distinguish three roughly identifiable stages in its evolution. The earliest of these, encompassing most witnesses of the 19th cent. up to the early 1970s, has been characterized as "The Hermeneutics of Recuperation." This effort viewed the biblical tradition as the authoritative source of truth but one whose interpretation needed a corrective emphasis. Effort was given to the reclamation of the role of the women of the Bible, such as the matriarchs of Israel and the women around Jesus. Many contemporary feminists consider these rereadings to be naïve, effacing cultural and historical differences in gender ideology, race, and ethnicity, and focusing on individuals rather than on systemic analysis of social roles of domination and subordination. A second stage, called "The Hermeneutics of Suspicion," "does not presuppose the feminist authority and truth of the Bible, but takes as its starting point the assumption that biblical texts and their interpretations are androcentric and serve patriarchal functions" (Schüssler Fiorenza). This hermeneutic goes further to argue that the key to the adequacy of texts of the Bible lies not in the text itself but in the way the text brings about, or hinders, the experience of political and social liberation. This has led to a critical interest in EARLY CHURCH history, to history writing (a thoroughly androcentric enterprise), and to the necessity of revalorizing the experience of women, not just to restore women to their rightful place in history but to "the theological center of revelation" (Brooten). A still more recent stage in the evolution of feminist biblical interpretation is termed "The Hermeneutics of Survival." It is less concerned with the critique of biblical texts than with "social and political institutions, forces, and processes of domination." The goal changes from understanding and claiming a rightful role in the world to "changing the world." At present all three hermeneutics have their advocates. (For this highly abbreviated sketch, see "Feminist and Womanist Criticism," in *The Postmodern Bible* (New Haven, Conn.: Yale University Press, 1995).

See also A. Walker, *In Search of Our Mothers' Gardens: Womanist Prose* (San Diego: Harcourt Brace Jovanovich, 1983); E. M. Townes (ed.), *Embracing the Spirit: Womanist Perspectives on Hope, Salvation, and Transformation* (Maryknoll, N.Y.: Orbis Books, 1997); Elisabeth Schüssler Fiorenza, *Bread Not Stone: The Challenge of Feminist Biblical Interpretation* (Boston: Beacon Press, 1984) and *Searching the Scriptures: A Feminist Commentary*, 2 vols. (New York: Crossroad, 1993–94); Mary Ann Tolbert, ed., *The Bible* and Feminist Hermeneutics (*Semeia* 28; Atlanta: Scholars Press, 1983); and the *Journal of Feminist Studies in Religion*.

Festschrift   A writing (Ger: *Schrift*) occasioned by the celebration (Ger: *Fest*) of a special event in the life of a famous scholar, often a birthday or retirement; usually a collection of essays by colleagues, students, and admirers.

Fifth Gospel (The),   as a name for the GOSPEL OF THOMAS, must be characterized as a marketing strategy rather than a consensus of scholarly opinion. The genre of the *Gospel of Thomas* has less in common with the canonical GOSPELS than with the hypothetically reconstructed Q source, a collection (whether written or oral) of the SAYINGS of Jesus employed by Matthew and Luke in the writing of their Gospels. A critical edition of the Coptic text, its translation back into Greek as well as German and English translations, is now included as an appendix in KURT ALAND's *Synopsis Quattuor Evangeliorum*, 15th rev. ed. (Stuttgart: Deutsche Bibelgesellschaft, 1996/1997), which is the standard parallel text of the four Gospels. *Note:* The term *fifth gospel* has been used with other referents in mind, such as the book of Isaiah, the experience of Black Americans, etc. See JESUS SEMINAR.

Figura etymologica.   See **Paronomasia.**

Five Scrolls, The.   See **Megillah.**

Floating Logion.   See **Logion.**

Florilegium   (pl.: -*ia*; Lat: a gathering of flowers) is a learned name for an anthology, being also the literal translation of the Greek word into Latin, from *antho* (flower) and *legein* (to gather). (Cf. *The Little Flowers [Fioretti] of St. Francis: Omnibus of Sources* [Chicago: University of Chicago Press, 1973], which is a collection of brief anecdotes about Francis.) Certain documents of the DEAD SEA SCROLLS are referred to as *Florilegia*, consisting of the *Eschatological Midrashim* (4QEschMidr), the *Patriarchal*

Blessings (4QPBless), and the *Testimonia* (4Qtestim).

Form Criticism   (Ger: *Formgeschichte, Gattungsgeschichte*) may be loosely defined as the analysis of the typical forms by which human existence is expressed linguistically; traditionally this referred particularly to their oral, preliterary state, such as LEGENDS, HYMNS, curses, LAMENTS, etc.

The term *form criticism* is a translation of the German word *Formgeschichte*, which literally means the "history of form." It first appeared in the title of MARTIN DIBELIUS's work, *Die Formgeschichte des Evangeliums* (1919; Eng: *From [Oral] Tradition to Gospel* [London: Ivor Nicholson & Watson, Ltd., 1934; repr. James Clarke, 1971; New York: Charles Scribner's Sons, 1935]). But the approach in biblical studies goes back to the OT scholar HERMANN GUNKEL (1862–1932), whose description of its principles and method (which he called GATTUNGS-GESCHICHTE, a history of [literary] types or "genres") is still basic though limited. (See "Fundamental Problems of Hebrew Literary History" in *What Remains of the Old Testament* [London: George Allen & Unwin, 1928].) For a more nuanced definition of the term, see M. J. Buss, *Biblical Form Criticism in Its Context* (JSOT 274; Sheffield: Sheffield Academic Press, 1999; 358).

The task of form criticism at the beginning of the 20th cent. was to go beyond LITERARY CRITICISM as then defined. Literary criticism had recognized the composite character of both OT and NT documents (see GRAF-WELLHAUSEN HYPOTHESIS; TWO SOURCE HYPOTHESIS), and it had proposed dates and places of authorship for the documents and their underlying sources. But literary criticism treated scripture, particularly the PENTATEUCH and the Synoptic GOSPELS, as the literary product of individual personalities and not as the repository of the living traditions of common people, traditions of shared experience and belief as varied as life itself. What was needed was an analysis of literary forms in order to rediscover the history of their development.

Gunkel himself noted two broad literary classifications, prose and poetry, the former including MYTHS, folktales, romances, legends, and historical NARRATIVE; the latter, wisdom and prophetic ORACLES, secular lyric poetry, hymns, thanksgivings, eschatological PSALMS, etc. Gunkel also noted that types are often recognizable by their introductory FORMULAS ("Sing unto the Lord," "How long, O Lord?" etc.); that each type emerges from a specific setting in the life of a people; and further that, because of this, a genre gives insight into the life situation (*SITZ-IM-LEBEN*) in which it arises, and the setting in turn illumines the content and intention of the genre itself.

As Gunkel put it, "To understand the literary type we must in each case have the whole situation clearly before us and ask ourselves, Who is speaking? Who are the listeners? What is the *mise en scène* [Fr: the setting on the stage] at the time? What effect is aimed at?" (*What Remains*, 62). Finally, Gunkel suggested that literary types evolve, that they arise, flourish, and die or are transmuted, and can therefore be placed in a chronological relationship as well as a formal relationship to each other. Forms provide the data for a literary history of Israel. He described the end of that history: "The spirit loses power. The types are exhausted. Imitations begin to abound. Redactions take the place of original creations. Hebrew ceases to be the living language of the people. By this time the collections [psalms, laws, legends, proverbs, etc.] are grouped together into larger collections. The canon has come into being" (66).

Gunkel applied the form-critical method to Genesis (*The Legends of Genesis* [New York: Schocken Books, 1966[2]; orig. 1901]) and to the Psalms with lasting results. But his hope for a literary history of Israel faded as form criticism became absorbed in pure formalism. TRADITION CRITICISM arose in the 1930s in a renewed effort to analyze the history of the transmission of traditions, with their varied settings and transmutations.

In more recent years, the methodological assumptions of form criticism have been challenged by RHETORICAL CRITICISM, structural LINGUISTICS (see STRUCTURALISM), et al. Under reexamination is the relation of genre to setting, of oral to written traditions, of form to content, of the conventional or typical to the unique within a text, etc. Form critics now suggest that the notions of genre, setting, and function are far more complex than traditional form criticism allowed, and that the typicality (or typicalities) that govern a text may include one or more factors other than pure MORPHOLOGY, such as setting, function, intention, STRUCTURE, etc.

The four more or less traditional steps of form-critical method have been outlined by Gene M. Tucker: (1) Structure: An analysis of the outline, pattern, or schema of a given genre; its opening and closing (*INCLUSIO*), conventional patterns (PARALLELISM, CHIASMUS, etc.), etc. (2) Genre: A definition and description of the unit according to its type (however that typicality is defined). (3) Setting: A determination of the social situation (or other factors, e.g., the "style of an epoch") or language (*langue*, in the structuralist sense) that gave rise to the genre, to other typicalities of the text, or to the individual text at hand. (4) Intention: A statement of the purpose and function, the mood and content, of the genre in general and specifically of the example under study. See Tucker, *Form Criticism of the Old Testament* (Philadelphia: Fortress Press, 1971). For a sketch of the history of form criticism, see *Old Testament Form Criticism*, ed. John H. Hayes (San Antonio: Trinity University Press, 1974), and more recently Buss, *Biblical Form Criticism in Its Context*. Buss begins his comprehensive study with ancient Greek reflection on the interrelationship of life experiences and activities, thoughts and moods, and linguistic forms, tracing that history through the centuries while reflecting on the context in which such form-critical study emerged. A COMMENTARY series with introductory articles on various genres is being published by Wm. B. Eerdmans Publishing Co. (Grand Rapids, Mich.) under the series title, Forms of the Old Testament Literature (FOTL, 1981–).

The literary forms of the OT, and the ORAL TRADITIONS behind them, present the critic with a vastly different problem from those of the NT. The OT, in many instances, has hundreds of years of oral tradition behind it; the Synoptic Gospels, with which NT form criticism began, have 30–60 years at most, the LETTERS of Paul even less. Furthermore, OT forms are numerous; NT forms relatively few. For this reason, and others, the two disciplines developed along lines independent of each other.

Form criticism in NT study began with the writings of K. L. Schmidt, Martin Dibelius (op. cit.), and RUDOLF BULTMANN (*History of the Synoptic Tradition* [Ger 1921; Eng.: New York: Harper & Row, 1963; Oxford: Basil Blackwell, 1963], still an indispensable tool of Gospel criticism). In England, Vincent Taylor (*The Formation of the Gospel Tradition* [London: Macmillan & Co., 1933]) became a cautious proponent of the method. Since these beginnings the method has been applied to a wide variety of NT and, more recently, extracanonical material.

As in OT studies, the purpose of NT form criticism as traditionally defined was to rediscover the origin and history of the individual units and thereby to shed some light on the history of the tradition before it took literary form, that is, to determine whether the various units are traceable to Jesus, to the EARLY CHURCH, or to the redactional (editorial) activity of the Gospel writers. Dibelius began with the assumption that the *setting in the life of the church* that gave rise to and formed much of the synoptic material was the sermon (KERYGMA) and Christian teaching (DIDACHE). Bultmann also attributed many of the forms to the church and to redactional activity; he concluded that nothing could be attributed to Jesus with absolute certainty (see CRITERIA OF AUTHENTICITY).

An impediment to form criticism after its initial thrust was the lack of terminological clarity. While some unanimity existed in identifying certain forms (narratives, SAYINGS, miracle stories, etc.) little agreement existed concerning the subdivision of these classifications or the terminology appropriate to them (see, e.g., APOPHTHEGM; PRONOUNCEMENT STORY; CHRIA; PARADIGM). What has endured are certain of form criticism's methodological assumptions, viz., that different linguistic forms arise from and elucidate different aspects of life; that differences in the synoptic material are due in part to oral transmission; that form, content, and function are related in varied ways, etc. As mentioned previously, however, these assumptions and others are being rethought. It can be said that on the one hand the initial thrust of form criticism further weakened the Gospels as historical sources for a biography of Jesus, on the other it elevated the importance of the PARABLES as that speech form most illuminative of the life and mind of Jesus. Finally, form criticism's fragmentary approach to the Gospels ignored the thought and setting of the Gospel writers themselves. This oversight was corrected by REDACTION CRITICISM. Structural linguistics challenges the basic assumption that written material can provide any access at all to the period of oral tradition. Others point out that "form" and "structure" are not objective realities but are related to an observer, and that, in any case form citicism cannot be executed in isolation but involves judgments and knowledge across the spectrum of human existence, from laws of social organization to laments of personal grief. See Edgar V. McKnight, *What Is Form Criticism?* (Philadelphia: Fortress Press, 1969); also *Interpretation*, 27 (Oct. 1973), and James L. Bailey and Lyle D. Vander Broek, *Literary Forms in the NT: A Handbook* (Louisville, Ky.: Westminster/John Knox, 1992). Rhetorical criticism, whose initial impetus is attributed to James Muilenburg ("Form Criticism and Beyond," *JBL* 88 (1969): 1–18, saw that form criticism disregarded the individual, personal, and unique features of a text, and with this insight attempted to go beyond it.

See in addition to terms noted BIBLICAL CRITICISM; QUEST OF THE HISTORICAL JESUS.

Formal Parallelism. See Synthetic Parallelism under **Parallelism.**

Formgeschichte (Ger: lit., "form history"). See **Form Criticism.**

Formula (pl.: -ae or -s); formulary. In FORM CRITICISM, a formula is a short literary form, usually not more than a brief phrase or sentence, established principally through use and employed to designate an action (as, e.g., a baptismal formulary) or otherwise introduce a longer literary type. The types of formulas are as varied as life: e.g., of asseveration, "Truly, I tell you" (Matt 18:3, 13, 18, 19, etc.); of accusation (Gen 3:13; 29:25; Num 23:11, etc.); prophetic, "Thus says the LORD of hosts" (Jer 19:11,15; 20:4, etc.); quotation (1 Kgs 11:41; 14:19, etc.); liturgical (Matt 28:18; 1 Cor 11:23–26) and so on. It is by way of such formulas that corporate life is formalized and thereby made possible. Though often loosely used in the sense above, the term *formulary* more precisely refers to a collection or system of formulas.

In the analysis of biblical poetry, the term *formula* has been defined as "a repeated group of words the length of which corresponds to one of the divisions in the poetic STRUCTURE" (usually a half line or line). Robert Culley has identified approximately 175 formulas or formulaic systems in the poetic material of the biblical PSALMS, e.g., "Incline your ear (to me; to my cry; O Lord)": Pss 31:2; 71:2; 102:2; 88:2; 116:2; 86:1. See R. Culley, *Oral Formulaic Language in the Biblical Psalms* (Toronto: University of Toronto Press, 1967).

Four Document (or Source) Hypothesis of the Synoptic Gospels as proposed by B. H. STREETER (*The Four Gospels* [London: Macmillan & Co., 1924]). (See chart below.)

The goal of the Four Document Hypothesis was to establish documentary sources essentially equal in antiquity and presumably therefore in authenticity to Mark and Q and thereby to widen the scope of the search for the historical Jesus; it was more widely accepted among English than German scholars. The issue of the sources used by the writers of the Synoptic GOSPELS is still debated in contemporary scholarship. See PROTO-LUKE; SYNOPTIC PROBLEM; TWO SOURCE HYPOTHESIS; *URMARKUS*.

Fourfold Sense of Scripture, The Also known as the *Quadriga* (Lat: a team of four horses), *The Fourfold Sense of Scripture* refers to a classification of the senses of scripture and their corresponding

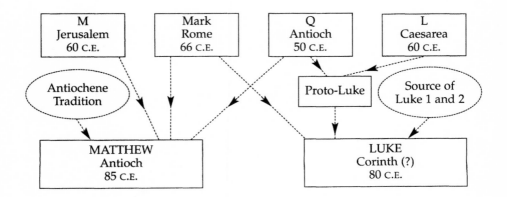

modes of interpretation first proposed by John Cassian (ca. 360–435) and prominent in the West from the medieval period to the Reformation and beyond. Like others before him, Cassian distinguished between the scripture's literal and spiritual senses, but then subdivided the spiritual more precisely into (1) tropological (= moral), (2) allegorical (also typological), and (3) anagogical (= pertaining to last or ultimate things). Cassian gave the following illustration: "One and the same Jerusalem can be taken in four senses: historically as the city of the Jews; allegorically as Church of Christ, anagogically as the heavenly city of God 'which is the mother of us all,' tropologically, as the soul of man, which is frequently subject to praise or blame from the Lord under this title." Generations of students committed *The Fourfold Sense* to memory with the help of an anonymous rhyme:

Littera gesta docet, quid credas allegoria,
Moralis quid agas, quo tendas anagogia.

("The letter shows us what God and our fathers did; the allegory shows us where our faith is hid; the moral meaning gives us rules of daily life; the anagogy shows us where we end our strife"; Grant and Tracy, *A Short History of the Interpretation of the Bible,* 2nd ed. [Minneapolis: Fortress Press, 1984, 85].)

Only one of several classifications of the sense of scripture proposed by the church fathers (ORIGEN and Ambrose distinguished a threefold sense), *The Fourfold Sense* is a rough and in part misleading characterization of the wide variety of patristic and medieval interpretive practice (see Frances M. Young, *Biblical Exegesis and the Formation of Christian Culture* (Cambridge: Cambridge University Press, 1997). Nevertheless, *The Fourfold Sense* testifies to a fundamental premise of EXEGESIS prior to the modern age, namely, that the meaning of a biblical passage is not exhausted by a single sense—that the Bible is sufficiently profound and complex to comprehend multiple valid senses. The Fourfold Sense

provided an influential point of reference for the development of hermeneutical theory in the West and was embraced by theologians such as John of Salisbury, Thomas Aquinas, Hugh of St. Cher, and Nicholas of Lyre. See LITERAL SENSE; *SENSUS PLENIOR.*

Frei, Hans   (1922–1988). Born in Breslau, Frei fled Germany before the Second World War, studied theology under H. Richard Niebuhr at Yale University, and there spent almost all of his teaching career. Influenced by the literary studies of Eric Auerbach (*Mimesis*) and the THEOLOGICAL INTERPRETATION of KARL BARTH, Frei wanted to understand why traditional modes of biblical interpretation had collapsed in the modern world and how they could be critically recovered. Traditionally, Frei believed, Christians read the GOSPELS as realistic NARRATIVES and accorded them interpretive priority within a reading of the Bible as a single, typologically unified book. Frei believed that this pattern of reading fell apart largely because early modern interpreters of the Gospels increasingly ignored their character as realistic narratives. That is, they ceased to read the Gospels as narratives that mean what they say and instead read them as historical sources or as symbolic or mythical expressions of truth, whose meaning consists in reference to historical events or spiritual truths that can also be expressed by other means. But a Gospel's meaning, Frei urged, consists precisely in the story that it tells, in its rendering of Jesus' identity through an account of his actions and reactions to persons and circumstances. "The location of meaning in narrative of the realistic sort is the text, the narrative structure or sequence itself" (*The Eclipse of Biblical Narrative* [New Haven: Yale University Press, 1984], 280). Frei did not hold that the Gospels are ahistorical or nonreferential, as is sometimes said, but rather that they confront the reader with Jesus' identity through the story they tell and not otherwise.

Neither a prolific nor an easily accessible writer, Frei was nevertheless one of the most seminal American theologians of his generation, providing decisive stimulus for renewed interest in the theology of Karl Barth, biblical narrative, and the postcritical recovery of traditional modes of biblical interpretation. See HERMENEUTICS.

Frühkatholizismus.   See **Early Church (The).**

G.   See **Grundlage**.

Gattung; Gattungsforschung; Gattungsgeschichte   (Ger: Gattung: form, type, genre. *Forschung:* research. *Geschichte:* history). In German, the term *Gattung* denotes a group of things or beings that have important or distinguishing (i.e., "typical") characteristics in common (Duden). In German BIBLICAL CRITICISM usage is disputed. *Gattung* is sometimes used to designate larger literary entities, such as GOSPEL, epistle, APOCALYPSE, historical writing, etc., in which case *Gattungsforschung* designates the study of these literary genres and *Gattungsgeschichte* the analysis of their historical origin, development, and death or transmutation into another literary genre or mixed genre (*Mischgattung*). Here, *Gattung* is distinct from the German *Form* (*Formen,* pl.), which is used to denote smaller literary units that primarily, but not exclusively, arise in ORAL TRADITION. Where *Form* ends and *Gattung* begins is obviously arbitrary, causing some scholars to reject the distinction altogether so that *Form* and *Gattung* are essentially identical. In recent structuralist theory, particularly applied to OT criticism, the term *Form* is used in reference to individual texts; the term *Gattung* either to a structural model or scheme (*Strukturmuster*) involving at least two exemplars, or to text type, i.e., the typicality by which a text is governed, whether that typicality be determined by a text's STRUCTURE, setting, concern, or a specific motif. (See Rolf Knierim, "Old Testament Form Criticism Reconsidered," *Interpretation* 27 [Oct. 1973]: esp. 463.)

In English, *Gattung* is now most frequently translated "genre." *Gattung* criticism becomes especially problematic when applied to the literature of the EARLY CHURCH because its most important documents, especially the Gospels, represent a new kind of literature, their closest parallels being the so-called aretalogy.

From the perspective of communication theory, a genre, according to M. Buss, "is best viewed as an open or virtual class which describes a possibility, rather than as a class of actual objects which meet a certain description." Such a view attempts to understand a given genre, such as a LAMENT psalm, in terms of its actual function in human life, that is, as an expectation of the speaker or hearer, rather than simply as a theoretical and closed construct constituted by the collective elements of all PSALMS of this type. See Martin Buss, ed., *Encounter with the Text* (*Semeia* Suppl.; Missoula, Mont.: Scholars Press, 1979). See ARETALOGY; FORM CRITICISM.

Gemara.   See **Talmud.**

Gemeindeordnungen; Gemeinderegeln   (Ger: *Gemeinde*: congregation/community. *Ordnungen/Regeln:* rules) are German words meaning "rules for the congregation" that connote a counsel of discipline designed for and originating within the earliest Christian communities, although the ethos that the rules embody may go back to Jesus. Matthew 18 (particularly vv. 15–18) is widely accepted as an example of *Gemeindeordnungen* placed back, for authority, on the lips of Jesus. *Gemeindeordnungen* are found throughout the writings of Paul (esp. 1 and 2 Cor), the PASTORAL EPISTLES (e.g., 1 Tim 2:1–15; 5:1–21; 6:1–2; 2 Pet 2:13–3:7), and THE DIDACHE (*Did.* 4:9–11). It should be noted that numbered among the DEAD SEA SCROLLS are writings known as the *Rule of the Congregation* and the MANUAL OF DISCIPLINE. See HOUSEHOLD RULES.

General Epistles.   See **Catholic Epistles.**

Genre.   (Fr: kind, sort, style). See **Gattung**.

Geschichte.   See **Historie**.

Gloss (fr. Lat: a difficult word requiring explanation). In the narrower sense, a gloss is a brief explanation or definition of a difficult word or a translation of a foreign word; more broadly, it is a comment or interpretation. In TEXTUAL CRITICISM it refers to a synonym or brief definition written above a word or in the margin of a text; if continued throughout, the original text is given an interlinear translation, e.g., a Greek MS "glossed" with Latin (so CODEX Sangallensis, 9th cent.; see Bruce Metzger, *The Text of the New Testament* [London and New York: Oxford University Press, 1964], plate 13). In copying MSS, scribes sometimes mistakenly incorporated glosses into the body of the text, thereby corrupting it. See ASSIMILATION; CONFLATION; INTERLINEAR (GREEK NT).

Glossolalia (fr. Gk: "speaking in tongues"). Ecstatic utterance associated with possession of the Holy Spirit, typically unintelligible in character (but compare Acts 2:4). Glossolalia was undoubtedly common within the EARLY CHURCH; its problematic features, its role in worship, and its status as a gift of the Spirit are discussed by Paul in 1 Cor 12–14.

***Gnosis;* Gnostic, Gnosticism** (Gk: knowledge). The nature and origin of *gnosis* and the terms by which it is discussed is a matter of scholarly debate. The central issue has been whether Gnosticism is a heretical outgrowth of 2nd-cent. Christianity (which is the traditional view apparently held by the early church fathers and by scholars up to the turn of the 20th cent.) or a recrudescence and resurgence of an ancient religion whose origins lay in the East and whose appeal came to rival that of Christianity.

What is indisputable is that there appeared in the 2nd cent. a heresy among Christians that the EARLY CHURCH termed false "*gnosis*" (or "knowledge"; 1 Tim 6:20) and which today, primarily in English language scholarship, is commonly referred to as Gnosticism. The nature of this heresy

has been fairly well known through the quotations of those who argued against it: Irenaeus, Hippolytus, ORIGEN. However, with the 1945–46 discovery near Nag Hammadi, Egypt, of some fifty gnostic texts, the prospect of detailing the nature of "Gnosticism" more precisely is now immeasurably enhanced. Some scholars use the term *gnosis* broadly as a fairly widespread and highly diverse but generalizable pre-Christian religious phenomenon. When *gnosis* is thus defined, the term "Gnosticism" is reserved as designating Christianized *gnosis*. This judgment may however be premature in light of work being done on the NAG HAMMADI CODICES. Currently it is common to distinguish between texts more mythically oriented from those more perspicuously Christian in content, the former referred to as "Sethian," the latter as "Christian Gnostic." One of the foremost examples of a "Sethian" text is the *Apocryphon of John.*

At this stage of understanding, then, how should *gnosis* be defined? No single term, such as philosophy, theology, or mysticism, suffices. It has been described as "a constellation of religious phenomena" (R. M. Grant) that consists of the following main points:

1. The true God, transcendent and unknowable, is utterly different from and not responsible for the visible creation, which is the work of the demiurge. (Some gnostic systems identify the demiurge with the God of the OT.)
2. Each person's true "self," the "I" of the gnostic, is a "spark of the divine"; it is therefore unalterably immortal but "fallen" and imprisoned in corporeality by the powers of this world and, like gold in mud, unable on its own to attain freedom.
3. Only a divine "call" can arouse a person from material stupor, giving him or her "knowledge" (*gnosis*) of the true self, of the self's home in the transcendent realm, and of the true God.
4. This return of the self occurs at the end of the individual life, when the soul travels

through the spheres, or at the end of the world, simultaneous with the relapse of materiality to its original chaos or impassivity; the return is therefore resisted by the evil spirits and powers of this world.

Apart from these common elements, there is no single gnostic system; just as there seems to be no single founder or text from which all the systems flow. There are many systems, each understanding itself to be an extension of the call which, in Christianized *gnosis,* proceeds from a Redeemer who has descended from the divine world, imparted *gnosis* and returned to the world above. Gnostic systems are often known by their founder or major teacher, such as MARCION, Basilides, and Valentinus; but the church fathers refer to others whose origins are unknown, such as the Ophites, Cainites, Naassenes, Peratae, Sethians, etc. (See Werner Foerster, *Gnosis: A Selection of Gnostic Texts,* Vol. 1: *Patristic Evidence;* 2: *Coptic and Mandean Sources,* trans. R. McL. Wilson [London and New York: Oxford University Press, 1972]; C. W. Hedrick and R. Hodgson, eds., *Nag Hammadi Gnosticism and Early Christianity* [Peabody, Mass.: Hendrickson, 1986]; H. Jonas, *The Gnostic Religion* [Boston: Beacon Press, 1963]); for additional bibliography, see NAG HAMMADI CODICES.

The question biblical interpreters face concerns the nature and role of *gnosis* in the NT and in the religious milieu to which these writings were addressed. Certainly *gnosis* in the broadest sense was present, even if incipient and partial, in the 1st cent. in Judaism, in the DEAD SEA SCROLLS, and in PHILO. Christian writings such as the GOSPEL of John and 1 John show a great affinity for concepts integral to 2nd-cent. Gnosticism: the descent and ascent of the Redeemer from and to the heavenly realm (John 1:18; 3:13; 6:33; 12:23, etc.); the revelation of truth about the unknown God (John 1:18; 3:31–36; 14:8–11, etc.); the division of humankind into those who accept and those who reject the truth (John 1:12–13; 8:23, 44; 17:16); the dualism of flesh and spirit (John 3:6; 6:63), of above

and below, and so forth. It has been argued that Paul struggles against *gnosis* in Corinth, having to defend the futurity of resurrection and its "bodily" form (1 Cor 15), and at Colossae, where he asserts the subjection of all earthly spirit powers by CHRIST, who is the mediator of creation (Col 2). By the time of the DEUTEROPAULINE PASTORAL EPISTLES, *Gnosticism,* has become a rival (1 Tim. 6:20), which Christians are admonished to avoid (1 Tim 4:1–16; 6:3–5; 2 Tim 2:14ff.; 4:1–5; Titus 3:9). See K. Rudolph, *Gnosis: The Nature and History of Gnosticism* (San Francisco: Harper & Row, 1984). See CHENOBOSKION.

Good News for Modern Man. See **Today's English Version.**

Gospel (OE: fr. *Godspell:* good news) is the Anglo-Saxon translation of the Greek word *euangelion,* which is used by the NT writers only in the sense of God's good news (lower case "gospel") to humankind (Mark 1:15; 10:29; Rom 1:1–3, 16; 1 Cor 4:15; 9:18, passim). The term later came to mean a book (upper case "Gospel") telling of the life and teachings of Jesus (*Did.* 8:2; 11:3; 15:3; Justin, *Apol.* 1. 66), perhaps following Mark 1:1. Some ancient writings, however, though called "gospels," in fact tell nothing of Jesus' life, e.g., the GOSPEL OF THOMAS. Whether or to what extent the four NT Gospels (Matt, Mark, Luke, John) constitute a distinct literary genre or have parallels in contemporary Hellenistic literature has been a lively question in BIBLICAL CRITICISM. See C. H. Talbert, *What Is a Gospel? The Genre of the Canonical Gospels* (Philadelphia: Fortress Press, 1977). See also ARETALOGY.

Gospel of Peter (The) Dating from the 2nd cent. and repudiated by Bishop Serapion of Antioch (ca. 190) as spurious, the *Gospel of Peter* is preserved only fragmentarily in a CODEX, from ca. 800. The extant passages constitute the earliest uncanonical account of the Passion. Although most scholars consider the work an imaginative retelling of the GOSPEL accounts with a decidedly anti-Jewish and Docetic cast, John Dominic Crossan argues for the historical authenticity of certain data within it. For text, see *The Apocryphal New Testament,* ed. J. K. Elliott (Oxford: Clarendon Press, 1993), and John Dominic Crossan, *The Cross That Spoke* (San Francisco: Harper & Row, 1988).

Gospel of Thomas (The) is a collection of 114 logia, or SAYINGS, "which the Living Jesus spoke and Didymos Judas Thomas wrote." A Coptic VERSION of the *Gospel of Thomas* was discovered near Nag Hammadi in Upper Egypt in 1945 along with a number of other GNOSTIC manuscripts now referred to as the Nag Hammadi library. Greek fragments of the document were found in the same region in 1898 and 1903, although their identity remained unknown. Since the work contains none of the typifying characteristics of the canonical GOSPELS, such as NARRATIVES of the birth, baptism, ministry, and Passion, it is a gospel in name only. As a collection of sayings, it is in form more to be equated with the hypothetical document scholars refer to as Q. Although highly gnostic in content, the logia form has led some scholars to speculate that some of the sayings are as old as the sayings of Q, encouraging the bolder among them to refer to the *Gospel of Thomas* as "THE FIFTH GOSPEL." Scholars generally date the *Gospel of Thomas* to a period ranging from 140 to 200 C.E., long after the completion of the canonical Gospels. Whereas some of the sayings closely resemble those of the canonical Gospels, others do not, for example, #114: "Simon Peter said to them: Let Mary go out from among us, because women are not worthy of the Life. Jesus said: See I shall lead her, so that I will make her male, that she too may become a living spirit, resembling you males. For every woman who makes herself male will enter the Kingdom of Heaven." For bibliography, see JESUS SEMINAR; NAG HAMMADI CODICES; QUEST OF THE HISTORICAL JESUS.

Gospel Parallel. See **Synopsis.**

Graf, Karl Heinrich (1815–1869). Born in Mülhausen in Elsass, Graf was a private tutor in Paris (1839–43) before becoming a teacher of Hebrew and French in Giessen (1847–68). His suggestion (1866) that the "Foundation Writing" (P) was the latest stratum of the PENTATEUCH became the basis of J. WELLHAUSEN's elaborated theory of 1872. See GRAF-WELLHAUSEN HYPOTHESIS; P: PRIESTLY CODE.

Graf-Wellhausen Hypothesis A theory concerning the origins of the PENTATEUCH that, though having numerous antecedents, was most persuasively argued by K. H. GRAF (1866) and JULIUS WELLHAUSEN (1876–1884); it added to the existing hypothesis the argument that written documents, combined and revised over several centuries from varying historical and theological points of view, could be (fairly) precisely dated and placed in an evolutionary sequence. A J (YAHWIST) document (ca. 850 B.C.E.) and an E (ELOHIST) document (ca. 750 B.C.E.) were, according to this hypothesis, combined by a REDACTOR (R^{JE}) around 650 B.C.E.; the DEUTERONOMIC CODE (621 B.C.E., called D) was added by a redactor (R^{D}) around 550 B.C.E.; the Priestly Code (ca. 450 B.C.E.) constituted the final document added by a redactor (R^{P}) around 400 B.C.E. Numerous revisions of this hypothesis, also called the "Newer Documentary Hypothesis," which dominated OT criticism until the rise of FORM CRITICISM, have been proposed. An argument for its rejection is found in R. N. Whybray, *The Making of the Pentateuch: A Methodological Study* (JSOTSup 53; Sheffield: Sheffield University Press, 1987). See D: DEUTERONOMIC CODE; E: ELOHIST; *GRUNDLAGE*; P: PRIESTLY CODE.

Griesbach, Johann Jakob (1745–1812). Professor of NT at the Universities of Halle (1771) and Jena (1775) in Germany. He is noted in both textual and LITERARY CRITICISM. He was the first to break with the *TEXTUS RECEPTUS* by developing a CRITICAL TEXT of his own supplemented with a CRITICAL APPARATUS; he was the first to reject the traditional explanation of the relationship of the first three GOSPELS (GRIESBACH HYPOTHESIS); and, denying the possibility of writing a HARMONY, he created the first SYNOPSIS of the

Gospels (Matt, Mark, and Luke) and the name "synoptic writer" (Ger: *Synoptiker*).

Griesbach Hypothesis (The) seeks to explain the literary relationship of the first three GOSPELS of the NT by assuming that Matt is the earliest Gospel, that it was used by Luke, and that Mark as the latest composition is a radical CONFLATION of both Matt and Luke. This proposal, made by J. J. GRIES- BACH in Germany in 1783, had been suggested earlier by the Englishman Henry Owen (*Observations on the Four Gospels* [London: T. Payne, 1764]) with little effect. The Griesbach hypothesis is a modification of Augustine's conjecture that each of the Gospel writers was dependent on the previous author(s), following the canonical order: Matt, Mark, Luke, John (cf. Augustine, *On the Harmony of the Evangelists* [*De Consunsu Evangelistarum*]). The Griesbach hypothesis was revived and revised by W. R. Farmer, (*The Synoptic Problem* [New York: Macmillan Co., 1964]; see also D. B. Peabody, "Augustine and the Augustinian Hypothesis" in W. R. Farmer, ed., *New Synoptic Studies* [Macon, Ga.: Mercer University Press, 1983]). See FOUR DOCUMENT HYPOTHESIS; SYNOPTIC PROBLEM; TWO SOURCE HYPOTHESIS; Q; *URMARKUS*.

Grundlage (Ger: basis; *siglum*: G). A hypothetical common basis behind the Pentateuchal traditions known as J and E, first proposed by MARTIN NOTH in 1948 to explain the large number of common elements in the two traditions. Noth designated this common basis *Grundlage*. (See Noth, *A History of Pentateuchal Traditions*, trans. Bernhard W. Anderson [Englewood Cliffs, N.J.: Prentice-Hall, 1971], 38–41.) However, the term may refer to any foundational text (written or oral) underlying a literary work.

Gunkel, Hermann (1862–1932) was born in Springe, Germany, and taught NT at Göttingen (1888) before turning to OT studies at Halle (1889–93); he became associate professor of OT in Berlin (1894–1907), a full professor in Giessen (1907–20), and ended his career in Halle (1920–27). Although Gunkel was overshadowed

by the influence of JULIUS WELLHAUSEN during most of his own lifetime, Gunkel's methodological insights and conclusions have withstood 20th-cent. criticism better than Wellhausen's. He has been called "the founder of form-critical and history-of-religions research in the OT" (Kümmel). He was the first to use the terms "*GATTUNGS- FORSCHUNG*" and "*SITZ-IM-LEBEN*" (setting-in-life), terms which were to redirect the development of LITERARY CRITICISM in NT studies as well. (See John H. Hayes, *An Introduction to OT Study* [Nashville: Abingdon Press, 1979], 121–149.) With WILHELM BOUSSET, Gunkel founded the series Forschungen zur Religion und Literatur des Alten und Neuen Testaments (FRLANT). (See his *The Legends of Genesis: The Biblical Saga and History*, trans. W. H. Carruth [1901] with an Introduction by WILLIAM F. ALBRIGHT [New York: Schocken Books, 1964, 1962]; and *The Folktale in the Old Testament* [Sheffield: Sheffield Academic Press, 1987; Ger 1921].) See FORM CRITICISM.

Haggadah (fr. Heb: *haggid*: to tell, narrate; pl. *haggadot*). In rabbinic tradition, *Haggadah* refers either to (a) that part of rabbinic literature that shapes and informs individual and communal life through folklore, legend, parable, anecdote, proverb, etc., (b) an individual literary unit of such character transmitted by the rabbis to interpret the written and/or oral TORAH, or (c) the specific extended collection of such units that frames the Passover Seder. As a descriptive term referring to the non-legal interpretive methods of rabbinic literature, *Haggadah* stands in contrast to *HALAKAH*. See *The Book of Legends*, eds. Hayim Hahman Bialik and Yehoshua Hana Ravnitzky (New York: Schocken Books, 1992), and Louis Ginsberg, *The Legends of the Jews*, 6 vols. (Philadelphia: Jewish Publication Society of America, 1936–42). See *HALAKAH*; MIDRASH; TORAH.

Hagiographa means in Greek "the holy (or sacred) writings" and is the name commonly given to the third Jewish division of the HB, also called in Hebrew

Ketubim, or "The Writings" (the "k" in TANAKH). The Hagiographa comprises, in varying order, the PSALMS, Proverbs, Job, Song of Solomon, Ruth, Lamentations, Ecclesiastes, Esther, Daniel, Ezra, Nehemiah, and 1 and 2 Chronicles.

Halakah (or *Halacha;* fr. Heb: *halak:* to go, to walk). In rabbinic tradition, *halakah* is a technical term that refers either to (a) that part of rabbinic literature that contains rules for the daily conduct of the individual's and the community's life, or (b) the rules and decisions themselves as handed down by the rabbis to be the authoritative interpretation of the written and/or oral TORAH. The plural form, *halakoth* (meaning "rules" or "decisions"), is used as a name for the various collections of these decisions. Where *halakah* stands as a plain statement of oral Torah, it is mishnaic; where it is derived from or attached to written Torah, it is midrashic. In the Talmudic and medieval periods, *halakah* was increasingly cast in midrashic form, while simultaneously there were developed mishnaic codes that summarized the *halakah* under topical categories. As a descriptive term referring to the legal interpretive methods of rabbinic literature, *halakah* stands in contrast to *haggadah.* See *HAGGADAH;* MIDRASH; MISHNAH; TORAH.

Hapaxlegomenon (pl.: -a) in Greek means "something said (only) once"; it usually refers to a word that appears but once in either the OT or NT as a whole; it may also be used in a more limited way of the writings of one person, e.g., the LETTERS of Paul. There are more hapaxlegomena in the OT book of Job than any other biblical writing, adding to the difficulty of translation.

Haplography is the name of an error in manuscript copying in which a syllable, word, or line is omitted by accidental oversight because of the identity or similarity of adjacent material; the opposite of DITTOG-

RAPHY. See ASSIMILATION; CONFLATION; *HOMOIOTELEUTON;* TEXTUAL CRITICISM.

Harmony (of the Gospels) In current usage, a harmony is a work that attempts so to interrelate the materials of the four GOSPELS that they tell a single and continuous story. The first and most famous was by TATIAN (2nd cent.), called the *Diatessaron.* The genre flourished especially in the century after the Reformation and gradually died out with the advent of HISTORICAL CRITICISM. In the modern period, the verb "to harmonize" has come to be used in a pejorative way to refer to forced attempts to establish literary or thematic unity between different biblical writings. The word *harmony* is at times used as synonymous with "SYNOPSIS," or "Gospel parallel," but it should be reserved for the former meaning.

Hatch and Redpath is the common call name of the Hatch-Redpath *Concordance to the Septuagint and Other Greek Versions of the OT* (including the APOCRYPHA) by Edwin Hatch and Henry A. Redpath, 2 vols. (Oxford: Clarendon Press, 1897; Suppl. 1906. Reprint. 3 vols. in 2. Grand Rapids: Eerdmans, 1983).

An Expanded Index of the Hatch-Redpath Concordance to the Septuagint (Jerusalem, Israel: Dugith Publishers, 1974) places the Greek words used in the LXX opposite their Hebrew equivalents.

Haustafeln. (Ger: rules of the house). See **Household Rules.**

Hebraism. See **Semitism.**

Hebrew Bible (HB) is a term chiefly at home in academic (in contrast to liturgical or religious) settings to refer to the sacred scriptures of Judaism as established by rabbinic authorities around 100 C.E. Comprised of thirty-nine books originally written in Hebrew and Aramaic (Daniel and brief portions of Ezra), it is more familiarly known in Judaism as the TANAKH, a name derived from the initial letters of its three divisions: TORAH or LAW, Nephiim or PROPHETS, and Ketubim or Writings. In

1988, the Jewish Publication Society issued an English translation of the HB under the title *Tanakh—The Holy Scriptures.* Begun in 1955 with the publication of *The Torah* in 1962 followed by *The Prophets* in 1978 and *The Writings* in 1982, the translation maintains a high literary level.

In recent years, the term Hebrew Bible has increasingly replaced Old Testament as the preferred scholarly designation for the first half of the Christian CANON, not least among Christian scholars (see OLD TESTAMENT/NEW TESTAMENT). However well intentioned, this usage is potentially misleading, for the Jewish canon is not identical in every respect with the body of writings traditionally known among the Christian churches as the OT. The canonical shape of the OT differs from the HB and among the Christian churches themselves due to two factors: (1) the SEPTUAGINT (LXX) formed the original basis of the church's canon, which included a number of works originally composed in Greek and ultimately rejected by normative Judaism (see APOCRYPHA); and (2) different churches have to different degrees "corrected" their OT canon in the direction of the HB while still following ancient ecclesial precedent in other respects (e.g., the order of the books). Today Orthodox churches follow the LXX most closely, using it even as the primary source text for translation, while Protestant churches hew most closely to the HB, excluding the APOCRYPHA altogether from most printed editions. In other modern translations of the Christian Bible, the Masoretic text of the HB is ordinarily used as the primary source text for the 39 books mentioned above, while the LXX provides the source text for books of the Apocrypha. It should be remembered that in Jesus' day and throughout the 1st cent., the limits of the canon of sacred scripture within Judaism were relatively fluid.

Heilsgeschichte   This compound German term has several English equivalents: redemptive history, salvation history, sacred history; the history of redemp-

tion/salvation; or the history of God's saving acts. The term achieved wide currency in OT and NT theology during the 1950s and '60s, particularly through the influence of GERHARD VON RAD's studies in Deuteronomy and the Hexateuch. In contrast to other "*-geschichte*" terms, *Heilsgeschichte* does not denote a methodology of BIBLICAL CRITICISM (such as *Formgeschichte* [FORM CRITICISM], *Redaktionsgeschichte* [REDACTION CRITICISM], etc.), but rather an approach to the THEOLOGICAL INTERPRETATION of scripture that emphasizes the ongoing story of God's redemptive activity in history (*Geschichte*). Or it may be used simply as a descriptive term referring to the theology of history found in both Testaments, esp. Deuteronomy and Luke-Acts.

Hendiadys   (Gk: "one through two [words]") is the name for a form of syntactic coordination in which two or more terms are joined by the use of "and" (*kai*), rather than by subordinating one term to the other, as, e.g., adjective to noun (BDF). A hendiadys is often obscured by translation, but cf. READINGS for Mark 6:26 in RSV/NRSV with TEV. See PARATAXIS.

Hermeneutic   (*n.*) (without the *s*) is a term proposed by American scholars in the 1960s to designate that modern approach to hermeneutics that conceives it as a theory of understanding in the broadest sense, in contrast to the traditional understanding of hermeneutics as the art of interpreting difficult texts (hermeneutics with the *s*). (See James M. Robinson, John B. Cobb Jr., *The New Hermeneutic* [New York: Harper & Row, 1964, ix.) Today the distinction is seldom observed and the nouns are used interchangeably. (Hermeneutic is also used as an adjective and is equivalent to hermeneutical.) See HERMENEUTICS; NEW HERMENEUTIC, THE.

Hermeneutical Circle   is a term that stems from Martin Heidegger (1889–1976), who used it to describe the partially predetermined yet open and revisable nature of human understanding. It has since passed into the general vocabulary of hermeneutics, where it refers to a number of different aspects of interpretation that have a reciprocal or mutually influencing character. Some of these aspects were recognized and described well before Heidegger.

Heidegger's point was that a person never comes to a text with a clean slate but instead always brings with her a certain preunderstanding (*Vorverständis*) of the issues at stake in the text. This preunderstanding may be challenged, however, when the person grasps the specific possibilities posed by the text, and this in turn may lead to a revision of the preunderstanding. The person's modified preunderstanding then becomes the basis for new investigation of the text, and so forth. For Heidegger, this hermeneutical circle represents the general structure of all meaningful activity and not just of the interpretation of texts.

Before Heidegger, SCHLEIERMACHER had already drawn attention to several aspects of the process of interpretation that have a circular or, more exactly, a mutually revising character. According to Schleiermacher, an interpreter's understanding of the meaning of a word in a text depends on his understanding of the text as a whole, and vice versa. A similar relationship exists between one text and other texts by the same author, and between a text and its historical environment. In each case, understanding is circular but in a mutually revising and nonvicious sense.

Drawing on Heidegger, RUDOLF BULTMANN argued that the decisive hermeneutical circle in the interpretation of the NT concerns the existential questions that the interpreter puts to the text and the NT's interpretation of existence (e.g., "What must I do to be saved?"; "Who do you say that I am?" [Mark 8:29b]). Trivial questions evoke trivial answers. Real questions, in contrast, are those in which the very existence of the reader is at stake.

FEMINIST BIBLICAL INTERPRETATION and other forms of ADVOCACY CRITICISM have expanded the notion of the hermeneutical circle to include analyses of how gender, class, ethnicity, etc., contribute to shaping an interpreter's approach to a text. See HERMENEUTIC; HERMENEUTICS; NEW HERMENEUTIC, THE.

Hermeneutics (Gk: *hermeneuein*: to express, to explain, to translate, to interpret). According to its older definition, hermeneutics means the "art of interpretation," that is, the rules and procedures for determining the sense of written texts. Christian and Jewish hermeneutics before the modern period presupposed scripture's unique status and inexhaustible truth and on that basis sought to describe the specific rules and procedures that were appropriate for unpacking its significance for the present time. The rise of modern culture eroded the theological premises of traditional hermeneutics and created a new climate in which many inherited hermeneutical rules and procedures seemed unworkable. The crisis stimulated a major transformation of hermeneutics that vastly expanded its definition and aims. In its modern form, hermeneutics seeks not merely to describe rules for appropriate interpretation but more basically to provide a general theory of human understanding that can support continued claims for the contemporary meaningfulness and possible truth of biblical (and other ancient) texts. This modern tradition is associated with the names F. D. E. SCHLEIERMACHER, WILHELM DILTHEY, Martin Heidegger, Hans Georg Gadamer, and Paul Ricoeur. In recent decades, this distinguished tradition has been subjected to sharp critique. Some seek to revise it from within in order to accommodate previously marginalized viewpoints and concerns (e.g., the FEMINIST BIBLICAL INTERPRETATION of Elisabeth Schüssler Fiorenza and others.). Others regard it as more radically flawed, whether for philosophical (e.g., POSTMODERN BIBLICAL INTERPRETATION, DECONSTRUCTION) or theological (e.g., HANS FREI, KARL BARTH) reasons.

Although biblical interpretation is as old as the Bible itself, hermeneutics as a theory of biblical interpretation first took shape around the beginning of the C.E.

Ancient Jewish hermeneutics assumes that sacred scripture embodies a truth that is inexhaustibly rich and supremely relevant to the present time. This theological conviction shapes such otherwise different hermeneutical approaches as Rabbi HIL-LEL's relatively simple "rules of interpretation" (ca. 20 B.C.E. to 15 C.E.) and the Hellenistic Jew PHILO's more philosophically adventurous use of ALLEGORY (ca. 20 B.C.E.–45 C.E.). The Christian church inherited Judaism's theological premises and also a wide range of Jewish and Hellenistic interpretive techniques. At the same time, the church transformed both in light of its conviction that JESUS CHRIST was the personal embodiment of God's truth and hence also the center or SCOPE of sacred scripture. For a comparison of early rabbinic and patristic hermeneutics, see Marc Hirshman, *A Rivalry of Genius: Jewish and Christian Biblical Interpretation in Late Antiquity*, trans. Batya Stein (Albany: State University of New York Press, 1996).

Many basic features of Christian hermeneutics achieved lasting shape during the 2nd cent. when the church defended the unity of its Bible against MARCION's rejection of the OT. Christian theologians argued that scripture possesses both literal and spiritual senses (cf. 2 Cor 3), and that a literal READING of the NT provides the key for unlocking the hidden spiritual meaning of the OT. In addition, they held that a correct perception of the Bible's unity depended on proper use of the "RULE OF FAITH," a short *précis* or summary of Christian belief that serves as a guide for interpretation. Adherence to the rule of faith provided a framework for debate, not a fixed outcome for every problem, as exemplified by the debate between the School of Alexandria (ALEXANDRIA, SCHOOL OF) and the School of Antioch over the proper limits of spiritual interpretation of the OT (ALLEGORY; TYPOLOGY). (See Frances Young, *Biblical Exegesis and the Formation of Christian Culture* [Cambridge: Cambridge University Press, 1997.)

In the medieval period theologians continued to cultivate allegorical reading in the Alexandrian tradition (see FOURFOLD SENSE OF SCRIPTURE) and also refined contemplative approaches to scripture such as LECTIO DIVINA, which moves from textual study to meditation or spiritual reflection on the divine thoughts clothed in scripture. In the High Scholastic period, theologians began to reassert the priority of the LITERAL SENSE over spiritual senses, a position that was taken up again and radicalized at the time of the Reformation. Yet even the Reformers did not so much break with the theological premises and specific practices of traditional hermeneutics as refocus them in the task of public preaching. Luther understood the *proclaimed* Bible as the living word of God in which CHRIST himself was present. Other hallmarks of Reformation hermeneutics—the priority of scripture's plain sense, the supremacy of the Word over human authority, renewed emphasis on philology—were conceived as flowing from and serving the proclamation of the GOSPEL.

The Enlightenment's spirit of emancipation provoked a prolonged crisis in biblical hermeneutics whose effects are still felt today. Emerging rationalism put on the defensive the ancient Jewish presupposition of sacred scripture's inexhaustible truth and significance. Gradually a new set of hermeneutical procedures grew up based on the belief that correct interpretation requires standards of judgment that are neutral, i.e., secular, nonsectarian, scientific, nontheological. For a time, theologians sought to protect the Bible's unique status by distinguishing between two sets of hermeneutical rules, one for scripture (*hermeneutica sacra*) and another for all other writings (*hermeneutica profana*). Still, it was inevitable that scholars should begin to read the Bible like any other ancient work and subject it to the same standards of evidence and verifiability. In the new environment, the inherited techniques of THEOLOGICAL INTERPRETATION such as typology proved largely unworkable, while new techniques such as HISTORICAL CRITICISM produced results that were often religiously inert or seemingly antithetical to faith.

F. D. E. Schleiermacher addressed the crisis in biblical interpretation and in so doing created hermeneutics in its modern, expansive form. Schleiermacher accepted the new anthropological orientation of modern thought and rejected the attempt to defend the Bible by appeal to supernatural authority. At the same time, Schleiermacher transformed Enlightenment rationalism by locating the power of reason within a basically religious conception of humankind's openness toward reality. On this basis Schleiermacher recast biblical hermeneutics as (a) part of a general theory of understanding that (b) describes the dialogical interaction between the contemporary interpreter and the text as an expression of a past religious consciousness and that thereby (c) allows for the irreducible meaningfulness of sacred texts. The new approach required Christians to apply the same methods of interpretation to the Bible as to all other literature, yet left open the question of its historical and religious uniqueness.

Heirs of Schleiermacher's approach to hermeneutics include WILHELM DILTHEY (1833–1911), Hans-Georg Gadamer (1900–), and Paul Ricoeur (1913–). All three continue Schleiermacher's program of describing human understanding as fundamentally dialogical in character and on that basis defending the irreducible meaningfulness of religious texts and forms of life. Dilthey extended the concept of hermeneutics from the interpretation of texts to the interpretation of all human acts and artifacts, and sought to describe the epistemological and cultural conditions that make such interpretation possible. Gadamer argued (*Truth and Method* [1960]) that the conditions that enable understanding include the interpreter's own prior location within a particular historical tradition. We understand a text when we understand it to make a true claim about something that is an issue for us in our own time and place. Paul Ricouer, in keeping with his APHORISM "the symbol gives rise to thought," has analyzed a range of biblical genres, especially METAPHOR and NARRATIVE, and sought to delineate how each creates a "proposed world," a world that "we may inhabit." (See *The Symbolism*

of Evil [Boston: Beacon Press, 1969]; *Essays on Biblical Interpretation*, ed. Lewis S. Mudge [Philadelphia: Fortress Press, 1980]), *Figuring the Sacred: Religion, Narrative, and Imagination*, ed. Mark I. Wallace [Minneapolis: Fortress Press, 1995]).

Other proponents of hermeneutics in the Schleiermacherian tradition include RUDOLF BULTMANN, Gerhard Ebeling, and the movement known as the NEW HERMENEUTIC, which took primary inspiration from them and flowered in the 1960s and '70s. (See EXISTENTIALIST; DEMYTHOLOGIZATION; HERMENEUTIC; HERMENEUTICAL CIRCLE.)

Yet the sway of modern hermeneutics has not been universal. In conservative Christian circles, traditional hermeneutics has survived. A classic American study is by Milton S. Terry, *Biblical Hermeneutics: A Treatise on the Interpretation of the Old and New Testaments* [1883; reprinted by Zondervan Publishing House, 1952]). On the other hand, in liberal Christian circles, biblical scholars throughout the 19th and 20th centuries have often been so captivated by the tools of historical criticism that they have neglected to bother with a theory of interpretation at all. They have been content to ascertain what they believe the text once meant and have left it for others to ask what it means (see BIBLICAL CRITICISM; HISTORICAL CRITICISM; HISTORICAL-CRITICAL METHOD).

In recent decades, dialogical hermeneutics in the Schleiermacherian tradition has come in for sharp criticism from at least three different perspectives. Many liberation and feminist theologians insist that the dialogical tradition is vulnerable to ideological distortion unless and until it is practiced from the perspective of a marginalized community and its aspirations for justice or liberation (see ADVOCACY CRITICISM). A proponent of this kind of immanent critique is Elisabeth Schüssler Fiorenza, who argues that mainstream hermeneutics is blind to the androcentric character of the Bible and needs to be corrected by a feminist hermeneutics that understands "the act of critical reading as a moment in the global praxis for liberation" (see Elisabeth Schüssler Fiorenza, *Bread Not Stone: The Challenge of Feminist Biblical Interpretation* (Edinburgh: T. & T. Clark, 1990).

Postmodern theorists such as Roland Barthes (1915–1980), Jean-François Lyotard (1924–) and others represent a more radical philosophical critique of dialogical hermeneutics. In their view, the tradition of dialogical hermeneutics rests on the foundation of a modern rationalism that is itself profoundly ideological in character and in need of unmasking. In particular, they question two key premises of modern hermeneutics, namely, the stability of the text as a "finished" product on the one hand and reason's competence to discover and apply stable canons of interpretation on the other. If dialogical hermeneutics can be said to *qualify* these two premises for the sake of a possible meeting or convergence between text and interpreter, postmodern theory rejects the premises altogether. They emphasize instead the creative and endlessly repeated act of interpretation (see METANARRATIVE).

Finally, the theologian Hans Frei (1922–1988) argued that the tradition of dialogical hermeneutics from Schleiermacher to Ricoeur was theologically problematic because it made a general philosophical anthropology the arbiter of biblical EXEGESIS. In this sort of hermeneutics, he held, general theory dictates to and indeed overwhelms exegesis and subject matter. In particular, he held that when this theory is applied to the genre of realistic narrative, "not only is the subject matter turned into something other than the story and what it depicts, but even what is supposed to be the true subject matter is nothing except in and by relation . . . between it and the interpreter" (*The Identity of Jesus Christ* [New Haven: Yale University Press, 1975], xvii). He called for the revival of biblical hermeneutics in a more modest, text- and tradition-specific vein, seeking only as much theory as was necessary for the particular text or texts in question.

A comprehensive bibliography of titles in hermeneutics may be found in A. C. Thiselton, *New Horizons in Hermeneutics— The Theory and Practice of Transforming Biblical Reading* (London: HarperCollins, and Grand Rapids: Zondervan, 1992). See POST-CRITICAL BIBLICAL INTERPRETATION.

Hermetic Literature   (also: Hermetica) arose in the 1st cent. B.C.E. to 2nd cent. C.E. within Greek theosophical circles superficially enamored with the gods and environs of Egypt. In content, Hermetic literature is essentially Greek. The term comes from Hermes Trismegistus (meaning "Thoth thrice greatest"), who is (in the main) the reputed author of the various treatises. The standard edition of the literature is the *Corpus Hermeticum* by A. D. Nock and A. J. Festugière (Paris: Société d'édition "Les Belles lettres," 1945–54; 1962²), which contains (1) the *Corpus Hermeticum*, also known as *Poimandrès* (18 tractates, poorly preserved), (2) a Latin RECENSION of a speech by Hermes T. to Asclepius (the latter being the name by which it is known), and (3) 29 extracts of the writings of Stobaeus (23–27 recount the teachings of Isis to Horus; the 23rd extract is known as *Kore Kosmou*). In addition to this collection and also belonging to the Hermetica are the Coptic Hermetica from CODEX VI of the Nag Hammadi texts, various Hermetically influenced LETTERS, and other papyri. (For a more recent translation, with extensive notes and introduction, see Brian P. Copenhaver, *Hermetica: The Greek Corpus Hermeticum and the Latin Asclepius in a New English Translation, with Notes and Introduction* [Cambridge: Cambridge University Press, 1992].)

These tractates, essentially devotional and occult in character, have the common themes of God, world, and humankind; their setting is mythical and fantastic, their symbolism dualistic (light-darkness, height-depth, birth-death), and in their dialogical character resemble the *Timaeus* and *Phaedo* of Plato, hence their characterization as "proletarian Platonism." For their relationship to the NT see esp. C. H. DODD, *The Interpretation of the Fourth Gospel* (Cambridge: Cambridge University Press, 1953).

***Hexapla*, Hexaplaric** (Gk: sixfold). The earliest and one of the greatest achievements of TEXTUAL CRITICISM, the *Hexapla* is ORIGEN's six-columned critical edition of the OT (ca. 245 C.E.), now extant only in fragments. Origen supplied the *Hexapla* with diacritical signs to exhibit relations between the Hebrew text of the OT and the SEPTUAGINT (LXX) and to provide a sound basis for the church's debates with Judaism, whose dislike for the LXX had grown with the church's preference for it. The six texts placed in parallel columns are Hebrew; a Greek TRANSLITERATION; AQUILA; SYMMACHUS; LXX; and THEODOTION. In textual criticism, the adjective hexaplaric is a pejorative term denoting those MSS of the LXX that have been corrupted by readings from the *Hexapla*.

Hieronymus.   See **Jerome.**

Hieros Logos   (Gk: *hieros*: holy, sacred; *logos*: word, doctrine; Herodotus, LCL 2.81: sacred LEGEND) is a technical term used to denote that which is told (*logos*) about an event and/or place in explanation of its sacred (*hieros*) origin and significance. It is used in OT studies, for example, in reference to the instituting words (*HL*) of the covenant (Joshua 24), the sacred legend concerning the sanctuary at Bethel (Gen 28:10–17), and that concerning the ark at Jerusalem (1 Sam 4:1–7:2; 2 Sam 6–7). The appropriateness of the term in specific instances is an issue of debate.

Higher Criticism.   See **Lower Criticism.**

Hillel   (60 B.C.E.–20 C.E.?). Also called "H. the Elder," Rabbi Hillel was one of the most important sages of the late 2nd Temple Period and shaped the school of Pharisaic rabbis that ultimately charted the course of Judaism after the destruction of the Temple

(ca. 70 C.E.). Hillel's name is disputedly associated with seven rules of biblical interpretation that are often cited as typical of rabbinic exegesis. The seven rules are (1) *Qāl wāḥōmer* (light and heavy): what applies in a less important case will certainly apply in a more important case; (2) *Gězērāh šhāwāh* (verbal analogy from one verse to another): where the same words are applied to two separate cases, it follows that the same considerations apply to both; (3) *Binyan ʾāb mikkātûb ʾeḥād* (building up a family from a single text): when the same phrase is found in a number of passages, then a consideration found in one of them applies to all of them; (4) *Binyan ʾāb mi-šěnê ketubim* (building up a family from two or more texts): a principle is established by relating two texts together; the principle can then be applied to other passages; (5) *Kělāl uperāt* (the general and the particular): a general principle may be restricted by particularization of it in another verse; or conversely, a particular rule may be extended into a general principle; (6) *Kayôṣēʾ bô běmāqôm ʾāher* (as is found in another place): a difficulty in one text may be solved by comparing it with another that has points of general (though not necessarily verbal) similarity; and (7) *Dābār hallāmēd mi-ʿinyānô* (explanation obtained from context): the sense of words or phrases may be defined by examining the grammatical parts of the immediate context as well as the literary context as a whole.

Hillel's rules provide standardized guidelines for interpreting scripture that sought to permit the written word of God to remain applicable to a variety of life situations. For this account and further discussion of the rules, see Herbert W. Bateman IV, *Early Jewish Hermeneutics and Hebrews 1:5–13* (New York: Peter Lang, 1997). On Hillel himself, see Jacob Neusner, *The Rabbinic Traditions about the Pharisees Before 70,* 3 vols. (Leiden: E. J. Brill, 1971).

Historic; Historical.   See ***Historie.***

Historical-Critical Method (The) is a term sometimes used erroneously as a synonym for the whole body of critical methodologies and approaches related to the discipline of BIBLICAL CRITICISM. This use is mistaken because a number of these claim not to be historical in nature, such as STRUCTURALISM, NARRATIVE CRITICISM, READER-RESPONSE CRITICISM, etc.; with others the issue is debated, e.g., FORM CRITICISM, and others still deny even the possibility of HISTORICAL CRITICISM, such as POSTMODERN BIBLICAL INTERPRETATION. Strictly speaking, the term *historical-critical method* refers to the specific procedures used by historical criticism; more broadly, it encompasses the underlying conception of the nature and power of historical reasoning on which historical criticism rests. This underlying conception came to full flower in the 19th cent. and typically embraces the following tenets: (1) that reality is uniform and universal; (2) that it is accessible to human reason and investigation; (3) that all events historical and natural occurring within it are in principle interconnected and comparable by analogy; and (4) that humanity's contemporary experience of reality can provide objective criteria by which what could or could not have happened in the past can be determined. As this description suggests, the historical-critical method rests on presuppositions whose validity cannot be demonstrated by historical investigation alone and that are finally philosophical and theological in character. Partly for this reason, there has of course never been *a* historical-critical method, any more than there has ever been *one* view of reality. The advocates of historical-critical method in the 19th cent. strenuously tried to avoid any trace of dogma or theological bias in their reconstruction of past reality, yet many also held that universal ethical values underlay the fluctuations of history and that these values were most purely expressed by Christianity in general and liberal Protestantism in particular. The corresponding portrait of ancient Judaism was often profoundly derogatory (see Jon Levenson, *The Hebrew Bible, The Old Testament, and Historical Criticism* [Louisville, Ky.: Westminster John Knox Press, 1993]). Others more skeptical of ecclesial tradition used historical-critical method to arrive at the remarkable conclusion that Jesus had never lived (see RADICAL CRITICISM).

Throughout the 20th cent. the role and basic assumptions of historical-critical method, as well as the constituent "methods" themselves have been energetically and constantly debated. Fundamental questions include: If historical-critical method by definition rules out God as an agent in history, of what help can it be to church or synagogue in understanding the Bible, since like the Bible itself these institutions view God and history precisely in that way? Further, if in fact every event in history is in some sense unique, of what value is the principle of analogy? And further still, is the meaning of an event reducible to that which is objectively verifiable? (See Werner G. Kümmel, *The New Testament: The History of the Investigation of Its Problems* [Nashville: Abingdon Press, 1972; London: SCM Press, 1973]; Edgar Krentz, *The Historical-Critical Method* [Philadelphia: Fortress Press, 1975].) More recently, some have questioned whether it is possible or even desirable to aspire to "objectivity" in the interpretation of history (HISTORIOGRAPHY) at all. According to some postmodern thinkers, no method can reconstruct past events on the basis of ancient texts, because the meaning of texts is inherently indeterminate and their interpretation is largely shaped by the prevailing norms of the society of the contemporary interpreter (see "Historiography," in A. K. M. Adam, ed., *Handbook of Postmodern Biblical Interpretation* [St. Louis: Chalice Press, 2000]). Most practitioners of historical-critical method acknowledge the limitations of historical method but eschew such extreme skepticism. See EXEGESIS; HERMENEUTICS; *HISTORIE*; LESSING; *WIE ES EIGENTLICH GEWESEN IST.*

Historical Criticism   Same as HISTORI-
CAL-CRITICAL METHOD. Narrowly defined,
that is, as limited to the domain of biblical
interpretation, historical criticism seeks to
understand the ancient text in light of its
historical origins, the time and place in
which it was written, its sources, if any, the
events, dates, persons, places, things, customs, etc., mentioned or implied in the text.
Its primary goal is to ascertain the text's
primitive or original meaning in its original
historical context (its "LITERAL SENSE," or
more precisely, its *sensus literalis historicus*).
Its secondary goals may include reconstructing the historical situation of the
author and recipients of the text and reconstructing the true nature of the events which
the text describes. In principle, the priority
of these goals may be reversed, in which
case the historical critic is chiefly interested
in the ancient text as a document, record, or
source for reconstructing the ancient past
rather than as a writing whose original
meaning is of interest in its own right. The
distinction between these two emphases
(which cannot, of course, be entirely separated) is evident in the older curricular division between "The Literature of Israel" and
"The History of Israel" that formerly existed
in colleges and seminaries.

The rise of historical criticism, which
began in the 17th cent. and achieved full
flower in the 19th and 20th centuries, is the
major transforming fact of biblical studies
in the modern period. It has contributed to
a vast increase in knowledge of the composite, multilayered, and heterogeneous
character of the biblical writings and of the
historical distances that separate the peoples and cultures of the BIBLE from the
modern interpreter. In addition, the rise of
historical criticism has profoundly shaped
how many modern readers conceive what
it means to "understand the Bible." Historical critics have often thought of themselves as continuing the aims of the
Protestant Reformation, above all, with
respect to historical criticism's commitment to the exclusive validity of the literal

(i.e., original) sense of the text, and the
necessity of interpreting the Bible free from
the influence of ecclesial tradition and control. Similarly, the theologian Gerhard
Ebeling, following RUDOLF BULTMANN, has
argued that there is a "deep, inner connection" between the historical-critical reading of scripture and the Reformers'
doctrine of justification by grace through
faith in that both function to remove all
false security (Ebeling, *Word and Faith*
[Philadelphia: Fortress Press, 1963]). At
the same time, historical criticism embodies substantial discontinuities with the
Reformers, and the Christian tradition
generally, on issues such as the meaning of
the literal sense, the place of tradition in
interpretation, the goal of reading scripture, and the role of the Holy Spirit in
understanding. See H. Graf Reventlow, *The
Authority of the Bible and the Rise of the Modern World*, trans. J. Bowden (Philadelphia:
Fortress Press, 1985).

Over the past century or more, historical
criticism has been refined into various partially overlapping subdisciplines or methodologies, including SOURCE CRITICISM, FORM
CRITICISM, REDACTION CRITICISM, and TRADI-
TION CRITICISM. Each of these attempts to get
to "the world behind the text." Meanwhile,
the interests of BIBLICAL CRITICISM have
extended well beyond the inaugurating
concerns of historical criticism, especially
so since 1945. A host of approaches are centrally concerned with "the world of the
text" independent of its historical origins,
such as STRUCTURALISM, NARRATIVE CRITI-
CISM, RHETORICAL CRITICISM, et al. Still other
approaches to the Bible are centrally concerned with neither the world "behind" nor
"in" the text, but rather with "the world in
front of the text." Some of these contend
that a text is so dependent on its interpreter
that its meaning becomes entirely a function of the interpreter's own interests and
context (POSTMODERN BIBLICAL INTERPRETA-
TION, READER-RESPONSE CRITICISM).

Note: The Journal of Higher Criticism was
founded in 1995 to discuss and promote the

assumptions, methods, and findings of historical criticism. See also HISTORICAL-CRITICAL METHOD; LITERARY CRITICISM.

Historie/Geschichte; historisch/geschichtlich (Ger: history/historic; historical). In mid-20th-cent. biblical theology a distinction was frequently made between, on the one hand, history as fact, external and verifiable, and, on the other, history as significance, internal and nonverifiable. German theologians used the word *Historie* to refer to the former; the word *Geschichte* to refer to the latter. That Jesus was a Jew who lived in 1st-cent. Palestine is a statement of *Historie:* it is a statement of historical fact verifiable by the same canons of historical reason by which any fact of the past is verified. That he was the Son of God is a statement of *Geschichte:* it is an interpretive statement about the significance of the man Jesus, the validity of which cannot be verified by historical method but only affirmed by faith. The distinction has its roots in the philosophy of Immanuel Kant (1724–1804), and it played an important apologetic role among theologians of a broadly Kantian orientation. It permits one to say that something (e.g., the resurrection of Jesus) is "true" in terms of history-as-significance that is "not true" in the sense of history-as-fact, i.e., objectively verifiable.

English approximates the German usage in the two adjectives, "historic" (*geschichtlich*) and "historical" (*historisch*). To say an event is historic is to note that it possesses great significance for a people; to say an event is historical is simply to note that it actually happened, without judgment concerning its significance.

In the second half of the 20th cent., many developments in theology, philosophy, and science have contributed to a marked decrease in enthusiasm for the distinction between *Historie* and *Geschichte* among theologians and biblical scholars. Greater appreciation for the theory-laden character of all HISTORIOGRAPHY has focused attention on the way perception of facts are shaped by prior judgments of sig-

nificance from the outset. The shift in perspectives can be seen by comparing two major NT theologians from the mid and late 20th cent. respectively, that of RUDOLF BULTMANN (*History and Eschatology* [Edinburgh: Edinburgh University Press, 1957]) and N. T. Wright (*The New Testament and the People of God* [Minneapolis: Fortress Press, 1992]). See JESUS CHRIST; QUEST OF THE HISTORICAL JESUS.

For the meaning and significance of *Historie* and *Geschichte* at mid-century, see Van Harvey, *The Historian and the Believer* (New York: Macmillan Co. 1966; London: SCM Press, 1967). For a more recent theological critique of the intellectual underpinnings of the distinction, see Lesslie Newbigin, *The Gospel in a Pluralist Society* (Grand Rapids: Eerdmans, 1989).

Historiography (fr. Gk: to write history) is of especial concern to OT scholars, since the history presented in the OT extends from Creation to the Maccabean Revolt (ca. 167 B.C.E.); it is of less concern to NT scholars, for, apart from the GOSPELS, only Acts purports to be a record of historical events, and it covers a span of less than 35 years, from the ascension of Jesus to the imprisonment of Paul in Rome (ca. 30–62 C.E.). (See Ward W. Gasque, *A History of the Criticism of the Acts of the Apostles* [Grand Rapids: Eerdmans, 1975].)

As a NARRATIVE of past events, historiography is undoubtedly older than writing itself, initially taking the form of ORAL TRADITIONS in which LEGENDS, MYTH, and history were interwoven without any awareness of the distinction between them. Modern historiography attempts to make such a distinction, one that tries to distinguish between "what actually happened" and the supra- or ahistorical causes and meanings attributed to it by the OT narrator(s). Historical methodology, which analyzes methods and perspectives employed in the interpretation of the texts and artifacts of history, is of primary interest to OT scholars. Four major approaches to OT history are said to exist at the present time:

1. The *orthodox* or *traditional* *approach* assumes that the Bible is of supernatural origin and, in its original wording, free from error. The task of the biblical scholar is therefore one of corroborating rather than questioning statements of scripture. See Harold Lindsell, *The Battle for the Bible* (Grand Rapids: Zondervan, 1976).
2. The *archaeological approach* contends that (a) the traditions of the OT embody historical memory and are in the main quite reliable, and that (b) archaeological remains provide an objective means for containing subjectivistic hypotheses whether literary, philosophical, or theological, regarding the history of Israel. This approach is most closely associated with W. F. ALBRIGHT and his school. See George E. Mendenhall, *The Tenth Generation* (Baltimore: Johns Hopkins University Press, 1973).
3. The *traditio-historical approach* received its initial impetus in the form-critical studies of HERMANN GUNKEL and is associated with the German scholars ALBRECHT ALT, MARTIN NOTH, and GERHARD VON RAD. More recently in this school of thought is the work of J. A. Soggin, *A History of Ancient Israel* (Philadelphia: Westminster Press, 1985). The traditio-historical approach rests on certain principles of analysis deduced from the form-critical study of scripture; these include the conviction that (a) OT traditions existed for centuries only in oral form, (b) the written documents found in the OT represent a late stage in the development of these traditions; (c) the traditions arose in specific settings in the life of the people and were shaped by generic and formal factors at the time; (d) such literary units or genres are the basic forms of the tradition; (e) the primary unit in the partriarchal traditions is the *Sage* (Ger: TALE or story; pl.: *Sagen*); (f) the function of the *Sagen* was not historical but aetiological, that is, they were designed to explain the origin of shrines, cultic practices, ethnic relationships, customs, etc.; (g) the *Sagen* were combined to form cycles of traditions; and (h) out of these came history writing in Israel. The consequence of these interpretive princi-

ples for the reconstruction of the history of Israel varies with each interpreter who employs them. For a description of the methodology and its history, see D. A. Knight, *Rediscovering the Traditions of Israel* (Missoula, Mont.: Scholars Press, 1973, 1975[2]).

4. The *socioeconomic approach* applies the theories of sociology to the reconstruction of Israel's history and claims as its initiator the work of the sociologist Max Weber (1863–1920). The socioeconomic approach differs with the other views in that it sees the origins of Israel not in nomadic tribes of the Mesopotamian-Palestinian regions, but in a pastoral-peasant class in Canaan whose revolt against oppressive overlords produced a tribal-covenantal society that subsequently decayed into a monarchical state. For further discussion and bibliography, see SOCIOLOGICAL INTERPRETATION.

For this typology and synopsis, see John H. Hayes and J. Maxwell Miller, eds., *Israelite and Judaean History* (Philadelphia: Westminster Press, 1977; reprint, Valley Forge: Trinity Press International, 1990). See also Miller's essay, "Reading the Bible Historically," in Steven L. McKenzie and Stephen R. Haynes, eds., *To Each Its Own Meaning: An Introduction to Biblical Criticisms and Their Application* (Louisville, Ky.: Westminster John Knox, 1999); also J. M. Miller and J. H. Hayes, *A History of Ancient Israel and Judah* (Philadelphia: Westminster Press, 1986), which discusses the historiographical issues involved. Attention is given to the role of women in ancient Israel in C. Meyers, *Discovering Eve* (New York: Oxford University Press, 1988).

History of Tradition. See **Tradition Criticism.**

Hittite; Hittitology The Indo-European people known as Hittites flourished in Anatolia (east central Turkey) from ca. 1700 B.C.E. to the time of their collapse as an empire ca. 1200 B.C.E. Remnants of the Hittite empire continued to form and re-form over the subsequent centuries in central Anatolia and northern Syria, but the name came to be associated with the geographical area, reaching down into Palestine, obscuring the political history of the region. References to Hittites are found in the HB (e.g., 2 Kgs 7:6; 2 Chr 1:17; 2 Sam 11:3; Gen 15:20), as well as in contemporary Egyptian and Assyrian hieroglyphic and cuneiform texts first deciphered in the 19th cent. With the discovery of the ancient Hittite capital Hattshua near Boghazköy in modern Turkey in 1893, and the decipherment of the numerous unearthed texts written in the Hittite language in 1915, the field of study known as Hittitology began. Under the influence of form-critical research in the second half of the 20th cent., scholars sought parallels between the Hittites and the Hebrews of the Mosaic age. Parallels have been drawn, with varying success, between covenant texts in the HB and the structure of Hittite vassal treaties as well as between a variety of historiographic, legal, and religious practices. A sampling of Hittite texts may be found in *ANET*. See H. A. Hoffner, "Hittites," *Peoples of the Old Testament World*, ed. A. J. Hoerth et al. (Grand Rapids: Baker Books, 1994).

Holiness Code   is the name applied by the German scholar A. Klostermann in 1877 to Lev 17–26. As a literary entity the Holiness Code is distinguished by its hortatory style, by its prescriptions for moral conduct and cultic purity and, particularly, by its use of the divine first person, as in the statement, "You shall be holy, for I the LORD your God am holy" (cf. NRSV: 19:2; 20:26). It seems probable that the code evolved gradually within the cult, perhaps in stages and around chs. 19 and 21, finally serving as a catechism for use by priests and Levites. See LAW.

Holtzmann, Heinrich Julius   (1832–1910). Born in Karlsruhe, Germany, Holtzmann was professor of NT in Heidelberg (1858–1873) and Strassburg (1874–1904). He is credited with establishing (in *Die syn-optischen Evangelien*, 1863) the TWO SOURCE HYPOTHESIS of the Synoptic GOSPELS (Mark and a common SAYINGS source [Q] underlying Matt and Luke), which has been the basis of synoptic criticism ever since, notwithstanding numerous attempts, even in recent decades, to provide a more convincing and useful alternative. See GRIESBACH HYPOTHESIS; Q.

Homoioteleuton; Homoioarchton (Gk: similar ending; similar beginning) are technical terms in TEXTUAL CRITICISM that denote scribal errors in copying MSS, in which words, parts of words, or lines are omitted because the transcriber's eye fell to a subsequent and similar ending (or beginning), whether of a syllable, word, or line. According to B. H. STREETER there are 115 instances of omission by *homoioteleuton* in CODEX SINAITICUS.

In RHETORIC, *homoioteleuton* is the name given to a form of artistic prose based on the assonance of the final syllables of certain key words (BDF, para. 488). Its presence in the original languages of the BIBLE is almost always lost in translation. For example, 1 Tim 3:16 contains in the Greek a highly stylized form of *homoioteleuton* with six aorist passive verbs, each ending with the same syllable of two letters. The RSV rendering of this passage, strictly speaking, retains *homoioteleuton* only in the first two past participles, though much of the poetic power of the passage is preserved by other kinds of assonance. "He was manifested in the flesh, vindicated in the Spirit, seen by angels, preached among the nations, believed on in the world, taken up in glory." Cf. Rom 12:15. See EPIPHORA.

Hort, Fenton John Anthony   (1828–1892). Collaborator with B. F. WESTCOTT, from 1870 to 1881, in editing the critical edition of the Greek NT which bears their names. Educated at Trinity College, Cambridge, where he was a Fellow (1852–1857), he taught at St. Ippolyts (1857–72) and Cambridge (1872–92; from 1887 as Lady Margaret Professor). See CRITICAL TEXT; TEXTUAL CRITICISM.

Household Rules, outlining the duties and responsibilities of husbands and wives, parents and children, masters and slaves, are found in Col 3:18–4:1; Eph 5: 22–6:9; 1 Pet 2:13–3:7. The lists belong to a widespread form of Hellenistic moral instruction concerning household management whose roots go back to Aristotle (*Pol.* 1.1253b 1–14). Such lists invariably exhibited a marked hierarchical and patriarchal structure. Their presence in early Christian literature suggests a concession on the part of the EARLY CHURCH to the social ethic of the 1st cent. Conversely, Christian household rules may implicitly critique contemporary conceptions of household obligations in certain respects. The term *household rules* is the common translation of the German word *Haustafeln* (lit., "house tablets [of rules]"), a designation that dates back to Martin Luther (16th cent.). Similar instructions for groups within the church (called GEMEINDEORD-NUNGEN) are found in 1 Tim 2:8–15; 5:1–2; 6:1–2; Titus 2:1–10; 3:1. See Elisabeth Schüssler Fiorenza, *In Memory of Her: A Feminist Reconstruction of Christian Origins* (New York, 1984); David L. Balch, "Household Codes," in *The New Testament and Graeco-Roman Literature,* ed. D. E. Aune (Atlanta: SBLSBS, 1988). See LASTERKATA-LOG; PARAENESIS.

Hymn (fr. Gk: *hymnos:* hymn, ODE, song of praise). In OT form-critical studies since the work of HERMANN GUNKEL, the term *hymn* (Ger: *Hymne*) is used to designate a song of praise that glorifies God as God, in contradistinction for example to a song of thanksgiving, which praises God for some specific act of grace on behalf of the nation or the individual. Gunkel listed as hymns Pss 8; 19; 29; 33; 65; 68; 96; 98; 100; 103; 104; 111; 113; 114; 115; 117; 135; 136; 145–150. To these he added Enthronement Songs (e.g., 93; 97; 99) and Songs of Zion (e.g., 46; 48; 76; 84; 87), which though hymnic in form constituted an identifiable subcategory in terms of content.

Form critics, however, have not agreed on terminology or on formal criteria for distinguishing between hymns, thanksgivings, prayers, and confessions. CLAUS WESTERMANN has suggested that since hymns and thanksgivings are both songs of praise the respective designations "descriptive" and "declarative" PSALMS of praise are more appropriate.

Hymns and hymnic themes are found outside the Psalter, e.g., Job 5:9–16; 9:5–12; 12:13–25; 26:5–14; 28; Prov 1:20–33; 8; Sir 1:1–10; 10:14–18; 16:18–19; 16:26–17:24; 17:29–30; 24:1–22; 39:12–35; 42:15–43:33; Wis 6:12–20; 7:22–8:21; 11:21–12:22, etc.

In the NT, hymns are referred to in Col 3:16 and Eph 5:19 along with psalms and spiritual songs with no clear distinction between them. Among NT critics perhaps greatest unanimity concerns the following as early Christian hymns: Luke 1:46–55 (*MAGNIFICAT*); 1:68–79 (*BENEDICTUS*); 2:14 (*Gloria*); 2:29–32 (*NUNC DIMITTIS*)—these may draw on pre-Christian antecedents in the Baptist movement or other Jewish circles; christological hymns: Phil 2:6–11; Col 1:15–20; Heb 1:(2)3(4); 5:5; 7:1–3; 1 Pet 3:18–22; Eph 2:14–16; 1 Tim 3:16; Rev 5:9–13; the *Logos* hymn (also perhaps pre-Christian): John 1:1–5, 9–14, 16; and hymns to God: Rev 4:8, 11; 7:10, 12; 11:17–18; 19:1b–3, 5, 6–8a. (See Jack T. Sanders, *The New Testament Christological Hymns* [Cambridge: Cambridge University Press, 1971].)

Hypocoristicon is the abbreviation of a name or its modification by the addition of a diminutive. In OT studies in particular the term is applied to the ancient practice of dropping off the name of the deity suffixed to a person's name, such as Adon for Adonijah. However, hypocoristicon by ETYMOLOGY (*hypo:* beneath, less than; *koros:* child) refers to the modification of names for children, e.g., Jonathan/Johnny/Jon.

Hypotaxis, the opposite of PARATAXIS, is a term used to describe "elaborate systems of grammatical subordination" (Eugene

Nida, *Toward a Science in Translating* [Leiden: E. J. Brill, 1964], 210), a style of writing highly developed in the literary Greek of antiquity and in modern (esp. 19th cent.) German prose. Hypotaxis is especially characteristic of the writings of the apostle Paul, perhaps due as much to the nature of his mind and temperament as to a desire for literary effect, e.g., Rom 1:1–7; 1 Cor 1:4–8; 1 Thess 1:2–7.

IB/NIB See *Interpreter's Bible, The; New Interpreter's Bible.*

IDB See *Interpreter's Dictionary of the Bible, The.*

Ideological Criticism As the name suggests, ideological criticism is an approach to biblical interpretation that is centrally concerned with laying bare the ideological dimensions of a text and its history of interpretation. In popular parlance, ideology often refers pejoratively to a system of belief that is oppressive or doctrinaire and infused with extremist passion. As employed by ideological criticism, however, ideology is not an exclusively pejorative concept. An ideology is a set of attitudes and ideas, consciously or unconsciously held, that reflects or shapes understandings (and misunderstandings) of the social and political world, and that serves to justify collective action aimed at preserving or changing it. According to G. A. Yee, the aim of ideological criticism is, in part, to "enable the exegete to become conscious of personal ideological blind spots and constraints and to produce a more ethically responsible reading" of the biblical text.

The term *ideology* was originally developed in the Marxist tradition in order to describe how cultures are structured in ways that enable dominant groups to exercise maximum control with the minimum of conflict. Quite aside from its deliberate intentions, a dominant group works through institutions and symbol systems to legitimate the social order it leads, especially through widespread teaching about

how the world "really" works and should work. These ideas orient people's thinking in ways that lead them to accept their current roles in society as "natural." It is through ideology, so conceived, that the fundamental structure of a society is defined and justified. Marxist analysis originally used *ideology* in a pejorative fashion to denote a false view of reality and confined its use to the legitimation of unjust political economies and class structures. In recent decades, the concept of ideology has been widely extended to encompass many other social structures marked by patterns of dominance and subordination, i.e., race, ethnicity, gender, religion, etc. Moreover, it has come to be used in a nonpejorative fashion to refer to any systematic framework for comprehending, evaluating, and acting on social and political realities. The concept of ideology remains a critical one, however, because it assumes that people are usually unaware of the ideological character of their own beliefs, for people tend to equate these beliefs with "how things really are."

Ideological criticism investigates three elements of every text: (1) the ideological context in which an author produces a text, (2) the ideology reproduced within the text itself, and (3) the ideology of a text's readers or "consumers." It asks questions such as, What assumptions are being made about what is natural, just, and right? What (and who) do these assumptions distort or obscure? What are the power relations? How are they made to appear as if they are normal or good? What negative aspects are excluded? Ideological criticism makes use of HISTORICAL and SOCIAL-SCIENTIFIC CRITICISM in its attempt to reconstruct the socioeconomic conditions in biblical times, focusing particularly on the means of production, the power structures of dominance and subordination it produced, and so forth. Various modes of LITERARY CRITICISM (STRUCTURALISM, NARRATIVE CRITICISM, RHETORICAL CRITICISM, DECONSTRUCTION, etc.) are employed to analyze how ideology functions within the confines of the text itself. Finally, ideological criticism attempts to overthrow, ameliorate, or otherwise disempower exploitative ideologies at work in a text's history of reception.

Like many other methods and approaches described in this book, ideological criticism serves best when used to supplement other perspectives rather than to provide an exclusive framework for interpretation. At its best, it gives methodological expression to two material concerns of biblical literature, namely, the propensity of the strong and dominant to exploit the weak, and the general human proclivity toward self-deception. At its worst, it tends to reduce all questions of truth to the struggle for power. See G. A. Yee, "Ideological Criticism," in John H. Hayes (ed.), DICTIONARY OF BIBLICAL INTERPRETATION (Nashville: Abingdon Press, 2000), and her essays, "Ideological Criticism: Judges 17–21 and the Dismembered Body," in *Judges and Method*, ed. G. A. Yee, (Minneapolis: Fortress Press, 1995), and "Ideology," in Frank Lentricchia and Thomas McLaughlin, *Critical Terms For Literary Study*, 2nd ed. (Chicago: University of Chicago Press, 1995). Also see David J. A. Clines, *Interested Parties: The Ideology of Writers and Readers of the Hebrew Bible* (JSOTSup 205; Sheffield: Sheffield Academic Press, 1995). The problem of definition is discussed in T. Eagleton, *Ideology: An Introduction* (London: Verso, 1991).

Idiom (Gk: one's own) may refer broadly to (a) the language peculiar to a people, or more narrowly to (b) an expression whose meaning cannot be derived from the customary meaning of the component words—also called in SEMANTICS an "exocentric expression" (the opposite of an "endocentric expression").

Idioms (definition b) abound in every language and can rarely be translated literally. Examples in scripture include "to close one's bowels" = to be lacking in compassion (1 John 3:17); to "heap burning coals upon his head" (NRSV) = to make him

ashamed (Rom 12:20); "our mouth is open to you" (RSV) = we have spoken very frankly to you (2 Cor 6:11; cf. NRSV); to be "before the Lord" (RSV) = "by the grace of the Lord" (Gen 10:9, NJV), or "with the Lord's approval" (Gen 27:7, NJV), or "by the will of the Lord" (Num 3:4, NJV).

The uncertain Hebrew of Song of Songs 1:7b ("one who wanders"—see RSV footnote ad loc.) becomes in the LXX, Latin VULGATE, and NRSV "one who is veiled," and in KJV "one that turneth aside"; but the NEB finds here the (ancient Hebrew?) idiom "that I may not be left picking lice"! Cf. JB: "wander like a vagabond."

Illustrative Story A name frequently given in NT PARABLE interpretation since the studies of ADOLF JÜLICHER (1886) to those "parables" of Jesus that present models of behavior, i.e., NARRATIVES in which "the moral lies in the narrative itself" (Vincent Taylor)—rather than outside the story as in the true parable: e.g., the good Samaritan (Luke 10:29–37), the rich fool (Luke 12:13–21), the rich man and Lazarus (Luke 16:19–31), and the Pharisee and the publican (Luke 18:9–14). No hard and fast line can be drawn between illustrative stories and "parables," and in contemporary discussions the distinction is often ignored.

Implied Author/Reader, The. See **Reception Theory; Narrative Criticism.**

Inclusio (Lat: a shutting off, confinement) is a technical term for a passage of scripture in which the opening phrase or idea is repeated, PARAPHRASED, or otherwise returned to at the close (also called a cyclic or ring composition), such as Psalm 1; 4:1a–3b; 8; 21; passim; Amos 1:3–5, 6–8, 9–15; Ezek 25:3–7, 8–11, 12–17; Jer 3:1–4:4 (cf. 3:1d with 4:1a, omitting prose insertions), etc. The presence of the *inclusio* can aid the critic in determining the limits of an idea or tradition, particularly in the analysis of material that is composite in nature, such as the prophetic literature (see the

Jeremiah passage cited previously). See RHETORICAL CRITICISM.

Interlinear (Greek NT/ Hebrew OT) An interlinear Greek NT is written in Greek with an English translation placed according to the Greek word order between the lines of the text; e.g., *The Interlinear Literal Translation of the Greek NT with the Authorized Version* (with a CRITICAL APPARATUS from Elzevir, GRIESBACH, LACHMANN, TISCHENDORF, Tregelles, Alford, and Wordsworth), by George Ricker Berry (Chicago: Wilcox & Follett, 1956 reprint). *The RSV-Interlinear Greek-English NT*, published by Zondervan Publishing House with a Nestle Greek Text, contains the RSV text in the margin with an interlinear English translation by Alfred Marshall (originally published in London by Samuel Bagster & Son, Ltd., 1958). J. D. Douglas has edited a new VERSION using the United Bible Societies' third edition of the CRITICAL TEXT with the NRSV (Wheaton, Ill.: Tyndale, 1990). *The Interlinear NIV Hebrew-English Old Testament*, 1 vol. ed., is published by Zondervan (1987). A number of other interlinear editions are available, such as the NKJV (Nashville: Nelson, 1994).

Internal Parallelism. See **Parallelism.**

Interpolation In TEXTUAL CRITICISM, the word *interpolation* denotes material inserted into the text in the process of scribal transmission, thereby altering the original READING. Interpolations in the text of the OT are difficult to ascertain because of the dearth of ancient MSS. In the NT the matter is different. Verses present in the later Byzantine MSS (used as the basis of the KJV) that are not found in the more ancient MSS of the NT are considered to be interpolations. Since most modern VERSIONS are based on the older MSS, the interpolated verses are often, but not always, omitted from the text and placed in a footnote. Over 70 verses or parts of verses contained in the KJV of the NT are interpolations; over 40 of these are in the Synoptic GOSPELS, e.g., Matt 1:16a; 6:13b; 12:47;

17:21; 18:11; 19:9b; 21:44; 23:14; 27:49b. See GLOSS; JOHANNINE COMMA.

Interpreter's Bible, The; New Interpreter's Bible, The Commonly abbreviated *IB, The Interpreter's Bible*, ed. George Arthur Buttrick (New York: Abingdon Press, 1951–57) is a twelve-volume commentary containing introductory articles on each book as well as general articles on biblical history, criticism, and theology. The first of its kind in English in over fifty years, the *IB* was a huge publication success and inspired a flood of works like it. Though in many respects dated, the *IB* remains a valuable tool for study. The work is famous for dividing entries into two sections written by different authors, one devoted to exegesis (written by an academician) and one to theological exposition (often by a noted homiletician). The format reflects the view that exegesis is an independent historical, philological, and literary exercise, whereas theological exposition is dependent and more subjective in nature. *The New Interpreter's Bible* (NIB) (1994—) differs from the *IB* in this respect by assigning both kinds of reflection to a single author, a change indicative of a broader recognition within the guild of biblical studies that exegesis can be informed by theological concerns from the outset. The *NIB* contains numerous introductory essays that treat the use of the Bible among women and ethnic groups scarcely visible in the *IB*, e.g., Asian Americans, Hispanic Americans, Native Americans, etc. Available on CD-Rom. See COMMENTARY; EXEGESIS; EXPOSITION.

Interpreter's Dictionary of the Bible, The Commonly abbreviated as *IDB*, the *Interpreter's Dictionary of the Bible: An Illustrated Encyclopedia in Four Volumes*, ed. George Arthur Buttrick (New York: Abingdon Press, 1962), remains an authoritative biblical dictionary. The original four volumes were supplemented with new and expanded articles in vol. 5, ed. Keith R. Crim (Nashville: Abingdon, 1976). Although still useful, the *IDB* has been supplanted by the six-volume *Anchor Bible Dictionary* (*ABD*).

Intertextuality As employed in contemporary literary theory and biblical studies, the term *intertextuality* ranges in reference from a general (and essentially untraceable) characteristic of all language to specific (and traceable) phenomena of language use. In its general sense, intertextuality refers to the fact that any given use of language (text) is intelligible only because and in terms of its interconnection with prior uses and understandings of its constituent METAPHORS, concepts, images, symbolic worlds, etc. The infinite diversity and contextuality of all prior uses, as well as the novelty of its new literary-social context (including the knowledge and understandings that the hearer/reader brings to the text) prohibits a text from being definitively intelligible in any given setting. The reason is that these same factors provide the text with an inexhaustible number of potential and therefore indefinite meanings. (See the symbols > and < in the Diagram of Biblical Interpretation, p. 235.) It is this aspect of language that in part explains why the BIBLE has, over the centuries, served as an inexhaustible source of meaning. Reflection on this aspect of language at its deepest level is found in the work of the Russian theorist M. M. Bakhtin, whom the French theorist Julia Kristeva credits with introducing the concept into literary theory. Kristeva coined the term *intertextuality* to describe Bakhtin's insight (see listing for P. K. Tull's article at end).

Both the phenomenon and the concept *mutatis mutandis* have long been recognized by literary theorists, exegetes, and theologians, permitting the term to be rather freely adapted to refer to a wide variety of intertextual connections. Rather than to Bakhtin, whose influence arrived in the West only in the late 20th cent., some scholars point to an essay by T. S. Eliot (1919) as generative of studies loosely classifiable as intertextual in nature. Eliot noted that texts do not arise de novo but are dependent on, extend, and renew the language, symbolic worlds, and metaphors of texts that preceded and, in their interaction with new social conditions, generated them. This is to suggest not only that texts have a past to which they are related but also, of equal interest, a future in whose creation they take part. The direction of this interrelation of texts is not to be taken as linear, as from past to future only; the meaning (and the future) of past texts are also transformed or renewed by their embodiment in subsequent settings. It is in reference to these dynamic interrelations that the term *intertextuality* is employed.

Some scholars interpret the term *text* to include not only literary but cultural, social, and political artifacts as well. For example, the generative and imaginative power of the exodus and the Promised Land as literary TROPES have caused them to be efficacious symbols of great rhetorical currency and social consequence throughout the ages. The Zionist Movement of the 19th and 20th centuries, like Martin Luther King Jr. and the American civil rights movement generally, employed these "tropes" as sacred texts in such a way that they were turned into political events, and from those events back again into novel texts. Compare, e.g., the crucifixion of Jesus as history and as text and the relation of both to Psalm 22.

Aspects of intertextuality in its less abstract, more concretely specific sense (citations, allusions, etc.) have been explored under other names, such as inner-biblical EXEGESIS. In this limited sense intertextuality has been a subject of study in more traditional methodologies, such as TRADITION HISTORY, comparative religions, and form and genre criticism. These approaches have tended to look on literary interrelations from a historical or evolutionary perspective, whereas newer methodologies and approaches, such as RHETORICAL CRITICISM, do not. Precritical interpreters of the Bible frequently demonstrated an unsurpassed sensitivity to the interconnectivity of scripture (see TYPOLOGY). This awareness is vividly evoked by George Herbert's (1593–1633) poem "The Holy Scriptures," which speaks of the Bible using the imagery of stars and constellations:

Oh that I knew how all thy lights combine,
   And the configurations of their glorie!
Seeing not onely how each verse doth shine,
   But all the constellations of the storie.

(Cited from *The Works of George Herbert*, intro. by Tim Cook [Ware, Hertfordshire: Wordsworth Editions Ltd., 1994], 49.)

Note: This article on intertextuality is also an illustration of the phenomenon to which it refers. Intertextuality is variously defined and differently rooted in literary theory, some to Bakhtin, others to Eliot, still others elsewhere, depending on how the term is heard and located by those who recontextualize it. The term cannot be contained or restricted because the linguistic phenomenon to which it points and the socio-literary contexts in which it occurs are larger, more diffuse, and untraceable than any single definition or attribution could contain. The same could be said of any universal symbol: creation, exodus, exile, crucifixion, resurrection, rebirth, etc.
   See Patricia K. Tull, "Rhetorical Criticism and Intertexuality," in *To Each Its Own Meaning: An Introduction to Biblical Criticisms and Their Application*, ed. by Steven L. McKenzie and Stephen R. Haynes (Louisville, Ky.: Westminster John Knox Press, Rev. and Expanded Ed., 1999), 156–180; *The Dialogic Imagination: Four Essays by M. M. Bakhtin*, ed. by Michael Holquist (Austin: University of Texas Press, 1981, 1994); *Reading Between Texts: Intertextuality and the Hebrew Bible*, ed. by Danna Nolan Fewell (Louisville, Ky.: Westminster/John Knox Press, 1992); and especially Michael Fishbane, *Biblical Interpretation in Ancient Israel* (Oxford: Clarendon Press, 1985). On Paul's use of scripture, see R. B. Hays, *Echoes of Scripture in the Letters of Paul* (New Haven, Conn.: Yale University Press, 1989).

Inverted Parallelism. See Chiastic Parallelism under **Parallelism** (synonymous).

Ipsissima verba; ipsissima vox   Latin phrases meaning "the very words" and "the very voice" respectively, often used in the context of the quest of the historical Jesus. *Ipsissima verba Jesu* refers to the words or SAYINGS that Jesus actually spoke in contradistinction to those merely attributed to him by subsequent tradition. Since Jesus probably spoke Aramaic and the New Testament is written in Greek, we probably do not have the *ipsissima verba Jesu* apart from a very few exceptions (*abba, ephphatha*). *Ipsissima vox* makes a lesser claim: it designates words or sayings that give the sense but not the exact linguistic form of Jesus' speech. Opinions vary widely in both regards and certainty is beyond the reach of any historical method. The same terms apply to OT study, particularly of the PROPHETS. See CRITERIA OF AUTHENTICITY.

Irony   (fr. Gk: *eironeia*: dissimulation). In common parlance, irony is the statement of one thing with the intention of suggesting something else. The word and its original meaning derive from a stock figure in early Greek COMEDY, the *eiron*, who mocks and finally triumphs over his boastful antagonist (*alazon*) by feigning ignorance and impotence. In manner and method, Socrates is the personification of the *eiron*; hence, the "Socratic irony." According to H. D. Betz, Paul's "dialogue" with the boastful charlatans of Corinth (2 Cor 10–13) is an intentional satire, full of irony and sarcasm in the Socratic tradition (see *Der Apostel Paulus und die Sokratische Tradition* [Tübingen: J. C. B. Mohr, 1972]). In the OT PROPHETS, as in Greek tragedy, irony dominates, as Israel, proud and willful like Oedipus, remains blind to the doom that is at hand. Ironic incongruity underlies both the teachings of Jesus ("The last will be first and the first last" [Matt 20:16]; "Blessed are you poor . . ." [Luke 6:20]; etc.) and his fate (the crucifixion of the Messiah). As literature the scriptures are also filled with dramatic irony in which the reader knows what the characters do not; e.g., David's self-condemnation (2 Sam 12:5–6), Jonah's futile flight (Jonah), Peter's asseveration of faithfulness (Mark 14:30), and Paul's appeal to Caesar (Acts 25:11c). Dramatic irony creates the possibility of multiple layers of irony in a single passage, e.g., "He saved others, he cannot save himself" (Mark 15:31). For the use of irony as an intentional literary device see John 4:12; 7:35, 42; 8:22; 11:50. (See Edwin M. Good, *Irony in the OT* [Naperville, Ill.: Alec R. Allenson, 1965]; P. D. Duke, *Irony in the Fourth Gospel* [Atlanta: John Knox Press, 1985].) See MEIOSIS.

Itacism (or iotacism) is a technical term in Greek phonology for certain vowels and diphthongs (ι, ει, η [η], οι, υ [υι]), all of which came to be pronounced like ι (i). The process of leveling out the phonetic distinctions present in classical (Attic) Greek and its consequent effect on spelling began in the 2nd and 3rd cents. B.C.E. and is essentially complete in modern Greek. As a phenomenon of spelling it is frequent in NT MSS.

Itala.   See **Old Latin MSS.**

J (Yahwist)   is the customary designation for one of the four major but hypothetical sources (with E, D, and P) used in the composition of the PENTATEUCH or Hexateuch. The unknown author of this source is called the Yahwist, from the English spelling of the author's preferred name for God in its vocalized (and conjectural) form (Yahweh). The symbol J, however, comes from the German spelling of the same name (*Jahve*). In English Bibles, YHWH is translated LORD. See TETRAGRAMMATON.

The existence, extent, date, and nature (whether written or oral) of the J source are widely debated. Nevertheless, many scholars believe that it was composed from ancient folk traditions during the 10th or 9th cent. B.C.E. in Judah, perhaps during the reign of Solomon as a charter of national faith. In style and subject the document can be described as an epic, at once patriotic and religious (Pfeiffer). It ascribes the origin and well-being of Israel to YHWH's promises to Abraham, viz., that his seed would become a great nation, that they would be a blessing to all nations, and that they would receive at the Lord's hand a land flowing with milk and honey (Gen 12:1–4a, 7). It sketches the long journey to the land of promise, from the patriarchs, to the vicissitudes in Egypt and in the wilderness, to the conquest of Canaan.

Of those who hold this view, most are of the opinion that this source was supplemented with a later, northern tradition (E) by a REDACTOR (R^{JE}) perhaps in the 8th cent. Others find an older tradition behind J, particularly in Genesis: Rudolf Smend used the symbol J^1 for this material; OTTO EISSFELDT extended it to other books, using the symbol L; R. H. Pfeiffer found an S source differing from both J^1 and L, and so forth. The following reconstruction of the J source is therefore not the final word but a once widely accepted hypothesis by a noted OT scholar.

The "J-Document" according to MARTIN NOTH: Gen 2:4b–4:26; 5:29; 6:1–8; 7:1–(3a) 5, 7 (8–9), 10, 12, 16b, 17b, 22–23; 8:6a, 2b, 3a, 6b, 8–12, 13b, 20–22; 9:18–27; 10:8–19, 21, 25–30; 11:1–9, 28–30; 12:1–4a; 12:6–13:5, 7–11a, 13–18 (15:1–2*); 15:3b–4, 6*, 7–12, 17–21; 16:1b–2, 4–14*; 18:1–19:28, 30–38; 20:1a, 7, 20–24; 24:1–67; (25:1–4); 25:5–6, 11b, 21–26a, 27–34; 26:1–33; 27:1–45; 28:10, 13–16, 19; 29:1–35; 30:4–5, 7–16, 20–21, 24–43; 31:1, 3, 17, 19a, 20–23, 25b, 27, 30a, 31, 36a, 38–40, 46–49, 51–53a; 32:3–13a, 22–32; 33:1–3, 6–7, 12–17, 18b; 34:1–31; 35:21–22a; 37:3a, 4–21, 25–28; 38:1–40:1; 41:34a, 35b, 41–45, 46b, 49, 55–57; 42:1b, 4–5, 8–11a, 12, 27–28a, 38; 43:1–34; 44:1–34; 45:1, 4–5a, 16–28; 46:5b, 28–34; 47:1–5a, 6b, 13–26, 29–31; 50:1–10a, 14.

Exod 1:8–12, 22; 2:1–22; 3:1–4a, 5, 7–8, 16–22; 4:1–9, 10–16, 19, 20a, 21–31; 5:1–6:1; 7:14–18, 20, 21a, 23–25; 8:1–4, 8–15a, 20–32; 9:1–7, 13–35; 10:1–11:8; 12:21–23, 27b, 29–39; 13:20–22; 14:5b, 6, 13–14, 19b, 20, 24,

25b, 27a, 30–31; 15:20–21, 22b–25a; 16:4–5, 28–31, 35b, 36; 17:2, 4–16; 19:2b (7–9*), 11b–13, 18, 20–25; 24:1–2*, 9–11*, 12–15a; 32:1a, 4b–6, 15–20, 25–35; 33 (problematic); 34:1–35.

Num 10:29–32, 33–36; 11:1–35 (composite, older traditions); 12:1–16; 13:17b–20, 22–24, 27–31; 14:1b, 4, 11–25, 39–45; 16:1b, 12–15, 25, 26, 27b–34; 20:19–20, 22a; 21:1–3, 4–9; 22:3b–8, 13–19, 21–37, 39–40; 23:28; 24:1–25; 25:1–5; 32:1, 16, 39–42.

Deut 31:14–15, 23 (JE)*; (34:1b–5a, 6, 10 JE).

See Martin Noth, *A History of Pentateuchal Traditions* (Englewood Cliffs, N.J.: Prentice-Hall, 1971), ch. 4 and Translator's Supplement. Passages marked with * indicate points at which, according to Bernhard Anderson, scholars deviate from Noth's analysis; parentheses indicate passages omitted by Noth. *Note:* With the beginning of the 21st cent., the theory outlined above has met with greater skepticism, placing the origins of these traditions much later in Israel's development and therefore casting greater doubt on their historical verisimilitude. See D: DEUTERONOMIC CODE; E: ELOHIST; P: PRIESTLY CODE; TETRATEUCH.

JB.   See **Jerusalem Bible.**

JBL.   See **SBL; Council on the Study of Religion.**

Jehovah.   See **Tetragrammaton.**

Jerome   (340/350–420 C.E.). The most learned biblical scholar of the Latin Church, Eusebius Hieronymus, in English called Jerome, was born in Strido in Dalmatia and died in Bethlehem, an ardent monastic and controversialist. Jerome was a great linguist who was proficient in Latin, Greek, and Hebrew. In Bethlehem he translated the OT from Hebrew into Latin and wrote philological studies on the OT that remained standard works for centuries. His translation of the scripture became the basis of the later Latin VULGATE, for almost 1500 years the official scriptures of Roman Catholicism.

Jerusalem   Bible/New   Jerusalem Bible   JB/NJB are the common abbreviations for the (New) Jerusalem Bible (Garden City, N.Y.: Doubleday & Co., 1966 and 1985). The JB is the English equivalent of *La Bible de Jerusalem (BJ)*, a translation of the Hebrew and Greek texts of the BIBLE with introductions and notes by the Roman Catholic Dominican Biblical School in Jerusalem, published by Les Editions du Cerf of Paris in 1956. The English text of the Bible, though in the main also a direct translation of ancient texts, is indebted to the French edition at many points; the introductions and notes of the JB are translations of those in the French edition, revised and updated under the general editorship of Père ROLAND DE VAUX, O.P. The NJB, published in 1985, was translated directly from the ancient languages but still turns to the 1973 revised French BJ "where the text admits of more than one interpretation." According to RAYMOND BROWN, the NJB is a "significantly improved translation." With its extensive scholarly notes and small type, it is principally a study Bible rather than one designed for public reading. See AMERICAN STANDARD VERSION; CONTEMPORARY ENGLISH VERSION; DOUAY; KING JAMES VERSION; LIVING BIBLE (PARAPHRASED); NEW AMERICAN BIBLE; NEW ENGLISH BIBLE; NEW INTERNATIONAL VERSION; NEW JEWISH VERSION; PARAPHRASE; REVISED STANDARD VERSION; TODAY'S ENGLISH VERSION; VERSION.

Jesus Christ   The central figure of Christian faith has always posed a challenge to the understanding of those who seek to know him. In the modern period, the challenge has frequently been formulated in terms of the contrast between "the Jesus of history" and "the CHRIST of faith." In reality, this contrast can be as much an obstacle to understanding as a clarification of it. In particular, the term "Jesus of history" conceals an important ambiguity. The term can refer to Jesus as he actually was, regardless of whether he can be known thus. Or it can refer to Jesus as historians can reconstruct his identity using the conventional methods of historical inquiry, regardless of whether this does justice to Jesus as he actually was. These two senses differ because historical research can never achieve more than approximate and probable knowledge of any figure of the past. More significantly, however, they differ because modern historical inquiry rests on premises that may in principle preclude knowledge of who Jesus actually was. For example, if the decisive factor in Jesus' identity was (and is) God's attitude toward and presence in him ("This is my Beloved Son"), then Jesus' actual reality will elude modern historical inquiry, simply on account of the latter's methodological atheism. For this reason, some have suggested that the term "the earthly Jesus" be used to refer to Jesus as he actually was, while the term "the historical Jesus" be reserved exclusively for the product of historical-critical research. This has the advantage of making clear that the contrast between "the Jesus of history" and "the Christ of faith" is not a contrast between a "neutral" and an "interested" approach to knowledge of Jesus Christ, but two different, interested approaches, and that the relation between them is finally as much a theological question as one of historical method. See HISTORICAL-CRITICAL METHOD; *HISTORIE/GESCHICHTE*; QUEST OF THE HISTORICAL JESUS.

Jesus Seminar (The) refers to an association of NT scholars founded (1985) and led by R. W. Funk to assess all SAYINGS attributed to Jesus, both canonical and extracanonical (e.g., the GOSPEL OF THOMAS), according to the probability of their authenticity. The procedures and findings of the seminar are recorded in its journal, *Foundations and Facets Forum*. The seminar sought and received considerable publicity (and notoriety) for its practice of voting on a scale of 1 to 4 (using colored balls) whether a given saying was to be accepted as authentic, inauthentic, or somewhere in between. For findings see,

e.g., Robert W. Funk et al., *The Parables of Jesus: Red Letter Edition. A Report of the Jesus Seminar* (Sonoma, Calif.: Polebridge Press, 1988); also representative, see Burton Mack, *A Myth of Innocence: Mark and Christian Origins* (Philadelphia: Fortress Press, 1988). The Jesus Seminar's operational presuppositions, methodology, and findings have been widely and severely criticized. See Timothy Luke Johnson, *The Real Jesus* (San Francisco: HarperSanFrancisco, 1995). See Q; QUEST OF THE HISTORICAL JESUS.

Johannine Comma (Lat: phrase). An INTERPOLATION in the text of 1 John 5:7f., viz. the italicized words in the following passage: "There are three that testify *in heaven, the Father, the Word, and the Holy Spirit, and these three are one. And there are three that testify in earth*: the Spirit and the water and the blood." Unattested by the oldest MSS and unknown to most church fathers prior to the 5th cent., the Johannine comma appears to be a GLOSS incorporated by scribal error into some Latin MSS of the NT around the 3rd or 4th cent. Erasmus omitted the Johannine comma from his earliest critical editions of the NT but restored it after an outcry, and it enjoyed widespread acceptance during the 16th and 17th cents.

Josephus, Flavius (37/38–ca. 110 C.E.). Jewish historian and apologist, though considered a traitor by his contemporaries. His histories of the Jewish revolt against Rome (66–73 C.E.; *De Bello Judaico* [*The Jewish War*], covering the period from Antiochus IV [d. 164 B.C.E.] to the fall of Masada in 73 C.E.) and of the Jews (*Antiquitates Judaicae* [*Jewish Antiquities*], from creation to the outbreak of the war), as well as his defense of Judaism (*Contra Apionem* [*Against Apion*]) and his biography (*Vita* [*The Life*]) are of incomparable value for reconstructing the history of the Jews in the first centuries B.C.E. and C.E.—even though the works are replete with gossip and LEGEND. Though a Pharisee and erstwhile military commander in Galilee early in the revolt, Josephus quickly sided with Rome, where he lived following the war under the patronage of Emperor Vespasian (whence his name Flavius). Three passages of particular interest to Christians, concerning Jesus, John the Baptist, and James the brother of Jesus, are found in *Ant. Jud.* (18.63f.; 18.116–119; 20.200–203). Of these, the first is widely held to be a later INTERPOLATION; the latter two, authentic. See *Josephus*, The Loeb Classical Library, 9 vols. (London: W. Heinemann; Cambridge, Mass.: Harvard University Press, 1926–65); P. Bilde, *Flavius Josephus between Jerusalem and Rome: His Life, His Works, and Their Importance* (Journal for the Study of the Pseudepigrapha, Sup. Series 2; Sheffield: Sheffield Academic Press, 1988); L. H. Feldman and G. Hata, eds., *Josephus, the Bible and History* (Detroit: Wayne State University Press, 1989).

Jülicher, Adolf (1857–1938). Born in Falkenberg near Berlin, Jülicher became a pastor in Rummelsberg (1882) and, on the basis of his book *The Parables of Jesus* (*Die Gleichnisreden Jesu*, 1888), was called to Marburg as professor of church history and NT (1888–1923), where he remained until retirement. All modern study of the PARABLES begins with Jülicher's massive work (vols. 1 & 2, 1899) of 970 pages (!); it repudiated the allegorical interpretation of parables while committing the error of overstatement by reducing every parable to a single point, invariably one simple moral maxim. In addition to his *An Introduction to the NT*, trans. J. P. Ward (New York: G. P. Putnam's Sons, 1904), Jülicher published important studies in church history and contributed to TEXTUAL CRITICISM by editing an Old Latin VERSION of the GOSPELS. As a historian, Jülicher was incensed by both ALBERT SCHWEITZER's *Quest of the Historical Jesus* and KARL BARTH's *Romans*.

Kaddish (Aram: "holy"). An ancient Jewish doxology now recited usually after the reading of scripture in synagogal worship or elsewhere, and including a congregational response. Its eschatological character and phraseology show affinities with the Lord's Prayer (Matt 6:9–13; cf. Ezek 38:23). The doxology, without the response, reads,

Glorified and sanctified be God's great name throughout the world which He has created according to His will.

May He establish His Kingdom in your lifetime and during your days, and within the lifetime of the entire house of Israel, speedily and soon; and say, Amen.

Kähler, Martin (1835–1912). Professor of NT and systematic theology at Halle (1867–1901), Kähler is especially remembered for his work *The So-Called Historical Jesus and the Historic Biblical Christ*, trans. Carl Braaten (Philadelphia: Fortress Press, 1964; Ger: 1892) in which he attacked the literary and theological premises of the quest of the historical Jesus, then at full bloom. Kähler's main interest was to establish that the real JESUS CHRIST is not the Jesus of historical reconstruction (the so-called *historische* Jesus) but rather the figure depicted in the GOSPELS and experienced as a contemporary reality by faith (the *geschichtliche* CHRIST). Kähler insisted on the irreducibly theological character of the Gospels and on the consequent futility and speculative character of the historical "lives of Jesus." His insights were taken up by KARL BARTH and RUDOLF BULTMANN, though in substantially different ways, and he was again "rediscovered" by the NEW HERMENEUTIC at mid-century. His question to NT criticism remains, "How can Jesus Christ be the real object of faith for all Christians if what and who he really was can be ascertained only by research methodologies so elaborate that only the scholarship of our time is adequate to the task?" See *HISTORIE*; QUEST OF THE HISTORICAL JESUS; SCHWEITZER.

***Kaige* Recension** (also: Proto-Theodotion recension). A VERSION of the OT in Greek that arose either as a direct translation of the Hebrew/Aramaic scriptures or as a revision of the Old Greek OT in the direction of the original. The name is derived from its unusual use of the Greek word *kaige* for the Hebrew word *gam* (also). A fragmentary scroll of this type containing portions of the Minor PROPHETS was found in 1952 at Nahal Hever (Wadi Khabra) in the Judean wilderness; it dates from the beginning of the 1st cent. C.E. or before. The *Kaige* recension stands in the same text tradition as that of "THEODOTION" in the 2nd cent. C.E.; hence it is commonly known as Proto-Theodotion.

Note: Study indicates that "Theodotion Daniel" (that is, the text of Daniel found in Theodotion's version of the Greek OT) may not be a part of the *Kaige* recension as heretofore believed, but a distinct and separate text type. Theodotion Daniel is the RECENSION quoted in NT citations of Daniel. See A. A. Di Lella's article "Daniel" in *IDBSup* vol. (5) (Nashville: Abingdon Press, 1976). See HEXAPLA; ORIGEN.

Kaine Diatheke is Greek for "New Testament" or "New Covenant"; see Heb 9:15. See OLD TESTAMENT/NEW TESTAMENT.

Kal wahomer (Heb: light and heavy). See **A minore ad majus.**

Käsemann, Ernst (1906–1998). Born in Dahlhausen near Bochum, Germany, Käsemann received his theological training in Bonn, Marburg, and Tübingen, studying under leading NT scholars of the time, esp. the pietist Adolf Schlatter and existentialist RUDOLF BULTMANN. A pastor in the *Evangelische Landeskirche*, he was imprisoned by the Nazis for several weeks, during which time he surreptitiously (though with the aid of guards) wrote *The Wandering People of God* (1938), a study of Hebrews. Following World War II he taught at Mainz (1946), Göttingen (1951), and Tübingen (1959), gaining international recognition as Bultmann's most famous

pupil and critic. Contrary to Bultmann's radical skepticism, Käsemann argued that something could be said about the historical Jesus. This interest led to the so-called "New Quest of the Historical Jesus" and to the effort to find the exegetical CRITERIA OF AUTHENTICITY by which the SAYINGS of Jesus were to be judged. Käsemann was principally an essayist with a deep concern for theological issues (see SACHEXEGESE, SACHKRITIK). His COMMENTARY on Romans was published following his retirement in 1970. It is characterized by its emphasis on the cross and on the radical distinction between letter and spirit, LAW and GOSPEL, justification by works and by faith— themes of the Reformation stressed by Martin Luther. Although Käsemann argued that the believer is totally dependent upon the word of God for salvation, a notion that is foolishness to the world, he wrote and spoke passionately of the need for social and political engagement with the world. His daughter was murdered in the 1970s by the military regime in Argentina for her social rights activism. His major works include *Essays on New Testament Themes* (London: SCM Press, 1964); *New Testament Questions of Today* (Philadelphia: Fortress Press, 1969); *Perspectives on Paul* (Philadelphia: Fortress Press, 1971); *Jesus Means Freedom* (Philadelphia: Fortress Press, 1968); and *Commentary on Romans* (Grand Rapids: Eerdmans, 1980).

Kerygma (Gk: proclamation; preaching) is a term derived from the Greek that in scripture and in modern biblical theology and criticism may refer either to the content of what is preached or to the act of preaching; hence kerygma in 1 Cor 1:21 may be translated, "It pleased God by the foolishness of *the preaching* [so Dodd; or KJV: *"of preaching"*] to save them that believe."

The realization within BIBLICAL CRITICISM since the turn of the 20th cent. that the GOSPELS are first of all theological and didactic and secondarily historical documents led to two diverse but related reactions: (1) the rise of biblical theology within Protestant circles that rediscovered the Pauline and Reformation emphasis on the preached word (the kerygma) and the decision of faith that the kerygma demands (so MARTIN KÄHLER, KARL BARTH, RUDOLF BULTMANN, Emil Brunner, et al.); and (2) the search for the earliest kerygma of the EARLY CHURCH. According to C. H. DODD (*The Apostolic Preaching and Its Development* [London: Hodder & Stoughton, Ltd., 1936; New York: Willett, Clark, & Co., 1937]) the kerygma is found in whole or in part in Acts 2:14–39; 3:13–26; 4:10–12; 5:30–32; 10:36–43; and 13:17–41; and in Paul's writings in Gal 3:1b; 1:3–4; 4:6; 1 Thess 1:10; 1 Cor 15:1–7; Rom 1:1–3; 2:16; 8:34a; 8:34b; 10:8–9. Here the kerygma opens with references to OT PROPHECY concerning the fulfillment of the age with CHRIST as its Lord, the fact of Jesus' powers and preaching, his crucifixion, resurrection, and exaltation, the promise of his coming, the call to repentance and the offer of forgiveness. The Gospel of Mark is the kerygma briefly elaborated, beginning with prophecy and ending with the promise of a CHRISTOPHANY.

Dodd's restrictive definition of the term *kerygma* served to point up again (1) the nonkerygmatic character of most contemporary preaching, and (2) the continuing riddle of Christian origins, viz., how Jesus who proclaimed the coming of the kingdom became the proclaimed Christ-who-is-to-come (again) of the church.

The resistance of biblical theologians and critics to leaving the riddle unsolved has caused the term *kerygma* to be more widely defined than Dodd's usage permits. Consequently, in its broader theological meaning it has also come to connote "the saving message"—as for example in the phrase, "The kerygma of Jeremiah." Similarly, both "the New Quest of the Historical Jesus" and its theoretical counterpart, "The NEW HERMENEUTIC," sought to reestablish the historical origins of Christian faith in the person of Jesus, and in the process broadened the parameters of the term *kerygma*.

Kethib and Qere   (Heb: "it is written"; "read" respectively) are terms employed in the study of the HEBREW BIBLE to distinguish the authoritative, consonantal writing of the text (the *Kethib*) from the corrected alternate pronunciation (the *Qere*), which was written in the margin of the text and was to be read in its place. The traditional text was thus "corrected" on various grounds: grammatical, aesthetic, or dogmatic. The variations, which number over 1300, were recorded in the MASORETIC TEXT (MT) over the course of centuries of scribal transmission. One noteworthy example concerns the personal proper name for God, YHWH, which Jews from the SECOND TEMPLE PERIOD onward ordinarily ceased to pronounce for reasons of reverence; hence, wherever YHWH appeared in the text, a different word was spoken in substitution, e.g., Lord (*Adonai*). Because the name of God appears so frequently in the BIBLE, scribes subsequently did not trouble to write the *Qere* in the margin. Instead, they merely added the vowel points of the word *Adonai* directly to the four consonants (YHWH) of the text. The *Qere* reminded knowledgeable readers to pronounce "Adonai" in place of YHWH but eventually gave rise in Christian circles (ca. 1300) to the erroneous TRANSLITERATION "Jehovah." A *Qere* required but not written in the margin because of frequency is called a *Qere Perpetuum*. See TETRAGRAMMATON.

Ketubim   (also *Ketuvim*; lit., writings). See **Hagiographa.**

Khirbet Qumran   is the name given to the ruins of an Essene community (Jewish monastics) on the northwestern coast of the Dead Sea, first occupied around 150 B.C.E. and destroyed in 68–70 C.E. during the suppression of the First Jewish Revolt (66–70 C.E.) by Rome. In its vicinity the DEAD SEA SCROLLS were found in 1947–56.

King James Version/New King James Version KJV/NKJV are the common abbreviations for the King James Version of the BIBLE published in 1611; though heeding the Hebrew and Greek texts at hand, it owed much of its English phrasing to antecedent translations and VERSIONS by Tyndale (1525); Coverdale (1535); Thomas Matthew (1537); as well as the Great Bible (1539); the Geneva Bible (1560); and the Bishop's Bible (1568). Of these the KJV is most dependent on Tyndale's translation, which in turn followed Martin Luther's German translation of 1534. In England the KJV is commonly known as the Authorized Version (AV). No single book has affected the language and culture of English-speaking peoples more than the KJV of the Bible. The same can be said of Luther's translation for the German language.

Two major factors led to the revision of the KJV: (a) the discovery in the 19th and 20th centuries of MSS far older than the MSS used in 1611 (see TEXTUAL CRITICISM) and (b) the increasingly archaic and obsolete character of the Elizabethan English in which the KJV was written. The following are examples of KJV words whose meaning has changed from their usage in 1611: Acts 21:15: carriages = baggage; Acts 17:23: devotions = objects of worship; Mark 6:8: script = wallet; 1 Tim 5:4: nephews = grandchildren; Mark 7:24: coasts = borders; 2 Thess 2:7: let = restrain; 1 Thess 4:15: prevent = precede; Mark 6:25: charger = platter; James 3:13: conduct = conversation.

The New King James Version (Nashville: Thomas Nelson; NT, 1979; OT, 1983) attempts to modernize the KJV language by omitting archaic pronouns (thee, thou, thy, thine) and verb endings (-eth, -est), and by replacing archaic and obsolete words with modern equivalents. Ironically, the participating scholars "signed a document of subscription to the plenary and VERBAL INSPIRATION of the original AUTOGRAPHS of the Bible," but chose to follow the "traditional Greek text underlying the 1611 edition" rather than follow the Hebrew and Greek MSS found since 1611 and antedating the "traditional text" by as much as 1,000 years and more. See PARAPHRASE; see also AMERICAN STANDARD VERSION; CONTEMPORARY ENGLISH VERSION; DOUAY; LIVING BIBLE (PARAPHRASED); NEW AMERICAN BIBLE; NEW ENGLISH BIBLE; NEW INTERNATIONAL VERSION; NEW JEWISH VERSION; REVISED STANDARD VERSION; TODAY'S ENGLISH VERSION.

Kittel, Gerhard (1888–1948). Son of Rudolf Kittel; professor of NT principally at Tübingen. Known for works on Tannaitic Judaism and early Christianity and as founder of the *Theologisches Wörterbuch zum Neuen Testament*, vols. 1–9 (Abbrev.: TWzNT; 1933–73); English translation by Geoffrey W. Bromiley, *Theological Dictionary of the New Testament*, vols. 1–9 (Grand Rapids: Eerdmans, 1964–74).

Kittel, Rudolf (1853–1929). Professor of OT principally in Leipzig (Germany); known for his Hebrew edition of the OT, the *Biblia Hebraica* (1906, 1909[2], 1929[3]), which bears his name.

***Koiné* Greek** (or more appropriately: *Koiné dialektos:* Gk: common language) is the term used to designate the language most widely used by Greek-speaking peoples of NT times that came into being following the extension of Macedonian hegemony throughout the ancient Near East by Alexander the Great, 323 B.C.E. Also called Hellenistic Greek, *Koiné* Greek arose as an amalgam of several dialects of which Attic, a minor member, proved dominant. The books of the NT were written in *Koiné* Greek.

Kompositionsgeschichte is an alternate and less widely used term in Germany for *Redaktionsgeschichte* (REDACTION CRITICISM) meaning "composition history/criticism," suggested by Ernst Haenchen (*Der Weg Jesu* [Berlin: Walter de Gruyter, 1968], 24); its English equivalent has been supported by some as preferable to redaction criticism, but it is also less widely accepted.

Kompositionskritik (Ger: composition criticism). In some German OT scholarship a distinction is made between LITERARY CRITICISM and *Kompositionskritik* in which the former is narrowly defined as the analysis of single, usually brief literary units and the latter as the analysis of those larger texts composed of at least two preexisting (whether oral or written) units. So defined, "composition" can occur at any of three stages: (a) at an oral or written stage prior to adoption by a writer; (b) at the time when the writer joins the units together in the process of composition, or (c) when a "REDACTOR" reworks a text, adding material to a preexisting literary unit. *Kompositionskritik* comes into play when a text shows that it has been formed by the joining together of partly literary and partly preliterary units. It seeks to explain how such units were joined together and how the compositor made changes in the preexisting material, and how and why he added his own. *Kompositionskritik* asks, What are the steps of composition? What is the function of the units within the composition? It may seek to determine the theological content of the various units, for they can vary greatly, along with perspective and intention. When *Kompositionskritik* investigates the redactional treatment of units or compositions and their function in larger works or books, it becomes virtually identical with *Redacktionskritik*. Examples of material studied include the Abraham and Jacob cycles, the NARRATIVE passages of the PENTATEUCH, 1 and 2 Kings, etc.

Redacktionskritik, by contrast, seeks to determine the extent and nature of the redactional elements in the text at hand. This can include marginal or interlinear GLOSSES, the addition of larger units or parts of texts (such as the HYMNS in the book of Amos), the transposition of texts, or alterations within the texts themselves, including the loss of portions thereof (e.g., Amos 2:12). The Pentateuch/Hexateuch and the Deuteronomistic redaction remain the areas of greatest complexity and inter-

est in this regard. (See, e.g., Otto Eissfeldt, "Die Komposition der Sinai-Erzählung Exodus 19–34," in his *Kleine Schriften*, vol. 4 [Tübingen: J. C. B. Mohr, 1968], 231–37.)

Kore Kosmou. See **Hermetic Literature.**

Kultgeschichtliche Schule (Ger: cult-history school) refers in German BIBLICAL CRITICISM to the application of certain insights, perspectives, and funds of cultic knowledge from the field of comparative religions to the study of OT and NT traditions. While the term is not often used today except in historical surveys, it refers to two related but disparate formulations of the method, viz., to (a) the so-called "Myth and Ritual School" in England, and (b) the "Uppsala School" in Scandinavia. The former is associated with the work of S. H. Hooke (*Myth and Ritual* [London: Oxford University Press, 1933]; also *Myth, Ritual, and Kingship* [Oxford: Clarendon Press, 1958]); Jane Ellen Harrison (*Ancient Art and Ritual* [New York: Henry Holt & Co., 1913]), et al. Throughout these works the ethnological studies of James Frazer's *The Golden Bough* (1890; 1911–15) is apparent. In Scandinavia, the chief representatives of this perspective (for which the term "school" is not particularly apt) are Wilhelm Grønbeck, SIGMUND MOWINCKEL, JOHANNES PEDERSEN, Aage Bentzen, Geo Widengren, Ivan Engnell, Alfred Haldar, and A. S. Kapelrud; see, e.g., Ivan Engnell, *Studies in Divine Kingship in the Ancient Near East* (Oxford: Basil Blackwell, 1943), and Sigmund Mowinckel, *The Psalms in Israel's Worship* (New York: Abingdon Press, 1962; Oxford: Basil Blackwell, 1963), the latter author being considered the most influential of all the Scandinavians.

The cult-historical method, as it is sometimes called, developed as a reaction to the limitations of LITERARY CRITICISM and to the evolutionistic rationalism typical of the Wellhausen School, which tended to reduce OT religion to matters of doctrine and ethics. In contrast, the *Kult-*

geschichtliche Schule (*KS*) influenced by FORM CRITICISM, lifted up the centrality of the cult, the communal and recurrent character of its sacred rites and festivals, and in particular the concept of sacral kingship and the role of the king in the cult drama.

Criticism of the *KS* perspective as practiced among OT scholars—principally the Scandinavians—is directed primarily against its extreme emphasis on kingship, the cyclical aspects of the cult, and the isolation of these concepts and motifs from their specific cultural and religious contexts.

In his study of the PSALMS, Mowinckel proposed the term *cult-functional method* as a corrective to the overemphasis of early form criticism on form alone, suggesting that psalms which outwardly appear to belong to different form categories nevertheless belong together, being governed by the same ideas, perhaps functioning as the psalms of a specific festival. In NT studies, the *KS* critics analyzed NT documents centering on the formative influences that baptism and the Lord's Supper especially had on the traditions (particularly 1 Peter, Ephesians, the passion narratives, etc.). See TRADITION CRITICISM.

Kunstprosa (Ger: artistic prose) is defined by Friedrich Blass as a writing "intended by an author technically trained in this regard, not only to instruct, nor merely to make an impression, but also to please" (BDF, para. 485). According to Blass, in the NT only the book of Hebrews fits the category of *Kunstprosa*.

Kunstspruch. See ***Volksspruch.***

Kyrios In modern English there is no precise equivalent for the Greek "*Kyrios*" as used in the NT period: "Lord" or "lord" in the Elizabethan period and "*Herr*" in German are much closer approximations. *Kyrios*'s semantic range includes "master" (Matt 13:27; 25:20; Luke 13:8), "owner" (Matt 20:8; 21:40), "Sir" (Matt 25:11; John 12:21), "Lord" meaning the exalted Jesus

(Acts 5:14; 9:10–11, 42; Rom 12:11; Gal 1:19; 1 Cor 8:5, passim), and "LORD" i.e., YHWH, the God of Israel (Matt 5:33; Mark 5:19; Luke 1:6, passim). In the last two instances especially the sense of *Kyrios* is colored to a greater or lesser degree by its use as a reverential paraphrasis for the personal proper name of Israel's God (cf. Phil 2:11). The NT frequently makes sophisticated use of the multivalence of *Kyrios* to display the contested nature of Jesus' identity and to suggest how the astonishing is made visible in the familiar and ordinary, cf. the rapid change in Mary Magdalene's use of *Kyrios* in John 20:15–20. When the term appears untranslated as a technical term in BIBLICAL CRITICISM, it almost invariably means "Lord," referring to the lordship of JESUS CHRIST. See Joseph A. Fitzmyer, "The Semitic Background of the New Testament Kyrios Title," in *A Wandering Aramean: Collected Aramaic Essays* (Missoula, Mont.: Scholars Press, 1979).

"L" is the symbol created by B. H. STREETER (1924) to designate material peculiar to Luke's GOSPEL alone, including such familiar passages as the PARABLES of the good Samaritan (10:29–37) and the prodigal son (15:11–32) but excluding the infancy NARRATIVES (chs. 1–2), composed by Luke from traditional material around 60 C.E. in the province of Caesarea by the Sea.

In OT TEXTUAL CRITICISM, L is the *siglum* for CODEX Leningradensis. Copied in Cairo in 1009 C.E. from a ben Asher MS of the OT, it was adopted as the base text for R. KITTEL's *Biblia Hebraica*, 3rd ed. (1929). See FOUR DOCUMENT HYPOTHESIS; GRIESBACH HYPOTHESIS; "M"; Q; SYNOPTIC PROBLEM; TWO SOURCE HYPOTHESIS.

Lachmann, Karl; "The Lachmann Fallacy" Professor of German and classical philology in Berlin (1825–51) and known as the founder of the modern era of TEXTUAL CRITICISM for his publication of the first CRITICAL TEXT based entirely on ancient MSS, Lachmann (1793–1851) argued for the existence of a source antedating the Synoptics whose order Mark best preserved (URMARKUS) and of a second source (called *Quelle*) to explain the parallels between Matt and Luke. The Lachmann Fallacy is a name in NT source criticism given to the argument that because Matt and Luke with few exceptions follow the order of Markan material and because wherever one disagrees with Markan order the other agrees, it follows that Matt and Luke are *dependent* on Mark (or a document very much like it) while being *independent* of each other (a conclusion Lachmann derived from other facts as well). Logically, however, the deduction is fallacious because it is but one of three possibilities, viz., that the order of dependence is (a) Matt → Mark → Luke, (b) Luke → Mark → Matt, or (c) Mark → Matt and Luke. Lachmann himself did not commit this mistake of reasoning, for he believed each of the GOSPELS to be dependent on a primitive Gospel (i.e., *Urmarkus*), but his contention that Mark best preserved its order naturally led to the acceptance of the priority of Mark once the hypothesis of an *Urmarkus* was abandoned. See TWO SOURCE HYPOTHESIS; GRIESBACH HYPOTHESIS.

Lacuna (pl.: lacunae; Lat: hole) is a technical term in TEXTUAL CRITICISM denoting a gap or missing portion of a text due to damage in the MS itself and caused by wear, decay, worms, mice, careless repair, or intentional alteration (e.g., cutting out illuminations).

Lament is occasionally used to translate the German word *Klage* in spite of its varied connotations in that language: (1) (a) complaint, (b) lament; (2) (a) grievance, (b) lawsuit, charge. In form-critical studies, the terms *dirge* (funeral song) and *complaint* are more precise than *lament*. For a critical analysis of the lament in the OT, see CLAUS WESTERMANN, *Praise and Lament in the Psalms* (Atlanta: John Knox Press, 1981). See PSALMS; *QINAH* METER.

Language event; Word event (Ger: *Sprachereignis*, WORTGESCHEHEN) are synonymous terms in the NEW HERMENEUTIC as developed by Ernst Fuchs (1903–1983) and Gerhard Ebeling (1912–) respectively. The concept of the language event, derived in part from German philosophers of language and existence, is based on the idea that for human beings reality *happens*— comes into being—through language, and that the creative eventfulness of language is the key issue in HERMENEUTICS. Language events have an ongoing residual effect in and as language, called language gain, that enables previously realized possibilities of human existence to be actualized again in new circumstances. For Fuchs and Ebeling, the NT is evidence of the coming-into-language (language gain) of the new reality known as JESUS CHRIST (language event). Cf. John 1:1–14.

Langue. See **Structuralism.**

Lasterkatalog (Ger: pl. *Lasterkataloge*; a catalog of vices) is a technical term in German NT studies frequently carried over into English without translation to designate the lists of vices enumerated by Paul and other NT writers in the context of ethical instruction (Rom 1:29–31; 13:13; 1 Cor 5:10–11; 6:9–10; 2 Cor 12:20–21; Gal 5:19–21; Eph 4:31; 5:3–5; Col 3:5, 8; Rev 21:8; 22:15). The *Lasterkatalog* constitutes a somewhat loosely delineable "gathering" or literary form that antedates Christianity, whether derived from the writings of Judaism (see PHILO's *de sacr. Abelis et Caini* 22, 27; Wis 8:7; 14:25ff.; 4 Macc 1:19, 26; *Jub* 21:21; 23:14; *1 Enoch* 10:20; 91:6–8; DEAD SEA SCROLLS 1QS IV, 9–11) or the ethical DISCOURSES of Greek antiquity, especially the Cynic-Stoic DIATRIBE, from which the asyndetic form of the *Lasterkatalog* found in the NT probably comes (see, e.g., Epictetus 1116.45; Stobaeus, *ecl.* II. 60, 9; Seneca, *de vit. beat.* VII. 3; X. 2; Lucian of Samasota's style is paratactic, e. g., *dial. mort.* X. 4, 6, 8). Nag Hammadi CODEX VI contains *Lasterkatalog*.

Frequently coupled with *Lasterkatalog* are catalogs of virtues (*Tugendkataloge*). See 2 Cor 6:6; Gal 5:22–23; Eph 4:2–3, 32–5:2;

Phil 4:8; Col 3:12; 1 Tim 6:11; 2 Tim 2:22; 1 Pet 3:8; 2 Pet 1:5ff.; also Epictetus 1.29.39; 2.14.8; 3.5.7; 20.5.14–15.

The ancient Hellenistic world commonly recognized four cardinal virtues: wisdom, righteousness (justice), manliness, and moderation (temperance); and four cardinal vices: folly, unrighteousness (injustice), cowardice, and licentiousness (intemperance). See Victor Furnish, *Theology and Ethics in Paul* (Nashville: Abingdon Press, 1968).

Late Judaism (fr. Ger: *Spät-Judentum*) is a term used to designate the Judaism of the NT (and TALMUDIC) period. In spite of wide use, the term, which appears in anti-Jewish tracts of the Reformation and post-Reformation period (F. C. Grant), is inaccurate and misleading and should be dropped. It suggests that Judaism faded away after the 1st cent. or that the church and not rabbinic Judaism was the only legitimate continuation of OT Israel. Preferred alternatives are "Ancient" or "early Judaism," or "Tannaitic Judaism," or simply "1st cent. Judaism."

Latinism Although the influence of Latin on the NT is not as great as that of Semitic languages, its presence is apparent in (a) military terminology: praetorium, legion, centurion, custodian; (b) legal and administrative language: Caesar, tax, colony, freedman, title; and (c) measurements and coins: liter, mile, denarius, drachma, etc. For example, see Mark 12:42 ". . . two *lepta* [Greek coins] that is, a quadrans [Roman coin]." See SEMITISM; SEPTUAGINTISM.

Law If the object of law is the ordering of life in community, the specific object of OT law is the ordering of Israel's life in communion with YHWH as the people of YHWH's free choosing. OT law is thus closely connected to covenant, and the revelation and restatement of law typically takes place in the context of God's making and renewing of covenant (cf. Exod 1–20; 2 Kgs 23:1–3; Jer 34:8–22; Ezra 9–10; Neh 9–13).

According to tradition Moses was the great lawgiver and at his hand the TORAH (PENTATEUCH) was written. LITERARY CRITICISM has shown, however, that the laws of the OT, concentrated almost entirely in the first five books, vary in age, form, and historical setting, and are the product of more than 1,000 years of social and religious development. In fact, it is not until the 6th cent. B.C.E., long after Moses' death, that the multiform civil and penal laws, cultic stipulations and prohibitions, moral and ethical commands, procedural rules, etc., were looked upon collectively as "Torah" or the Law (see Deut 17:19; 27:3; 28:61).

Literary criticism, prior to the advent of FORM CRITICISM, identified five "codes" or collections of law: the Covenant Code (Exod 20:22–23:33), the DECALOGUE (Exod 20:2–17; Deut 5:6–21), the DEUTERONOMIC CODE (Deut 12–26), the HOLINESS CODE (Lev 17–26), and the Priestly Code (Exod 25:31; 34:29–Lev 16; and portions of Numbers). Form criticism has since shown, however, that these codes are made up of individual laws and units of laws that often considerably antedate the period of their codification.

The antiquity of certain OT law is revealed by its similarity (and dissimilarity) with other ancient law codes discovered in the Near East: the Sumerian codes known as Ur-Nammu (ca. 2050 B.C.E.) and Lipit-Ishtur (ca. 1975 B.C.E.); the Akkadian codes known as Eshnunna (ca. 1700 B.C.E.) and the Hammurabi Code (ca. 1700 B.C.E.); Middle Assyrian codes (ca. 1450–1000 B.C.E.), Hittite codes (ca. 1500 B.C.E.), and Neo-Babylonian codes (ca. 600 B.C.E.). English translations of these codes can be found in J. B. Pritchard's *Ancient Near Eastern Texts* (Princeton: Princeton University Press, 1958, 1971[5]). See APODICTIC LAW; CASUISTIC LAW; P: PRIESTLY CODE.

Law, The. See **Pentateuch; Torah.**

LB(P); NLT. See *Living Bible (Paraphrased). The; New Living Translation, The.*

Leben-Jesu Forschung. See **Quest of the Historical Jesus.**

Lectio difficilior probabilior   (Lat)
is a rule of thumb in TEXTUAL CRITICISM dating from J. A. Bengel (1687–1752) and J.
Mill (1645–1707) which states that when a
choice is to be made between two or more
renderings of a text "the more difficult
reading is the more probable," i.e., more
likely to be original. The logic of the rule is
based on the assumption that subsequent
copyists would attempt to eliminate from
the text grammatical, historical, or theological errors or ambiguities.

Lectio divina   (Lat: sacred reading)
refers to the meditative study of scripture,
especially as this was originally developed
and practiced in the medieval monastic
tradition. The 12th-cent. Carthusian writer
Guigo II (*The Ladder of Monks*) distinguished four stages in *lectio divina*: reading
(*lectio*), reflection (*meditatio*), prayer (*oratio*), and contemplation (*contemplatio*). The
aim of *lectio divina* was to combine meditative reading with purity of life and knowledge of God, so that scripture provided a
flexible guide for the whole of life.

Lectionary   (Lat: a reader). A lectionary
is a collection or list of selected passages
(PERICOPES) from scripture arranged according to the liturgical year for use in worship or private devotion. There is evidence
for a fixed pattern of readings from the LAW
and PROPHETS in synagogue worship from
the beginning of the 3rd cent. C.E., and the
practice may be substantially older. In the
Christian tradition, the use of fixed readings for public worship is also quite
ancient. The lectionary system still in use
in the Orthodox Church took shape
between the 4th and 7th centuries (it
excludes the book of Revelation for a variety of historical and theological reasons).
The practice of fixed readings gave rise to
the production of special MSS that contain
passages from the GOSPELS and Epistles
arranged not according to canonical order
but according to either the church year
(called the synaxarion) or the calendar year
(called the menologion). The former runs
from Easter to Easter and contains readings for specified Saturdays, Sundays, and
weekdays of the ecclesiastical year, while
the latter starts on September 1 and contains readings for feast days, saints' days,
and other special occasions. Lectionaries
represent a considerable portion of all
extant MSS of the NT. Since lectionaries are
thought to be highly resistant to change,
they are an important source for TEXTUAL
CRITICISM in ascertaining early variants of
scriptural texts. In CRITICAL APPARATUSES,
they are given the *siglum* 1 followed by the
number of the MS. See Bruce M. Metzger,
"Greek Lectionaries and a Critical Edition
of the Greek New Testament," in K. Aland,
ed., *Die alten Übersetzungen des Neuen Testaments, die Kirchenväterzitate und Lektionare*
(Berlin: De Gruyter, 1972).

Legend   (Lat: *legenda:* "what is to be
read"; ME: *legende*). In the usage of the Middle Ages, "*legenda*" referred to the NARRATIVE read on the feast day of a holy figure,
telling the story of his or her life and death.
Over time and by the 17th cent., the term
had come to refer to a popularly believed
but nonhistorical story (*ABD*). Nineteenth-
and 20th-cent. LITERARY CRITICISM sought to
refurbish the term by employing it as a formal category applicable across national literary and linguistic traditions, but it did so
with limited, often confusing, results, as
explained below. It is currently proposed in
some quarters that the term be restricted to
its original meaning as a narrative about a
holy person told for edificatory purposes,
using the term *Sage* or folk story for the
bulk of OT narratives (so J. J. Sullion, *ABD*).
  Acknowledging that the lines between
them are fluid and permit no strict delineation, early form critics attempted to differentiate between legends, fairy tales (see
MÄRCHEN), and MYTHS. Fairy tales are here
defined as entertaining and fanciful creations that tell of "once upon a time in the
land of make believe" where virtue is
miraculously rescued from evil and all
"live happily ever after." No narrative of
scripture falls totally within this genre.

However, according to E. Jacob (*RGG*[3]), the miraculous rescues of Moses and of Elijah, the peril of great beauty (Sarah, Rebekah), the victory of the weak over the strong (Joseph, Gideon, David), and the quarrel between two wives (Sarah and Hagar) are "fairy-tale like" (Ger: *märchenhaft*).

Confusion arose among form critics because the term *legend* was used in English-language form-critical studies as a translation of (a) the Latin technical term *legenda*, (b) the Norse "saga," and (c) the German *Sage* (Ger.: tale, story; pl. *Sagen*), terms that denote diverse literary genres. As noted, in the Middle Ages the term *legenda* referred to the lives of the martyrs and saints read in the context of community worship or for purposes of private devotion; sagas are narrative compositions in prose that were written in Iceland or Norway during the Middle Ages; *Sage* denotes any popular story, set in the past and rooted in reality (e.g., by the use of actual person and place names) that has been worked over by poetic imagination, i.e., having elements of the "fabulous" or "fantastic."

What must be remembered is that what is usually connoted in popular use by the English *legend*—"an inauthentic and unhistorical story"—has not been the intended connotation in the context of literary or FORM CRITICISM. However, the disparity between popular and scholarly usage is no small part of the problem of formal category and nomenclature in the domain of form criticism.

The listing below principally follows the practice of the famed Scandinavian form critic SIGMUND MOWINCKEL (*IDB*), in part for historical interest. No effort is made here to resolve the issues of form and nomenclature. Study of the passages cited will give insight into the formal nature of the material and the problems inherent in any effort at classification.

A. *Etiological Legends:*

1. *Natural Phenomena.* The Dead Sea (Gen 19), the salt "pillar" (Gen 19), the stone of Makkedah (Josh 10), the megalith of Bashan (Deut 3), etc.

2. *Persons or Place Names.* The tower of Babel (Gen 11), the tell of Ai (Josh 7–8), the well of Kadesh (Gen 16)—over forty-five such legends are to be found in Gen alone.

3. *Cult Objects, Practices, and Places.* OT: The bronze serpent (Num 21:4–9), the ark of God (1 Sam 4–6; 2 Sam 6), circumcision (Gen 17; Exod 4; Josh 5), Passover (Exod 1–15), Bethel–Jacob (Gen 28; 35), Sinai–Moses (Exod 19), Jer-usalem–David (2 Sam 5–7); NT: EUCHARIST (Mark 14:22–26 pars.; 1 Cor 11:23–25; also Mark 14:12–16), Baptism of the Holy Spirit (Acts 2).

4. *Culture Heroes.* The originator of towns (Enoch, Gen 4:17), tent dwelling and the breeding of cattle (Jabal, Gen 4:20), musical instruments (Jubal, Gen 4:21), blacksmithing (Tubal-cain, Gen 4:22).

B. *Ancestor or ethnological legemds*, explaining the origin or characterizing traits of a nation, tribe, or city: Cain (Gen 4), Canaan (Gen 9), Noah's sons (Gen 10), Abraham (Gen 12), Ishmael (Gen 16), etc.

C. *Hero tales*, containing perhaps historical kernels, e.g., stories of the Judges (see esp. Judg 14–16), of Saul and David (esp. David and Goliath).

D. *Legends proper* (so Mowinckel), i.e., a story with an "edifying devotional tendency" possessing a nucleus of historical fact: Elijah ("a masterpiece of epic art," 1 Kgs 17ff.) and the more popularized accounts of Elisha (2 Kgs). The latter may also properly be classified an aretalogy.

Legends of the NT dealing with persons can in the main be listed here: the accounts of Jesus' birth, the explanation of Mary's virginity (Matt 1:1 8ff.), the magi (2:1ff.), the slaughter of the children and the flight into Egypt may have originated with the school of Matt; the Lukan narratives on the other hand show evidence of tradition reaching back to John the Baptist (Luke 1:14–17). The story of Jesus in the temple, the temptation, the accounts of the empty tomb and of the Emmaus disciples bear the same devotional motifs—whatever historical fact underlies them.

Persons surrounding Jesus are treated in a similar fashion by Luke, e.g., Mary and Martha (10:38–42), Zacchaeus (19:1–10), Peter (5:1–10; Acts 12:1ff.), Paul (Acts 9:1ff.), Paul and Silas (Acts 16:19–40), Stephen (Acts 7:54–60), Cornelius (Acts 10), etc.

See also GATTUNG.

Lessing, Gotthold Ephraim (1729–1781). In the area of BIBLICAL CRITICISM, Lessing is accorded notice for publishing posthumously portions of the writing of H. S. REIMARUS that, according to ALBERT SCHWEITZER at least, inaugurated the "Lives-of-Jesus Research" of the 19th cent.; for proposing an UREVANGELIUM behind the Synoptics to explain their interrelationships; and, in biblical theology, for his axiom concerning the relationship of history to revelation, called by Lessing "the ugly broad ditch [*garstige breite Graben*] which I cannot get across," viz.: "Accidental truths of history can never become the proof of necessary truths of reason . . ." ("*Zufällige Geschichtswahrheiten können der Beweis von notwendigen Vernunftswahrheiten nie werden*" ["On the Proof of the Spirit and of Power"]). He is also known for his argument that the RULE OF FAITH and not the scriptures themselves was the source and norm of faith for the earliest Christians, and for his insistence that a distinction had to be made between a miracle and a story about a miracle. In all these points Lessing remains one of the conversants in 21st-cent. Christian theology. See HERMENEUTICS; HISTORICAL-CRITICAL METHOD; *URMARKUS*.

Letter   As a literary form, none of the writings of the OT is a letter; several of the books contain letters, e.g., 2 Sam 11:14–15; 1 Kgs 21:8–11; and 2 Kgs 10:1–2. In the NT the situation is quite different; twenty of twenty-seven writings are, or bear semblances of, letters and two additional books contain letters (Acts 15:23–29; 23:26–30; and Rev 2–3). None of the NT letters is, strictly speaking, private correspondence; all were intended for the larger community, even Philemon, which deals with a personal matter. The typical Pauline letter contains an opening (including the name of the sender, the recipient, and a greeting; e.g., Rom 1:1–7; Phil 1:1–2); a thanksgiving or blessing (missing in Gal; cf. Heb, Jas, et al.), which may include a prayer of intercession (e.g., Rom 1:9–10) and an eschatological climax (e.g., 1 Cor 1:8–9); the body of the letter with some kind of formulary opening (e.g., Rom 1:13–15; Phil 1:12–18), eschatological conclusion (e.g., Gal 6:7–10), and a travelogue (e.g., Phil 2:19–24); PARAENESIS (e.g., Gal 5:13–6:10); and a closing, including greetings, a doxology, and a benediction (e.g., Phil 4:21–22). See William G. Doty, *Letters in Primitive Christianity* (Philadelphia: Fortress Press, 1973); Stanley K. Stowers, *Letter Writing in Greco-Roman Antiquity* (Philadelphia: Westminster Press, 1986).

Lexeme.   See **Structuralism.**

Lexicon   (pl.: lexica; Gk: word) has several connotations of which two are pertinent to BIBLICAL CRITICISM: (a) it is used most frequently to designate a dictionary of Hebrew, Greek, or Latin words found in the scriptures or the church fathers, such as Brown-Driver-Briggs (OT Hebrew) or Bauer-Arndt-Gingrich-Danker (NT Greek); or (b) it may be used in a broader sense to denote any specialized vocabulary of a particular field of knowledge—this *Handbook* is in part a highly selective lexicon of biblical criticism.

In addition to BDB see *A Concise Hebrew and Aramaic Lexicon of the Old Testament*, ed. William L. Holladay (Grand Rapids: Eerdmans, 1971; 1974^2); it is based on the 1st–3rd editions of the Koehler-Baumgartner *Lexicon in Veteris Testamenti Libros,* a German-English lexicon of the Hebrew and Aramaic OT, subsequently revised by J. J. Stamm, and now more recently edited under the supervision of M. E. J. Richardson in 5 vols. (Leiden: Brill, 1994–2000). See LIDDELL-SCOTT-JONES

Lex talionis   (Lat: law of retaliation). "An eye for an eye and a tooth for a tooth" is the traditional expression of the *lex talionis;* it is characteristic of the Code of Hammurabi and has its parallel in OT LAW (e.g., Exod 21:23–25). An enlightened law, it was designed to *reduce* bloodshed by prescribing the extent of retaliation. See *SÄTZE HEILIGEN RECHTES*.

Liber antiquitatum Biblicarum. See **Pseudepigrapha**.

Liberal Lives of Jesus. See **Quest of the Historical Jesus.**

Liddell-Scott-Jones is the common call name of *A Greek-English Lexicon*, compiled by Henry George Liddell and Robert Scott; revised and augmented by Henry Stuart Jones (2 vols.; Oxford: Clarendon Press, 1925–40). *A Supplement*, ed. E. A. Barber, was published by Oxford in 1968; revised for the 9th ed., 1996. Liddell-Scott-Jones is the standard Greek-English LEXICON for classical and Hellenistic Greek; it appears also in two abridged editions (known to students as "the middle Liddell" and "the little Liddell," the full edition being "the Great Scott"). *A Patristic Greek Lexicon*, ed. G. W. H. Lampe (Oxford: Clarendon Press, 1961), contains the theological and ecclesiastical vocabulary of post-Greek Christian authors from Clement of Rome to Theodore of Studium (d. C.E. 826). See EXEGESIS.

Lightfoot, Robert Henry (1883–1953). Born in Wellingborough, England, the son of an Anglican priest, Lightfoot was a Fellow of Lincoln College (1919–21) and New College (1921–50), Oxford University, where he became Dean Ireland Professor of EXEGESIS and Holy Scripture (1934–49). An early English advocate of FORM CRITICISM, he also recognized the necessity of giving place to the theological and literary tendencies of the GOSPEL writers (later called REDACTION CRITICISM). See *History and Interpretation in the Gospels* (Bampton Lectures for 1934; New York: Harper & Brothers, 1934); *The Gospel Message of St. Mark* (New York: Oxford University Press, 1950); and published posthumously by C. F. Evans, *St. John's Gospel* (New York: Oxford University Press, 1956); Lightfoot was also editor of the *Journal of Theological Studies*, 1941–53.

Linguistics is the study of language; it seeks to describe and explain human speech in terms of its internal characteristics, its function, and its role in society. Linguistics is both empirical and theoretical in that it gathers observable data and clarifies that data according to a general theory of linguistic STRUCTURE. In recent decades, the field has become exceedingly diverse and complex, since language in all its aspects can be subsumed under this one rubric. It includes the theoretical study of signs (SEMIOTICS); communication theory (and media); language structure (see STRUCTURALISM) and systems; social settings (sociolinguistics); psychological setting (psycholinguistics); geographical setting (dialectology, linguistic geography); language development; the characteristics of individual languages and their relationship to other languages (comparative linguistics); and the fundamental commonality of all languages.

The common subdivisions of linguistics include phonetics, phonology, MORPHOLOGY, SYNTAX (grammar), SEMANTICS (SEMASIOLOGY, lexicology, lexicography, etc.), and pragmatics.

Whereas in early decades of the 20th cent., linguistics concentrated on the speech act, on RHETORIC and stylistics, as well as on historical (DIACHRONIC) aspects of language generally, emphasis in recent decades has been on the structure of language (i.e., its SYNCHRONIC aspects). The former is sometimes termed "classical linguistics," the latter, "modern linguistics." Further, concentration on the sentence as the basic semantic unit has given way to increased attention to texts (text linguistics) and (more recently still) to complete "speech acts." This broadening of the scope of linguistics to macrosyntactic units, specifically to texts as such, has caused biblical critics and theologians (as well as sociologists, psychologists, neophysicists, etc.) to become interested in developments in modern linguistics. (See Theodor Lewandowski, *Linguistisches Wörterbuch* 2 [Heidelberg: Quelle & Meyer, 1976²].) Two journals joining the broad ranges of linguistics to biblical interpretation (among other interests) are SEMEIA (published by the SOCIETY OF BIBLICAL LITERATURE, 1974–) and *Linguistica Biblica*, ed. Erhardt Güttgemanns (Bonn, W. Germany, 1970–). For studies related to the Bible, see Walter R. Bodine, ed., *Linguistics and Biblical Hebrew* (Winona Lake, Ind.: Eisenbrauns, 1992); Stanley E. Porter and D. A. Carson, eds., *Linguistics and the New Testament: Critical Junctures* (JSNTSup 168; Sheffield: Sheffield Academic Press, 1999).

Literal Inspiration. See **Verbal Inspiration.**

Literal Sense   (Lat: *sensus literalis*). The literal sense of scripture has been understood in various ways from age to age. Definitions have included "the sense the author intended," "the verbal or grammatical sense," "the sense for the writer's public," "the sense that God intends," "the sense a text has when included in the canon," and "the sense church authorities designate." As this list suggests, "The search for the literal sense of the text may seem to some to be a first and elementary step in biblical interpretation, but actually its discernment lies at the heart of one of the most difficult and profound theological questions in the entire study of the Bible" (Childs).

In early Christian tradition, the literal sense of scripture was distinguished from its spiritual sense. Generally speaking, the literal sense is the grammatical sense of a passage that is accessible to a properly attentive reader; the spiritual sense refers to a deeper level (or levels) of truth hidden in the text (see FOURFOLD SENSE OF SCRIPTURE). From the 2nd cent. onward, Christians have given strong preference to the literal sense when reading the NT while giving much broader scope to the spiritual sense when reading the OT. In effect, a literal reading of the NT provided Christians

the key for unlocking the hidden spiritual truths contained elsewhere in scripture. In the patristic period, the School of Alexandria (ALEXANDRIA, SCHOOL OF) and the School of Antioch (ANTIOCH, SCHOOL OF) debated how closely one should hew to the literal sense when interpreting the OT, the former granting wide latitude for allegorical READINGS, the latter insisting on a more limited typological approach. Yet both schools treated literal and spiritual senses as interlocking parts of a theologically interested and christologically centered approach to the canon.

The hermeneutical priority of the literal sense was affirmed by both medieval and Reformation theologians, albeit in different ways. Thomas Aquinas (1225–1274) held that all spiritual interpretation depended on the literal sense intended by the human author, from which alone theological argument could be drawn. But Thomas also held that because God is the ultimate author of scripture, the authorial intention that determines the literal sense of scripture extends beyond the human author's reference to things and encompasses whatever God wishes to signify by the things themselves (*Summa Theologiae* 1a. q. 10). Reformers such as Luther and, even more, Calvin deemphasized the traditional spiritual senses altogether, but they did so in keeping with their conviction that the literal sense of scripture was itself the sufficient, ordinary medium of the Spirit's witness, even in the case of the OT. (For the implications for OT interpretation, see James S. Preus, *From Shadow to Promise: Old Testament Interpretation from Augustine to the Young Luther* [Cambridge: Harvard University Press, 1969]). When scripture is properly heard as witness to God's Word, the literal sense *is* the spiritual sense.

Throughout the modern period, the appeal to the literal sense of scripture has frequently embodied an emancipatory impulse that seeks to free the Bible from the overlay of ecclesial interpretation and control. Eighteenth-century biblical critics defined the literal sense as the *sensus literalis historicus*, the sense intended by the original human author in historical context. As BIBLICAL CRITICISM matured, enormous exegetical energy and acumen was channeled into determining the original sense of scripture by illuminating the biblical text's literary origins and historical horizons. The results were impressive but contributed to an awareness of the vast gulfs of time that separated biblical writers from the modern reader. Meanwhile, the theological meaning of scripture was regarded as a problem to be addressed by a separate discipline after biblical critics had established the literal, i.e., original historical, sense.

In recent decades, the modern identification of the literal sense with the original historical sense has been challenged from numerous, often conflicting, perspectives. Some have argued that the literal sense of the Bible can be determined only by the interpreter who enters directly and personally into a consideration of the subject matter that the biblical writers address (see *SACHEXEGESE*). Others have argued that the literal sense of scripture is determined by its present placement in the canon, with the result that literal sense may exceed or contravene the original intention of its authors (see CANONICAL CRITICISM). Still others have suggested that the very notion of "literal sense " is problematic because textual meaning is inherently unstable and indeterminate (see POSTMODERN BIBLICAL INTERPRETATION, READER-RESPONSE CRITICISM, INTERTEXTUALITY).

At present, one can distinguish three main approaches to "the literal sense" of the Bible, depending on whether the emphasis is placed on the text's origin (the world behind the text), its content or subject matter (the world of the text), or its present use (the world in front of the text). Understood in terms of origin, the literal sense is the sense that the author intended. Understood in terms of content, it is the sense communicated by the words taken as a sufficient testimony to their own subject matter. Understood in terms of use, it is whatever sense is assigned interpretive priority by the community that reads it and that exercises a critical role over against further possible interpretations (Tanner). Arguably, an adequate understanding of the literal sense requires that some attention be given to all three of these dimensions.

See Brevard S. Childs, "The *Sensus Literalis* of Scripture: An Ancient and Modern Problem," in Herbert Donner et al., eds., *Beiträge zur Alttestamentlichen Theologie* (Göttingen: Vandenhoeck & Ruprecht, 1977), 80–93; Kathryn E. Tanner, "Theology and the Plain Sense," in Garrett Green, ed., *Scriptural Authority and Narrative Interpretation* (Philadelphia: Fortress Press, 1987). Also see *PESHAT; SENSUS PLENIOR*.

Literary Criticism has at least three quite different definitions according to its 19th-cent., early-and-mid-20th-cent., and contemporary usages. All three remain in use today, making literary criticism one of the most potentially ambiguous terms in the field of biblical studies. (1) Originally, it referred to a particular approach to the historical study of scripture that appeared in systematic form in the 19th cent. and that is now more familiarly known and practiced as SOURCE CRITICISM. (2) In the early and mid 20th cent., literary criticism began to be used to refer to attempts to explicate a biblical author's intention and achievements through a detailed analysis of the text's rhetorical elements and literary structure. (3) In contemporary usage, it often refers quite broadly to any attempt to understand biblical literature in a manner that parallels the interests and theories of modern literary critics and theorists generally, such as those of I. A. Richards, T. S. Eliot, N. Frye, J. Derrida, M. M. Bakhtin, et al. Definition no. 1 falls under the rubric of HISTORICAL CRITICISM; definition no. 3 denotes an approach to scripture that is often ahistorical in interests and method; and definition no. 2 falls somewhere in between.

During the last half of the 20th cent., a veritable host of diverse approaches to the text have appeared, all of which, with varying degree of appropriateness, are commonly placed within the category of literary criticism under definition no. 3 above. Many of these approaches are discussed separately, such as STRUCTURALISM, NARRATIVE CRITICISM, DECONSTRUCTION, RECEPTION THEORY, and READER-RESPONSE CRITICISM. See also INTERTEXTUALITY.

Litotes. See **Meiosis.**

Little Apocalypse. See **Apocalypse, The; The Little Apocalypse.**

Living Bible (Paraphrased), The; New Living Translation, The. LB(P), with or without the parentheses, is a common abbreviation for *The Living Bible, Paraphrased* (Wheaton, Ill.: Tyndale House, 1971), and *The Living New Testament, Paraphrased* (Tyndale House, 1967) by Kenneth N. Taylor. The *LBP* is fundamentally a PARAPHRASE of the KING JAMES VERSION and the AMERICAN STANDARD VERSION of 1901, with only a limited indebtedness to the original languages. The *LBP* is not a standard translation approved by an authorized committee of scholars and churchmen (such as KJV, ASV, RSV/NRSV, NEB/REB, etc.) but an interpretive translation by an individual. Its working principle is that "when the Greek is not clear, then the theology of the translator is his guide . . ." ("Preface," *LNT*[*P*], 1967). Regrettably, interpretations often occur without notation. Elsewhere the *LBP* provides a footnote explaining the literal meaning of the text or suggesting that the new reading is implied. Involved may be historical assumptions (e.g., Luke 23:5, 14; John 13:23–26; 1 Pet 5:1; 1 John 5:6–8) or theological ones (e. g., Luke 4:19; 17:26; Mark 10:12; Heb 5:7; Gal 1:6; Rom 3:21–26; Rev 1:1).

The theological point of view of the *LBP* is explicitly conservative. In the NT, for example, this means that the divine nature of Jesus is introduced or heightened at points or in ways not found in the Greek text (e.g., Mark 1:2; 2:10; 8:38; Matt 9:13; John 8:59; 2 Tim 2:8); that the Holy Spirit in the sense of a person of the Trinity appears where no such reference exists in the Greek (e.g., John 4:21–23; Luke 24:49; Rom 8:4; Rev 1:4; 4:5); that the concept of "scripture" is expanded to include either the OT or the Bible as a whole when neither existed at that time in the modern sense of those terms (e.g., Matt 5:17; 13:52; Luke 24:27; 2 Tim 3:16); and that the return of CHRIST (e.g., Luke 17:26, 30), the role of Satan (e.g., Luke 8:27ff.; 11:15; 1 John 5:18–19), and salvation as "going to heaven" (e.g., Rom 1:16; 3:21) are all introduced into the paraphrase or otherwise emphasized in a manner not found in the text itself. In short, the *LBP* often reads not as the original texts but as a 20th-cent. conservative theologian wishes they had. Among linguists this type of translation (or paraphrase) is called a "cultural translation" because it introduces cultural ideas that are either absent in or foreign to the culture of the text.

The New Living Translation (*NLT*; Wheaton, Ill.: Tyndale House Publishers, 1996), is a reworking of the *LBP* by ninety conservative scholars "who began their work by carefully comparing the text of *The Living Bible* with the original Greek and Hebrew texts" (Jacket). The *NLT* refers to itself as a translation, not a paraphrase. The resulting differences with the *LBP* are notable and laudatory. The *NLT* achieves a more consistent literary style than its predecessor with notably less theological intrusion into the wording of the text. It often chooses to translate biblical METAPHORS, giving the text a clarity not found in NIV or NRSV. Nevertheless, the committee's express intent "to translate terms shrouded in history or culture in ways that can be immediately understood by the contemporary reader" makes the *NLT* unsuitable for scholarly use despite its evident popularity. The window that the original texts provide on the life and mind of the biblical writers has been painted with a silverizing brush, turning the text into a mirror of contemporary evangelical thought. For these reasons, the *LBP* and the *NLT* serve the student of scripture poorly and should always be used in conjunction with one or more of the standard translations (RSV/NRSV, NIV).

Lives of Jesus Research (trans. of Ger: *Leben-Jesu Forschung*). See **Quest of the Historical Jesus.**

Locus (pl.: loci; Lat: place; cf. Gk: *Topos;* pl.: *Topoi:* place[s]). The term *loci* in its Greek form (see *Topos, Topoi*) has a special meaning and function in rhetorical/literary studies and is discussed separately. The Latin term *loci* is primarily of historical interest, though in substance significant to EXEGESIS.

The concept of *loci* (or *Topoi*) is derived from the notion that the mind is analogous to a spatial entity in which individual thoughts are separately located and preexistent, ready at hand for use. This follows Plato's understanding of knowledge in which ideas are not created but remembered (anamnesis). Thoughts hidden in their various *loci* within the mind are called to remembrance through appropriate questions, as in the Socratic method.

According to Lausberg (pars. 40–41), the questions have been encapsulated since the 12th cent. in the following hexameter: *quis, quid, ubi, quibus auxiliis, cur, quomodo, quando?* The questions, their corresponding *loci*, and their translations are as follows:

Although the Latin terms and the theory behind them are no longer in use, the questions themselves are still a part of an exegetical approach to a text, whether that approach be historical or rhetorical.

Locus classicus (Lat: classical source or place) is the academician's jargon for that passage of scripture or literature generally most frequently cited as the best illustration or explanation of a subject; Rom 3:21–26 is the *locus classicus* of Paul's understanding of justification by faith; Eccles 3:1–9 of the Hellenized Jew's pessimistic view of history.

Logion (pl.: logia; Gk: a saying). In its singular form, logion means "a saying" and in its technical sense is almost always used in reference to an utterance of Jesus characterized by brevity and succinctness in contrast to longer SAYINGS such as PARABLES or DISCOURSES (as in John's GOSPEL). A "floating" or "migrant" logion is one that appears in a variety of settings in the Gospel tradition, due either to its location within the ORAL TRADITION or to the judgment of the Gospel writer. Two such "floating logia" are "He who has ears to hear, let him hear" (Mark 4:9, 23; Matt 11:15; 13:9) and "The first shall be last and the last first" (Matt 19:30; 20:1).

In its plural form (logia), the term usually refers to a hypothetical collection of sayings antedating the Gospels. According to Papias (ca. 60–130 C.E.), Matt compiled

a.	*quis*	= *locus a persona*	—Who?
b.	*quid*	= *locus a re*	—What?
c.	*ubi*	= *locus a loco*	—Where?
d.	*quibus auxiliis*	= *locus ab instrumento*	—By what means?
e.	*cur*	= *locus a causa*	—Why?
f.	*quomodo*	= *locus a modo*	—How?
g.	*quando*	= *locus a tempore*	—When?

the logia of Jesus in Hebrew, but their precise identity has not been established. According to some scholars, the reference is to Q (*Quelle:* source), a collection of sayings and additional materials found in both Matt and Luke. The *Gospel of Thomas*, which is not a gospel at all in the literary sense, is a good example of logia, though of highly disputed authenticity; fragments of this gospel were found at Oxyrhynchus, Egypt, in 1897 and 1904 and were sometimes referred to subsequently as "the *Logia* of Jesus." See FORM CRITICISM.

Loisy, Alfred (1857–1940). French Roman Catholic theologian and biblical critic, excommunicated in 1908 for his views on BIBLICAL CRITICISM; called the father of the modernist movement in Roman Catholicism. For an overview and bibliography, see *DBI*.

LORD. See J (YAHWIST); KYRIOS; TETRAGRAMMATON; TETRATEUCH.

Lower Criticism is an unhappy term, now of infrequent parlance, characterizing TEXTUAL CRITICISM in contrast to so-called "higher" criticism, i.e., all other forms of BIBLICAL CRITICISM. The term is falling into disuse because of its pejorative sound coupled with the increasing acknowledgment that textual criticism is both important and complex.

Lucianic Text. See **Byzantine Text.**

Luke's Great Omission refers to Luke's apparent disuse of Mark 6:45 (53)–Mark 8: (21)26, which is to be explained either by (a) the *URMARKUS* hypothesis, which states that the original form of the GOSPEL used by Luke lacked this section, or by (b) assuming the mutilation of Luke's copy of Mark, or by (c) Luke's intentional disuse of this material because of parallel materials, or by (d) Mark's being a RECENSION of Luke. Of these (c) is most widely accepted.

LXX (Seventy). See **Septuagint.**

"M" is the symbol created by B. H. STREETER (1924) to designate material peculiar to Matt's GOSPEL alone, including the

PARABLES of the laborers in the vineyard (20:1–16), the hidden treasure and the pearl of great price (13:44–46), but excluding the infancy NARRATIVES (chs. 1–2). According to Streeter, it was composed in Jerusalem around 60 C.E. from traditions preserved by Jewish Christians associated with James the brother of Jesus. See FOUR DOCUMENT HYPOTHESIS; "L"; SYNOPTIC PROBLEM.

Magnificat is the traditional name of Mary's song of praise recorded in Luke 1:46–55, from the opening word of the Latin text: "*Magnificat anima mea Dominum*" ("My soul magnifies the Lord"). Also called the "Song of Mary." The language of the HYMN is styled after the Greek OT and hence offers one of the best examples of "SEPTUAGINTISM" in the NT. See *BENEDICTUS; NUNC DIMITTIS.*

Major Prophets is a designation based purely on length for the books of Isaiah, Jeremiah, and Ezekiel, as distinct from the shorter and therefore "Minor" PROPHETS, which are Hosea, Joel, Amos, Obadiah, Jonah, Micah, Nahum, Habakkuk, Zephaniah, Haggai, Zechariah, and Malachi. The terms have nothing to do with the significance of the writings themselves.

Makarism (or *Makarismos*) is a TRANSLITERATION of the Greek word meaning "blessing" (cf. Rom 4:6, 9; Gal 4:15). It is sometimes used in form-critical studies as a technical term to denote sayings of this type. See BLESSINGS.

Manual of Discipline is the name of one of the most important of the documents known as the DEAD SEA SCROLLS; it contains the rules by which the Essene community of KHIRBET QUMRAN lived and a treatise about the community's theological beliefs. See James A. Charlesworth et al., eds., *The Dead Sea Scrolls: Rule of Community* (Philadelphia: American Interfaith Institute, 1996).

Märchen (Ger: fairy TALE, folktale, legendary fiction). A literary genre within folk literature first studied as such principally by Wilhelm (1786–1859) and Jacob

(1785–1863) Grimm (Germany) and Hans Christian Andersen (1805–1875, Denmark). In German OT FORM CRITICISM, the term is generally retained for those stories not identified with any specific person, place, or time; HERMANN GUNKEL included Jonah, for example, in this category. According to some scholars, the term is best translated "folk tale," as it now appears in the English translation of his classic 1917 study *The Folktale in the Old Testament* (Sheffield: Sheffield Academic Press, 1987). However, no complete uniformity of definition or translation exists. See LEGEND; MYTH.

Marcion   (ca. 85–160 C.E.). Though celebrated as "the first Protestant" by Adolf von Harnack for his radical interpretation of the Pauline distinction between LAW and GOSPEL, Marcion was the most formidable heretic of the 2nd cent. and the spiritual father of a perennial danger for Christian theology. Marcion dismissed the God of the OT as a vengeful demiurge and proclaimed Jesus to be the noncarnate manifestation of the true, transcendent, and hitherto unknown God. Marcion's rejection of the OT and the formation of his own CANON of scripture, made up of an abbreviated Gospel of Luke (called the *Gospel of Marcion*) and ten edited LETTERS of Paul (called the *Apostolikon)*, contributed both to his expulsion from the church of Rome in 144 C.E. and to the formation of a canon within orthodox Christianity (von Campenhausen). Marcion's gospel and *Apostolikon* are important for source and TEXTUAL CRITICISM. See Adolf von Harnack, *Marcion: The Gospel of the Alien God* (Durham: Labyrinth Press, Ger: 1921; ET: 1990); John Knox, *Marcion and the New Testament* (Chicago: University of Chicago Press, 1942); and R. J. Hoffman, *Marcion: On the Restitution of Christianity* (Chico, Calif.: Scholars Press, 1984).

Mari Tablets,   some 20,000 in number, were found in the palace archives of Zimri-Lin (ca. 1730–1700 B.C.E.) at Tell el-Hariri, the ancient dynastic city of Mari situated on the Middle Euphrates in Mesopotamia. The tell (or "mound") was excavated by

the French archaeologist André Parrot between 1933 and 1955. The tablets, which are written in Akkadian, contain contracts, diplomatic correspondence, inventories, lists of male and female workers, private LETTERS, etc. They are of significant value in reconstructing the Amorite (Northwest Semitic) culture during the early centuries of the 2nd millennium B.C.E., the period of the biblical patriarchs as recorded in Genesis. For the original texts and French translation, see *Archives royales de Man*, vols. 1–19 (Paris: Imprimerie Nationale, 1950–79); for a few texts in English, see *ANET*. The legacy of the Mari Tablets discovery is discussed in *Biblical Archaeologist* 47/2 (1984).

Mashal   is a Hebrew word denoting a wide category of linguistic forms, such as taunt (Isa 14:4), riddle (Ps 49:4), ALLEGORY (Ezek 17:2–3), byword (Deut 28:37), dirge (Mic 2:4), etc. In each case, the Greek VERSION of the OT (the SEPTUAGINT) translates *mashal* with *parable*. See PARABLE.

Masoretic Text   (abbrev.: MT) refers to the received text of the Hebrew OT as annotated for punctuation (with accents) and vocalization (with "points") by the Masoretes (or Masorites), the authoritative teachers of scriptural tradition (Heb: *Masorah*).

By 500 C.E, two schools of Masoretes had emerged, one in the West (Palestine/Tiberias), the other in the East (Babylonia/Sura). The consonantal text (without vowel points) was preserved from emendation by Masoretic notations in the margin (*Masora marginalis*) and at the end of books or at the end of the whole OT (*Masora finalis*). Marginal notes written at the side of the text are called *Masora parva* (Mp), while those at the top and bottom are called *Masora magna* (Mm). The rules governing the consonantal text were laid out in two tractates, *Seper Torah* and *Soperim*. It was not until the 9th and 10th centuries that the vocalization of the Hebrew text practiced in the West by the leading Masoretic families of ben Asher and ben Naphtali became dominant. In the 14th cent. these two traditions were joined to form a kind of mixed text, called the TEXTUS RECEPTUS or "received text," on which the first two editions of the *Biblia Hebraica* were based. Subsequent editions follow the ben Asher text of the Leningrad CODEX B 19[A] (*siglum* L), which dates from the first quarter of the 11th cent. An earlier but incomplete ben Asher text, the Aleppo Codex (A) is the basis for the edition being prepared by the Hebrew University Bible Project. See KITTEL, RUDOLF; TEXTUAL CRITICISM; SEPTUAGINT.

Megillah   (pl.: *Megilloth*; Heb: Scroll) in Jewish tradition usually refers to the book of Esther, but applies as well to the *Megilloth* (or *Megillahs*) also called the Five Scrolls, including, with Esther, the Song of Songs, Ruth, Lamentations, and Ecclesiastes.

Meiosis   (Gk: a lessening). In RHETORIC, *meiosis* refers to understatement, of which litotes (a positive affirmation by the negation of an antonym or contrary expression) is a common type, e.g., "For Christ did not please himself" (Rom 15:3a), or "For I am not ashamed of the gospel" (Rom 1:16a). Thus, litotes is a form of periphrasis, usually for emphasis. Cf. 2 Cor 11:21. See DIATRIBE; IRONY.

Messiah.   See Christ.

Messianic Prophecies   Passages in the OT that speak of a future bearer of salvation and traditionally interpreted by Christians as referring to JESUS CHRIST, the Messianic King, include Gen 49:9–10; Num 24:17ff.; Isa 7:14; 9:1–6; 11:1–5; Mic 5:1ff.; Jer 23:4; Ezek 17:22–23; 34:23–24; Zech 9:9–10; Pss 2; 72; 110. For a contemporary sifting of the difficulties and possibilities inherent in this tradition, see Paul M. van Buren, *According to the Scriptures: The Origin of the Gospel and the Church's Old Testament* (Grand Rapids: Eerdmans, 1998). See also Fredrick Carlson Holmgren, *The Old Testament and the Significance of Jesus: Embracing Change— Maintaining Christian Identity: The Emerging Center in Biblical Scholarship* (Grand Rapids: Eerdmans, 1999). See CHRIST.

Messianic Secret   refers to a discernible phenomenon in the GOSPELS, most especially in the Gospel of Mark, in which Jesus explicitly conceals his messianic character and power until the closing period of his ministry. The term *messianic secret* entered NT criticism with the epoch-making work of WILLIAM WREDE (*Das Messiasgeheimnis in den Evangelien: Zugleich ein Beitrag zum Verständnis des Markusevangeliums* [Göttingen: Vandenhoeck & Ruprecht, 1901]; Eng: *The Messianic Secret*, trans. J. C. G. Grieg [London: James Clarke, 1971]). Wrede argued that the messianic secret, as it is found in Mark, is a product of Mark's own interpretive editing of traditional materials and therefore belongs to the history of theology and not to the life of Jesus. Key passages in Mark are (a) the demons' recognition of the Messiah (1:23–25, 34; 3:11–12; 5:2–19; 9:20) and (b) injunctions and acts designed to keep Jesus' messiahship secret: (1) injunctions addressed to demons in cases involving exorcism (1:25, 34; 3:12); (2) injunctions following other miracles (1:43–45; 5:43; 7:36; 8:26); (3) injunctions following Peter's confession (8:30; 9:9); (4) intentional acts to preserve Jesus' incognito (7:24; 9:30–31); and (5) prohibitions by others (10:47–48). Wrede further argued that, according to Mark's theory of the messianic secret, Jesus' PARABLES were purposely obscure in order to keep the messianic secret from all but the disciples (4:10–13, 33–34), who nevertheless did not readily comprehend who Jesus was, some not believing in spite of his resurrection from the dead. See QUEST OF THE HISTORICAL JESUS; SCHWEITZER.

Metalanguage   (adj.: metalingual or metalinguistic) refers to language devised in order to describe language itself. Terms such as sentence, clause, distich, anaphora, and pronoun are metalinguistic, as also are theories about language, e.g., STRUCTURALISM.

Metanarrative   (Fr: *grand récit*) is a NARRATIVE that grounds or legitimates a way of life, its social institutions, and corresponding forms of knowledge. Jean-François Lyotard, French philosopher and theorist of postmodernism, gave currency to the term in a now famous definition of the postmodern. "Simplifying to the extreme, I define postmodern as incredulity toward metanarratives. . . . The narrative function is losing its functors, its great hero, its great dangers, its great voyages, its great goal. It is being dispersed in clouds of narrative language elements—narrative, but also denotative, prescriptive, descriptive, and so on. . . . Each of us lives at the intersection of many of these. However, we do not necessarily establish stable language combinations, and the properties of the ones we do establish are not necessarily communicable" (Lyotard, *The Postmodern Condition: A Report on Knowledge,* trans. Geoff Bennington and Brian Massumi [Minneapolis: University of Minneapolis Press, 1984]. The deliberate subversion of prominent metanarratives in favor of localized and heterogenous "little narratives" is supposed to be a prominent aim of postmodernism; whether "postmodernism" itself is not at present one such prominent metanarrative ripe for subversion is an open question. In any case, some biblical scholars have pointed out that the Bible's frequently iconoclastic narratives are at least as prone to subvert legitimating systems as to support them. See Walter Brueggemann, *Theology of the Old Testament: Testimony, Dispute, Advocacy* (Minneapolis: Fortress Press, 1997); Regina M. Schwartz, "Adultery in the House of David: The Metanarrative of Biblical Scholarship and the Narratives of the Bible," in SEMEIA 54:36–55 (Atlanta: Scholars Press, 1991). See DECONSTRUCTION; POSTMODERN BIBLICAL INTERPRETATION.

Metaphor (Gk: transfer). A figure of speech in which a word or phrase literally denoting one kind of object is used in place of another in order to suggest comparison between them: "God is *light* and in him is no *darkness* at all." (1 John 1:5b). Following I. A. Richards, it is customary to distinguish between a metaphor's *vehicle* or image (light/darkness) and its *tenor* or theme (truth/falsehood, etc.) (see C. K. Ogden and I. A. Richards, *The Meaning of Meaning* [New York: Harcourt, Brace & Co., 1938; London: Routledge & Kegan Paul, 1949]). According to Janet Martin Soskice, "A metaphor has one true subject which tenor and vehicle conjointly depict and illumine" (*Metaphor and Religious Language* [New York: Clarendon Press, 1985], 47). One implication of this analysis is that metaphors are not mere ornaments for ideas that might just as well be expressed literally but communicate in ways that cannot be duplicated in nonmetaphorical terms.

Grammatically, a metaphor is defined as "a simile without 'like' or 'as.'" The rhetorical difference between a simile and a metaphor, however, lies partly in the fact that metaphors set no limits on how far the proposed comparison might be extended (Barbour). For example, "Be wise as serpents and innocent as doves" (Matt 10:16) is a simile. The qualities that "serpents" and "doves" connote are made explicit (wisdom and innocence) and thus limits are set to the comparison. The metaphor in John's GOSPEL "Here is the Lamb of God who takes away the sin of the world" (1:29) sets no such limits. It sets in motion a comparison between Jesus and a sacrificial lamb whose extension defies clear delimitation. Indeed, John's metaphor (in this case as elsewhere in the Gospel) ultimately puts in question the distinction between literal and figurative speech on which metaphors are thought to depend (see TYPOLOGY).

The fecundity of metaphorical speech is suggested by the variety of analyses it has inspired. In *Metaphor and Reality* (Bloomington, Ind.: Indiana University Press, 1962), Philip Wheelwright distinguishes two broad types of of metaphor, which he terms *epiphor* and *diaphor*. The former bears the usual understanding of metaphor as the transference of something relatively well known to something less well known though of greater importance (the sacrifice of lambs//the sacrifice of CHRIST). The diaphoric metaphor refers to a semantic movement (*phora*) through (*dia*) ordinary experience that produces "new meaning by juxtaposition." These two types of metaphor can be seen in the Song of Songs, diaphoric metaphor particularly in 4:1–7; 5:10–16; 6:4–7; and 7:2–8 (see R. N. Soulen, "The Waṣfs of the Song of Songs and Hermeneutic," *JBL* 86 [1967]: 183–190).

More recently, many theologians and biblical interpreters have argued that metaphor provides the key for a general theory of religious language. According to this view, which appears in many variations, all religious language is essentially metaphorical in character, because it seeks to illumine the less well known (God) by terms drawn from the known (the world) (cf. Sallie McFague, *Metaphorical Theology: Models of God in Religious Language* [Philadelphia: Fortress Press, 1982]). One weakness of this theory as applied to the Bible is that it effaces differences among the varieties of biblical genres (e.g., NARRATIVE, LAW code, LAMENT, geneaology, LEGEND, ORACLE, song, epistle, etc.). All of these genres are integral to the Bible's witness to God, but many of them communicate in ways other than metaphor. For a classic proposal suggesting that realistic narrative rather than metaphor is the central genre for Christian HERMENEUTICS, see HANS W. FREI, *The Identity of Jesus Christ: the Hermeneutical Bases of Dogmatic Theology* (Philadelphia: Fortress Press, 1975).

In addition, see Paul Ricoeur, *The Rule of Metaphor: Multi-Disciplinary Studies of the Creation of Meaning in Language*, trans. Robert Czerny et al. (Toronto: University of Toronto Press, 1977); Ian G. Barbour, *Myths, Models, and Paradigms: A Comparative Study in Science and Religion* (New York: Harper & Row, 1974); and Garrett Green, *Imagining God: Theology and the Religious Imagination* (San Francisco: Harper & Row, 1989).

Metaphrase.   See **Paraphrase.**

Meter   (fr. Lat: to measure) refers to any specific form of poetic rhythm (OED). The modern analysis of meter in early Hebrew poetry extends back two centuries and remains an issue of scholarly debate because (a) the current vocalization of the Hebrew text dates only from the early Mid-

dle Ages, and (b) the exact reading of the original consonantal Hebrew text is a matter of conjecture.

According to Douglas K. Stuart, four schools of thought concerning meter in early Hebrew poetry are discernible. The schools and their principal exponents are:

1. *The Traditional School:* J. Ley, *Die metrischen Formen der hebräischen Poesie* (Leipzig: B. G. Tuebner, 1886); K. Budde, "Das Hebräische Klagelied," *ZAW* 2 (1882): 1–52; and E. Sievers, *Metrische Studien I & II* (Leipzig: B. G. Tuebner, 1901, 1904). The Traditional School argued that Hebrew meter is accentual rather than syllabic or quantitative, and that units of stress (called feet) may vary in content from one to six syllables. Most Hebrew poetry was observed to be written in two or three parallel lines (BICOLON/TRICOLON), the cola being either of equal (2 + 2; 3 + 3; 4 + 4, etc.) or unequal (2 + 3; 3 + 2; 3 + 4; 4 + 3; etc.) length, e.g., Ps 29 = 2 + 2; Job, Proverbs, and most PSALMS = 3 + 3.

2. *The Semantic PARALLELISM School:* Robert Lowth, *The Sacred Poetry of the Hebrews* (Lat: Oxford: Clarendon Press, 1753; Eng: 1787; reprint: N.Y.: Garland Press, 1971); G. B. Gray, *The Forms of Hebrew Poetry* (London/ New York: Hodder & Stoughton, 1915; reprint: KTAV, 1972); and T. H. Robinson, *The Poetry of the Old Testament* (London: Gerald Duckworth & Co., 1947). The Semantic Parallelism School suggested that the determining factor in Hebrew meter is to be found in the PARALLELISM of semantic units rather than in phonetic phenomena. The counter argument is that semantic parallelism is an element of style and not of meter.

3. *The Alternating Meter School:* S. MOWINCKEL, "Zum Problem der hebräischen Metrik," *Festschrift Alfred Bertholet* (Tübingen: J. C. B. Mohr [Paul Siebeck], 1950), 379–94; and S. Siegert, "Problems of Hebrew Prosody," *SVT* 7 (1960): 283–91. The Alternating Meter School, though not uniform, sees Hebrew poetry as characterized by a regular interchange of toned and untoned syllables, the basic Hebrew foot being iambic, occasionally trochaic. In most instances, Alternate Meter theorists

relied on the vocalization of the Masoretic Text.

4. *The Syllabic School:* P. Haupt, essays in *AJSL* 19 (1903): 129–42; 20 (1904): 149–72; 26 (1910): 201–52; *Biblische Liebeslieder* (Baltimore: Johns Hopkins Press, 1907); W. F. Albright, *Yhwh and the Gods of Canaan* (Garden City: Doubleday, 1968; note bibliography). Though closely related to the Traditional School, the Syllabic School bases its approach on a syllabic scansion of the text and is not dependent on Masoretic vocalization. This method is relatively more exact, since it identifies cola (see Colon) according to precise numbers of syllables (four to thirteen or more) rather than simply noting them to be short (2 stresses) or long (4 or 5 stresses).

For an overview of these schools and an elaboration and defense of the last, see Douglas K. Stuart, *Studies in Early Hebrew Meter* (Missoula, Mont.: Scholars Press, 1976). James L. Kugel critiques metric theories in *The Idea of Biblical Poetry: Parallelism and Its History* (New Haven, Conn.: Yale University Press, 1981); metric interpretation is defended by W. G. E. Watson, *Classical Hebrew Poetry: A Guide to Its Techniques* (Sheffield: Sheffield Academic Press, 1984). See QINAH METER.

Metonymy is a figure of speech in which a word is substituted for the thing it is intended to suggest. APOCALYPTIC literature makes frequent use of metonymy and its close parallel, SYNECDOCHE, as do the PROPHETS, PSALMS, and WISDOM LITERATURE. In the book of Revelation, terms such as "head" or "crown" are pseudocryptic substitutes for Caesar (Rev 13:3); similarly the use of Mt. Zion for Jerusalem, heaven for God, and the bottomless pit for hell, or saying that one is reading Job or Mark or Paul instead of saying "the book of . . . ," are all examples of metonymy. See TROPE.

Midrash (pl. midrashim; fr. Heb: *darash:* to search, inquire). Midrash is the rabbinic term for the exegesis or interpretation of scripture. It may refer to a particular instance of scriptural interpretation,

or, more precisely, to a literary work of scriptural commentary. (See, e.g., 2 Chr 24:27 and 13:22 in the Jerusalem Bible; cf. RSV.) A midrash may be either halakic (legal, procedural) or haggadic (nonlegal, illustrative, etc.) in content; exegetical, homiletical, or narrative in form.

However, it is always commentary on scripture, i.e., on a fixed text regarded by the interpreter as the revealed word of God. The dating and more precise definition of midrashim are debated. Some employ the term broadly to include early Jewish exegesis of scripture from the postexilic period onward, thereby allowing for the possibility of midrashic activity in the HB itself (e.g., Chronicles). Others reserve the term for the exegesis of scripture produced by and characteristic of rabbinic Judaism. Examples of midrashim in the broader sense include the midrash of the *Passover Haggadah* (see the *Encyclopaedia Judaica*, ad loc.), the several "pesharim" or commentaries in the Dead Sea Scrolls, the Wisdom of Solomon (chs. 11–19), 1 Cor 10, and perhaps John 6. See HALAKAH; HILLEL.

Minor Prophets. See **Major Prophets.**

Minuscule denotes a MS written in small cursive or "running" letters, first used for codices of the Bible ca. 800 C.E. The style predominated after the 10th cent. and now constitutes more than nine-tenths of all known MSS. The earliest dated MS of the NT is a minuscule bearing the year 835 C.E. The most important minuscules are the Lake group, known also as FAMILY 1 (*siglum:* λ) and the Ferrar Group, known also as Family 13 (*siglum:* φ). Minuscules are designated by arabic numerals without a preceding zero, e.g., 1, 118, 131, 209, etc., extending at present to ca. 2860 for the NT. See LECTIONARY; PAPYRUS MANUSCRIPTS; TEXTUAL CRITICISM.

Miracle Story. See **Aretalogy.**

Mishnah (fr. Heb: *shanah:* to repeat, i.e., to learn). An authoritative collection of mostly halakic (legal and procedural) material developed within the oral traditions of pharisaic and rabbinic Judaism, and arranged and revised by Judah ha-Nasi in the first decades of the 3rd cent. The Mishnah provides the foundation for and the structure of the Talmud. It is divided into six orders (or *sedarim*) containing a total of sixty-three tractates: (1) *Zeraᶜim* (seeds), (2) *Moᵓed* (set feasts), (3) *Našim* (women), (4) *Neziqin* (damages), (5) *Qodašim* (holy things), and (6) *Ṭeharot* (cleannesses). Its form, content, and organization represent a significant departure from earlier and contemporary Jewish literature, but scholarship is not yet agreed on the meaning of its difference. "One may say that just as the New Testament is represented by Christianity as the conception and fulfillment of the Old Testament, so the Mishnah is understood by Rabbinic Judaism as the other half of *Tanakh*" (Neusner). See *The Literature of the Sages*, ed. Shmuel Safrai (CRINT; Philadelphia: Fortress Press, 1987). See TALMUD; *HALAKAH*; MIDRASH.

Monograph (Gk: a single writing). A scholarly, documented study of a specific and limited subject, in contradistinction to a general introduction, COMMENTARY, collection of essays, etc.; for an example of a monograph see Patrick D. Miller, *They Cried to the Lord: The Form and Theology of Biblical Prayer* (Minneapolis: Fortress Press, 1994). See COMMENTARY; EXEGESIS; *FESTSCHRIFT*.

Morpheme (Fr: form + *-eme*: unit, thing). One of the two basic units of linguistic description (with PHONEME), morphemes can be loosely defined as "the smallest meaningful units in the STRUCTURE of a language" (Gleason). Prefixes (a-, bi-, in-, etc.) and suffixes (-ed, -ly, -tion, etc.) as well as freestanding words (year, love, etc.) are all morphemes, because they are indivisible units of meaning, indispensable to the sense of the utterance of which they are a part. (See H. A. Gleason, Jr., *An Introduction to Descriptive Linguistics* [New

York/London: Holt, Rinehart & Winston, 1955, 1961²].) See STRUCTURALISM.

Morphology   is the descriptive analysis of words; it is the study of MORPHEMES and their arrangements in forming words (Nida). The combination of words into phrases and sentences is treated under SYNTAX, but in some languages, word STRUCTURE and phrase structure are almost impossible to distinguish. See Eugene Nida, *Morphology* (Ann Arbor: University of Michigan Press, 1949²).

Mowinckel, Sigmund Olaf Plytt (1884–1965). Born in Kjerringy, Norway, Mowinckel was from 1917 professor of OT in Oslo. Though he wrote on subjects ranging over the whole OT and its environment, he is especially noted for his studies of the PSALMS and the PROPHETS. Influenced by the form-critical studies of HERMANN GUNKEL and by the cult-centered studies of Wilhelm Grønbeck and JOHANNES PEDERSEN, Mowinckel combined both perspectives in his work on the cultic origin and setting of the Psalms and prophetic preaching. (See *The Psalms in Israel's Worship* [Nashville: Abingdon Press, 1962; Oxford: Basil Blackwell, 1963]; *Prophecy and Tradition* [Oslo: I kommisjon hos J. Dybwad, 1946]; also *He that Cometh* [Nashville: Abingdon Press, 1956; Oxford: Basil Blackwell, 1956].) See *KULTGESCHICHTLICHE SCHULE*; MYTH; TRADITION CRITICISM.

MT.   Abbreviation for Masoretic Text.

Mujerista Biblical Interpretation (fr. Span: *mujer*: woman) "has as its goal the survival—the liberation—of Hispanic women." Biblical "interpretation, appropriation, and usage" are thus seen as "tools" in the "struggle for survival" (Isasi-Díaz).

The BIBLE has not often played a central role in the traditional faith development and expression of most Hispanic *mestizo* Christians, in part because of certain traditional features of their Roman Catholic heritage. Bible study and biblical-centered devotion have been looked on as quite secondary to the immediacy and intimacy of private devotion and corporate worship. It is the American religious cultural milieu, and especially the rapid growth of Hispanic participation in Protestant and evangelical churches, that has brought the Bible into an unaccustomed prominence and has given rise to mujerista biblical interpretation. In particular, it is Hispanic women's (or Latinas') experience and particularly their struggle for survival that have provided the impetus and language of theological expression, and it is this experience of struggle that has formed the need and the questions for interpreting and appropriating the Bible into daily life. A prominent practitioner of mujerista biblical interpretation declares that it "accepts the Bible as part of divine revelation and as authoritative only insofar as it contributes to Hispanic women's struggle for liberation" from oppression. It is a struggle looked on as "a matter of physical and cultural survival" (Isasi-Díaz).

See A. M. Isasi-Díaz, "La Palabra de Dios en Nosotros: The Word of God in Us," *Searching the Scriptures*, 2 vols., ed. Elisabeth Schüssler Fiorenza (New York: Crossroad, 1993); also her article "Mujerista Biblical Interpretation," in DICTIONARY OF BIBLICAL INTERPRETATION, ed. John H. Hays (Nashville: Abingdon Press, 1999).

Myth; Mythology In popular usage the term *myth* connotes something untrue, imaginative, or unbelievable; or, in older parlance, "a purely fictitious NARRATIVE usually involving supernatural persons, actions, or events" (OED). (Deferring to this usage and to the Christian religion, standard Western encyclopedias of mythology omit from their discussion any reference to the narratives of the Bible.)

However, in the realm of biblical studies and theology, just as in contemporary anthropology, philosophy, and literature, the term *myth* is often used in a less pejorative fashion to describe an important if provisional way of perceiving and expressing truth. There is, however, no agreed-on definition, whether in terms of its form

(that is, its relationship to fairy TALES, LEGENDS, tales, epics, etc.), or in terms of its content and function.

HERMANN GUNKEL defined *myth* as a story involving at least two gods and on this basis denied that the OT contains true myths but, at most, "faded out" myths or "mythic torsos" (e.g., Gen 6:1–4). SIGMUND MOWINCKEL identified myth with narrative belonging to a cult: myth tells in epic form the "salvation" reactualized and experienced in the cult. Israel "historicizes" myth by having the cult myth refer not to a "timeless time" distinct from historical time, as in Babylonian cult myths but to the history of Israel itself. History, not nature, is the subject of the cultus. Here YHWH is enthroned in power, is victorious over the gods of Babylonian and Canaanitic mythology (Leviathan, Baal, etc.), delivers Israel from bondage, leads it to the Promised Land, and so on (cf. Ps 44:2; 74:12–17; 89:10ff.; Job 26:12–13; 7:12, etc.). Myth is thus used to destroy myth; it becomes "iconoclastic, that is mythoclastic" (Wilder).

In NT criticism D. F. STRAUSS (1808–1874) traced the NT's reports of miracles not to deliberate fraud and chicanery (as Enlightenment foes of Christianity had charged) but to the mythic consciousness of the first Christians. The resulting furor ended his academic career and led to the de facto banishment of the term "myth" from NT studies for a hundred years. RUDOLF BULTMANN introduced it again in a prominent way in his program of DEMYTHOLOGIZATION. Bultmann defined myth as a way of speaking about the transcendent in terms of the immanent, the world beyond in terms of this world. He suggested that biblical myths need to be interpreted in terms of their understanding of existence if they are to be meaningful to contemporary humans. For example, hell is to be understood not as a place but as a human condition connoting separation from God.

The function of myth in individual and corporate life has been summarized by Ian G. Barbour: myths (1) order experience by providing a vision of the basic structure of reality, (2) inform humanity about itself, its identity, nature, and destiny, (3) express a saving power in human life, whether in the form of a redeemer, or a law, a ritual, or a discipline, (4) provide patterns for human actions, and (5) are enacted in ritual. (See Ian G. Barbour, *Myths, Models, and Paradigms* [London: SCM Press, 1974; New York: Harper & Row, 1974].)

The term *mythology* refers both to the study of myth and to the corpus of myths within a given religious tradition.

Myth and Ritual School. See **Kultgeschichtliche Schule.**

NAB. See **New American Bible.**

Nag Hammadi Codices (abbrev.: NHC; older abbrev.: CG: Cairensis Gnosticus). A collection of GNOSTIC and other writings dating from the 4th cent. C.E. reportedly discovered in 1945–46 in an ancient tomb-cave near the modern town of Nag Hammadi, located on the Nile some forty air miles northwest of Luxor in Upper Egypt. The extant inscribed pages number more than 1,100 and represent somewhat less than 90 percent of what originally was one tractate and twelve codices (bound volumes), of which one is quite fragmentary. Although some of the writings were previously known in whole or in part, the find provides primary documentation of Gnosticism in late antiquity and is therefore of great importance for understanding a strand of religious development that was divergent from and competitive with both orthodox Christianity and Judaism.

The Facsimile Edition of the NHC is published by E. J. Brill (Leiden), 1972ff., under the auspices of the Department of Antiquities of the Arab Republic of Egypt and UNESCO, James M. Robinson, Secretary to the Editorial Board. For a bibliography of texts, translations, and secondary literature, see David M. Scholer, *Nag Hammadi Bibliography 1948–1969* (Leiden: E. J. Brill, 1971), supplemented each year in *Novum Testamentum* (1971ff. [except for 1976]) and published separately by Brill, D. M. Scholer, ed., 1970–1994 (1997).

The texts with brief introductions are available in translation in *The Nag Hammadi Library in English*, ed. by James M. Robinson, 4th rev. ed. (Leiden: Brill, 1996). The collection includes related and previously known tractates of the gnostics known as PAPYRUS Berolinensis 8502. Each codex contains several tractates, the current (1996) standard numbering, titles, and abbreviations as follows. It should be noted that tractates bearing the same name may not be identical in content.

The codices and tractates are:

I,1	*Prayer of the Apostle Paul*	*Pr. Paul*
I,2	*Apocryphon of James*	*Ap. Jas.*
I,3	*Gospel of Truth*	*Gos. Truth*
I,4	*Treatise on the Resurrection*	*Treat. Res.*
I,5	*Tripartite Tractate*	*Tri. Trac.*
II,1	*Apocryphon of John*	*Ap. John*
II,2	*Gospel of Thomas*	*Gos. Thom.*
II,3	*Gospel of Philip*	*Gos. Phil.*
II,4	*Hypostasis of the Archons*	*Hyp. Arch.*
II,5	*On the Origin of the World*	*Orig. World*
II,6	*Exegesis on the Soul*	*Exeg. Soul*
II,7	*Book of Thomas the Contender*	*Thom. Cont.*
III,1	*Apocryphon of John*	*Ap. John*
III,2	*Gospel of the Egyptians*	*Gos. Eg.*
III,3	*Eugnostos the Blessed*	*Eugnostos*
III,4	*Sophia of Jesus Christ*	*Soph. Jes. Chr.*

III,5	Dialogue of the Savior	Dial. Sav.
IV,1	Apocryphon of John	Ap. John
IV,2	Gospel of the Egyptians	Gos. Eg.
V,1	Eugnostos the Blessed	Eugnostos
V,2	The Apocalypse of Paul	Apoc. Paul
V,3	(First) Apocalypse of James	1 Apoc. Jas.
V,4	(Second) Apocalypse of James	2 Apoc. Jas.
V,5	Apocalypse of Adam	Apoc. Adam
VI,1	Acts of Peter and the Twelve Apostles	Acts Pet. 12 Apos.
VI,2	Thunder: Perfect Mind	Thund.
VI,3	Authoritative Teaching	Auth. Teach.
VI,4	Concept of Our Great Power	Great Pow.
VI,5	Plato, Republic 588b–589b	Plato Rep.
VI,6	Discourse on the Eighth and Ninth	Disc. 8–9
VI,7	Prayer of Thanksgiving	Pr. Thanks.
VI,8	Asclepius 21–29	Asclepius
VII,1	Paraphrase of Shem	Paraph. Shem
VII,2	Second Treatise of the Great Seth	Treat. Seth
VII,3	Apocalypse of Peter	Apoc. Pet.
VII,4	Teachings of Silvanus	Teach. Silv.
VII,5	Three Steles of Seth	Steles Seth
VIII,1	Zostrianos	Zost.
VIII,2	The Letter of Peter to Philip	Ep. Pet. Phil.
IX,1	Melchizedek	Melch.
IX,2	Thought of Norea	Norea
IX,3	The Testimony of Truth	Testim. Truth
X	Marsanes	Marsanes
XI,1	Interpretation of Knowledge	Interp. Know.
XI,2	A Valentinian Exposition	Val. Exp.
XI,2a	On the Anointing	On Anoint.
XI,2b	On Baptism A	On Bap. A
XI,2c	On Baptism B	On Bap. B
XI,2d	On the Eucharist A	On Euch. A
XI,2e	On the Eucharist B	On Euch. B
XI,3	Allogenes	Allogenes
XI,4	Hypsiphrone	Hypsiph.
XII,1	Sentences of Sextus	Sent. Sextus
XII,2	Gospel of Truth	Gos. Truth
XII,3	Fragments	Frm.
XIII,1	Trimorphic Protennoia	Trim. Prot.
XIII,2	On the Origin of the World	Orig. World
BG,1	Gospel of Mary	Gos. Mary
BG,2	Apocryphon of John	Ap. John
BG,3	Sophia of Jesus Christ	Soph. Jes. Chr.
BG,4	Act of Peter	Act Pet.

See C. W. Hedrick and R. Hodgson, eds., *Nag Hammadi Gnosticism and Early Christianity* (Peabody, Mass.: Hendrickson, 1986). See GNOSIS; CHENOBOSKION.

Narratio. See **Rhetorical Analysis.**

Narrative, used as a noun ("a narrative"), is in the broadest sense an account of events, whether actual or fanciful, reported in any way for any reason. Used as an adjective, narrative may denote a part of such an account. More narrowly, narrative is distinguished from other literary genres (lyric poem, law code, etc.) by the presence of plot, a sequence of connected action that brings together character, place, and circumstance and that leads through dramatic conflict to some sense of resolution.

The Bible is a book of many narratives which may also be viewed as strands in one great narrative that recounts God's history with Israel and the world. "When one regards the biblical canon as a whole, the centrality to it of a narrative element is difficult to overlook: not only the chronological sweep of the whole, from creation to new creation, including the various events and developments of what has sometimes been called 'salvation history,' but also the way the large narrative portions interweave and provide a context for the remaining materials so that they, too, have a place in the ongoing story, while these other materials—parables, hymns, prayers, summaries, theological expositions—serve in different ways to enable readers to get hold of the story and to live their way into it" (Charles Wood, *The Formation of Christian Understanding* [Philadelphia: Westminster Press, 1981], 100).

Yet if narrative has long been crucial for the THEOLOGICAL INTERPRETATION of the Bible, it has not always been adequately attended to by modern BIBLICAL CRITICISM. Paradoxically, the rise of HISTORICAL CRITICISM in the modern period has been charged with contributing to "the eclipse of biblical narrative" (HANS FREI). Interest in the prehistory of the text and in the reconstruction of past events frequently overshadowed the literary character of the narratives themselves. Yet numerous countervailing pressures have helped restore biblical narrative to prominence over the course of the twentieth cent. Among the earliest of these were developments within historical criticism itself, such as FORM CRITICISM, which studied small narrative units such as LEGEND, PARABLE, etc., and REDACTION CRITICISM, which examined how such units were shaped into larger narrative wholes (e.g., a GOSPEL). Other important impulses for the recovery of biblical narrative have come from theology (KARL BARTH, H. R. Niebuhr, Hans Frei), HERMENEUTICS (Amos Wilder, Paul Ricoeur), literary studies (Erich Auerbach, Robert Alter, Frank Kermode), and ethics (Alasdair MacIntyre).

In the study of the HB, form critics such as HERMANN GUNKEL distinguished narrative as a distinct literary type from law, prophecy, psalms, and wisdom. In addition, form critics categorized different types of narrative, such as legends, fables, MYTHS, and novellas (stories). They pointed out that HB narratives often incorporate nonnarrative genres (blessings, commands, laws, prophecies, etc.) or may contain smaller narrative forms possessing their own distinct elements (dreams, visions, miracle stories, parables, etc.). Some scholars contrast poetic narratives (myths, legends, etc.) with historical narratives (popular history, prophetic AUTOBIOGRAPHY, reports of dreams and visions, etc.). More recently, questions of genre have given way to intensive study of the inner workings of the stories themselves and to the complexity of meaning they produce. See J. P. Fokkelman, *Narrative Art and Poetry in the Books of Samuel*, 4 vols. (Assen: Van Gorcum, 1981–93); M. Sternberg, *The Poetics of Biblical Narrative* (Bloomington, Ind.: Indiana University Press, 1985); Phyllis Trible, *Texts of Terror* (Philadelphia: Fortress Press, 1984).

In NT studies, form critics sought to categorize and describe the smaller narrative units visible in the Synoptic Gospels, although, as in OT criticism, no common agreement was achieved as to the classification and nomenclature of narrative types. RUDOLF BULTMANN distinguished two main types of narratives in the Synoptic Gospels: (a) miracle stories (miracles of healing, e.g., Mark 5:1–20, and nature miracles, e.g., Mark 4:37–41; the form critic MARTIN DIBELIUS called them PARADIGMS and novellas [*Novellen*] respectively), and (b) stories and legends, such as the infancy narratives, those dealing with the baptism to the triumphal entry, passion and Easter narratives (called legends, passion stories, and myths by Dibelius). (See Bultmann, *The History of the Synoptic Tradition* [New York: Harper & Row, 1963; Oxford: Basil Blackwell, 1963].) In the 1950s redaction criticism directed attention from small narrative units to the finished literary product. H. Conzelmann, for example, argued that Luke had arranged traditional material so as to depict a "history of salvation" consisting of three periods: the era of Israel, the time of Jesus, and the period of the church. As in OT criticism, more recent studies give detailed attention to the literary artistry of gospel narrative, as, for example, J. D. Kingsbury, *Matthew as Story* (Philadelphia: Fortress Press, 1988); D. Rhodes and D. Michie, *Mark as Story: An Introduction to the Narrative of a Gospel* (Philadelphia: Fortress Press, 1982).

The major recent interpretations of narrative from the perspectives of theology and the philosophy of religion respectively are those of Hans Frei and Paul Ricoeur. Frei, who gave a major impetus to what is commonly known as narrative theology, argued that the Gospels are "realistic narratives" that render Jesus as a unique and unsubstitutable human agent, rather than as a symbol, myth, or cipher for a mode of being-in-the-world. Ricoeur's very extensive investigations on narrative explore how the invention of plots—or, more generally, the telling of stories—permits humans to "refashion the field of human action and refigure the temporality of human existence." See Hans Frei, *The Identity of Jesus Christ* (Philadelphia: Fortress Press, 1975); Paul Ricoeur, *Time and Narrative*, 3 vols. (Chicago: University of Chicago Press, 1984–88); and *Why Narrative? Readings in Narrative Theology*, ed. by Stanley Hauerwas and L. Gregory Jones (Grand Rapids: Eerdmans, 1989). See APOPHTHEGM; ARETALOGY; KERYGMA; METANARRATIVE; NARRATIVE CRITICISM; PERIPETEIA; STRUCTURALISM.

Narrative Criticism   is less a methodology than a focus of inquiry employing and contributing to the methods and insights of STRUCTURALISM, RHETORICAL CRITICISM, READER-RESPONSE CRITICISM, et al. It does have its own vocabulary, such as narrator, character, plot, *mise en scène*, etc., but they are not discussed here. Arising particularly in the 1980s and '90s as a self-conscious discipline, narrative criticism has concentrated on the GOSPELS and Acts in the NT and, perhaps to a lesser extent, on the NARRATIVES of the HB. Narrative criticism is interested in narrative as narrative, not first of all as a source for understanding the historical circumstances in which the narrative was produced, the identity of its author, or the audience to which the text was originally addressed—although these questions may indeed be of exegetical interest and importance. In this regard narrative criticism begins with the assumptions of structuralism that such information adds nothing to the meaning of a narrative nor aids in its interpretation. Like reader-response criticism, it contends that quite apart from a narrative's real (historical) author, who may or may not be identifiable, there is nevertheless an "implied author" within the text. The implied author is simply the discernible perspective from which the narrative is told. That perspective is built into the narrative itself and is independent of the conscious intention of the real author and of the historical circumstances of the real audience being addressed. Equally important to narrative criticism, as in reader-response criticism, is the "implied reader" who is also to be found within the narrative. Unlike AUDIENCE CRITICISM in which specific historical groups are the object of inquiry, narrative criticism is interested in reconstructing the effect the narrative is intended to have on its readers in terms of their value judgments, beliefs, and perceptions. This construct is called "the implied reader." The "implied readers" are therefore those who would "actualize the potential for meaning in texts, who respond to texts in ways consistent with the expectations ascribed to their implied authors" (M. A. Powell).

Narrative criticism concentrates on the story being told, on the events that occur within it, the spatial and temporal settings of these events, and the characters who inhabit the story, including their social location, values, etc. It asks, "What is the plot? How are the characters developed? What is the setting for the events of the narrative?" etc. It also notes the role of rhetorical devices in the narrative, such as IRONY, PARONOMASIA, etc., and the effect they are intended to have on the implied reader. Narrative criticism argues that narrative is a fundamental character of human being, which finds the meaning of human existence in story form, as in the world renown physicist Stephen Hawkins's book *A Short History of Time.* Narrative criticism has been particularly interested therefore in restoring the narrative character of the Bible, and the way in which the actors of the story inhabit the overarching METANARRATIVE of the beginning and end of time.

See M. A. Powell, *What Is Narrative Criticism?* (Guides to Biblical Scholarship, NT Series; Minneapolis: Fortress Press, 1990); J. D. Kingsbury (ed.), *Gospel Interpretation: Narrative-critical and Social-scientific Approaches* (Harrisburg, Pa.: Trinity University Press, 1997). A precursor to recent narrative criticism is the classic study by Erich Auerbach, *Mimesis: The Representation of Reality in Western Literature,* trans. W. Trask (Garden City, N.Y.: Doubleday & Co., 1957; Ger: 1946).

NAS (New American Standard Bible, 1963). See **ASV.**

Naturweisheit (Ger: knowledge of nature). See **Onomasticon**.

NEB/REB. See **New English Bible/Revised English Bible.**

Nebiim (Heb: prophets). See *Ketubim;* **Pentateuch; Prophets; Tanakh.**

Neofiti I. See **Targum.**

Nestle, Eberhard (1851–1913). Born in Stuttgart, Germany, Nestle was professor of OT at Ulm for two periods (1883–89 and 1893–98), separated by an interlude as visiting professor of Semitic languages at Tübingen (1890–93); thereafter he accepted posts at the Evangelical Seminary at Maulbronn (1898–1913). After devoting his earlier years to the study of Syriac and the LXX, Nestle turned to editing a CRITICAL TEXT of the Greek NT for which he is best known, commonly called the NESTLE TEXT.

Nestle Text A critical text of the Greek NT by EBERHARD NESTLE (see previous entry) based on prior editions by TISCHENDORF (1869) and WESTCOTT and HORT (1881), which in turn followed primarily the text of CODEX VATICANUS (B). Nestle consulted a third scientific edition (ed. by R. H. Weymouth, 1886; from the 3rd edition on, ed. by BERNHARD WEISS, 1894–1900) in order to get a majority reading in those cases where the editions of Tischendorf and Westcott-Hort differed. First published in 1898, the NT has continually been revised: 10th–21st editions (1914–52) by his son Erwin Nestle; 22nd–25th editions (1956–63) by Erwin Nestle and KURT ALAND. The twenty-fifth edition of the Nestle-Aland Text shows 558 variants from Westcott-Hort. Beginning with the twenty-sixth edition, the Nestle-Aland text is identical to the Greek NT published by the American Bible Society (1966), both being edited by the same group of scholars. They differ only in their CRITICAL APPARATUS.

Neutral Text, The (also called Alexandrian, Egyptian, or Beta Text). See **Alexandrian Text.**

New American Bible   NAB is the common abbreviation of this Roman Catholic translation of the Bible, including the APOCRYPHA, by members of the CATHOLIC BIBLICAL ASSOCIATION OF AMERICA, begun in 1944 and completed in 1970. It is based on a critical use of the best texts available. The NT, considered inferior to the OT translation, was revised in 1987 with a modest effort toward inclusive language but "in the direction of a formal-equivalence approach to translation, matching the vocabulary, structure, and even word order of the original as closely as possible" in order to maintain the translation suitability for liturgical proclamation as well as for purposes of private devotion and study (Preface). See CONTEMPORARY ENGLISH VERSION; DOUAY; JERUSALEM BIBLE; LIVING BIBLE (PARAPHRASED); NEW ENGLISH BIBLE; NEW INTERNATIONAL VERSION; NEW JEWISH VERSION; KING JAMES VERSION; PARAPHRASE; REVISED STANDARD VERSION; TODAY'S ENGLISH VERSION; VERSION.

New English Bible; Revised English Bible   NEB is the common abbreviation of the New English Bible, a translation of the Bible from the original tongues by British scholars with C. H. DODD as Director (1947–65) and as Joint Director with G. R. Driver from 1965, under the auspices of a Joint Committee of the non–Roman Catholic Churches of the British Isles (NT, 1961; OT and APOCRYPHA, 1970). Roman Catholic scholars did join in the revision of the NEB, published as the REB (Revised English Bible) in 1989. The REB is considered a major revision of the NEB, particularly in the text of the OT where archaism and controversial READINGS were abandoned for more traditional readings. The REB also eliminated much male-oriented language, but not as consistently as the NRSV, which substitutes all third-person masculine pronouns with generic third-person plurals. See VERSION; PARAPHRASE; EXEGESIS.

New Hermeneutic, The   The New Hermeneutic is the name of a movement influenced by Martin Heidegger and RUDOLF BULTMANN, whose leading representatives were Ernst Fuchs (1903–1983) and Gerhard Ebeling (1912–). The movement grew out of and in response to the "dialectical theology" of the 1920s, which, following the thought of the Protestant Reformers, held that God speaks through (*dia*) his Word (*logos*), which is attested in scripture and made present in proclamation. The New Hermeneutic accepted these theological assertions but went on to insist (contra, e.g., KARL BARTH) that it was necessary to inquire into their basis in philosophical anthropology. Drawing on Heidegger's later writings, the New Hermeneutic analyzed the relationship of language to understanding and to reality. Out of this analysis came the terms LANGUAGE EVENT and *language gain* and, in part, "the New QUEST OF THE HISTORICAL JESUS."

Together with Heidegger, Bultmann, and others, the New Hermeneutic helped give currency to the terms *hermeneutic problem* and *hermeneutic principle* in theological discussion. According to the New Hermeneutic, the hermeneutic problem, or the problem of interpretation, exists wherever meaning is in doubt. Thus it is not only a linguistic problem that arises in the case of texts whose language and culture have long since disappeared but exists as well in the interpretation of everyday conversation (of special interest to SCHLEIERMACHER), of art and history (DILTHEY), of dreams as expressions of humanity's inner psychic nature (Freud), of Being itself (Heidegger), and so on.

The New Hermeneutic gave a similarly broad imprint to the idea of a hermeneutic principle. A hermeneutic principle, in the broadest sense, is simply a rule that guides how one approaches and interprets a text. So understood, hermeneutic principles are as various as the history of interpretation itself. The New Hermeneutic, however, frames the discussion of hermeneutic principles in terms of the historically shaped preunderstanding that the interpreter inevitably brings to the task of interpretation. According to the New Hermeneutic, the preunderstanding is the "key" or "principle" by which the process of understanding is initiated.

A good introduction to the New Hermeneutic is Paul Achtemeier's *An Introduction to the New Hermeneutic* (Philadelphia: Westminster Press, 1969). A more indigenously American approach to the New Hermeneutic was developed by process theologians; see, e.g., David R. Griffin, *A Process Christology* (Philadelphia: Westminster Press, 1973). See HERMENEUTIC; HERMENEUTIC CIRCLE; HERMENEUTICS.

New International Version   NIV is the common abbreviation of the New International Version of the Bible (NT, 1973; OT, 1978). The NIV was prepared by more than 100 scholars from more than a dozen conservative evangelical denominations in the U.S. and abroad "united in their commitment to the authority and infallibility of the Bible as God's Word in written form" (Preface, 1978). The NIV "came into being as a result of the repudiation of the RSV by the majority of conservative Protestants" in the U.S. and in an effort to provide a translation of the Bible that might correct the perceived mistranslations or misleading translations of the RSV. Assuming, for example, the inerrancy of the scriptures, the NIV frequently translates OT passages so as to conform to their rendering in the NT (e.g., Isa 7:14 is made to conform to Matt 1:23 and Ps 16:10 to Acts 2:27, although there is no textual support for doing so). A gender inclusive edition of the NIV has been distributed in Britain, but objections from conservative circles has prohibited its release in the U.S. (see *Christianity Today*, Oct. 27, 1997). Ironically, the NIV is now closer in style and content with the RSV than with any other recent VERSION of the Bible. For a critical review article, see *The Duke Divinity School Review* (Spring 1979), 164–79. See KING JAMES VERSION; LIVING BIBLE (PARAPHRASED); PARAPHRASE; TEXTUAL CRITICISM.

New Jewish Version of the Hebrew Scriptures   NJV is the common abbreviation for the New Jewish Version of the Hebrew Scriptures being prepared by the Jewish Publication Society and appearing piecemeal since 1962: *The Torah* (Genesis–Deuteronomy), 1962; *The Five Megilloth and Jonah* (Esther, Lamentations, Ruth, Ecclesiastes, and the Song of Solomon), 1969; *The Book of Psalms*, 1973; and *The Prophets–Nevi'im*, 1978. The remaining books of the *Kethubim*, or "Writings" (Job and Proverbs) are still to be published. For a critical review, see *The Duke Divinity School Review* (Spring 1979), 180–91. See JERUSALEM BIBLE; KING JAMES VERSION; NEW AMERICAN BIBLE; NEW INTERNATIONAL VERSION.

New King James Version.   See **King James Version.**

New Living Translation, The.   See *Living Bible (Paraphrased), The; New Living Translation, The.*

New Testament.   See *Kaine Diatheke;* **Old Testament, New Testament.**

NIB.   See *Interpreter's Bible; New Interpreter's Bible, The.*

NIV.   See **New International Version.**

NJB.   See **Jerusalem Bible. New Jerusalem Bible.**

NJV.   See **New Jewish Version of the Hebrew Scriptures.**

NLT.   See **LB(P).**

Nomina Sacra   (Lat: the Holy Names) is a term coined by L. Traube (1907) to denote a limited number of words, at most fifteen, that always appear in abbreviated form in virtually all ancient Christian manuscripts of the Bible. A horizontal line is placed above the abbreviation as a warning that the word cannot be pronounced as written, e.g., $\overline{KS}$ instead of KYRIOS. The words in question divide into three classes. The first class consists of four words that are always abbreviated: Jesus, Christ, Lord, and God; the second class consists of three words that are frequently abbreviated in relatively early MSS: Spirit, *anthropos*, and cross; and the third class consists of the remainder (father, son, savior, mother, heaven, Israel, David, and Jerusalem). The origins and purpose of the *nomina sacra* are unknown, though scholars have often suggested a connection of some kind with "the reverence with which the Sacred or Divine Name YHWH was held by the Jews" (Nevius). C. H. Roberts suggests the *nomina sacra* embody "the embryonic creed of the first church." See C. H. Roberts, "*Nomina Sacra*: Origins and Significance," in *Manuscript, Society and Belief in Early Christian Egypt* (London: Oxford University Press, 1979), 26–48. See TETRAGRAMMATON.

Noth, Martin (1902–1968). Born in Dresden, Germany, Noth (pronounced Note) was *Privatdozent* at Greifswald and Leipzig before becoming professor of OT at Königsberg (1930–44) and Bonn (1945–65); thereafter he was Director of the Institute for the Study of the Holy Land in Jerusalem until his death. A prolific writer, Noth is best known for *The History of Israel* (Ger: 1950; Eng: New York: Harper & Row, 1958; London: A. & C. Black, 1960), *A History of Pentateuchal Traditions* (Ger: 1948; Eng: Englewood Cliffs, N.J.: Prentice-Hall, 1971), and his commentaries on *Exodus* (Ger: 1959; Eng: Philadelphia: Westminster Press, 1962), *Leviticus* (Ger: 1962; Eng: Westminster Press, 1965; London: SCM Press, 1965), and *Numbers* (Ger: 1966; Eng: Westminster Press, 1968; SCM Press, 1968). Two of his theories received the greatest attention: (1) that "Israel" came into being as a tribal "amphictyony" (religious confederation) that followed the invasion of Canaan by the tribe of Joseph, and that no reliable information concerning its prehistory, including the figure of Moses, exists; and (2) that the book of Deuteronomy is to be understood as a kind of preamble to the historical books of the OT (Joshua–2 Kings) and not as an addendum to the TETRATEUCH (Genesis–Numbers). See E: ELOHIST; J (YAHWIST); P: PRIESTLY CODE; TRADITION CRITICISM; DEUTERONOMIST (-IC HISTORY).

Novelle (Ger: novelette, short story) is a word employed by MARTIN DIBELIUS as a form-critical term, translated by the English word "tale" (*From Tradition to Gospel* [Ger: 1919, 1933²; Eng: London: Ivor Nicholson & Watson, Ltd., 1934; repr. James Clarke, 1971; New York: Charles Scribner's Sons, 1935]).

In OT FORM CRITICISM the term is used perhaps in a manner more consistent with its original sense, that is, a novelette or short story. GERHARD VON RAD, for example, contends that the story of Joseph in Genesis is more appropriately called a *novelle* rather than "Tale" (Ger: *Sage*) as some form critics had earlier suggested. (Von Rad, "Biblische Joseph-Erzählung und Joseph-Roman," *Neue Rundschau*, 76 [1965]: 546–559.) See TALE.

NRSV. See **Revised Standard Version/New Revised Standard Version.**

Nunc Dimittis is the traditional name of Simeon's prayer uttered according to Luke at the dedication of the infant Jesus in the Temple, recorded in Luke 2:29–32, from the first two words of the Latin text: "*Nunc dimittis servum tuum Domine . . .*" ("Lord, *now lettest* thou thy servant *depart* in peace . . ."). See BENEDICTUS; MAGNIFICAT.

Ode (Gk: song). A poem intended to be sung, expressive of the poet's feelings, and generally possessing an irregular metrical form. In the LXX and in the Greek NT, the term refers to a song of praise to God (e.g., Exod 15:1) or to CHRIST (Rev 5:9; 14:3). That the odes mentioned in Eph 5:19 and Col 3:16 are qualified as "spiritual" suggests that not all odes were sacred. In the LXX, thirty-six PSALMS are identified as odes in their title (4; 17; 29; 38; 44; 47; 64–67; 74; 75; 82; 86; 87; 90–92; 94; 95; 107; 119–133). Its usage in the LXX is somewhat arbitrary perhaps since it is not used as the exclusive translation of any one Hebrew term.

OED Oxford English Dictionary.

Old Latin MSS   (also called Itala; *siglum:* it). The name given to approximately 30 MSS that antedate or are otherwise independent of the Latin VULGATE *(siglum:* vg), the *VORLAGE* of which JEROME completed in 405 C.E. . The Old Latin texts are highly divergent, and no single MS contains the whole NT. The oldest, CODEX Vercellensis *(siglum:* a), dates from the 4th cent. The *sigla* for Old Latin MSS are lower-case letters: a, b, c, etc.

Old Testament; New Testament are traditional Christian designations for the two major parts of the Christian Bible, the propriety of which has recently become the subject of debate in both scholarly and religious circles. Although the terms themselves are of biblical derivation (cf. Jer 31:31; 2 Cor 3:14; Heb 8:6–8, etc.), Christians first used them to designate the two parts of their canon as literary entities in the latter half of the 2nd cent. The adoption of the terms meant that "[e]ach part of the Scripture has acquired a new name which simultaneously unites the two and distinguishes between them. It is no longer possible to divorce the New Testament from the Old, as Marcion had tried to do; but it is even less possible simply to put the two collections on the same level, as if there were no difference between them" (H. von Campenhausen, *The Formation of the Christian Canon* [Philadelphia: Fortress Press, 1972], 268).

In recent decades, the terms, and especially the "Old Testament," have come under attack, although for different reasons that are not always adequately distinguished. One line of criticism holds that the terms are unacceptable because they are incompatible with a scientific or critical understanding of the Bible in its historical context, being irreducibly Christian and theological in character. This perspective typically holds that at a minimum "Old Testament" be replaced by "HEBREW BIBLE" or "Hebrew Scriptures," a term at home among neither Jewish nor Christian readerships. Whatever the merits of this argu-

ment, it is well to remember that differences of scope and sequence have existed and continue to exist between Judaism's canon of sacred scriptures and the body of writings traditionally known among the churches as the Old Testament, so that the application of a single term to both entities is potentially misleading.

A quite different line of criticism holds that the terms are unacceptable for reasons that are specifically Christian and theological in nature, e.g., because they minimize the contemporary importance of the Old Testament as a witness to God, or because they imply that the church has replaced the Jews as heirs of the scriptures and as God's people. Proposed alternatives include "First Testament and Second Testament," "Shared Testament and New Testament," "Scriptures and Apostolic Writings" (P. van Buren), "Scriptures and Apostolic Witness" (R. K. Soulen). By the nature of the case, proposals for new nomenclature that are designed to address the first objection are unlikely to satisfy the second, and vice versa.

At present, it appears that no theologically satisfactory alternative to the traditional paired terms has won widespread acceptance among Christians. Moreover, it is by no means universally conceded that the contested terms should be abandoned. In this book, the authors have made use of the term Old Testament (OT) where a Christian interpretive context is presupposed or where a Christian form of the canon is in question while employing the term Hebrew Bible (HB) in other contexts.

For an argument in favor of retaining the Christian use of the term "Old Testament" by one of its early critics, see Paul M. van Buren, *According to the Scriptures: The Origin of the Gospel and the Church's Old Testament* (Grand Rapids: Eerdmans, 1998). See also Jon Levenson, *The Hebrew Bible, the Old Testament, and Historical Criticism* (Louisville, Ky.: Westminster/John Knox Press, 1993); John J. Collins and Roger Brooks, eds., *Hebrew Bible or Old Testament? Studying the Bible in Judaism and Christianity* (University of Notre Dame Press, 1990). See TANAKH.

Onomasticon (pl.: -a; Gk: consisting of names) is a learned term for a list of names, particularly of the proper names within a given culture as a philological aid to their meaning and ETYMOLOGY, as found for example in Plato's *Cratylus*. The *Onomasticon* of Julius Pollux (2nd cent.) is a ten-volume LEXICON containing the most important words related to a wide range of subjects (music, theater, politics, nature, crime, religion, etc.) with short explanations, illustrated with quotations from ancient writers. It is suggested that onomastica were used in wisdom writing, e.g., Job 28; 38–39; 41; Wis 7:17–23; Sir 43, etc. Cf. the *Onomastica* of Amenemope (*ANET*, 421–425). Each of these deals with knowledge of the wonders of nature (*Naturweisheit*, Ger: knowledge of nature). The onomasticon of Eusebius, published about 328 C.E. , is a treatise on the names and places of the Bible; it was translated into Latin by JEROME.

Onomatopoeia (Gk: lit., "to make a name"). Strictly speaking, onomatopoeia is the creation of a word in imitation of a sound (whack, swish); in RHETORIC, however, it refers to the use of a word whose sound is used for its own effect or that suggests the intended sense (e.g., the Hebrew words *thohu wavohu* in Gen 1:2 suggest to the ear what the English translation communicates only conceptually: "without form and void").

Oracle (Lat: *oraculum*, which denoted both a divine message and the place or medium by which it was communicated). In OT LITERARY CRITICISM the term has often been used broadly as any oracular communication of God *to* humans, in contrast to prayers in which humans communicate *with* God. Omens (e.g., Gen 30:27; 44:5; Num 17:1–11; 2 Sam 5:22–24), dreams, and visions are not classed as oracles, although the accounts of dreams or visions may be incorporated into the body of a prophetic oracle.

A distinction was formerly made between the priestly (cultic) oracle and the prophetic oracle; recent scholarship, however, generally ties both prophet and priest closely to the cult, although the question of the prophet's setting in the life of Israel is still debated. It may be that originally the cultic (or priestly) oracle was little more than a "yes" or "no" reply to specific inquiries of the deity by a priest, in Israel principally through the use of sacred dice or lots called Urim and Thummim (see 2 Sam 23:2, 11; 28:6). Eventually, the mechanical use of lots seemed a poor substitute for the word of an inspired individual (prophet) of God; nevertheless, the use of lots did not entirely disappear with the rise of PROPHECY (see Jer 3:16; Acts 1:26).

The earliest account of a prophetic oracle is recorded in the autobiographical NARRATIVE of Wen-Amon, an official in the court of the Egyptian god Amon at Karnak. It dates from the 11th cent. B.C.E. (See *ANET*, 25–29, "The Journey of Wen-Amon to Phoenicia.")

By the 9th cent. B.C.E., the prophetic oracle attained such distinction in style and content as to be preserved in written form as an identifiable genre, although at times incorporating other rhetorical forms, such as PARABLE, vision, dialogue, song, etc. After the classical period of prophecy in the 8th–6th cents. B.C.E., the prophetic *oracle* slowly disappeared, giving way to priestly prayer and the APOCALYPTIC vision.

In recent NT criticism, the term *oracle* has been used to characterize those SAYINGS of Jesus that contain elements of judgment, as in the prophetic oracle.

Oral Tradition   refers to any body of material handed down from generation to generation by word of mouth, or to the process thereof; the stories of creation and of the patriarchs in Genesis, of the exodus and Moses in the PENTATEUCH, the deeds and teachings of Jesus in the GOSPELS, and the accounts of the rise of the EARLY CHURCH in Acts were all shaped by the laws of oral tradition, explication of which is one of the goals of FORM CRITICISM. Theories concerning the nature of oral tradition have occupied

Scandinavian scholars in particular; see Birger Gerhardsson, *Memory and Manuscript* (Uppsala, 1961); SIGMUND MOWINCKEL, *Prophecy and Tradition* (Oslo: I kommisjon hos J. Dybwad, 1946); and Eduard Nielsen, *Oral Tradition* (Chicago: Alec R. Allenson, 1954). See Q; SYNOPTIC PROBLEM; TRADITION CRITICISM.

Origen   (ca. 185–251/254 C.E.). Born in Alexandria, Egypt, of Christian parents, Origen is generally recognized as the most brilliant biblical scholar and theologian of early Christianity, even though his views were later condemned by the Council of Constantinople (553). In addition to voluminous biblical commentaries, his chief works include his monumental HEXAPLA, a pioneering example of TEXTUAL CRITICISM, his *De Principiis* (ca. 230), the first great systematic presentation of Christian theology, and his *Against Celsus* (ca. 247), a reply to the Platonist Celsus in defense of Christian beliefs. Origen died, probably in Caesarea, as a result of persecution initiated by the Roman Emperor Decius (249–251).

For much of the modern period, Origen has served as the whipping boy of critical exegesis on account of his robust use of allegorical interpretation, which was judged to destroy the text's plain or historical sense. Typical is the verdict of R. P. C. Hanson, who judged that "Origen's use of allegory, with the exception of those few cases where he is confusing allegory with simple metaphor, is today widely regarded as wholly indefensible and as merely a process by which Origen misled himself and others. At best we might describe it as quaint and sometimes poetical; at the worst it is a device for obscuring the meaning of the Bible from its readers" (*Allegory and Event* [London: SCM Press, 1959]). Yet Origen, who held that "the passages which hold good in their historical acceptation are much more numerous than those which contain a purely spiritual meaning" (*De Princ.* Bk. 4), possessed a theory and practice of biblical interpretation that is more rigorous and supple than is often rec-

ognized, and that has in any case attracted a more sympathetic analysis in recent decades. For example, Origen shows a sense for the historical and even cosmic sweep of Paul's argument in Rom 9–11 that is often missing in later interpreters. See Peter Gorday, *Principles of Patristic Exegesis: Romans 9–11 in Origen, John Chrysostom, and Augustine* (New York: Edwin Mellen Press, 1983); Karen J. Torjesen, *Hermeneutical Procedure and Theological Method in Origen's Exegesis* (Berlin: De Gruyler 1986); Henri Crouzel, *Origen: The Life and Thought of the First Great Theologian* (San Francisco: HarperSanFrancisco, 1989).

Ostraca   (Gk: shell) in TEXTUAL CRITICISM refers to small pieces of pottery, usually fragments of vases, pots, plates, etc., used in antiquity for writing brief notes, LETTERS, receipts, school exercises, religious maxims, HYMNS, etc. Written mostly in Greek, but also in Coptic and Latin, ostraca are more important for gaining knowledge of the EARLY CHURCH, its liturgy and its milieu, esp. Coptic, than for restoring the original text of the NT.

Otto, Rudolf   (1869–1937). Professor of systematic theology at Göttingen, Breslau, and Marburg in Germany, Otto's influence in NT criticism and interpretation came primarily from his books, *The Idea of the Holy* (1917; Eng: London: Oxford University Press, 1923) and *The Kingdom of God and Son of Man: A Study in the History of Religion* (1934; Eng: London: Lutterworth Press, 1938); the former expounds the nature of religious experience as an encounter with the numinous, the *mysterium tremendum et fascinans*, the "Wholly Other"; the latter rejects the radical skepticism of RUDOLF BULTMANN and attempts to reconstruct the self-consciousness of Jesus as the suffering servant of Isaiah.

Oxymoron   (Gk: lit.: sharp + dull) is the immediate juxtaposition of contradictory terms for effect, such as Jesus' reference to "living water" (John 4:10, 11, 14), or Paul's proclamation of "Christ crucified" (1 Cor 1:23); MARTIN DIBELIUS's description of

Mark's GOSPEL as a "book of secret epiphanies" is a modern example.

Oxyrhynchus Papyri   A treasure trove of ancient PAPYRUS fragments, numbering in the thousands, first discovered by B. P. Grenfell and A. S. Hunt (1897–1907) at Oxyrhynchus, near Behnesa in Upper Egypt. The papyri, dating from 2nd cent. B.C.E. to 7th cent. C.E. and written in Greek, Latin, Egyptian, Coptic, Hebrew, and Syriac, contain all varieties of texts, including fragments of the OT and NT and APOCRYPHAL literature, such as the GOSPEL OF THOMAS, the last being found intact at Nag Hammadi in 1946. See NAG HAMMADI CODICES.

P: Priestly Code; Priestly Document; Priestly Narrative; Priestly Writer   According to the majority of OT scholars, P represents the latest stratum of material used in the formation of the PENTATEUCH (or Hexateuch), deriving its name from the Hebrew priests whose traditions and theological point of view it contains.

The existence of this tradition, later designated "P," was first proposed in 1853 by Hermann Hupfeld, who thought it the earliest rather than the latest material in the Pentateuch as subsequently proposed by the GRAF-WELLHAUSEN HYPOTHESIS (DOCUMENTARY HYPOTHESIS) later in the same century. In the documentary view, which stresses the creative individuality of an unknown author, the P Code is described as a product of historical and legal (cultic) erudition, as evidenced by its concern for genealogies, tables of nations, dates and measurements, cultic ordinances, and literary FORMULAS (e.g., Gen 2:4a; 5:1; 6:9; 10:1; 11:10, 27; 25:12, 19; 36:1; 37:2), and in its repetitious and judiciously exact diction (e.g., Gen 1:11–12; Exod 7:9–10; 8:1–2, 12–13, etc.). In content, the P Code sketches the origins of the people of God, their sacred institutions and cultic laws from the creation of the world (Gen 1: 1–2:4a) to the settlement of the Promised Land, a history divided into four great periods marked by the revelation of divine law first

to Adam, then to Noah, to Abraham, and finally, to Moses. One representative of the traditional view has thus called the P Code "the charter of Judaism" or "the constitution of a theocratic state" (R. Pfeiffer).

In recent decades, however, the precise nature, date, and content of P, and the age and origin of the traditions it contains, have been heatedly debated. A modification of the Documentary Hypothesis is found in the work of MARTIN NOTH, whose traditio-historical criticism, though affirming a final literary stage in the exilic period (586–539 B.C.E.), stresses the *preliterary* history of the traditions. Noth suggests that P is but one of three (not four) distinct literary strands in the Pentateuch (apart from Deuteronomy), that it is principally a NARRATIVE that forms the framework of the Pentateuch and into which (older?) *legal* material (e.g., Lev 1–7) was subsequently added. The narrative emphasizes the establishment of the cult at Sinai (Exod 25–31; 35–40; Lev 8–9) and the formation of the twelve-tribe confederacy (Num 1–9).

According to Noth, the content of P is (with minor omissions):

Gen 1:1–2:4a; 5:1–28, 30–32; 6:9–22; 7:6, 11, 13–16a, 18–21, 24; 8:1–2a, 3b–5, 7, 13a, 14–19; 9:1–17, 28–29; 10:1–7, 20, 22–23 (24), 31–32; 11:10–27, 31–32; 12:4b–5; 13:6, 11b–12; 16:1a, 3, 15–16; 17:1–27; 19:29; 21:1b–5; 23:1–20; 25:7–11a, 12–17, 19–20, 26b; 26:34–35; 27:46; 28:9; 31:18; 33:18a; 35:6, 9–13, 15, 22b–29; 36:1–14; 37:1–2; 41:46a; 46:6–27; 47:27–28; 48:3–6; 49:1a, 29–33; 50:12–13.

Exod 1:1–7, 13–14; 2:23–25; 6:2–7:13, 19, 20a, 21b, 22; 8:5–7 (16, 19); 9:8–12; 11:9–10; 12:1–20, 28, 40–51; 14:14, 8–10*, 15–18, 21–23, 26, 28–29; 15:22a, 27; 16:1–3, 6–27, 32–35a; 17:1; 19:1–2a; 24:15b; 25:9–31:18; 35:1–40:38.

Lev (chs. 1–7 are additions to P) 8:1–10:20 (chs. 11–15 are additions); 16:1–34 (chs. 17–27 are additions).

Num 1:14:49 (chs. 5–6 are additions); 7:1–89 (8:14* is an "isolated piece"); 8:5–10:28; 13:1–17a, 21, 25–26, 32–33; 14:1a, 2–3, 5–10, 26–38; 16:1a, 2–11, 16–24, 27a,

---

Asterisk (*) marks major passages that, according to B. W. Anderson, are disputed by other scholars.

35–50; 17:1–18:32 (ch. 19 is an addition); 20:1–13, 22b–29; 22:1(25:6–18* may be an addition to the completed Pentateuch; 26:1–27:11, an addition to P); 27:12–23 (chs. 28–36, except 32:1, 16, 39–42 [J] are additions to P).

Deut (other scholars add: 32:48–52) 34:1a (5b), 7–9.

See Martin Noth, *A History of Pentateuchal Traditions* (Englewood Cliffs, N.J.: Prentice-Hall, 1972); this volume contains a helpful "Analytical Outline of the Pentateuch" by the translator, B. W. Anderson.

Paleography is the study of ancient writing, its history and development, as a means of deciphering and dating ancient texts; it is used in TEXTUAL CRITICISM to date biblical MSS, now with the DEAD SEA SCROLLS, extant from the mid-3rd cent. B.C.E. to the appearance of the printing press in the 15th cent. C.E. See Frank Moore Cross and David Noel Freedman, *Early Hebrew Orthography: A Study of Epigraphic Evidence* (New Haven, Conn.: American Oriental Society, 1952), and F. M. Cross, *Qumran and the History of the Biblical Text* (Cambridge: Harvard University Press, 1975).

Palestinian Talmud. See **Talmud.**

Palimpsest In Gk *palimpsest* literally means "rubbed (smooth) again" and denotes a MS of parchment from which the original text has been erased and a second text placed on top of it. The earlier and sometimes more significant text is recoverable by various means, particularly infrared or ultraviolet photography. CODEX EPHRAEMI RESCRIPTUS (C) is a palimpsest with parts of the OT and NT dating from the 5th cent.; the upper writing is a 12th-cent. Greek translation of the homilies of Ephraem Syrus (a Syrian church father who died in 373 C.E.). There are over 50 palimpsest MSS of the NT earlier than the 11th cent.

Papyrus (Lat: *Cyperus papyrus*) is a perennial plant of the Nile Delta whose long triangular stems (known in Greek as *papyros* and *byblos*) were cut into thin strips and glued together to form sheets for writ-

ing. Papyrus, known also as the paper-reed or paper-rush, was widely employed for writing throughout the Mediterranean from the 4th cent. B.C.E. to the 7th cent. C.E.

Papyrus Manuscripts The papyrus MSS of the NT are its earliest extant witnesses and are therefore of great significance for the early history and restoration of the original text. Discovered primarily in the 20th cent. in Egypt, they now number 81, each bearing the *siglum* P plus a numerical identification. The oldest fragment (P^{52}), found in a mummy cartonage, contains a small portion of John 18 and is dated ca. 125. Several papyrus MSS come from ca. 200: P^{32} (fragment of Titus), $P^{64,67}$ (fragment of Matt 3; 5; and 26), P^{46} (sections of Rom 5ff.; Heb, 1 and 2 Cor, Eph, Gal, Phil, Col, and 1 Thess—all with lacunae), and P^{66} (ca. 2/3 of John). P^{75}, also ca. 200 now in the Bodmer Library (Geneva), contains most of Luke and more than half of John. P^{45}, P^{46}, and P^{47} constitute the so-called Chester Beatty Papyri, purchased by Beatty in Egypt in the 1930s. Together they contain fragments of all the books of the NT. Of more recent discovery are the Martin Bodmer papyri (P^{66}, P^{72}, P^{74}, P^{75}—above), which have been published since 1954. There are also papyrus MSS of the OT and of many "literary" works from antiquity (of which Homer is the most frequently attested). See MINUSCULE; TEXTUAL CRITICISM; UNCIAL.

Par(s). In NT criticism, par. is an abbrev. meaning "and its parallel" and refers to a passage of scripture to be found in two or more of the Synoptic GOSPELS; an equivalent symbol is //, e.g., Mark 4:35–41//. In general usage, however, par(s). (or para.) is the abbreviation for paragraph(s).

Parable; Parabolic Sayings (Gk: *parabole*). Broadly speaking, parabolic SAYINGS constitute a type of figurative speech involving a comparison that is distinguishable from the simple METAPHOR on the one hand and ALLEGORY on the other yet contains, or may contain, elements of both, particularly the "shock" quality of metaphor and, occasionally, several points of comparison (see TERTIUM COMPARATIONIS, BILD-HÄLFTE) as in allegory. The parabolic sayings of Jesus (our focus here) have been categorized as the "similitude" (an "extended metaphor" or "metaphor extended into a picture"), the "parable proper" (a metaphor extended into a story—so C. H. DODD), and the "example story," which are often omitted from discussions of parables though sometimes called a parable in scripture, e.g., "The rich fool" (Luke 12:16–20). The images employed are drawn from nature and everyday life. Some scholars suggest that the similitude relates typical, recurrent events; the parable proper, particular and therefore nonrecurring ones (so JÜLICHER; Via); however, no general agreement exists.

The use of the term *parabole* in the SEP-TUAGINT and in the Greek NT offers no help in definition; it is used to translate the Hebrew word MASHAL which, being a very broad term, refers to a variety of linguistic forms, such as taunt (Isa 14:4), riddle (Ps 49:4), allegory (Ezek 17:2–3), byword (Deut 28:37), dirge (Mic 2:4), proverb (Luke 4:23), etc. Until the late 18th cent., the parables of Jesus were frequently treated as allegories, following Mark 4:10–12, 13–20 pars. The modern basis of parable criticism was laid by Adolf Jülicher (*Die Gleichnisreden Jesu*, 1888, 1899), whose study brought an end to a long history of allegorical interpretation. But, as the history of BIBLICAL CRITICISM attests, old issues thought settled tend to reemerge in new dress. Whether any of the parables themselves contain aspects of allegory and whether they stand within the Jewish prophetic tradition and as such have APOCALYPTIC dimensions are questions of the current debate.

Because the parables are thought to provide the best access to the historical Jesus, the study of their interpretation since Jülicher is highly illuminative of the changing perspectives and methodologies of NT criticism. The parables have been interpreted as (a) vehicles of moral teaching, (b) weapons of self-defense, (c) calls to deci-

sion, (d) witnesses to Jesus' faith, (e) gifts of time, (f) invitations to a new reality, etc. Significant studies include C. H. Dodd, *The Parables of the Kingdom* (1935; London: Nisbet, 1955; rev. ed., New York: Charles Scribner's Sons, 1961); Joachim Jeremias, *The Parables of Jesus* (Scribner's, 1970[8]; London: SCM Press, 1972); Dan O. Via, Jr., *The Parables: Their Literary and Existential Dimension* (Philadelphia: Fortress Press, 1967); John D. Crossan, *In Parables: The Challenge of the Historical Jesus* (New York: Harper & Row, 1973); eds., Robert W. Funk et al., *The Parables of Jesus: Red Letter Edition. A Report of the Jesus Seminar* (Sonoma, Calif.: Polebridge Press, 1988); Craig L. Blomberg, *Interpreting the Parables* (Leicester: Apollos Press, 1990); etc.

For an account of the parables that challenges two recent trends of parable research, according to which parables are creative works of art or mysterious utterances that hide truth from "outsiders" even as they reveal it to initiates, see Andrew Parker, *Painfully Clear: The Parables of Jesus* (Sheffield: Sheffield Academic Press, 1996). Parker holds that Jesus' parables were not riddles, but uncomfortably penetrating pieces of self-authenticating logic that compelled the hearer to face a twisted attitude and straighten it out.

Adolf Jülicher's listing of parabolic sayings follows on pp. 130 and 131. Most of Jülicher's *Gleichnisse* are now considered simple metaphors or similes. Jülicher's terminology is in parenthesis.

Paradigm (adj.: paradigmatic; Gk: pattern, model, example). *Paradigm* commonly means "model," as in "a paradigm of literary craftsmanship" (*JBL*), but it also appears in biblical studies in three more specialized senses, listed here in chronological order beginning with the oldest.

1. The student of language finds the term used for an example or pattern of the conjugation or the declension of a word in its various inflected forms.
2. The NT form critic encounters *paradigm* used as a technical term for (*Continued on p. 132*)

A. Similitudes and Similes (*Gleichnisse*)

[1. Concerning Salt	Matt 5:13	Mark 9:49–50	Luke 14:34–35
**[2. Concerning Light(s)	Matt 5:14, 16	Mark 4:21	Luke 8:16; 11:33
3. The Eye as Light of Life	Matt 6:22–23		Luke 11:34–36
4. Concerning the Fig Tree	Matt 24:32–33	Mark 13:28–29	Luke 21:29–31
5. The Servant's Wages			Luke 17:7–10
6. The Playing Children	Matt 11:16–19		Luke 7:31–35
[7. The Petitioning Son	Matt 7:9–11		Luke 11:11–13
[8. The Pupil and His Teacher	Matt 10:24–25		Luke 6:40
[9. The Blind Leading the Blind	Matt 15:14		Luke 6:39
[10. On What Defiles a Person	Matt 15:10–20	Mark 7:14–23	
[11. On Revealing What Is Hidden	Matt 10:26–27 12:2–23	Mark 4:22	Luke 8:17;
[12. Concerning Two Masters	Matt 6:24		Luke 16:13
[13. The Tree and Its Fruit	Matt 7:16–20; 12:33–37		Luke 6:43–45
[14. The Householder	Matt 13:51–52		
[15. The Eagles	Matt 24:28		Luke 17:37
*16. The Watchful Householder	Matt 24:43–44		Luke 12:39–40
17. The Faithful and Wise Servant	Matt 24:45–51		Luke 12:41–48
18. The Coming of the Householder		Mark 13:33–37	Luke 12:35–38
[19. On Healing Oneself			Luke 4:23
[20. The Physician and the Sick	Matt 9:12–13	Mark 2:17	Luke 5:31–32
[21. The Bridegroom	Matt 9:14–15	Mark 2:18–20	Luke 5:33–35
[22. Old Cloth and Old Wine Skins	Matt 9:16–17	Mark 2:21–22	Luke 5:36–39
23. On Building Towers and Going to War			Luke 14:28–33
[24. On Beelzebul	Matt 12:22–30, 43–45	Mark 3:22–27	Luke 11:14–26
25. On the Way to the Judge	Matt 5:25–26		Luke 12:57–59

Key:
[Metaphor or simile omitted by Jeremias from the category "Parable."
(Added by Jeremias.
**   Treated as two separate *Gleichnisse* by Jülicher.
*   Parallels in the GOSPEL OF THOMAS: #16: 85:7–10; 98:6–10. #33: 98:22–27. #36: 93:1–18. #37: 92:10–35. #43: 83:3–13. #44: 85:15–19. #46: 81:28–82:3. #47: 84:26–33; 97:2–6. #48: 98: 31–99:3; 94:14–18. #52: 92:3–10.

26. Places at the Feast			Luke 14:7–11, 12–14
[27. On Crumbs under the Table	Matt 15:26–27	Mark 7:27–28	

B. Parables Proper (*Parabeln*)

28. A House Built on Sand	Matt 7:24–27		Luke 6:47–49
29. The Importunate Friend			Luke 11:5–8
30. The Unjust Judge			Luke 18:1–8
31. The Two Debtors			Luke 7:36–50
32. The Unmerciful Servant	Matt 18:21–35		
*33. The Lost Sheep and Lost Coin	Matt 18:10–14		Luke 15:1–10
34. The Lost Son			Luke 15:11–32
35. The Two Sons	Matt 21:28–32		(Luke 7:29–30)
*36. The Wicked Tenants	Matt 21:33–46	Mark 12:1–12	Luke 20:9–19
*37. The Great Supper (2)	Matt 22:1–10 (11–14)		Luke 14:15–24
38. The Unfruitful Fig Tree			Luke 13:6–9
39. The Ten Virgins	Matt 25:1–13		(Luke 13:23–30)
40. The Laborers in the Field	Matt 20:1–16		
41. The Pounds	Matt 25:14–30		Luke 19:11–27
42. The Unjust Steward			Luke 16:1–12
*43. The Sower	Matt 13:3–9; 18–23	Mark 4:3–9, 14–20	Luke 8:5–8, 11–15
*44. The Seed Growing Secretly		Mark 4:26–29	
45. The Wheat and the Tares	Matt 13:24–30, 36–43		
*46. The Dragnet	Matt 13:47–50		
*47. The Mustard Seed and the Leaven	Matt 13:31–33	Mark 4:30–32	Luke 13:18–21
*48. The Treasure and the Pearl	Matt 13:44–46		
(49. The Last Judgment	Matt 25:31–46		

C. Example Stories (*Beispielerzählungen*)

50. The Good Samaritan			Luke 10:29–37
51. The Pharisee and the Publican			Luke 18:9–14
*52. The Rich Fool			Luke 12:16–21
53. The Rich Man and Lazarus			Luke 16:19–31

See ESCHATOLOGY.

(*Continued from p. 129*) a brief NARRATIVE that culminates in a saying of Jesus; roughly synonymous terms include APOPHTHEGM (RUDOLF BULTMANN) and PRONOUNCEMENT STORY (V. Taylor). MARTIN DIBELIUS introduced this use of paradigm in his form-critical study *From Tradition to Gospel* (Ger: 1919; Eng: New York: Charles Scribner's Sons, 1935; repr. James Clarke, 1971). Dibelius defined *paradigm* as "a short illustrative notice or story of an event, not more descriptive than is necessary to make the point for the sake of which it is introduced" (p. xii). According to Dibelius, the "setting-in-life" of the paradigm was the sermon. Dibelius discovered, in all, eighteen paradigms, including eight of "noteworthy purity" in Mark: "The Healing of the Paralytic" (2:1ff.); "The Question of Fasting" (2:18–19); "Plucking Wheat on the Sabbath" (2:23ff.); "The Healing of the Withered Hand" (3:1ff.); "The Relatives of Jesus" (3:31–35); "Blessing the Children" (10:13–16); "The Tribute Money" (12:13–17); and "The Anointing in Bethany" (14:3–7).

3. Of most recent parlance, the word *paradigm* means "an interpretive framework." This usage stems from T. S. Kuhn's classic but disputed study *The Structure of Scientific Revolutions* (Chicago: University of Chicago Press, 1970). Famously, Newton, Einstein, and quantum mechanics, and super string theory each represent "paradigm shifts" in the way physicists think about reality. According to some, paradigm shifts in science find their corollary in paradigm shifts in biblical interpretation. (See Vern S. Poythress, *Science and Hermeneutics: Implications of Scientific Method for Biblical Interpretation* [Grand Rapids: Zondervan, 1988].)

See FORM CRITICISM.

Paradosis (Gk: that which is handed down or delivered) is usually translated "tradition" (so, e.g., Mark 7:5, 8, 9, 13; Matt 15:2, 3, 6; Col 2:8, etc.). In English the verbal forms of paradosis are rendered by "deliver" (RSV), "passed on" (Phillips), "handed on" (NEB), etc.; these translations have the disadvantage of losing the connotations surrounding the more technical term "tradition." See DOUBLE TRADITION; ORAL TRADITION; TRIPLE TRADITION.

Paradox (fr. Gk: beyond or contrary to expectation; unbelievable). An apparent contradiction; that is, a statement that, though false to common opinion, proves to be unexpectedly but profoundly true. In the NT generally, and in Paul in particular, the central paradox is the GOSPEL of a crucified Messiah (1 Cor 1:22–25); it is presented as the resolution of prior paradoxes pertaining to the nature of God, viz., that God is both just and merciful; that although God makes absolute moral demands (Exod 20; Matt 5:20–48), his forgiving love is also infinite (Hos; Luke 15); that although God is exalted above the heavens, he identifies with the weak (Ps 113; Phil 2:5–7). Jesus' teachings are filled with paradoxes: "For all who exalt themselves will be humbled, and those who humble themselves will be exalted" (Luke 14:11; cf. Mark 8:35; Luke 18:14; Matt 5:3–5, etc.). Paul often cites paradoxes and glories in them (e.g., 1 Cor 7:22; 2 Cor 4:8–11; 5:17; 12:10b; Phil 3:7). Compare Paul's paradoxical antitheses in 2 Cor 6:9–10 with Epictetus 11–19. 24–26: "Show me a man who though rich is happy, though in danger is happy, though dying is happy, though condemned to exile is happy, though in disrepute is happy. Show him! By the gods, I fain would see a stoic . . . , which to this very day I have never seen." See IRONY.

Paraenesis (also parenesis; Gk: exhortation, advice, counsel) is a technical term in FORM CRITICISM, principally introduced by MARTIN DIBELIUS in his studies of the Epistle of James, to denote a text containing a series of admonitions, usually ethical and eclectic in nature and without any reference to concrete situations. The paraenetic passages of the NT outside Jas are varied: in 1 and 2 Thess; Gal 5–6; Rom 12–13; Col 34; and Eph 4–6, paraenesis follows a theological discussion; Paul admonishes the believers to become what the faith declares the believer to be already in CHRIST (cf. Rom 6:1–14; 8:12–13; 1 Cor 5:7–8; 6:9–12, 15–20, etc.); in 1 and 2 Cor and Phil, the paraenesis contains concrete pastoral advice for specific situations.

The Epistle to the Hebrews, which moves back and forth between theological reasoning and paraenesis, is by its own author called a "word of exhortation" (NRSV), i.e., its main purpose is paraenetic. In 1 Peter, paraenesis finds its setting, some suggest, in a baptismal homily (cf. also 1 Cor 5:9; Eph 2:1–10; 5:1–21; Col 3); in 1 John, Jude, and 2 Peter in the dangers of heresy; in the PASTORAL EPISTLES in the responsibilities of the various church orders. For a hypothesis concerning the role of paraenesis in the formation of the GOSPEL tradition, see Dibelius, *From Tradition to Gospel* (London: Ivor Nicholson & Watson, 1934; repr. James Clarke, 1971; New York: Charles Scribner's Sons, 1935), chap. 9.

The place of paraenesis, in the sense of homiletic exhortation, is also important in OT studies, particularly in regard to that tradition surrounding or otherwise related to the covenant renewal festivals in Jerusalem. GERHARD VON RAD interprets Deuteronomy, for example, as basically a collection of sermons ostensibly in the form of a single sermon by Moses but in fact attributable to Levitical circles active prior to the exile. Paraenesis, as a "summons to obedience," reaches its high point in the commandment to love YHWH "with all your heart and with all your soul and with all your might" (Deut 6:4–5; cf. 10:12; 11:13; 13:4, etc.). Paraenesis is also found in the prose sections of Jeremiah; whether patterned after or serving as a pattern for the Deuteronomic paraenetic style is a matter of debate. Elsewhere, cf. also Prov 8:1–21,32–36, etc.

See Leo G. Perdue and John G. Gammie, *Paraenesis: Act and Form* (SEMEIA 50; Atlanta: Scholars Press, 1990).

Paralipomenon (pl.: -mena; Gk: thing[s] left out). The SEPTUAGINT and Latin VULGATE name for the two books of the OT otherwise known in English as 1 and 2 Chronicles; the term, which implies that the works are supplementary to 1 Samuel–2 Kings, is still occasionally used by the Roman Catholic and Eastern Orthodox churches.

Parallel, A.   See **Synopsis.**

Parallelism (*parallelismus membrorum*) is a word used to designate a formal characteristic of Hebrew poetry, though it is found somewhat in Greek, particularly Greek influenced by Semitic IDIOM as in the NT. Parallelism (or *parallelismus membrorum*, the Latin technical term first employed by Robert Lowth [1753] meaning "parallelism of members") takes three major forms: synonymous, antithetic, and synthetic.

1. Synonymous parallelism describes a couplet or bicolon (two cola or half-lines of a poem and occasionally three lines or tricolon) in which the idea expressed in the first line is repeated in the second (or third) with equivalent but different words. Ps 114 contains this form throughout; note, e.g., the two bicola of vv. 3–4:

The sea looked and fled,
    Jordan turned back.
The mountains skipped like rams,
    the hills like lambs.

According to C. F. Burney (*The Poetry of Our Lord* [Oxford: Clarendon Press, 1925], 17), synonymous parallelism is most perfectly exemplified in those instances in which the subject, verb, and object of the first line are paralleled in the second; e.g., Ps 19:1:

The heavens are telling the glory of God;
    and the firmament proclaims his
        handiwork.

In Hebrew the parallel members are expressed a b c d: a´ b´ c´ d´; in English the line reads, a´ b´ d´ c´. So also Ps 94:9, 16; 101:7; Num 23:7–10. Synonymous parallelism appears in prophetic literature: Amos 5:21–24; Isa 40:29–31; 55:6–7, passim. It should be noted that parallelism of this type can vary greatly in degree of completeness.

It is a curiosity of Matt's description of Jesus' entry into Jerusalem that he fails to recognize the synonymous parallelism of the OT passage he is quoting: Zech 9:9; see Matt 21:4–7. For examples in John see 2:11; 4:36; 6:35; 55; 7:34; 13:16.

2. Antithetic parallelism describes a parallelism of thought in which the second line is posed as a contrast to the first. For example, Ps 1:6; 10:16; 11:5; 20:8, etc. The form is especially frequent in WISDOM LITERATURE:

Prov 10:12: Hatred stirs up strife, but love covers all offenses.
Prov 10:20: The tongue of the righteous is choice silver; the mind of the wicked is of little worth.
Cf. 1 Cor 7:29b—31, 32–34; 9:19–22; 10:6–10; 12:15–26, etc.; also John 3:18; 8:35; 9:39.

3. In synthetic parallelism (also called formal, numerical, or constructive parallelism) the parallelism involved is not of thought but of form and is in part discernible by identity of rhythm marked off by a clear break between bicola; in its thought, however, the second line is seen to supplement or complete that of the first (Burney, 21), e.g., Ps 3:2, 4 (in Hebrew, 3:3, 5); 14:1–2; 40:1–3 (in Hebrew, 40:24); Prov 6:16–19, etc. In NT, John 8:44.

Step parallelism is a type of synthetic parallelism usually of three or more cola, in which the thought of the unit is advanced with each line. Since one or more members of the initial line is often repeated, step parallelism bears a resemblance to synonymous parallelism as well, e.g., Ps 29:1–2; 3:1–2. In NT, John 1:1–5, 10–12,14; 6:37; 8:32; 13:20; 14:21.

A parallelism that exists within a bicolon or tricolon (2 or 3 lines) is sometimes called internal parallelism; one that exists between two or more bi- or tri-cola is called external parallelism.

A study of HB parallelism that finds significance not in parallelism itself but in what takes place *within* parallelistic lines is James L. Kugel's work *The Idea of Biblical Poetry* (New Haven: Yale University Press, 1981). See CHIASMUS; COLON.

Paraphrase   Commonly, a paraphrase is a free rendering of the sense of a difficult passage or text into another form in the same language. Within the context of Bible translation, paraphrase generally refers to a style of translation in which clarity is given precedence over fidelity to the original phrasing and vocabulary. The word paraphrase, its meaning and proper use, however, is a frequent subject of debate. Some argue that all translation is paraphrase; others, that a paraphrase is an interpretive translation while *metaphrase* is a slavishly literal translation—good, faithful translation being somewhere in between. J. B. Phillips (*The New Testament in Modern English*) admits to an occasional paraphrase "because a literal translation of the original Greek would prove unintelligible" ("Translator's Foreword"), but his translation is nevertheless usually termed a paraphrase.

The Living Bible, Paraphrased defines *paraphrase* "as a careful restatement of the author's thoughts," that "does not attempt to translate word by word, but rather thought by thought." The *LB(P)* calls itself an "interpretive translation"—a description that Phillips explicitly rejects for the *NTME*.

Cf. John 1:1a in NRSV: "In the beginning was the Word"; Phillips: "At the beginning God expressed himself'; *LB(P)*: "Before anything else existed, there was CHRIST." See LIVING BIBLE (PARAPHRASED); VERSION; EXEGESIS.

Parataxis   (Gk: to place beside). In grammar generally parataxis refers to the coordination of clauses without indicating their syntactic relation; in NT study it more often refers to the simple coordination of words, clauses, sentences, or paragraphs with "and" (*kai*). Parataxis is especially characteristic of Semitic style and, in the NT, is the most distinguishing characteristic of Mark, of whose 88 sections (as found in the WESTCOTT and HORT Greek text) 80 begin with "and" (Hawkins, 151). Asyndetic parataxis refers to the conjoining of parallel syntactic elements (whether words, phrases, or sentences) without a connective (such as and, but, or therefore). The opening verse of Ps 23 is an example of asyndetic parataxis and can be properly translated "Since the Lord is my shepherd, I shall not be in need" (Eugene Nida, *Toward a Science in Translating* [Leiden: E. J. Brill, 1964], 210). See HYPOTAXIS; PROSTAXIS.

Parchment.   See **Vellum.**

Parole.   See **Structuralism**.

Paronomasia   broadly defined is a play on words, a pun; in a more technical sense it is "the recurrence of the same word or word stem in close proximity" (BDF, 258). Paronomasia, whether appearing in the Hebrew OT or the Greek NT, is usually lost in translation, as, e.g., in the NT: Matt 21:41; 2 Cor 4:8 (NEB: "Hard-pressed on every side, we are never hemmed in"); Phil 3:2–3 (see KJV and the circumlocution of NEB). Other NT paronomasia include Mark 5:26; Rom 1:23, 25, 27, 28; 5:16, 19; 12:3, 15; 13:7; 14:22–23; 1 Cor 8:2–3; 9:19–22; 11:31–32; 13:6; 15:50; 2 Cor 3:2; 7:5; 8:22; 9:8; Acts 21:28; 23:3, etc. In Hebrew paronomasia is natural and ubiquitous. For example, Gen 1:2 describes the earth as *"thohu wavohu"*; here the sense of chaos is conveyed through ONOMATOPOEIA; in Gen 2:7, Adam is made of *Adamah* (ground), an etiological pun; Gen 4:1; 19:30–21:24; Job 3:25, etc., are etymological puns (or *figura etymologica*), in which substantives are derived from verbs.

Related to paronomasia is *antistasis:* the use of a word twice in close proximity with a sharp shift in meaning, e.g., Matt 10:39: "He who finds his life will lose it, and he who loses his life for my sake will find it." Cf. 1 Cor 1:21; 2:16, etc. Similarly: *antana-*

clasis, in which the shift in sense is not so sharp, e.g., Matt 8:22; 13:9 (KJV); Luke 10:16; 13:30, etc. Though neither term is current, the phenomena they describe are worth noting.

Parousia   (Gk: presence; cf. apousia: absence). In primitive Christianity, Parousia referred to the triumphant return of CHRIST at the end of the age (see the prayers in 1 Cor 16:22b and Rev 22:20; cf. 22:7, 12). The expectation of Jesus' return, coupled with his nonappearance (called "the delay of the Parousia"), had a profound effect upon the life and thought of the NT church (see e.g., 2 Pet 3:3–13; 2 Thess 2:1–12; Luke 21:7–9; Mark 13; Matt 24). However, the proper definition of Parousia, its relationship as an idea to Jesus' self-understanding, whether the Parousia refers to an event continuous with historical time or discontinuous, etc., are all highly debated subjects within BIBLICAL CRITICISM and theology. See, e.g., what is a countervailing argument to most 20th-cent. NT scholarship: N. T. Wright, *Jesus and the Victory of God* (Minneapolis: Fortress Press, 1996). See APOCALYPTIC; ESCHATOLOGIZE; ESCHATOLOGY.

Partitio.   See **Rhetorical Analysis.**

Pasce oves pericope   (Lat: Feed [my] lambs; PERICOPE: Gk: passage). See John 21:15–17.

Pastoral Epistles   consist of 1 and 2 Timothy and Titus in the NT; the title is derived from the "pastoral" advice which the author is writing to the recipients. The epistles are thought by many to be pseudonymous (or eponymous) though perhaps containing fragments of authentically Pauline LETTERS. See CATHOLIC EPISTLES; DEUTEROPAULINE.

Pedersen, Johannes Peder Ejler (1883–1977). Born in Illebolle, Denmark, Pedersen was lecturer in OT EXEGESIS at the University of Copenhagen (1916–22) and later professor of Semitic philology (1922–50). His major work (*Israel: Its Life* *and Culture*, vols. 1–4 [Eng: 1926–40; reprinted: Atlanta: Scholars Press, 1991]) greatly influenced subsequent OT research, particularly in Scandinavia, for its descriptive rather than historical approach to Israelite religion and for its emphasis on the role of the cult and primitive psychology in the formation of OT traditions. See KULTGESCHICHTLICHE SCHULE.

Pentateuch is a name derived from Greek for the first five books of the OT commonly known in Hebrew as the *Humash* ("the five fifths"); it is the first of three divisions of the Jewish Scriptures and is also called the LAW or the TORAH. The Pentateuch occupies a special place within the canon of the HB for several reasons. First, the events it relates are presupposed by the rest of the Jewish scriptures and are often explicitly mentioned or alluded to by them (e.g., Josh 24:2). Second, the Pentateuch enjoys a special place in Jewish religious tradition, both because the events it narrates are decisive for Jewish memory (cf. the Passover *HAGGADAH*) and because the body of law it contains is central to what eventually became normative Judaism. Finally, the Pentateuch has enjoyed a special place in history of modern biblical scholarship, since questions of its authorship and development were among the inaugurating themes of the field. (Richard Elliott Friedman, ad loc. ABD). See PROPHETS; TANAKH; HAGIOGRAPHA; E: ELOHIST; J (YAHWIST); P: PRIESTLY CODE; D: DEUTERONOMIC CODE; GRAF-WELLHAUSEN HYPOTHESIS.

Pericope (Gk: lit., "cut around") appears as a technical term in Hellenistic RHETORIC (3rd cent. C.E.) for a short section or passage of a writing and is carried over into Latin by JEROME to designate portions of scripture; use of the term in this way preceded the division of scripture into chapters (the PENTATEUCH first being divided into 175 pericopes) and subsequent to that, the pericope came to be used as a "lesson" for reading in public worship and later as the unit for preaching. In BIBLICAL CRITICISM,

the term is often used to refer to any self-contained unit of scripture.

Pericope de adultera refers to John 7:53–8:11, the account of the woman caught in adultery, which is absent from all MSS of John's GOSPEL prior to ca. 350 C.E. See DEUTEROCANON; PERICOPE; TEXTUAL CRITICISM.

Peripeteia (also peripetia, peripety) is a Greek technical term used in LITERARY CRITICISM to denote a sudden or unexpected turn of events or reversal of circumstances in a literary work; as in 2 Sam 12:1–15; Luke 12:13–21; Mark 8:27–33, etc.

Peroratio. See **Rhetorical Analysis.**

Peshat (Heb: simple meaning) has long been defined as the simple or plain meaning of a text, as opposed to the *derash*, or its homiletical interpretation. So defined, *peshat* is roughly equivalent to the LITERAL SENSE of scripture. Recent work, however, has demonstrated that early Jewish exegetes did not conceive the *peshat* along the lines of modern HISTORICAL CRITICISM as the most primitive meaning of a text or the meaning intended by the author. Rather, the *peshat* was the familiar and traditional teaching of scripture that was recognized by the community as authoritative in a given time and place, and which already implies concern for a text's contemporary religious significance. See Raphael Loewe, "The 'Plain' Meaning of Scripture in Early Jewish Exegesis," *Papers of the Institute of Jewish Studies in London*, vol. 1 (Jerusalem, 1964), 140–185; Stephen Garfinkel, "Applied *Peshat*: Historical-Critical Method and Religious Meaning," *Journal of the Ancient Near Eastern Society* 22 (1993):19–28. See MIDRASH; HILLEL.

Pesher (pl.: *pesharim*; Heb: interpretation, COMMENTARY). A technical term from Hebrew meaning commentary and applied by modern scholars as a descriptive designation to certain documents among the DEAD SEA SCROLLS: the *pesharim* on Habakkuk (1QpH), Nahum (4QpNah), Isaiah (1QpIsa), etc. The *pesharim* of the

DSS are haggadic MIDRASH, that is, scriptural commentary of a nonlegal nature; they are, however, commentaries of a special character in that they view the prophetic books of the HB as containing divine mysteries that pertain to the last days in which the Qumran sectarians believed themselves to be living and that therefore call for divinely illuminated interpretation. The Aramaic equivalent, *peshar*, is used 31 times in the Aramaic portions of the book of Daniel, the great APOCALYPTIC interpretation of history of the 2nd cent. B.C.E. It is well to remember that the term *pesher*, used to refer to a genre of literature, was coined by modern scholars and does not necessarily designate a classification that the authors of the relevant documents would have recognized. See *HALAKAH*.

Peshitta (syᴾ; also Peshitto: "simple"). The authorized Bible of the Syrian Church, dating from the latter 4th or early 5th cent. and traditionally ascribed to Rabbula, Bishop of Edessa (d. 435). Omitted from early MSS of the Peshitta are 2 Peter, 2 and 3 John, Jude, and Revelation, which the Syrian Church did not accept as canonical.

Philo of Alexandria (ca. 20 B.C.E.–45 C.E.). A Hellenistic Jewish philosopher and biblical exegete of the 1st cent., who lived in Alexandria, Egypt, the member of a wealthy and influential family and, significantly, a contemporary of Jesus (d. ca. 30 C.E.) and Paul (d. ca. 65 C.E.). Called a "man of two worlds," Philo was loyal to Jewish institutions and practices and thoroughly at home in Hellenistic philosophy, and he devoted much of his literary activity to the EXPOSITION of the LXX in terms indigenous to Platonic and Stoic thought. Philo was a skilled practitioner of allegorical EXEGESIS who sought to uncover the higher moral and cosmological lessons hidden above all in the PENTATEUCH, yet generally in a manner that preserved the validity of the LITERAL SENSE, especially in matters of ritual observance (see, e.g., *de migrationi Abrahami* [*On the Migration of Abraham*], 89–93).

Though quickly forgotten by his native Judaism, Philo's works were preserved by the Christian church, where they proved enormously influential, fundamentally shaping the ALEXANDRIAN SCHOOL of interpretation and earning for Philo himself the standing of "honorary Father of the Church" (Runia).

See Samuel Sandmel, *Philo of Alexandria: An Introduction* (New York: Oxford University Press, 1979); *Studia philonica* (published by the Philo Institute, Chicago, vols. 1–6, 1972–1980; dealing with "Hellenistic Judaism in general and with the works of Philo Judaeus in particular"), and *Studia philonica Annual* (1989–1998); for Philo's influence on Christian biblical interpretation, see D. H. T. Runia, *Philo and the Church Fathers* (Leiden: E. J. Brill, 1995).

Phoneme (Gk: sound). In LINGUISTICS a phoneme is "the maximum feature of the expression system of a spoken language . . . " According to H. A. Gleason there are 46 phonemes in the English language: 24 consonants, 9 vowels, 3 semivowels (including two consonants), 1 open transition, 4 stresses, 4 pitches, and 3 clause terminals—each of which is an indispensable part of the English system of verbal communication. See H. A. Gleason, *An Introduction to Descriptive Linguistics* (New York and London: Holt, Rinehart & Winston, 1961²). See MORPHEME; STRUCTURALISM.

Plain Sense. See **Literal Sense.**

Pleonasm (Lat: more than enough) is a technical term denoting a real or apparent redundancy of expression. The repetition of an idea by way of synonyms, particularly in poetry, is characteristic of Hebrew and is not duplicated in precise manner or extent in Greek. Consult a SYNOPSIS of the GOSPELS and note the following pleonasms in Mark that (assuming the priority of Mark) are eliminated in the Matthean parallel: Mark 2:25; 3:26; 4:2; 7:15, 21; 9:2; 14:1, 61; 15:26. Some pleonastic formulations may be for precision; see Mark 1:28, 32, 35, 38, passim.

Pneumatophany. See **Theophany.**

Poimandrès. See **Hermetic Literature.**

Polyglot is a Greek word meaning "many tongues" or "languages." As a noun it is used most frequently in reference to a Bible with the text in several languages placed in parallel columns. The most famous of these date to the 16th and 17th centuries and are known by the city in which they were published: Complutensia (Alcalá, Spain; 6 vols., 1522), Antwerp (8 vols., 1572), Paris (9 vols., 1645), and London (6 vols., 1657).

Postcolonial Biblical Interpretation is "an umbrella term that covers a multitude of literary practices and concerns of diverse races, empires, colonies, geographical centers, times, and genres. . . . [I]t emphasizes the pervasiveness of imperialism and relates imperial expansion, impact, and response to certain literary practices and practitioners. . . . [Hence, it] situate[s] almost all reading and writing of the past three to four hundred years within the parameters of imperial and colonial currents of dominance and resistance, challenging all readers and writers to examine their practices for imperial and colonial currents of domination and suppression" (Dube Shomanah).

The term *postcolonial* was introduced by political scientists in the early 1970s to denote the condition of Third World political systems after decolonization by the Western powers (i.e., Western Europe, Great Britain, and the United States.) It first came to be widely adopted as the name for a diverse family of critical perspectives in the late 1980s. Generally, postcolonialism grapples with the history and effects of Western imperialism and colonialism on a variety of levels, focusing as much on the ideology of colonialism as on the material consequences of colonial subjugation. It addresses themes such as slavery, migration, diaspora, oppression and resistance, identity and hybridity, ethnicity, gender, race, and place. In addition, postcolonialism addresses the West's continuing power and authority in global affairs and explores various strategies for resisting and appropriating Western ideas and influence.

Postcolonial biblical interpretation focuses on the use of the Bible in the context of Western colonialism and its aftermath. It demonstrates how Christian missionaries, official representatives of the colonizing powers, and colonized peoples themselves used the Bible in ways that legitimated colonialism. For this reason, a large number of postcolonial biblical interpretations deal less with the biblical texts themselves than with the readings of biblical texts by colonial and postcolonial missionaries up to the present. The Bible figures not as an ancient document to be investigated, or as a source of faith to be interpreted, but as an instrument of colonial power to be unmasked and deflected. Frequently, postcolonial biblical interpretation registers a similarly negative verdict against modern Western BIBLICAL CRITICISM, whose pretensions to universal validity are viewed as complicit with imperial expansion and colonial rule. Nevertheless, exceptions to this generalization are abundant, and many practitioners of postcolonial biblical interpretation are also concerned with developing approaches that reclaim the Bible's role for communities of faith.

Postcolonial biblical interpretation is diverse in methodology and approach. Examples include (a) the use of a comparative religions approach to read indigenous MYTHS and stories on equal footing with those of the Bible; (b) feminist analysis of male privilege in the HB and NT; (c) Afrocentric interpretation that seeks to give proper place to the role of Egypt and Ethiopia in the biblical story; (d) folklore studies that illumine biblical stories through the use of local folktales and thereby give recognition to the value of the interpreters' culture.

Evaluated from the perspective of the Bible's own formative traditions, the urgency of postcolonial biblical interpretation's central concern can scarcely be denied, viz., its determination not to accept the ideological distortion of God's word as God's word. While not all postcolonial practitioners find the relevant criterion for distinguishing between these two in the Bible itself, those that do continue in the tradition of biblical interpreters who have found the most powerful critique of the Bible's misuse in the Bible's own witness to God. See ADVOCACY CRITICISM; IDEOLOGICAL CRITICISM; FEMINIST BIBLICAL INTERPRETATION.

See B. Ashcroft, G. Griffiths, and H. Tiffin, *The Post-colonial Studies Reader* (London: Routledge & Kegan Paul, 1994); F. Segovia and M. A. Tolbert (eds.), *Reading from This Place*, 2 vols. (Minneapolis: Fortress Press, 1995); Fernando F. Segovia, *Decolonizing Biblical Studies: A View from the Margins* (New York: Orbis Press, 2000); also *Semeia* 72 (1995) and 73 (1996); and Musa W. Dube, *Postcolonial Feminist Interpretation of the Bible* (St. Louis: Chalice Press, 2000).

Postcritical Biblical Interpretation

designates an approach to scripture undertaken by a community of interpreters "for whom returning to the biblical text embodies, beyond all scholarship, a living relationship with God and humankind." Their shared conviction, whether Jewish or Christian, is that "the reality of God is simply a fact of common sense, that this God is as near to us as a touch," and that all biblical scholarship fails when this reality is forgotten (P. Ochs).

Postcritical biblical interpretation is not "post" critical because it rejects outright critical methodologies and their guiding philosophical assumptions. It acknowledges that critical methodologies, both historical and literary, can be used to "honor the divine word" and should not be ignored but held in ongoing conversation. The inadequacy of critical methodologies lies rather in the fact that they often willfully bracket out questions of ultimate meaning and too often devolve into interminable scholastic debates about the methodological legitimacy or adequacy of this or that approach. Questions of ultimacy receive scant hearing. Thus it is not so much what critical methodologies do but what they fail to do that calls for a "postcritical" return to the text. The paradigmatic examples of this return in the 20th cent. are KARL BARTH (1886–1968) and Hans Rosenzweig (1886–1929). Both men, one Christian and one Jewish, were fully conversant with the regnant philosophies and BIBLICAL CRITICISMS of the day, but turned to the text in a "postcritical" way to hear the Bible's own word on ultimate matters, not to force it into the Procrustean Bed of critical methods. Postcritical biblical interpretation also looks to other figures who embodied a kind of "postcritical" spirit in their own day, such as ORIGEN, Augustine, Johann Georg Hamann, Søren Kierkegaard, and others.

As a contemporary movement, postcritical biblical interpretation does not subscribe to the view, characteristic of much HISTORICAL CRITICISM, that "the most primitive meaning of the text is its only valid meaning, and the historical-critical method is the only key which can unlock it" (Steinmetz). Unlike methodologies such as SOURCE and FORM CRITICISM, which disintegrate the text into its antecedent kernels, postcritical biblical interpretation assumes that the canonical form of the text was designed to convey a message, and that finally the Bible itself is a text in its own right in which all discernible units large and small take on new hues and connotations within the whole. And just as the Bible's canonical shape was determined not by a single individual but by a community, so also interpretation of the Bible today properly takes place not "monologically," in isolated autonomy, but within a community of shared inquiry, as in a religious community or a community of scholars. Finally, postcritical biblical interpretation holds that the aim of interpretation "is never a mere matter of handling text and the relationships between texts. It is above all a matter of being in the presence and open to the handling of the One who, in some sense, is the final 'author' of its message" (Trevor Hart). The postcritical approach to the Bible thus presupposes a threefold relation between word (text), community of interpretation, and God. According to postcritical biblical interpretation, apart from this threefold relation, "the meaning of the Bible" can scarcely be understood.

The specific methods appropriate to postcritical biblical interpretation are various. Generally speaking, practitioners look to the scripture itself and to precritical EXEGESIS (e.g., rabbinic writings and the church fathers) to find models of scriptural interpretation that can be imitated as "vaguely defined principles of conduct." The work of the Jewish scholar Michael Fishbane on "inner-biblical" interpretation has found resonance among Jewish and Christian scholars (*Biblical Interpretation in Ancient Israel* [Oxford: Clarendon Press, 1985]). (See INTERTEXTUALITY.) Briefly, Fishbane argues that the Bible itself embodies patterns of biblical interpretation (cf. the prophet Jeremiah on the ark of the covenant [Jer 3:16] or the exodus [Jer 16:14–15]), and that these patterns in turn anticipate and shape subsequent patterns of postbiblical interpretation as they are found, for example, in rabbinic writings. This biblical and postbiblical tradition of interpretation can in turn provide a model for the contemporary practice of postcritical biblical interpretation. In rereading, the tradition is kept alive; the past is incorporated as part of a greater and living whole. "The reintroduction of the elements [separated by the fragmenting influence of historical criticism] to one another is a return from exile, both for the elements and for the reader who is thereby returned not only to the Bible as a whole but also to him- or herself as an agent of active interpretation and to the community of readers in which that interpretation finds its antecedents, guides, and meaning" (Ochs).

Interest in postcritical biblical interpretation is being aided by such guilds as the Society for Scriptural Reasoning, which has as one of its aims to recover the practices of hearing God's speech that both preceded and still provide the terms for modern thinking.

For this synopsis see Peter Ochs, "Returning to Scripture: Trends in Postcritical Interpretation," *Cross Currents* 44 (1994/95): 437–53; also by Ochs, *Return to Scripture in Judaism and Christianity* (New York: Paulist Press, 1993). For a discussion of three distinct varieties of postcritical biblical interpretation, see George Lindbeck, "Postcritical Canonical Interpretation: Three Modes of Retrieval," in *Theological Exegesis*, ed. by Christopher Seitz and Kathryn Greene-McCreight (Grand Rapids: Eerdmans, 1998). See THEOLOGICAL INTERPRETATION.

Postmodern Biblical Interpretation

Just as there is no single definition of the modern, there is no single definition of the postmodern. Commonly speaking, however, postmodern refers to a style of thought that is suspicious of modern rationalist accounts of truth, reason, and objectivity; that distrusts single explanatory frameworks or METANARRATIVES; that sees the world and personal identities as diverse, dispersed, indeterminate, and ungrounded; and that celebrates (or is resigned to) an approach to life and thought that is playful, eclectic, pluralistic, and subversive of traditional boundaries.

In the broadest sense, the term *postmodern* can be applied to any perspective that adopts at least some of these features. In this sense, for example, KARL BARTH is sometimes held to be a postmodern thinker, even though clearly not all of his commitments are postmodern in character (cf. Scott C. Saye, "The Wild and Crooked Tree: Barth, Fish, and Interpretive Communities," in *Modern Theology* 12, no. 4 [October, 1996]: 435–58). More narrowly, however, the term *postmodern* is reserved for perspectives that embrace many or most of the relevant features in a programmatic way.

A postmodern approach to biblical interpretation typically proceeds by drawing attention to what it regards as the problematic or unsustainable premises of modern BIBLICAL CRITICISM. These premises are often said to include (1) the view that biblical texts are artifacts that have a single, stable, meaning; (2) that a text's meaning, though initially hidden from the modern interpreter by temporal and cultural distances, can be recovered by historical reconstruction; and (3) that the benefits of critical methods accrue over time as methods become more sophisticated and as data increase.

By contrast, postmodern biblical interpretation contends that the meaning of a text is not "in" the text waiting to be recovered through the use of neutral, generally applicable criteria. Rather, textual meaning is constructed through the interplay of a text's semantic and rhetorical aspects and the reader's own life-world. In effect, the reader constructs the meaning of a text by creative use of the language, nuances, and conventions in which the reader is immersed. Thus postmodern biblical interpretation shifts the focus of attention from the historical origins of a text ("the world behind the text") and even from the text itself ("the world of the text") to the reader's use of a text within a given community of interpretation ("the world in front of the text").

Two characteristic emphases accompany a postmodern insistence on the "constructed" character of the biblical text. First, postmodern biblical interpretation emphasizes the particularity and distinctiveness of different communities of biblical interpretation and insists that no single such community can claim to enjoy privileged knowledge of the text. It seeks to dismantle the academy's (and the church's) claim to "insider" status with respect to the Bible's meaning. It challenges what it regards as modernity's unwarranted "hegemony of the expert" that has served to discount equally valid but differently formulated interpretations. And it seeks to empower interpretive communities whose voices have been marginalized, and/or to employ nontraditional media of interpretation, such as art, film, drama, etc.

Second, postmodern biblical interpretation emphasizes that interpretation is not only a matter of textual construction but also a process of self-location in which the reader lays bare his or her interests in the act of reading itself. Modern biblical criticism's ideal of a disinterested reading is an illusion that masks the presence of hidden interests (typically, of race, gender, class, sexuality, institutional location). A postmodern approach insists that these be acknowledged and dealt with in the interpretative process. It summons marginalized elements of the reader's life-world to interpret the biblical text in ways that subvert universalizing or stabilizing perspectives, and in this way seeks to celebrate an eternally open, because eternally indeterminate, text.

Despite its commitment to difference, postmodern biblical interpretation at times seems to exert a curiously homogenizing influence on the actual practice of interpretation, "constructing" a remarkably similar set of concerns irrespective of the particular biblical text in question. Perhaps this is symptomatic of a wider trend in biblical scholarship characterized by loss of interest in the biblical text itself in favor of preoccupation with the interpreter and the act of interpretation. Be that as it may, the fruitfulness of a postmodern approach for the practice of biblical interpretation seems likely to remain an open question for some time to come. From this description it is clear that postmodern biblical interpretation shares many ideas in common but is not synonymous with READER-RESPONSE CRITICISM, DECONSTRUCTION, IDEOLOGICAL CRITICISM, POSTCOLONIAL BIBLICAL INTERPRETATION, etc. However, if it is not contained in any single method, approach, or PARADIGM, then this description too is but an approximation that must be revised in light of any specific example.

See A. K. M. Adam, *What Is Postmodern Biblical Criticism?* Guides to Biblical Scholarship, ed. Dan O. Via (Minneapolis: Fortress Press, 1995); *The Postmodern Bible: The Bible and Culture Collective*, ed. Elisabeth A. Castelli et al. (New Haven, Conn.: Yale University Press, 1995), includes extensive bibliography; Stephen D. Moore, *Mark and Luke in Poststructuralist Perspectives: Jesus Begins to Write* (New Haven, Conn.: Yale University Press, 1992); Walter Brueggemann, *Texts Under Negotiation: The Bible and Postmodern Imagination* (Minneapolis: Fortress Press, 1993).

Pre-Pauline   The term is perhaps self-explanatory, except that it is frequently misunderstood by the beginner in NT criticism, for in normal use it refers to doctrines, FORMULAS, ideas, etc., that were in existence within the church prior to Paul's *use* of them, rather than being prior to Paul himself or to his conversion. See DEUTERO-PAULINE; TRADITION CRITICISM.

Primitive Christianity.   See **Early Church, (The).**

Probatio.   See **Rhetorical Analysis.**

Prolepsis   (adj.: proleptic; Gk: a taking beforehand; anticipation; preconception). In LITERARY CRITICISM, *prolepsis* is a technical term for the type of prophetic speech that treats as past that which in fact is still only a future possibility. For example, in Amos 5:1–3 the prophet laments the fall of Israel as an accomplished fact though it is yet to occur and in Matt 23:38 Jesus laments the fall of Jerusalem, which does not take place until 40 years after his crucifixion. However, the latter may be a *VATICINIUM EX EVENTU* placed on the lips of Jesus by the GOSPEL writer. More generally, the adjective proleptic can be applied to events or depictions of events that anticipate the future, e.g., Matthew's infancy NARRATIVE has been described as a "proleptic Passion."

Pronouncement Story   is the name given by English scholar Vincent Taylor (*The Formation of the Gospel Tradition* [London: Macmillan & Co., 1933]) to 35–40 brief NARRATIVES in the synoptic tradition that embody as their raison d'être a pronouncement-type saying of Jesus. An example of the pronouncement story "at its best" concerns tribute to Caesar (Mark 12:13–17). Taylor's *pronouncement story* is essentially equivalent to what MARTIN DIBELIUS termed "PARADIGMS" and BULTMANN termed "APOPHTHEGMS." In English scholarship the term *pronouncement story* has perhaps gained the greater currency. In contrast to Dibelius, Taylor did not believe that these narratives were primarily the product of the EARLY CHURCH's need for sermonic illustration; in contrast to Bultmann, he did not believe the narrative settings of the pronouncement SAYINGS were "ideal" or "fictitious" but, in large measure at least, historical. See Robert C. Tannehill (ed.), *Pronouncement Stories* (*Semeia* 20; Atlanta: Scholars Press, 1981); also Vernon D. Robbins, *The Rhetoric of Pronouncement* (*Semeia* 64; Atlanta: Scholars Press, 1994). See FORM CRITICISM.

Prooemium.   See **Rhetorical Analysis.**

Prophecy   (Gk: *propheteia*) is an utterance, whether originally oral or written, of a prophet (Gk: *prophetes*, lit.: "one who speaks for another"). In biblical tradition, a prophet (Heb: *nabi'*) was one who proclaimed the will or mind of God—whether to an individual (such as the king; see 2 Sam 12; 1 Kgs 21:17–24) or to the nation, even if he spoke falsely (1 Kgs 22:13–36; esp. v. 23) or was in service to false gods (such as Baal; see 1 Kgs 18:22). Since the prophet's interpretation of divine will often pertained to the future, the identification of prophecy with foretelling future events naturally followed (1 Sam 9:9 states that "he who is now called a prophet was formerly called a seer" [Heb: *rō'eh*]). This aspect of prophecy, however, is often considered a secondary and later characteristic. In any case, OT prophecy normally saw the future not as predetermined by divine foreordination but as a just consequence of past and present actions on the part of the individual or of Israel as a whole.

The origins of prophecy, its relation to divination and sorcery, its role in the cult, and the role of ecstasy in prophetic inspiration are uncertain due to the fragmentary and ambiguous evidence of scripture itself. First Sam 10:6 identifies prophecy with ecstasy and frenzy that caused the spirit-possessed to change "into another person." Ecstatic utterances by their very nature can scarcely be preserved in writing. OT prophecy in the classical sense (see following) is by contrast intelligible speech, poetic in form, and thus susceptible to repetition, reinterpretation, and reapplication. Prophecy as rational speech also explains the rise of schools of PROPHETS, with master-disciple relationships, which in turn accounts for the collection, redaction, and preservation of the great prophetic ORACLES and traditions. The period of Israelite prophecy appears to have run from the 11th to the 2nd cent. B.C.E. The classical period of prophecy occurred during the 8th to the 6th cent. B.C.E. and is represented predominantly by the OT books of Amos, Micah, Hosea, Isaiah, Jeremiah, and Ezekiel. The book of Daniel (ca. 165 B.C.E.), though numbered among the minor prophets, marks the ascendancy of a new worldview and a new literary mode divergent from that of classical prophecy and known as APOCALYPTIC.

In OT FORM CRITICISM, prophecy constitutes a separate category of literature distinct from NARRATIVE, LAW, PSALMS, and WISDOM. Prophecy is not a strictly formal category, however, since the *means* by which a prophet received a divine revelation (dreams, visions, ecstasies, or mystical experience) did not necessarily determine the *form* by which the prophecy itself was to be communicated. Prophecy could take the form of symbolic names (e.g., Isa 7:3), a play on words (apparent only in Hebrew;

e.g., Amos 8:1–3; Jer 1:11–12, etc.), a song (Isa 5:1–7; 23:16), a symbolic act (Hos 1; 3; Isa 20:1–6; Jer 32:6ff.), a funeral elegy (Isa 14:4a–21; Amos 5:1–2; Ezek 19, etc.), an ALLEGORY (Ezek 16; 20; 23), a report, such as an account of a vision or dream (Amos 7:1–9; 8:1–3; Jer 13:1–11, etc.), and so on.

Early form-critical studies, especially that of HERMANN GUNKEL, concentrated on the analysis of prophetic SAYINGS; later form criticism turned to the study of prophetic narratives. The latter have been divided into three major forms: (A) AUTOBIOGRAPHY or "private oracle," such as (1) reports of visions (see previous), of which a special type in terms of content is the prophet's call (Isa 6; Jer 1; Ezek 1–2, etc.), and (2) accounts of symbolic acts (in addition to the previous, see Isa 7:3; 8:1–4; Jer 16:1–9, etc.); (B) biographies of the prophets (Jer 26–28; 36–45, etc.); and (C) LEGENDS about the prophets, e.g., Ahijah the Shilonite (1 Kgs 11:29ff.), Samuel (1 Sam 3:1–18, etc.), Elijah (1 Kgs 17:1–16, 17–24, etc.), and Elisha (2 Kgs 2:19–22, 23–24; 4:1–7, etc.).

Form critics have identified two major types of prophetic sayings (speeches or oracles): (a) the prophecy of judgment (or disaster) and (b) of salvation. According to CLAUS WESTERMANN, the former can be divided between the "Judgment-speech to the individual" (e.g., 1 Kgs 21:18–19; 2 Kgs 1:34; Amos 7:14–17; Isa 22:15–25; 37:22–29; Jer 20:1–6; 22:10–12, 13–19, and passim) and the "Judgment-speech to the nation" (e.g., Amos 4:1–2; Hos 2:5–7; Isa 8:5–8; 9:7–11, 17–20; 22:8–14; 28:7–13; 29:13–14; 30:12–14, 15–17; Mic 2:14; 3:1–2, 4, 9–12; Jer 5:10–14, and passim). Westermann further suggests that such oracles have a set STRUCTURE that includes (1) an introduction (e.g., "Hear," "Woe"); (2) an accusation (oppression, harlotry, etc.); (3) a development of the accusation; (4) a messenger FORMULA, such as "Thus says the LORD" (e.g., Amos 1:3, 6, 9, 11, 13; called a *kōh ʾamar* formula) or "The word of the LORD came to me, saying . . . " (e.g., Jer 1:4, 11, 13; 2:1, and passim) or simply "Therefore" (Hos 2:6; Isa 8:7); (5) an announcement of God's intervention (e.g., "the days are coming upon you," Amos 4:2); and (6) the results of intervention (e.g., "Jerusalem shall become a heap of ruins," Mic 3:12). The early form critic Hermann Gunkel considered (2) and (3), and (5) and (6) to be two originally separate and distinct prophetic types, the former called a "reproach" or "invective" (Ger: Scheltrede), and the latter called a "threat" (Ger: Drohrede). Westermann's study intended to show this not to be the case.

A variant or secondary form of the prophetic oracle of judgment is the Woe-oracle (Heb: hôy), which has been identified by Westermann and others in Amos 5:18–20; 6:1–7; Isa 5:8–23; 28:1–31:9; Hab 2; Mic 2:14, etc. (See Claus Westermann, Basic Forms of Prophetic Speech, trans. Hugh Clayton White [Philadelphia: Westminster Press, 1967].)

According to Klaus Koch, the prophecy of salvation bears a structure similar to that of the prophecy of judgment; it may be found in Jer 28:24; 32:14–15, 36–41; 34:4–5; 35:18–19; 1 Kgs 17:14; 2 Kgs 3:16–19, etc. (See Koch, The Growth of the Biblical Tradition, trans. S. M. Cupitt [New York: Charles Scribner's Sons, 1969; London: A. & C. Black, 1969].) In addition to the prophecy of salvation, Westermann further distinguishes between the oracle of salvation (e.g., Isa 41:8–13, 14–16; 43:14, 5–7; 44:1–5) and the proclamation of salvation (e.g., Isa 41:17–20; 42:14–17; 43:16–21; and 49: 7–12), the former dealing with the present, the latter with a distant future, the former connected with a priest in the setting of individual LAMENT, the latter with a prophet and community lament.

Paul Hanson suggested that the origin of apocalyptic ESCHATOLOGY is to be traced to the joining of the prophetic oracle of salvation (blessing) with the oracle of judgment (curse). This salvation-judgment oracle (e.g., Isa 58:1–12) constitutes a new genre and corresponds to the apocalyptic outlook that part of Israel would be saved, part damned with the coming of the Day of YHWH (see Paul Hanson, The Dawn of Apocalyptic [Philadelphia: Fortress Press, 1975]).

Form critics have identified other forms among the prophetic speeches of the OT that may be borrowed from various settings within the culture. These "secondary" forms, which help shape the content and meaning of the passage in question, include the "trial speech" patterned after Israel's legal procedures (e.g., Isa 1:18–20; 3:13–15; Mic 6:1–5; Hos 2:4–17; 4:1–3, 4–6; 5:3–15, etc.); the "disputation" or "controversy" (Ger: STREITGESPRÄCH; e.g., Mic 2:6–11; Jer 2:23–25; 3:1–5; 8:8–9, etc.); the "PARABLE" (e.g., Isa 5:1–7; 2 Sam 12); the "lament" (e.g., Amos 5:1–3; Jer 8:4–7, 18–23; 9:17–21; 10:19–20; 12:7–13; 13:18–19; 15:5–9; 18:13–17, etc.); and the "prophetic TORAH" (e.g., Isa 1:10–17; 8:11–15; Jer 7:21–23). (See Westermann, op. cit., 199ff.) The form receiving the greatest attention in recent years is the rib or "covenant lawsuit" (see RIB PATTERN).

For an overview of the status and history of the form-critical study of OT prophecy, see Old Testament Form Criticism, ed. John H. Hayes (San Antonio: Trinity University Press, 1974), and his article on prophecy in DBI (2000).

The presence of prophets and the phenomenon of prophecy in the EARLY CHURCH is abundantly attested to by the NT. Both John the Baptist and Jesus are called prophets (Luke 1:76; Matt 14:5; 21:26 //Matt 16:14; 21:11, 46; Mark 8:28; Luke 7:16, 39; 9:19; cf. John 1:21, 25; 6:14, etc.). The apostle Paul lists prophecy among the gifts of the Spirit (1 Cor 14; cf. 1 Tim 1:18; 4:14), and he names prophets along with apostles and teachers as a ministry appointed by divine calling (1 Cor 12:28–29). But later NT writers warn of false prophets (e.g., Matt 7:15; 24:11; 1 John 4:1; Rev 2:20; 16:13; 19:20; 20:10), and Paul himself is compelled to contrast the edification that comes from true prophecy with the pandemonium (1 Cor 14:23) of speaking in tongues (1 Cor 14), intimating the close connection between ecstasy and prophetic inspiration (Acts 2:4ff.; 19:6). According to Paul, the function of Christian prophecy is essentially pastoral; it is one means by which the Lord says to the church what he has to say. In this sense, chaps. 2 and 3 of the book of Rev and chap. 22:6–19, which proclaims the nearness of the PAROUSIA, are appropriately termed prophecy; by contrast, the remainder of Rev is apocalyptic in character. Other examples of early Christian prophecy have been identified by ERNST KÄSEMANN in 1 Cor 3:17; 14:38; 16:22, etc. (see *SÄTZE HEILIGEN RECHTES*).

The nature and incidence of Christian prophecy and its relation to apocalyptic are widely debated; so, too, is the question of the relationship of Jesus' proclamation of the kingdom of God to the prophetic and to the apocalyptic worldviews. Prophecy sees the future as the divinely ordered consequence of human past and present actions; apocalyptic sees the future in sharper discontinuity with the present, as the divine breaks into and thus totally dissolves the human sphere or radically transforms it.

Note: All of the issues discussed here, including form-critical analysis, are subjects of continuing scholarly debate. Y. Gitay (ed.), *Prophecy and Prophets: The Diversity of Contemporary Issues in Scholarship* (*Semeia*, Atlanta: Scholars Press, 1997); R. P. Gordon, ed., *"The Place Is Too Small for Us": The Israelite Prophets in Recent Scholarship* (Winona Lake, Ind.: Eisenbrauns, 1995); and J. L. Mays and P. J. Achtemeier, eds., *Interpreting the Prophets* (Philadelphia: Fortress Press, 1987). See GLOSSOLALIA; MAJOR PROPHETS.

Prophetic Eschatology. See **Eschatology**

Prophetic Lawsuit. See *Rib* **Pattern.**

Prophets, The   In Judaism: the second of the three divisions of the HB, known in Hebrew as the *Nebiim* and comprising the Former PROPHETS (Joshua, Judges, 1 and 2 Samuel, 1 and 2 Kings), and the Latter Prophets (Isaiah, Jeremiah, Ezekiel, Hosea, Joel, Amos, Obadiah, Jonah, Micah, Nahum, Habakkuk, Zephaniah, Haggai, Zechariah, and Malachi).

In Christian tradition, the designation "the Prophets" does not include the so-called historical books of Joshua–2 Kings. As in Judaism, the remainder are divided into the Major Prophets (Isa, Jer, and Ezek) and the twelve Minor Prophets (Hos–Mal). See TANAKH.

Propositio.   See **Rhetorical Analysis.**

Prostaxis   is a term in LINGUISTICS used to identify "a particular way of combining clauses into long strips of relatively coordinate expressions (Eugene Nida, *Toward a Science in Translating* [New York: W. S. Heinman Imported Books, 1964], 210). Formally speaking, such clauses are coordinated by the use of continuative particles (such as "and"), but semantically speaking these serve to mark the divisions between clauses and therefore "function more like periods than conjunctions." According to Nida, prostaxis can be found in both biblical Hebrew and Greek. In Hebrew, "the clause initial *waw* is often merely a signal of a clause beginning, and does not really link the clause in any coordinate way to the previous clause" (ibid.). In Greek, the opening verses of Mark may also be an example of prostaxis, since, it can be argued, the *kai* ("and") forms are not used to construct one long sentence of many clauses but function to set the clauses off from each other. Prostaxis is a dominant characteristic of Mark's Greek and suggests a lack of literary skill. See HYPOTAXIS; PARATAXIS.

Protasis   In a conditional sentence, the conditional clause is called the protasis and in English usually begins with "If." The main clause, called the apodosis, states a conclusion conditioned on the fulfillment of the supposition stated in the subordinate (conditional) clause; e.g., Gal 1:10b: "If I were still pleasing men [protasis], I should not be a servant of Christ [apodosis]." See *A MINORE AD MAJUS*.

Protevangelium   (Gk: the first, or earliest form of, the GOSPEL) refers to Gen 3:15, in which God announces that the offspring of Eve will crush the offspring of the serpent, interpreted as God's first promise of CHRIST's (or, as suggested by the VULGATE, Mary's) future victory over evil. (See *The Jerusalem Bible* note ad loc.) The understanding (though not the term) goes back to at least the 2nd cent. and offers a good example of typological interpretation (cf. Irenaeus, *Against Heresies* 5.21). The *Protevangelium* should be distinguished from *The Protevangelium of James*, an APOCRYPHAL NT infancy NARRATIVE. See TYPOLOGY.

Proto-Lucian.   See **Septuagint.**

Proto-Luke, meaning "the earliest form of Luke," denotes a hypothetical document proposed by B. H. STREETER (*The Four Gospels* [London: Macmillan & Co., 1924]) composed of Q and "L" only, exclusive of any Markan materials and of Luke 1–2. It was deduced to account for the verbal differences between Q as found in Matt and Luke and to establish a source equal in antiquity and authenticity to Mark yet independent of it. The hypothesis lacks general acceptance. See FOUR DOCUMENT HYPOTHESIS; "M"; TWO SOURCE HYPOTHESIS.

Proto-LXX.   See **Septuagint.**

Proto-Theodotion.   See *Kaige Recension.*

Psalms   (Gk: *psalmoi:* songs accompanied by stringed instruments). The Hebrew title for the collection is *tehillim*, praises. The Psalter is artificially divided into five books modeled on the five books of the Torah: Book I: Pss 1–41; Book II: 42–72; Book III: 73–89; Book IV: 90–106; Book V: 107–150. Each book ends with a doxology. The collection evidences a long and complex history of transmission and editing. For example, Ps. 72:20, which ends Book II, declares that "the prayers of David, the son of Jesse, are ended," yet psalms of David (*ledavid*) are found in Book V. This means that only at one stage in the history of transmission did the psalms of David end with Ps. 72. Various mini-collections of psalms are found, such as Songs of Ascents, 120–134, and psalms connected to the various Levitical guilds in the Temple: Asaph, Korah, and Heman. Most of the psalms cannot be dated with any precision, given their often highly figurative language. Because Jewish tradition (MT) counts the superscriptions of psalms as verse 1, Hebrew versification does not coincide with most English translations.

Psalm superscriptions offer one way that the psalm may be understood. The superscription of penitential lament Ps 51, for example, reads, "A psalm of David, when the prophet Nathan came to him, after he had gone in to Bathsheba." Seventy-three psalms are connected to David, not necessarily in terms of his authorship but as an acknowledgment of his connection to the cultic life of Jerusalem as an archetypal figure. Musical notations in the superscriptions, e.g., "according to the Hind of the Dawn" (Ps 22) may indicate tunes to which the psalm was sung. The term *selah* may indicate a break in the recitation of the psalm, during which a choir, instrumentalists, or dancers would perform.

Until recent years much psalms scholarship was focused on the form-critical analysis of psalms pioneered by HERMANN GUNKEL, in which recurring psalm types or genres were tied to particular settings in worship (see *SITZ-IM-LEBEN*). Gunkel's categories are still operative in many psalm commentaries: individual and communal LAMENTS, thanksgivings, HYMNS, royal psalms, wisdom/Torah psalms, psalms of trust, prophetic exhortations, and entrance liturgies. Scholars disagree as to which psalms belong in each category. More recent scholarship has focused on the editorial shaping and purpose of the Psalter, which can best be seen at the "seams" of the collection, i.e., the beginning and end of books. Royal psalms connected to the king appear at the beginning of Book I and at the end of Books II and III; royal Pss 2 and 72 and 2 and 89 form an envelope for Books I–II and I–III, respectively. The intimate relationship of God with the king in Ps 2 deteriorates to God's rejection of the Davidic king in Ps 89:38ff. Books I–III document the failure of the Davidic covenant as experienced in the destruction of Jerusalem and exile in 587 B.C.E., and call out for the response in Books IV–V of the proclamation of God's reign (enthronement psalms 93, 96–99, etc.). Some scholars hold that the editorial placement of Ps 1 at the head of the Psalter removes the psalms from the sphere of worship to the sphere of personal meditation on God's Torah/instruction.

In his POSTCRITICAL reading of the psalms, Walter Brueggemann crosses over form-critical categories to group psalms according to the themes of orientation, disorientation, and new orientation that express the season of faith. He aims to tie together critical psalm categories with the realities of corporate and personal faith. The people of God move constantly out of settled orientation (hymns, wisdom psalms) to the chaos of disorientation (laments), and out of disorientation to the surprise of new orientation (thanksgivings, enthronement psalms). This approach allows room for the use of laments, which comprise more than a third of the Psalter and can serve as valuable paradigms for the exercise of pastoral care in the congregational context.

Pivotal works available in English are Hermann Gunkel, *The Psalms: A Form-Critical Introduction*, trans. Thomas M. Homer; Introduction by James Muilenburg (Philadelphia: Fortress Press, 1967, 1972³); and SIGMUND MOWINCKEL, *The Psalms in Israel's Worship*, trans. D. R. Ap-Thomas, 2 vols. (New York: Abingdon Press, 1962; Oxford: Basil Blackwell, 1962); CLAUS WESTERMANN, *Praise and Lament in the Psalms*, trans. Keith Crim and Richard N. Soulen (Atlanta: John Knox Press, 1981). More recently, see Walter Brueggemann, *The Message of the Psalms* (Minneapolis: Fortress Press, 1984); Denise Dombkowski Hopkins, *Journey through the Psalms* (New York: United Church Press, 1990), and *Psalms* (St. Louis: Chalice Press, 2002), and Patrick D. Miller, *They Cried to the Lord: The Form and Theology of Biblical Prayer* (Minneapolis: Fortress Press, 1994).

Pseudepigrapha (Gk: falsely entitled). In Protestant tradition since the 17th cent., the term *Pseudepigrapha* has been used to designate those ancient Jewish and Hellenistic Jewish writings not in the OT canon or in the APOCRYPHA and whose authorship is falsely ascribed to a famous person. Since the content of the Apocrypha in fact varies according to ecclesiastical tradition, and even within a given tradition, no universally accepted listing of Pseudepigrapha exists. Some scholars would include writings found among the DSS as well as certain books sometimes numbered among the Apocrypha. The potential group includes over 100 texts or TEXT FRAGMENTS.

The criteria currently employed (see James H. Charlesworth following) are (1) the work must be at least partially Jewish or Jewish-Christian; (2) it should date from the period 200 B.C.E. to 200 C.E.; (3) it should claim to be inspired; (4) it should be related in form or content to the OLD TESTAMENT; (5) it ideally is attributed to a figure of the HB.

The following titles and their abbreviations are of texts chosen to appear in an English edition of the Pseudepigrapha, to be translated by an international team of scholars, and edited by J. H. Charlesworth.

The publisher is Doubleday & Co.

1.	*Apocalypse of Abraham*	*ApAb*
2.	*Testament of Abraham*	*TAb*
3.	*Apocalypse of Adam*	*ApAdam*
4.	*Life of Adam and Eve*	*LAE*
	(Apocalypse of Moses)	*ApMos*
5.	*Ahiqar*	*Ah*
6.	An Anonymous Samaritan Text	AnonSam
7.	*Letter of Aristeas*	*LetAris*
8.	*2 (Syriac) Baruch*	*2 Bar*
9.	*3 (Greek) Baruch*	*3 Bar*
10.	*4 Baruch (Paraleipomena Jeremiou;* sometimes called *The Rest of the Words of Baruch, 2 Baruch, 3 Baruch, Christian Baruch)*	*4 Bar*
11.	*Apocalypse of Elijah*	*ApEl*
12.	*1 (Ethiopic) Enoch*	*1En*
13.	*2 (Slavonic) Enoch (Book of the Secrets of Enoch)*	*2En*
14.	*3 (Hebrew) Enoch (Sepher Heikhalot)*	*3En*
15.	*Apocalypse of Ezekiel*	*ApEzek*
16.	*4 Ezra (4, 5, 6 Ezra; 2 Esdras, 4 Esdras, Apocalypse of Ezra)*	*4 Ezra*
17.	*Greek Apocalypse of Ezra*	*GkApEzra*
18.	*Questions of Ezra*	*QuesEzra*
19.	*Vision of Ezra*	*VisEzra*
20.	Fragments of Historical Works	FrgsHistWrks
21.	*Testament of Isaac*	*TIsaac*
22.	*Ascension of Isaiah (Martyrdom of Isaiah, Treatment of Hezekiah, Vision of Isaiah)*	*AscenIs*
23.	*Ladder of Jacob*	*LadJac*
24.	*Testament of Jacob*	*TJac*
25.	*Jannes and Jambres*	*JanJam*
26.	*Testament of Job*	*TJob*
27.	*Joseph and Asenath*	*JosAsen*
28.	*Prayer of Joseph*	*PrJos*
29.	*Jubilees*	*Jub*
30.	*3 Maccabees (Ptolemaika)*	*3Mac*
31.	*4 Maccabees (Concerning the Supreme Power of Reason)*	*4Mac*
32.	*Prayer of Manasseh*	*PrMan*
33.	*Assumption of Moses (Ascension of Moses, Testament of Moses)*	*AsMos*
34.	Pseudo-Philo (Liber Antiquitatum Biblicarum)	Ps-Philo (LAB)
35.	Pseudo-Phocylides (*Poiemo Nouthetikon*)	Ps-Phoc Ps-Phoc

36. Fragments of Poetic Works   FrgsPoetWrks
37. *Lives of the Prophets (Deaths/*   *LivPro*
      Triumphs of the Prophets, Pseudo-
      Epiphanius)
38. *Apocalypse of Sedrach*   *ApSedr*
39. *Treatise of Shem (Book of Shem)*   *TrShem*
40. *Sibylline Oracles*   *SibOr*
41. *Odes of Solomon*   *OdesSol*
42. *Psalms of Solomon*   *PssSol*
43. *Testament of Solomon*   *TSol*
44. *Five Apocryphal Syriac Psalms*   *5ApocSyrPss*
      (*Five Psalms of David,* Psalms
      151–155)
45. *Testaments of the Twelve Patriarchs*   *T12P*
46. *Apocalypse of Zephaniah*   *ApZeph*
      (*Apocalypse of Saphonias*)
47. *Apocalypse of Zosimus*   *ApZos*
      (*Narrative/Testament of Zosimus,*
      The Abode of the Blessed)

Other pseudepigrapha, extant only in small fragments, are not included in the above; for a complete listing, see *The SBL Handbook of Style: For Ancient Near Eastern, Biblical, and Early Christian Studies* (Peabody, Mass.: Hendrickson, 1999). For bibliography, see James H. Charlesworth, *The Pseudepigrapha and Modern Research* (SBLSCS 7; Missoula, Mont.: Scholars Press, 1976; *Supplementary Volume,* 1981; and his *The Old Testament Pseudepigrapha and the New Testament* (Cambridge: Cambridge University Press, 1985); also, D. S. Russell, *The Old Testament Pseudepigrapha* (Philadelphia: Fortress Press, 1987); H. F. D. Sparks, ed., *The Apocryphal Old Testament* (Oxford: Oxford University Press, 1984); and *Bulletin of the International Organization for Septuagint and Cognate Studies,* esp. vol. 10 (1977) and vol. 11 (1978). See APOCALYPSE.

Pseudo-Jonathan.   See **Targum.**

Pseudonymity   (Gk: lit., using a false name). The practice of ascribing a writing to someone other than its real author. In the OT (e.g., Daniel and certain PSALMS), in the PSEUDEPIGRAPHA (Wisdom of Solomon, Additions to Esther, etc.), in the NT (John [?], 2 and 3 John [?], the PASTORAL EPISTLES, 1 and 2 Pet, Jas, Jude), and in the NT APOCRYPHA, the pseudonym is always of some ancient worthy or of a leading apostle. Pseudonymity in these instances is probably not to be thought of from a modern (cynical) point of view as a means of gaining authority and wide circulation for a work but rather as a product of the sincere conviction that truly inspired scripture was not of one's own doing but God's, or the Holy Spirit's, and must therefore be attributed to an acknowledged instrument of revelation. Within the spectrum of early Christian literature, the pseudonymous writings stand somewhere between the anonymous GOSPELS and Acts (to which names were affixed subsequently by tradition) and the work of apologists and church leaders who defended the gospel in their own name (cf. Justin Martyr, Irenaeus, etc.).

Pseudopauline.   See **Deuteropauline.**

Psychological Biblical Criticism applies contemporary psychological theory to the literature of the BIBLE and to its traditional and modern interpretation. It stands in continuity with a broad and even ancient interest in analyzing the human *psyche* (Gk: "soul") as it is displayed in biblical texts. The term "psychology" goes back to Philip Melanchthon in the 16th cent., and of course theological treatises on the nature of the human soul are quite ancient (cf. Tertullian's *De anima* ["Concerning the Soul"] and Augustine's *De anima et eius origine* ["Concerning the Soul and Its Origin"]). The attempt to establish pyschology as a modern empirical discipline in line with other natural sciences is often dated to Wilhelm Wundt of Leipzig in the latter third of the 19th cent. In subsequent decades many psychological studies were produced on key biblical figures, particularly Jesus. ALBERT SCHWEITZER analyzed these works with characteristic perspicuity in 1913 (ET, *The Psychiatric Study of Jesus: Exposition and Criticism* [Boston: Beacon Press, 1948]). The studies of this period illustrate the skeptical, even hostile, attitude of nascent psychology toward religion, which it viewed as a kind of pathology. Biblical scholars and theologians returned the skepticism in kind, as the largely pejorative term PSYCHOLOGICAL RECONSTRUCTION attests. The mutual suspicion between the fields began to be overcome only after 1960, though it persists in considerable measure to this day. It must be said that Wundt's hope to establish psychology as a pure natural science has never been realized, in part because the human psyche is both the subject and the object of investigation (Jung).

Depth psychology, so named because of its exploration of the unconscious, appeared in the first half of the 20th cent. and is closely associated with the names of Sigmund Freud and Carl Jung. Both wrote on biblical figures, though only Jung devoted extensive attention to the Bible, and his followers produced the greater number of studies on biblical texts. For the early Freud, religion was akin to a cultural neurosis, a view later moderated only in part. (See S. Freud, *Moses and Monotheism*

[New York: Vintage Books, 1955]; D. L. Miller, ed., *Jung and the Interpretation of the Bible* [New York: Continuum, 1995]; W. G. Rollins, *Jung and the Bible* [Atlanta: John Knox Press, 1983].)

During the second half of the 20th cent., post-Freudian and post-Jungian psychological analysis turned to biblical texts in a variety of ways, from the psychological analysis of biblical phenomena, key figures, and symbols, to analysis of biblical literature and its interpretation, even its use in pastoral counseling. For many the interpretation of the Bible as a record of the early development of human consciousness has been of major interest (so Jung, Erich Fromm, Lynn Bechtel, et al.) while the applicability of its insights for hermeneutical theory has been important to others (P. Ricoeur, P. Homans, et al.).

Wayne Rollins, a leading advocate of psychological biblical criticism, has recently stated that "the goal of a psychological-critical approach is to examine texts, their origination, authorship, modes of expression, their construction, transmission, translation, reading, interpretation, their transposition into kindred and alien art forms, and the history of their personal and cultural effect, as expressions of the structure, processes, and habits of the human psyche, both in individual and collective manifestations, past and present" (*Soul and Psyche: The Bible in Psychological Perspective* [Minneapolis: Fortress Press, 1999]). Such a broad statement suggests that psychological biblical criticism is not a method but an approach to scripture that seeks to add its perspective (the psychological dimension of human expression) to essentially all the avenues of BIBLICAL CRITICISM, whether concerned with authors or readers or critics (feminist, ideological, postmodern, etc.).

A frequently applauded example of psychological biblical criticism is Gerd Theissen's *Psychological Aspects of Pauline Theology* (Philadelphia: Fortress Press, 1987); for a survey of the field and its challenges, see D. Andrew Kille, *Psychological Biblical Criticism*, Guides to Biblical Scholarship (Minneapolis: Fortress Press, 2000); and for a historical sketch, bibliography, and proposal, see Rollins, noted previously. These works have been used extensively in this brief description.

Psychological Reconstruction is a pejorative term in BIBLICAL CRITICISM that refers to the attempt to reconstruct the thought processes of a historical personage (Jesus, Paul, Jeremiah, etc.) on the basis of conjecture and a modern psychological theory of personality or of human behavior. Although no book influenced the diminution (not the demise) of the psychological reconstruction of Jesus more than did ALBERT SCHWEITZER's *The Quest of the Historical Jesus* (Ger: 1906), it, too, succumbed to the temptation to go beyond what a historian can reasonably know or justifiably assume. In recent decades a renewed and more sophisticated effort to join psychological theory with biblical criticism has been undertaken (see PSYCHOLOGICAL BIBLICAL CRITICISM). Also see HERMENEUTICS; HISTORICAL-CRITICAL METHOD; QUEST OF THE HISTORICAL JESUS.

Q (also called "SAYINGS source"; Ger: *Redenquelle*; and simply: The Double Tradition), from the German word *Quelle* meaning "source," is the symbol used loosely to mean (a) all the material held in common by Matthew and Luke but not found in Mark; or more specifically, (b) a hypothetical *written document* lying behind and accounting for material which Matt and Luke have in common and including certain passages found also in Mark; or, finally, (c) a variation of the preceding, including theories concerning stages of oral and written tradition, translations of earlier sayings collections to account for differences, etc. The Q hypothesis rests on two main arguments: (1) The degree of verbal agreement between Lukan and Matthean non-Markan material is so high that it can be explained only by the use of a common source; and (2) the order of this non-Markan material is so

often the same that only a (written?) common source can account for it.

According to the TWO SOURCE HYPOTHESIS, Q antedates Mark. There is, however, no universal agreement as to its origin, date, and content, or how the document itself and the Jesus who stands behind it are to be characterized. Some have argued that Q is a scholarly fiction; others, in increasing numbers, particularly among International Q Project (IQP) participants, not only assert its existence as a document but find stages in its redaction prior to its incorporation in Matt and Luke. These hypothetical stages are commonly referred to as Q1, Q2, Q3, which in turn are sometimes correlated with perceived strata in the tradition itself, such as wisdom, prophetic, APOCALYPTIC, etc. Which stratum is to be identified with the earliest stage in Q's development, and therefore with the Jesus of history is the question (that is, whether Jesus was a sage, a prophet, an apocalypticist, or as one unknown). The answer given depends on the interpreter's theological perspective. Interest in Q in the first and last quarters of the 20th cent. was shaped by the QUEST OF THE HISTORICAL JESUS, and in the middle quarters by FORM CRITICISM and REDACTION CRITICISM. Q research has received major impetus from the JESUS SEMINAR and the organization, in 1989, of the IQP, which produced a critical edition of Q in 1999 and is publishing (1996–) a multivolume database of its reconstruction as proposed by various scholars since 1838. Acceptance of the notion that Q existed in documentary form has also been greatly increased by the role allotted to the GOSPEL OF THOMAS by recent historical Jesus research. The *Gospel of Thomas* is a collection of sayings comparable to Q, although the dating of its content is highly controversial. (See NAG HAMMADI CODICES.)

The following are proposed reconstructions of Q's content as found in Luke. The IQP assigns high probability to unbracketed verses, less probability to bracketed verses, and places braces around those deemed probably not belonging to Q.

A. Streeter	B. Schulz	C. IQP
Luke 3:2a–9	Luke 3:7–18	Luke 3:2b–3, 7–9
(10–14)		
16–17		16b–17
21–22		[21–22]
4:1–16a	4:1–13	4:1–13, 16
6:20–49	6:20b–23	6:20b–23
		{24–26}
	27–49	27–28, 35c
		29, [Q/Matt 5:41]
		30, 31, 32–33/34
		{35ab}, 36, 37
		{38ab}, 38c
		39–45, 46–49
7:1–10	7:1–10	7:1b,3
		{4–6a}, 6b–10
18–35	18–28	18–19, {20–21}
		22–23, 24–28
		{29–30}
	31–35	31–35
9:(51–56)		9:{1–2}
57–60	9:57–60	57–60
(61–62)		
10:2–16	10:11–16	10:2–3, 4–6, [7a], 7b-[8]
(17–20)		9–11, 12–15
		{Matt 11:23b–24}
21–24	21–24	16, 21–22, {Matt 11:28–30}
		23–24, {25–28}
11:9–52	11:9–26	11:2–4, {5–8}, 9–13, 14–15
		17–20, [21–22], 23, 24–26
	29–35, 39	[27–28], 16, 29–32,
		33–35, [36], 39a
	42–44	42, 39b–41, 43–44
	46–52	46, 52, 47–51
12:1a–12	12:2–11	12:2–12, {Matt 10:23}
22–59	22–31	{12:13–14, 16–21}
		22–31, {32}
	33–34, 39–40	33–34, {35–38}, 39–40
	42b–47	42b-46, [49], {50}
	51–53	51–53, [54–56]
	57–59	58–59
13:18–35	13:18–21	13:18–19, 20–21
	23–24	24, 25,
	26–29	26–27, 28–29, [30]
	34–35	34–35
		14:{1–4}, [5], {6}
14:11	14:11; cf. 18:14	14:11/18:14; 14
	16–24	[16–24]

26–27	26–27	26–27
		17:33
34–35	34–35	14:34–35
	15:4–7	15:4–7, 8–10
16:13, 16–18	16:13, 16–18	16:13, 16, 17, 18
17:1–6	17:3–6	17:1b–2, 3b–4, 6b
		{20–21}
20–37	23–24	23–24, 37b
	26–27, 30	26–27, {28–29}, 30
		{31–32}
	33–36	34–35
19:11–27	19:12–27	19:12–13, 15b–26
	(22:28–30)	22:28–30

A. Burnett H. Streeter, *The Four Gospels: A Study of Origins* (London: Macmillan & Co., 4th rev. ed., 1930), 291.
B. Siegfried Schulz, *Q: Die Spruchquelle der Evangelisten* (Zürich: Theologischer Verlag Zürich, 1972).
C. International Q Project.

Concerning stages in the formation of Q see esp. J. S. Kloppenborg, *The Formation of Q: Trajectories in Ancient Wisdom Collections* (Philadelphia: Fortress Press, 1987); C. M. Tuckett, *Q and the History of Early Christianity* (Peabody, Mass.: Hendrickson, 1996), and, for a critique, see H. A. Attridge, "Reflections on Research into Q," *Semeia* 55 (1992): 223–234. See "L"; "M"; PROTO-LUKE.

Qinah Meter (Heb: *Qinah*: lament) is the name given to the rhythmic pattern 3 + 2, because of its dominance in the book of Lamentations and because the imbalance in the lines seems to capture the tension of extreme emotion like grief (but also joy, e.g. Ps 65). The METER is usually lost in translation, but cf. "My eyés are spént with weéping my sóul is in túmult" (Lam 2:11, RSV). The interpretation of the "*Qinah* meter" is debated. (See N. K. Gottwald, "Poetry, Hebrew," *IDB.*)

Qoh Abbrev. for Qoheleth, or Koheleth; better known by the Greek name Ecclesiastes, or "The Preacher."

Quadriga, The (Lat: a team of four horses). See FOURFOLD SENSE OF SCRIPTURE, THE.

Quelle (Ger: Source). See **Q.**

Qere. See **Kethib.**

Quest of the Historical Jesus (The); Leben-Jesu Forschung; Liberal Lives of Jesus; The New Quest, The Third Quest The *Quest of the Historical Jesus* is the English (1910) title of ALBERT SCHWEITZER's critical history of 19th-cent. biographies of the life of Jesus, entitled in German *Von [H. S.] Reimarus zu [William] Wrede* (1906).

Since Schweitzer's epoch-making work, the various attempts to write a historical biography of Jesus, whether of the 19th or 20th cent., have been referred to, sometimes pejoratively, as *Leben-Jesu Forschung* ("Lives of Jesus Research"), which is a phrase taken from the German subtitle. The phrase is however also used broadly to refer to any search for the historical Jesus, however fragmentary and tentative the expected results might be.

Schweitzer (1875–1965) characterized those works written after D. F. STRAUSS's final *Life of Jesus* (1864) as the "Liberal Lives of Jesus," because they attempted to limit the explanation of Jesus' actions and the events of his life to natural, psychological causes and motivations and completely ignored the profoundly eschatological setting of Jesus' teachings and actions (see ESCHATOLOGY). The term "Liberal Lives of Jesus" is frequently expanded to include studies of Jesus' life by the American social movement through the 1930s, including Shailer Mathews's *Jesus on Social Institutions* (New York: The Macmillan Co., 1928), and SHIRLEY JACKSON CASE's *Jesus: A New Biography* (Chicago: University of Chicago Press, 1927).

Two key assumptions of the 19th-cent. quest were (a) the objective recoverability of the past by critical historiographical means and (b) the adequacy of the Synoptic GOSPELS as sources for the historical reconstruction of the life of Jesus, at least of his public ministry. Schweitzer himself largely accepted these assumptions for his own sketch of the life of Jesus (*Quest of the Historical Jesus*, ch. 19). Building on JOHANNES WEISS's *Jesus' Proclamation of the Kingdom of God* (Philadelphia: Fortress Press, 1971; London: SCM Press, 1971; Ger: 1892) and WILLIAM WREDE's notion of the MESSIANIC SECRET (from Wrede's *The Messianic Secret* [Naperville, Ill.: Alec R. Allenson, 1972; Ger: 1901]), Schweitzer proved to most of the scholarly world that Jesus' eschatological outlook determined his actions and teachings. Thus placed squarely in the thought-world of the 1st cent., Jesus becomes "as One unknown" to the 20th (p. 403). This portrait of Jesus as an eschatological preacher replaced the picture of 19th- and early- 20th- cent. liberalism of Jesus as moral and religious exemplar, if not immediately, then at least by the time of the rise of FORM CRITICISM in Germany (1920s–) and in English-speaking lands (1930–). But it is one of the ironies in the history of BIBLICAL CRITICISM that Schweitzer's own picture of Jesus as a religious fanatic who died disillusioned on a cross merely became an additional witness to the questionable assumptions on which all such "Lives" were based (see above) and to the dubious character of any quest built on

similar grounds. In Germany, then, the original quest ended with Schweitzer's book and was not initiated again for fifty years, and then on different grounds. The two major factors contributing to the end of the first quest were (a) skepticism that the Gospels provided suitable or sufficient material for historical reconstruction of Jesus, a skepticism reinforced by the rise of source and form criticism, and (b) disinterest in the historical Jesus for purely theological reasons, both on the part of dogmatic theologians such as KARL BARTH and on the part of NT scholars such as RUDOLF BULTMANN. In Protestant scholarship outside Germany, however, the matter was quite different; here the so-called quest continued.

A New Quest of the Historical Jesus (NQ) designates one of two distinct but interrelated approaches by which students of Bultmann in Germany and Switzerland sought to reestablish historical and theological grounds for identifying the Jesus of history with the CHRIST proclaimed by Christian faith. The term was coined by the NT scholar James M. Robinson and is the title of his sketch of the discussion and contribution to it, *The New Quest for the Historical Jesus* (London: SCM Press, 1959). Bultmann had argued that nothing could be said about the relation between "the historical Jesus" and "the Christ of faith" beyond Christian faith's sheer assertion *that* they were identical. He held that both the authenticity of the KERYGMA and the integrity of historical inquiry were fatally compromised by the desire to say more. Unsatisfied with this answer, the NQ sought to establish a "thicker" continuity between the historical Jesus and Christian faith, primarily by working on the historical side of this issue. The NQ has sought criteria for judging the authenticity of SAYINGS attributed to Jesus in order to provide an objective basis for showing how he became the object of Christian faith (see CRITERIA OF AUTHENTICITY). This aspect of the NQ is associated with ERNST KÄSEMANN

(*Essays on New Testament Themes* [London: SCM Press, 1964]); Gunther Bornkamm (*Jesus of Nazareth* [New York: Harper & Row, 1961; London: Hodder & Stoughton, 1973]); and outside Germany, Norman Perrin (*Rediscovering the Teaching of Jesus* [New York: Harper & Row, 1967; London: SCM Press, 1967]), and a host of others.

The philosophical and theological side of the effort to explain how the crucified Jesus came to be proclaimed as the risen Lord is more commonly known as the NEW HERMENEUTIC. In brief, the New Hermeneutic addresses the problem from the standpoint of a phenomenology of language. It contends that there is an identity between the *event of faith* that came to expression in the acts and teachings of Jesus as recorded in the Gospels (see LANGUAGE EVENT) and the *event of faith* that is articulated in Christian proclamation about Jesus. Here the New Quest and the New Hermeneutic overlap. See Gerhard Ebeling's *Word and Faith* (Philadelphia: Fortress Press, 1963), Ernst Fuchs's *Studies of the Historical Jesus* (London: SCM Press, 1964), and Robert W. Funk's *Language, Hermeneutic, and Word of God* (New York: Harper & Row, 1966), etc.

If theological disinterest and historical skepticism characterized the early decades of the 20th cent., the opposite characterized the century's close. A trickle of books in the 1960s became a flood by the 1980s. The term "The Third Quest" was coined by N. T. Wright (1982) to designate a perspective in principal accord with A. Schweitzer's depiction of Jesus as a prophet of the end time in the context of Jewish eschatological expectation. This perspective (with which he agrees) views Mark's Gospel, and its eschatological portrayal of Jesus, as essentially authentic. Within this category Wright placed such diverse historical reconstructions of Jesus as those by O. Betz, G. Vermes, B. F. Meyer, M. Borg, E. P. Sanders, G. Theissen, J. Charlesworth, et al. All other works on Jesus are said to be variations on an older skeptical position

that saw Mark as a literary fiction and its eschatology reflective of the mind of the EARLY CHURCH, not Jesus. Into this category Wright placed the JESUS SEMINAR, whose literary products he categorized, without success, as "the New Quest renewed." (See S. Neill and N. T. Wright, *The Interpretation of the New Testament 1861–1986*, 2nd ed. [Oxford: Oxford University Press, 1988], and N. T. Wright, *Christian Origins and the Question of God*, vol. 1, *The New Testament and the People of God* [Minneapolis: Fortress Press, 1992]; and vol. 2, *Jesus and the Victory of God* [1996].)

The term "The Third Quest," so defined, has not broadly held. It is sometimes used simply to designate all current research on the historical Jesus unrelated to the particular theological matrix and critical skepticism of the Bultmannian school so characteristic of the NQ. Current research is wide-ranging but, in the main, purports to employ the critical tools of secular HISTORIOGRAPHY, uninfected by theological biases or ulterior agendas. Here greater weight has been given to sociological methodologies, social history, and social description; and greater attention has been given to noncanonical and EXTRACANONICAL sources. As a result, the wardrobe of Jesus purchased by the labor of 19th-cent. scholars has been refurbished with the habits of the Cynic, the Peasant Revolutionary, the Peripatetic Magician, the Wisdom Teacher, the Social Prophet, the Wandering Hasid, et al. Among the most widely acclaimed and also the most tenuously hypothetical of these works is that of John Dominic Crossan, *The Historical Jesus: The Life of a Mediterranean Jewish Peasant* (San Francisco: HarperSanFrancisco, 1991); see also his *The Birth of Christianity: Discovering What Happened in the Years Immediately after the Execution of Jesus* (San Francisco: HarperSanFrancisco, 1998). For representative positions see John Dominic Crossan, Luke Timothy Johnson, and Werner W. Kelber, *The Jesus Controversy: Perspectives in Conflict* (Harrisburg, PA: Trinity Press International, 1999).

Note: Major works of the 19th-cent. Quest and other notable studies of Jesus are available in the Lives of Jesus Series, General Ed. Leander Keck, published by Fortress Press. See also JESUS CHRIST; PARABLE.

Qumran. See **Khirbet Qumran.**

Rabbinic Interpretation. See **Hillel.**

Rad, Gerhard von (1901–1971). Born in Nürnberg, von Rad studied theology at Erlangen and Tübingen, becoming in 1925 a curate in the *Landeskirche* (Lutheran Church) in Bavaria. Disturbed by the anti-OT sentiments of the German Christian Church, he turned to OT studies and became one of the leading OT theologians of the mid-20th cent. He taught at Erlangen (1929; tutor), Leipzig (1930–34; *Privatdozent*), Jena (1934–45; professor), Göttingen (1945–49), and Heidelberg (1949–67). He maintained that the compiler of the Hexateuch joined two streams of tradition (a Sinai tradition and an exodus-conquest tradition) into a unified theology of history (*HEILSGESCHICHTE*), of which the cultic CREDO in Deut 26:5–11 is the most succinct formulation. His major works include *Deuteronomy* (London: SCM Press, 1966; Philadelphia: Westminster Press, 1966); *Genesis* (Westminster, 1961; 1973; SCM Press, 1972); *Old Testament Theology*, 2 vols. (New York: Harper & Row, 1962–64); *The Problem of the Hexateuch* (New York: McGraw-Hill, 1966); and *Wisdom in Israel* (London: SCM Press, 1972). See J. L. Crenshaw, *Gerhard von Rad* (Makers of the Modern Theological Mind; Waco, Tex.: Word Publishers, 1978). See TRADITION CRITICISM.

Radical Criticism According to W. G. Kümmel, a distinction is to be made between "the radically historical approach" to the BIBLE (which characterized the work of WELLHAUSEN, WREDE, BOUSSET, Goguel, LOISY, GUNKEL, et al.) and the totally ill-founded "radical criticism" of Bruno Bauer (1809–1882) and of those Dutch, French, German, and English scholars at the turn of the 19th/20th cent. who

denied both the existence of Jesus and the authorship of almost all the LETTERS ascribed to Paul. This special use of the term has now slipped into the past. See BIBLICAL CRITICISM; HISTORICAL CRITICISM; HISTORICAL-CRITICAL METHOD.

Ras Shamra Texts discovered in 1929 in the ruins of the royal palace and temple environs of ancient Ugarit, a Phoenician city on the Syrian coast bearing the modern name Ras Shamra, which means "Hill of Fennel." These Ugaritic and Akkadian texts, numbering in the hundreds and dating, in the main, ca. 1400–1200 B.C.E., are unequaled in their importance for understanding Canaanitic culture and hence the milieu of Hebrew history and religion. In addition to providing knowledge of the Canaanitic pantheon (El, Baal, Anath, Dagon, Mot, etc.) and the ritual MYTHS that surrounded them, the texts disproved WELLHAUSEN's evolutionary theory of cultic development, which gave a postexilic date to the P: PRIESTLY CODE. There are in fact innumerable linguistic and other parallels between the Ras Shamra texts and both the OT and NT; one example is Ps 29, which has a parallel in Ugaritic literature, with the name Baal appearing in place of YHWH. For a translation of some of the religious texts and a discussion of their interrelation, see J. C. de Moor, *An Anthology of Religious Texts from Ugarit* (Leiden: E. J. Brill, 1987), also (ed.), *Intertextuality in Ugarit and Israel* (OTS 40; Leiden: E. J. Brill, 1998).

Reader-Response Criticism refers to a literary approach that is centrally concerned with the reader and the process of reading rather than with the author or the text as a self-contained unity. Although similar in many respects to the movement known as RECEPTION THEORY, from which it in part derives, reader-response criticism is a much more pluralistic phenomenon that lacks a single focused methodology. Nevertheless, practitioners generally subscribe to two key premises. First, the meaning of a literary text does not reside "within" the text as a self-contained unity but is actualized or created by the interaction of the reader and the text. Literature is like a performative art, analogous to the performance of a musical work or the staging of a drama. Second (and accordingly), the meaning of a text can differ from reader to reader and indeed from "performance" to "performance," as different readers perform the text in different circumstances to different ends. While reader-response criticism stems from general literary theory, it has become increasingly prominent in biblical studies in the last two decades. Its insights have been applied to the study of a variety of biblical genres, from PARABLES to GOSPELS to the biblical canon as a whole.

While all reader-response criticism recognizes the key role of the reader, it encompasses a "spectrum of positions" (McKnight) on the question of the degree to which a text can be said to enjoy a certain relative autonomy in the dialogical relation between text and reader. At one end of the spectrum are those who continue to find it useful to investigate a text's original meaning for its original audience, as this can be reconstructed by the traditional methods of HISTORICAL CRITICISM; here the concerns of reader-response criticism coincide with those of AUDIENCE CRITICISM. At the other end are those who emphasize the wholly indeterminate character of texts apart from their use by a given reader in a given community and context (in this form sometimes designated radical reader-response); here concerns largely overlap with the interests and positions of POSTMODERN BIBLICAL INTERPRETATION. Others hold that while a text possesses no single privileged meaning it does encode a relatively stable set of instructions that the reader or the community of interpretation can perform well or badly.

See Edgar V. McKnight (ed.), *Semeia* 48: *Reader Perspectives on the New Testament* (Atlanta: Scholars Press, 1989; esp. art. by W. Wuellner; also, Edgar V. McKnight,

"Reader-Response Criticism," *Dictionary of Biblical Interpretation*, ed. by John H. Hayes (Nashville: Abingdon Press, 1999). For a sense of the diversity of reader-response theory and its shortcomings from a postmodernist point of view, see chap. 1: "Reader-Response Criticism," in *The Postmodern Bible: The Bible and Culture Collective*, ed. by Elizabeth A. Castelli et al. (New Haven, Conn.: Yale University Press, 1995). See AUDIENCE CRITICISM; NARRATIVE CRITICISM.

Reading   In TEXTUAL CRITICISM a reading is a variant VERSION of a given passage of scripture as it is found in a particular text, e.g., a variant and less ancient reading of Matt 5:22 adds "without cause" to "if you are angry with a brother or sister . . ." (cf. KJV with NRSV) and thereby provides an effective escape from the harsher command. Significant VARIANT READINGS of biblical texts often appear in footnotes to the text in study editions of the Bible.

Realized Eschatology   is a technical term coined by C. H. DODD (*The Parables of the Kingdom* [London: Nisbet & Co., 1935]) to characterize the ministry of Jesus in which "the *eschaton* has moved from the future to the present, from the sphere of expectation into that of realized experience" (p. 50). Dodd argued that in the unprecedented and unrepeatable events of Jesus' life "the powers of the world to come" are present and made real. See ESCHATOLOGY; EXISTENTIALIST; PARABLE; QUEST OF THE HISTORICAL JESUS.

REB. See **New English Bible; Revised English Bible.**

Recension   (Lat: a review, reassessment). Meaning "an editorial revision of a text," the term was first used in the text-critical studies of KARL LACHMANN (d. 1851); it is sometimes applied more generally to any handwritten copy of a text in the broad sense that every MS is a "recension" of the original AUTOGRAPH and is not identical with it. The recension of the book of

Acts in CODEX D is one-tenth longer than that of Codex G; explaining and evaluating the differences in these recensions is in part the task of TEXTUAL CRITICISM.

Reception Theory (reception analysis; Ger: *Rezeptionsasthetik*) refers to a literary theory that first emerged in the 1960s in Germany and Czechoslovakia that focused on the reception (interpretation) of a work rather than on the historical factors that gave rise to it (as e.g. in HISTORICAL CRITICISM) or on the text itself as a self-contained unity (as e.g. in STRUCTURALISM). Reception theory was a precursor of READER-RESPONSE CRITICISM, though in comparison with the latter it was a more unified movement. Its principal exponents were Robert Jauss and Wolfgang Iser.

According to reception theory, "the historical and cultural reality which we call the 'literary work' is not exhausted in the text. The text is only one of the elements of a relation. The literary work consists of the text (the system of intra-textual relations) in its relation to extra-textual reality: to literary norms, tradition and the imagination" (J. M. Lotman). Thus a distinction must be drawn between the text as written document ("Text$_1$" or "artifact") and the "metatext" ("Text$_2$") or "aesthetic object" that is created in the act of reading and interpretation. The meaning of Text$_1$ remains open and indeterminate until closed in the act of reading that forms Text$_2$. As these "READINGS" are concretized in new texts, they become the subject matter of a history of reception (Ger: *Rezeptionsgeschichte*). Both the original text (Text$_1$) and its interpretations (Text$_{2,3}$, etc.) are the object of study for reception theory.

Reception theory pursued its distinctive interests in a manner that retained contact with other text-oriented methodologies, including historical criticism and structuralism. It shared historical criticism's concern for the text as a historically conditioned artifact, but rather than seeking the causative factors that gave rise to the text, it examined the text as a sign system (phonological, lexical, syntactic, or thematic) related to other contemporaneous synchronous systems outside the text that serve to determine the sense of the text in its epoch (see INTERTEXTUALITY). Reception theory shared structuralism's concern for SYNCHRONIC relations but sought to trace the text's reception through successive epochs. It also sought to preserve a measure of objectivity for the text over time by holding that it establishes a horizon of possibilities that while multivalent are not panvalent.

A lasting contribution of Wolfgang Iser has been his concept of the "implied reader" (also called the model/ideal/encoded reader). If the real author and the real reader refer to persons outside the text, the implied author and implied reader refer to perspectives that are implicit in the organization of the text itself. The notion of the implied reader attempts to describe how the text employs various literary and rhetorical devices to invite real readers to adopt certain attitudes in the act of reading it. According to Iser, the implied reader is thus both a STRUCTURE of the text and a vantage point with which actual readers may (or may not) align themselves.

See Wolfgang Iser, *The Art of Reading* (Baltimore: Johns Hopkins University Press, 1978); Robert Jauss, *Aesthetic Experience and Literary Hermeneutics* (Minneapolis: University of Minneapolis Press, 1982). For an extensive bibliography, see D. W. Fokkema and Elrud Künne-Ibsch, *Theories of Literature in the Twentieth Century* (London: C. Hurst & Co., 1977).

Redaction Criticism (fr. Ger: *Redaktionsgeschichte*) is a method of BIBLICAL CRITICISM that seeks to lay bare the historical and theological perspectives of a biblical writer by analyzing the editorial (redactional) and compositional techniques and interpretations employed in shaping and framing the written and/or ORAL TRADITIONS at hand (see Luke 1:1–4).

Redaction criticism, which in NT study pertains above all to the Synoptic GOSPELS, is generally conceived as a logical and therefore methodological correlative to FORM CRITICISM, the latter dealing with the identification of formal elements in a composition, the former with their use and interpretation within the total literary unit as a coherent and meaningful whole. Form criticism, which in NT studies began in the 1920s, fragmented the Synoptic Gospels into a multitude of disparate linguistic forms (e.g., PARABLE, miracle stories, SAY-INGS, etc.) in an effort to distinguish between "redactional" elements on the one hand and earlier traditional forms on the other, the latter being considered to be of greater historical value. Consequently, form criticism tended to treat the synoptic writers as mere "collectors," "editors," or "TRADITIONISTS," who were "only to the smallest extent authors" (MARTIN DIBELIUS, *From Tradition to Gospel* [London: Ivor Nicholson & Watson, Ltd., 1934; repr. James Clarke, 1971; New York: Charles Scribner's Sons, 1935], 3). The author's use of his materials was thus disregarded. Interest centered on rediscovering the hypothetical setting within the life of the church (see *SITZ-IM-LEBEN*) that purportedly gave rise to the forms themselves. The literary setting given to the traditions by the Gospel writers, and the function and meaning of the traditions within that setting, were all passed over as irrelevant. Redaction criticism, however, deals positively with the redactional framework into which the traditions have been placed; it therefore provides a corrective to the methodological imbalance of form criticism. It is the EVANGELIST's use, disuse, or alteration of the traditions known to him that is in view, rather than the form and original setting of the traditions themselves. The redaction critic asks, for example, Why does Luke alter the Markan tradition concerning John the Baptist as Elijah? (Cf. Mark 6:15–16 with Luke 9:7–9; Mark 6:17–29 and 9:9–13 are absent from

Luke.) Why does he have Satan present at the beginning and end of Jesus' ministry and not during it? (Luke 4:1–13; 22:3, but cf. Mark 8:31–33 with Luke 9:21–22.) Why does he restrict the appearances of the risen Lord to Jerusalem and its environs? (Cf. Mark 16:7 with Luke 24:6–7, 46–49; Acts 1:4.) In answering these questions and countless others like them, redaction critics have effectively restored the synoptic writers to their rightful place as theologians of the EARLY CHURCH. They are, in one scholar's words, the "earliest exegetes" of the Christian tradition, not merely its first editors.

Redaction criticism functions, then, only where identifiable sources are present within a composition, such as the Gospels and the book of Acts in the NT or Deut and Judg in the OT. It is important to note that redaction criticism as applied to the Synoptic Gospels is based on the TWO SOURCE HYPOTHESIS that names Mark and Q as sources in the writing of Matt and Luke. Should the priority of Matt be established, as some suggest (see SYNOPTIC PROBLEM), the redaction-critical analysis of the Synoptics would have to begin all over again. Redaction criticism has also been applied to the Gospel of John; see J. Louis Martyn, *History and Theology in the Fourth Gospel* (New York: Harper & Row, 1968).

The term *Redaktionsgeschichte* was coined by Willi Marxsen (1954), and his book, *Mark the Evangelist* (Nashville: Abingdon Press, 1969; Ger: 1956) is one of its earliest exemplars, along with *Tradition and Interpretation in Matthew* by Günther Bornkamm, Gerhard Barth, and H. J. Held; trans. Percy Scott (Philadelphia: Westminster Press, 1963; London: SCM Press, 1972; Ger: 1948), and Hans Conzelmann's *The Theology of St. Luke*, trans. Geoffrey Buswell (New York: Harper & Row, 1961; London: Faber & Faber, 1971; Ger: 1954). Redaction criticism, as represented by these inaugural works, is not without its antecedents in both OT and NT scholarship. In NT studies historians point to WILLIAM

WREDE's *The Messianic Secret* (see MESSIANIC SECRET) and R. H. LIGHTFOOT's *History and Interpretation in the Gospels* (Hampton Lectures for 1934; New York: Harper & Brothers, 1934), as well as to Adolf Schlatter's studies in Matthew. (See esp. Norman Perrin, *What Is Redaction Criticism?* [Philadelphia: Fortress Press, 1969]; and Joachim Rohde, *Rediscovering the Teaching of the Evangelists* [Philadelphia: Westminster Press, 1969, 1974[2]; London: SCM Press, 1969; Ger: 1966].)

Redaction criticism has been applied to noncanonical works with particularly provocative results by John Dominic Crossan. See his *Four Other Gospels: Shadows on the Contours of the Canon* (Minneapolis: Winston-Seabury, 1985) and *The Cross That Spoke: The Origins of the Passion Narrative* (San Francisco: HarperSanFrancisco, 1988).

The term COMPOSITION CRITICISM, coined by E. Haenchen, has enjoyed only modest currency to refer to the total effect of redactional techniques employed by an author, the implication being that redaction criticism deals with parts, composition criticism with the whole. The distinction, however, has been thought to be too closely drawn. In addition to the work of Haenchen, see R. F. O'Toole, *The Unity of Luke's Theology: An Analysis of Luke-Acts* (Wilmington, Del.: Michael Glazier, 1984).

Antecedents in OT research, which included the perspectives and concerns of redaction criticism in fact if not in name, date back centuries, but in modern scholarship they include GERHARD VON RAD's work in the PENTATEUCH and MARTIN NOTH's studies in Deuteronomy and the Former PROPHETS (Josh–2 Sam). Strictly speaking, *Redaktionsgeschichte* as the "history of redaction" applies as a term more appropriately to OT research than to NT research because the Gospels (except perhaps John) are the work of one REDACTOR and not several redactors over a period of time as is the case with many OT writings. This fact alone, however, invites disagreement, resulting in an absence of unanimity concerning what in a text is to be regarded tradition, composition, and redaction. See R. Knierim, "Criticism of Literary Features: Form, Tradition, and Redaction," in *The Hebrew Bible and Its Modern Interpreters* ed. D. A. Knight and G. M. Tucker (Atlanta: Scholars Press, 1985), 123–66; M. E. Biddle, *Polyphony and Symphony in Prophetic Literature: Rereading Jeremiah 7–20* (Macon, Ga.: Mercer University Press, 1996).

Note: The presumption that, properly applied, redaction criticism leads to an understanding of the author's intention in writing the text and therefore provides a key to the text's real meaning is rejected by some scholars; the presumption is called "the intentional fallacy." Recent approaches to the text, such as postmodern criticism, reject the premises of redaction criticism for this and other reasons. See CRITERIA OF AUTHENTICITY; DEUTERONOMIST (-IC HISTORY); TRADITION CRITICISM.

Redaction History. See **Redaction Criticism.**

Redactor One who arranges, revises, edits, or otherwise shapes oral and literary materials into a final composition. See REDACTION CRITICISM.

Redaktionsgeschichte (Ger: redaction/COMPOSITION CRITICISM). See **Redaction Criticism.**

Refutatio. See **Rhetorical Analysis.**

Reimarus, Hermann Samuel (1694–1768), teacher of Oriental languages in Hamburg, is treated as the initiator of "Lives of Jesus Research" by SCHWEITZER and accorded special honor by him for recognizing that Jesus' thought-world was essentially eschatological, a fact overlooked until the end of the 19th cent. The portions of Reimarus's study on Jesus that were published were done so posthumously by G. E. LESSING in 1774–78 as "Fragments by an Unknown Author." While demurring at Schweitzer's exalted assessment, W. G. Kümmel acknowledges that Reimarus saw the need to distinguish between the proclamation of the historical Jesus and the proclamation of the EARLY CHURCH and to ask to what extent Jesus himself is the origin of his followers' break with Judaism. Since the answer is one of interpretation, the question remains a lively issue for scholars. See QUEST OF THE HISTORICAL JESUS.

Reitzenstein, Richard (1861–1931). Born in Breslau, Germany, where in 1888 he became a *Privatdozent* for classical philology, Reitzenstein taught in Rostock (1889–92), Giessen (1892–93, becoming a full professor), Strassburg (1893–1911), Freiburg im Breisgan (1911–14), and Göttingen (1914–31). As a leading member of the "Comparative Religions School" (*RELIGIONSGESCHICHTLICHE SCHULE*), Reitzenstein contributed significantly to the understanding of the Hellenistic mystery religions, GNOSTICISM, and Mandaism and thus to the cultic background of the NT generally. His continued importance for NT study is reflected in the republication of his major works in Germany (1962–66) and by the appearance in English of his major work, *Hellenistic Mystery-Religions: Their Basic Ideas and Significance*, trans. John E. Steely (Pittsburgh Theological Monograph Series, 15; Pittsburgh: Pickwick Press, 1978). For a bibliography, see *Festschrift Richard Reitzenstein zum 2. April 1931*, ed. E. Fraenkel et al. (Leipzig and Berlin; B. G. Tuebner, 1931).

Religionsgeschichte is a German term without a single English equivalent. It is translated most accurately and literally as "the history of religion(s)." In broadest terms, it refers to the historical study of the origin, development, and interrelationship of religious movements. As such it can be differentiated (though often now only loosely and with difficulty) from the phenomenology-, psychology-, sociology-, and philosophy of religion. *Religionsgeschichte* is also frequently translated as

"comparative religions," which, in English at least, often connotes an anthropological approach to general religious subjects without concern for historical relativity. Properly speaking, comparative religions (Ger: *Religionsvergleichung*) is but a part of "the history of religions" approach, the former presupposing a detailed knowledge of the history of the specific religions being compared. See *RELIGIONSGESCHICHTLICHE SCHULE*.

Religionsgeschichtliche Schule (Ger: "history of religions school") is the name given to a group of Protestant scholars in Germany who, at the turn of the 20th cent., sought to understand the history and literature of ancient Israel, Judaism, and early Christianity by situating them within the history of ancient Near Eastern religions generally. The approach is associated with the names of HERMANN GUNKEL, JOHANNES WEISS, WILHELM BOUSSET, Wilhelm Heitmüller, Hugo Gressmann, ALBERT EICHHORN, et al. In one sense, the *Religionsgeschichtliche Schule* simply advocated the consistent application of historical method to the study of biblical religion. Nevertheless, the approach differed radically from the dominant HISTORIOGRAPHY of late 19th-cent. German Protestant liberalism (e.g., Harnack, Ritschl), which was Christian and apologetic in temperament. It advocated replacing a theological perspective with a purely historiographical one, a church-centered approach with one oriented toward human history in general. The scholars' work threw light on early Christianity's relationship to other religions of the time (e.g., Hellenistic mystery religions), and on the immense distances that separate both from the modern world. The perceieved sterility and ecclesial ineffectiveness of the approach bred dissatisfaction that helped ignite a more avowedly theological approach to biblical studies in the 1930s (see BIBLICAL THEOLOGY, BIBLICAL THEOLOGY MOVEMENT). See also RUDOLF

BULTMANN; FORM CRITICISM; HISTORICAL-CRITICAL METHOD.

Religious Studies News is a quarterly publication of the American Academy of Religion and the SOCIETY OF BIBLICAL LITERATURE that "seeks to communicate the important events, announcements, dates, and issues for persons involved in the academic study of religion, especially those in the learned societies of the field." Address: *RSN,* 825 Houston Mill Road NE, Atlanta, GA 30329.

Revised English Bible. See **New English Bible.**

Revised Standard Version/New Revised Standard Version RSV is the common abbreviation for the Revised Standard Version of the BIBLE (NT, 1946; 1971²; OT, 1952; APOCRYPHA, 1957; expanded edition with Apocrypha, 1977), being a revision of the AMERICAN STANDARD VERSION (1901), which in turn was a revision of the KING JAMES VERSION of 1611. The RSV sought to retain as much of the elevated style characteristic of the KJV as possible so that it would be suitable for public worship. The text of the RSV is closer to the original than the KJV, since ancient MSS far older than those available in 1611 have been (and are still being) discovered (see DEAD SEA SCROLLS; TEXTUAL CRITICISM). A Catholic Edition of the RSV NT appeared in 1965, containing 67 slight alterations in wording; the entire Bible, including the 1957 RSV edition of the Apocrypha, appeared in 1966. The RSV "Expanded Edition" (1977) includes the OT, NT, and Apocrypha of Catholic and Protestant tradition as well as 3 and 4 Maccabees and Ps 151 of the Orthodox (= SEPTUAGINT) tradition.

The New Revised Standard Version (NRSV), published in 1989 by the National Council of Churches (U.S.), is a full revision of the RSV. It seeks to retain the flavor of the King James Vesion while eliminating archaisms and making selective revisions in the direction of inclusive language. Though essentially a literal translation

rather than a PARAPHRASE, it does employ paraphrastic renderings "in order to compensate for a deficiency in the English language—the lack of a common gender third person singular pronoun." Similarly, the Greek "brothers" (cf. Rom 15:14) is rendered as "brothers and sisters," etc. The male pronoun for God is retained. See Bruce M. Metzger et al., *The Making of the New Revised Standard Version of the Bible* (Grand Rapids: Eerdmans, 1991); also AMERICAN STANDARD VERSION; CONTEMPORARY ENGLISH VERSION; DOUAY; JERUSALEM BIBLE; LIVING BIBLE (PARAPHRASED); NEW AMERICAN BIBLE; NEW ENGLISH BIBLE; NEW INTERNATIONAL VERSION; NEW JEWISH VERSION; TODAY'S ENGLISH VERSION; VERSION.

Rhetoric In the broadest sense, rhetoric is the "art of speaking" and is practiced, well or poorly, by everyone who participates in social life. The term *rhetoric,* therefore, may encompass all forms and aspects of human communication (philosophical, historical, critical, etc.), from speaker and speech to audience and reader. See *The Prospect of Rhetoric,* ed. Lloyd F. Bitzer and Edwin Black (Englewood Cliffs, N.J.: Prentice-Hall, 1971) and Richard Harvey Brown, *Society as Text: Essays on Rhetoric, Reason, and Reality* (Chicago: University of Chicago Press, 1987).

In the narrower, classical sense, rhetoric, often called "School Rhetoric," is the art of persuasive speech (as practiced by politicians, lawyers, etc.) and as a field of study traceable to the Sophists of the 5th cent. B.C.E., its most classical expression being Aristotle's *Rhetoric.* Scripture can be analyzed or described with the technical terminology of school rhetoric insofar as scripture is apologetic in nature or persuasive in intent. See, e.g., Y. Gitay, "A Study of Amos's Art of Speech: A Rhetorical Analysis of Amos 3:1–15," *CBQ* 42 (1980): 293–309). Interest in such analysis has burgeoned in recent decades and along with it an expansion of its definition and scope. See RHETORICAL ANALYSIS and RHETORICAL CRITICISM.

The question that divides philosophers and riles biblical critics is not whether all speech is rhetorical, but whether all speech is *only* rhetorical, that is, *only* persuasive in intent. Those who regard all speech as only rhetorical hold that concepts such as truth and reality are but further instruments in the rhetorician's bag of tricks, while those who hold that not all speech is *only* rhetorical hold that such concepts designate an independent object of human interest, concern for which rhetoric ignores at its own peril. For a synopsis of the philosophical discussion concerning truth and rhetoric, see Stanley Fish, "Rhetoric," in *Critical Terms for Literary Study*, 2nd ed., ed. Frank Lentricchia and Thomas McLaughlin (Chicago: University of Chicago Press, 1995).

Rhetorical Analysis is sometimes distinguished from RHETORICAL CRITICISM as a whole in order to denote that specific form of inquiry that is concerned with the rhetorical STRUCTURE of a text, that is, with RHETORIC as the art of composition. This distinction is by no means universally acknowledged. The analysis of rhetorical structures, particularly of the HB, date to the 18th cent., and to the work of Robert Lowth and Johann-Albrecht Bengel, who noted features of Hebrew poetry such as PARALLELISM and CHIASMUS. These discoveries seeded further insights in the 19th cent. leading to the comprehensive study by Nils W. Lund, *Chiasm in the NT* (Chapel Hill: University of North Carolina Press, 1942; repr. 1992). Lund, and his adherents, sought to identify rules of biblical, i.e., Hebrew, rhetoric, distinct from those governing classical Greco-Roman traditions. A proposal, sympathetic to Lund, concerning the rules of biblical/oral rhetoric and the technical terminology associated with them may be found in Roland Meynet, *Rhetorical Analysis: An Introduction to Biblical Rhetoric*, JSOTS 256 (Sheffield: Sheffield Academic Press, 1998). Renewed interest in rhetorical structures and styles in biblical literature

is commonly attributed to James Muilenburg. See RHETORICAL CRITICISM.

Quite apart from Hebrew rhetoric, the prescriptive nature of classical rhetoric has led scholars to test whether any biblical texts, particularly the LETTERS of Paul, show evidence of classical influence. For this reason the technical terms of classical rhetoric are listed here. They are derived in the main from that phase of classical speech preparation termed *inventio* (to which the second [*dispositio*] and third [*elocutio*] phases are closely related; they are not discussed separately as such in the *Handbook*, nor are the fourth [*memoria*] and fifth [*pronunciatio*]). *Inventio*, as the discovery of ideas appropriate to the intended goal of the speaker, and *dispositio*, as their selection and arrangement, are for practical purposes not separable insofar as the different parts of an address (including the letter form) present different ideas (so Lausberg; see Major Reference Works Consulted).

The parts of an address and their technical names from classical school rhetoric are as follows:

1. *Exordium*, or *prooemium*: the brief introductory section designed to catch the hearer's attention, his goodwill and acceptance.
2. The central section has the form: *propositio + rationes.*
   (a) *Propositio* has the function of presenting the goal to be achieved. It can be expanded or even replaced by the following:
      (i) *partitio*: a detailing of points;
      (ii) *narratio*: a rehearsal of the course of events pertinent to the *propositio*.
   (b) *argumentatio* has the function of carrying out the various (intellectual or affective) proofs. *Refutatio* is that part of the *argumentatio* given to refuting the arguments of the opponent.
3. The (short) conclusion (*peroratio*) corresponds to the *conclusio* and assumes that the proofs provided in the *argumentatio* are now certain. The speaker thereby requests a judgment in his favor. The *peroratio* has two functions:
   (a) To show the agreement between the *propositio* and the *conclusio*; and,

(b)   To repeat briefly (*recapitulatio*) the *argumentatio*.

The intended result is of course that the hearer judges in the speaker's favor.

Some suggest that Paul's Letter to the Galatians is a "defense speech" cast in the form of a letter; it essentially fits the above scheme, as follows: *Prooemium* (1:6–10), *narratio* (1:10–2:14), *propositio* (2:15–21), *argumetatio* or *probatio* (3:1–4:31); the final section (5:1–6:10) is called PARAENESIS. An epistolary frame is given by the "prescript" (1:1–5) and the "postscript" (6:11–18). See Hans Dieter Betz, *Galatians* (*Hermeneia*; Philadephia: Fortress Press, 1979); Philip H. Kern, *Rhetoric and Galatians: Assessing an Approach to Paul's Epistle* (Cambridge: Cambridge University Press, 1998); and George A. Kennedy, *New Testament Interpretation through Rhetorical Criticism* (Chapel Hill: University of North Carolina Press, 1984).

Rhetorical Criticism is a term adopted in 1968 by the OT scholar James Muilenburg to denote a methodological approach to scripture designed to supplement that of FORM CRITICISM. Its task, he suggested, is to exhibit the structural patterns (PARALLELISM, CHIASMUS, *INCLUSIO*, etc.) employed in the fashioning of a literary unit, whether prose or poetry, and to discern the various devices (such as anaphora, EPIPHORA, PARONOMASIA, etc.) by which the predications of the composition are formulated and ordered into a unified whole ("Form Criticism and Beyond," *JBL* 88 [March 1969]: 1–18). Whereas form criticism, traditionally defined, seeks the typical and representative, rhetorical criticism, as Muilenburg conceived it, seeks what is distinctive, unique, and personal within the text in order to trace the movement of the writer's thought. RHETORIC, as the art of composition, becomes in rhetorical criticism the method by which the content, structure, and style of the composition are laid bare in order to discover "the writer's intent and meaning." [*Note:* In classical rhetoric, content, structure, and style were

known as *inventio, dispositio,* and *elocutio,* but these terms are rarely used and, unlike *inclusio* and chiasm have come to serve little functional purpose in BIBLICAL CRITICISM; see RHETORICAL ANALYSIS above). Muilenburg himself developed no comprehensive critical system but pursued his interest in rhetorical criticism through the EXEGESIS of specific biblical texts.

Since Muilenburg, rhetorical criticism has developed into "a full-fledged biblical discipline" but one that is "practiced in different ways" (Trible). These differences stem in part from two distinct but interrelated understandings of rhetoric: the art of composition and the art of persuasion. In the former, the intent of the author is in focus; in the latter, the audience and the response the text (speech) is structured to elicit. Such differences in focus have led to different emphases in analysis and different terminologies, leading to different results—and even "to a confusion of tongues" (Trible). This is due in part to different national (and therefore linguistic, e.g., German, French, British, American, etc.) academic traditions, which are slowly being transcended by the globalization of scholarship. But more significantly the different practices within rhetorical criticism find root in the fact that the HEBREW BIBLE is the product of a rhetorical tradition distinct from that of Hellenism, yet one that was nowhere reflected on in a manner comparable to the classical traditions of Greece and Rome, Aristotle's *Rhetoric* being the foundation. As noted previously, classical rhetoric is essentially prescriptive and modern rhetorical criticism/analysis descriptive, leaving the terminology of classical rhetoric only partially applicable to the latter.

If rhetoric as the art of composition dominated earlier decades, rhetoric as the art of persuasion has received increased attention recently since the latter easily moves into questions concerning the rhetorical context of a text, here relying on various forms of sociohistorical analysis and AUDIENCE CRITICISM. Still more recently concern has expanded to include the context of the interpreter of the text, that is, the interpreter's social location is considered to be as important as that of the text itself, given the increasingly accepted conviction that "what one sees depends on where one stands."

Note: For a historical overview and detailed illustration of rhetorical criticism at work, see Phyllis Trible, *Rhetorical Criticism: Context, Method, and the Book of Jonah,* Guides to Biblical Scholarship, ed. Gene M. Tucker (Minneapolis: Fortress Press, 1994). See POSTMODERNISM; SOCIOLOGICAL INTERPRETATION; STRUCTURALISM.

Rib Pattern   (Heb: complaint; lawsuit) is a technical term in form-critical studies of the OT for the complaint that one member of a covenant (usually YHWH or his prophet) issues against the offending member. Also called the Prophetic Lawsuit or the COVENANT LAWSUIT. The pattern of the complaint generally includes the following elements: (a) summons to the offending party, (b) recitation of beneficent acts bestowed in former times on the offender, (c) accusations against the offender, and (d) call to witnesses of the covenant both in heaven and on earth. (See, e.g., Jer 2:4–13; Isa 1:2–9; Hos 4:1–10; Mic 6:1–8; Ps 50.) Walter Bruggemann has adopted the *rib* pattern as an organizing motif in his OT theology, cf. *Theology of the Old Testament: Testimony, Dispute, Advocacy* (Minneapolis: Fortress Press, 1997).

RSV (NRSV).   See **Revised Standard Version.**

Rule of Faith   (fr. Lat: *regula fidei*). A brief summary of the Christian confession, especially one that is flexible in wording but authoritative in content, and that is intended to serve as a guide to the interpretation of the scriptures. In the early patristic period, Irenaeus and Tertullian above all emphasized the indispensability of the Rule of Faith for the proper (i.e., Christian or ecclesial) interpretation of the

Bible. For them, the Rule of Faith was a flexible précis of God's identity and of the beginning, turning point, and anticipated outcome of God's action. It did not settle questions of method or points of detail but enabled interpretation by supplying the "overarching story" in which the quest for meaning could take place (see R. A. Greer, "The Christian Bible and Its Interpretation," in *Early Biblical Interpretation,* ed. J. L. Kugel and R. A. Greer [Philadelphia: Fortress Press, 1986]; Frances M. Young, *Biblical Exegesis and the Formation of Christian Culture* [Cambridge: Cambridge University Press, 1997]). Irenaeus compares GNOSTICS who interpret the scriptures without the Rule of Faith to those who take mosaic pieces, intended to form the image of a king, and rearrange them to form a dog or fox (*Adv. Haer.* 1.8.1).

Long viewed as incompatible with the critical study of the Bible, the hermeneutical contribution of the Rule of Faith has recently been the subject of renewed attention and debate, due to increased interest in patristic, theological, and postcritical modes of interpretation. See E. Radner and G. Sumner, *The Rule of Faith: Scripture, Canon, and Creed in a Critical Age* (Harrisburg, Pa.: Morehouse Publishing, 1998). See SCOPE.

RV   (Revised Version). Common abbreviation for the British revision of the KING JAMES VERSION of the Bible (1611), completed in 1885 (NT, 1881). It is a woodenly literal translation of the Hebrew and Greek texts purposely cast, as much as possible, in 16th-cent. English following the KJV and earlier VERSIONS. The AMERICAN STANDARD VERSION (1901) is a revision of the RV.

Sachexegese   (Ger: lit. subject exegesis). A term that stems from German theology of the early 20th cent., *Sachexegese* designates the effort to interpret the words of the BIBLE in light of the Bible's own central concern, i.e., God. The term is approximately equivalent to theological exegesis or THEOLOGICAL INTERPRETATION. *Sachexegese* regards the contribution to exegesis of philological and historical studies as indispensable but not sufficient. A thorough exegesis requires that the biblical text be interpreted in a manner consistent with the Bible's own central concerns, which are finally theological in nature. A BIBLICAL CRITICISM that stops short of theological engagement with the Bible's subject matter is *less*, not *more*, "objective" or "critical" than *Sachexegese*, because it interprets the Bible from a viewpoint that is in the end external to the Bible's own concerns, and hence arbitrary. This was the point of KARL BARTH's famous remark *"Kritischer müssten mir die Historisch-Kritischen sein!"* ("Historical-critical scholars need to be more critical!"). The necessity of *Sachexegese* was an insight common to the dialectical theologians of the 1920s (K. Barth, E. Thurneysen, F. Gogarten, E. Brunner, R. BULTMANN), and its absence from the historical-critical approaches of the older liberal theology was regarded by them as one of liberalism's chief failings. See *SACHKRITIK*.

Sachhälfte. See *Bildhälfte.*

Sachkritik (Ger: lit. subject criticism) is a concept stemming from RUDOLF BULTMANN (1884–1976), who defined it as a criticism "which distinguishes between what is said and what is meant and measures what is said by what is meant" ("The Problem of a Theological Exegesis of the New Testament," in *The Beginnings of Dialectical Theology*, ed. J. M. Robinson [Richmond: John Knox Press, 1968]). The first half of this definition is consistent with *SACHEXEGESE* and ennunciates a principle that Bultmann shared with KARL BARTH and other adherents of "Dialectical Theology": the text should be understood in light of its subject matter (e.g., God, the GOSPEL, justification by faith, etc.). The second half of the definition identifies the specific point of *Sachkritik*: the text's subject matter must be used as a standard for assessing the text, i.e., for judging to what extent the text's words and sentences give adequate

expression to the subject matter. According to Bultmann, it is impossible to assume that the biblical author was able to give adequate expression to his theological concern at every point. Hence it must be possible to criticize a biblical text from the point of view of its own central theological concern. Bultmann regarded Barth's failure to perform *Sachkritik* as the main deficiency of his EXEGESIS. Barth regarded Bultmann's notion of *Sachkritik* as indicative of Bultmann's subordination of the biblical message to a general anthropology. Bultmann's project of "DEMYTHOLOGIZATION" can be understood as his mature effort to apply a comprehensive *Sachkritik* to the NT as a whole.

Saga. See **Legend.**

Salvation History. See *Heilsgeschichte.*

Samaritan Pentateuch (*siglum:* SP) is a RECENSION of the first five books of the OT, written in Hebrew and preserved as the sacred scriptures of the Samaritans, a religious sect in Palestine (centered in Nablus) that has claimed since biblical times to be the faithful remnant of ancient Israel. In NT times the former region of Israel was called Samaria, its inhabitants Samaritans (see Matt 19:1; Luke 10:25–39; 17:11; John 4:4–9; etc.). Although the best extant recension of the SP (the Abisha Scroll at Nablus) is in part of great antiquity, corroborating READINGS in the LXX and the DSS, its value for OT TEXTUAL CRITICISM is limited. Of its six thousand variants from the MT, many are religiously motivated: e.g., the Hebrew name for God is changed from plural (Elohim) to singular form (Gen 20:13; 31:53; 35:7; Exod 22:8); the reference to "the angel who has redeemed me" (Gen 48:16) becomes "the king who has redeemed me," and so on.

See J. D. Parvis, *The Samaritan Pentateuch and the Origin of the Samaritan Sect* (Harvard Semitic Monographs, 2; Cambridge: Harvard University Press, 1968); and R. J. Coggins, *Samaritans and Jews* (Atlanta: John Knox Press, 1975).

Sätze heiligen Rechtes (Ger: "precepts of holy law"). A technical term, occasionally left untranslated, proposed by ERNST KÄSEMANN (1954) to denote what he considered to be the earliest form of Christian law, antedating the subsequent development of administrative, disciplinary, and canon law. The laws are a chiastic form of *jus talionis*: "If anyone destroys God's temple, God will destroy him" (1 Cor 3:17). Also 1 Cor 14:38; 16:22; Gal 1:9; Rev 22:18–19; cf. Rom 10:11, 13; Gal 3:12; Mark 8:38; Matt 10:32–33. According to Käsemann, these utterances come from the early Christian prophets who, filled with the Spirit and in anticipation of the imminent *Eschaton* (the final coming of the Lord), pronounced a blessing or curse on those who broke divine law. In this way the Christian prophet, particularly in circles outside the apostles, gave leadership and order to communities prior to the formal structuring of ecclesiastical authority. (See Ernst Käsemann, *New Testament Questions of Today* [London: SCM Press, 1969], ch. 3.)

Sayings In form-critical analyses of scripture, the term *sayings* is used to designate that speech which in form and content "stands midway between prose and poetry, between the story and the song" (EISSFELDT). In content it is often exalted or solemn, in form it may be free or formal (rhythmic). Categories of sayings usually include the aphorism, blessing, curse, exhortation, invective, legal demand, threat, and prophetic ORACLE.

Biblical sayings are generally attributed to one of three sources: the lawgiver, the prophet, or the sage (revelation; inspiration/vision; observation). In the OT, collections of legal sayings are found primarily in Exod, Lev, and Deut; collections of prophetic sayings in Isa, Jer, etc.; and collections of wisdom sayings in Prov. The NT depicts Jesus as lawgiver, prophet, and sage and records sayings appropriate to each role. The Epistle of James is not a LETTER but a collection of sayings, as is the GOSPEL OF THOMAS.

It is said that NARRATIVE "contribute(s)" to the unity and coherence of the biblical world," whereas sayings express "the fragmentariness of existence" (Beardslee). It must be averred, however, that sayings can also point toward universal dimensions of experience (e.g., proverbs), just as narrative can express the uncanny and incomplete (e.g., the end of the Gospel of Mark). See AGRAPHA; LOGION; Q.

Sayings Source. See Q.

SBL. See **Society of Biblical Literature.**

Schleiermacher, Friedrich Daniel Ernst (1768–1834). Born in Breslau, Germany, and raised in a Moravian community from which he later broke, Schleiermacher was a pastor in Berlin and Stolp before becoming professor of theology at Halle (1804) and later at the newly founded University of Berlin (1810), where he remained. He preached regularly throughout his life. Known as the "Father of Modern Protestantism" for his seminal theological writings (beginning with *On Religion: Speeches to Its Cultured Despisers* [1799]), Schleiermacher is with equal justification hailed as the creator of a distinctively modern approach to HERMENEUTICS. Long a largely practical art, hermeneutics was by his day a battleground in the contest between a moralistic rationalism and a defensive supernaturalism on issues like scriptural authority and revelation. Schleiermacher sought to transcend the conflict by recasting hermeneutics as (a) a general theory of understanding that (b) allowed for the possibility of meaningful religious speech. Thus he transformed the traditional division between secular and sacred hermeneutics into the modern division between general and special hermeneutics. The former is devoted to general principles of understanding applicable to the interpretation of all languages and writing; the latter to particular books and classes of writings (e.g., legal, religious, folkloric, etc.). The new approach required the interpretation of scripture in the same manner as all other literature yet left open the question of its historical and religious uniqueness. Heirs of Schleiermacher's approach include figures such as WILHELM DILTHEY, Hans-Georg Gadamer, and Paul Ricoeur. Schleiermacher is also remembered for having been the first to deliver lectures on the life of Jesus (1819).

Scholion   (pl.: scholia; Gk diminutive: "little lecture"; Lat: *scholium*). An annotation by an ancient or medieval scholar on a historical text for the purpose of instructing the reader, such as ORIGEN's note (scholion) to Ps 118:1 (LXX) in his HEXAPLA. CODEX Mosquensis (K^{ap}), dating from the 9th or 10th cent., contains scholia attributed to John Chrysostom, the great scholar-preacher of the 4th cent. When scholia accompany the whole text and are not simply random or marginal notations, the work is called a COMMENTARY. (See Bruce M. Metzger, *The Text of the New Testament* [London and New York: Oxford University Press, 1964].)

Schweitzer, Albert   (1875–1965). Born in Kayersberg (Oberelsass, Germany); *Privatdozent* for NT (1902–12) and assistant pastor at St. Nicholas' Cathedral (1903–6) in Strassburg; began medical studies in 1905 with the intention of becoming a medical missionary, which he realized in 1913, founding a hospital in Lambarene, French Equatorial Africa (now Gabon). In this period he wrote a doctorate in philosophy (1899), became a Licentiate in theology (1900), and completed his Habilitation (requirement for teaching on the university level) in 1902. An accomplished organist, he published a study on J. S. Bach (Fr: 1905; Ger: 1908) and on German and French organ construction (1906), the latter appearing in the same year as the first edition of his epoch-making *The Quest of the Historical Jesus*. Before his departure to Africa and in addition to lecture and recital tours, he published *Paul and His Interpreters* (Ger: 1911; Eng: London: A. & C. Black,

1912) and *The Psychiatric Study of Jesus* (Ger: 1913; Eng: 1948). Interned during WW I in Europe (1917) and unable to return to Lambarene for lack of funds until 1924, Schweitzer turned to writing, this time to philosophical and autobiographical works. His last major contribution to biblical studies, *The Mysticism of Paul the Apostle* (London: A. & C. Black), appeared in 1930.

Perhaps more than any other man Schweitzer characterized NT studies at the turn of the century. His *Quest* embodied 19th-cent. synoptic methodology even as it cataloged its inadequacies, yet his argument for the eschatological character of Jesus' proclamation won the day and thereby anticipated all dominant forms of biblical theology in the first six decades of the 20th cent.

Of all the contributors to modern BIBLICAL CRITICISM, Schweitzer remains unsurpassed in breadth of genius, audacity of vision, and courage of moral action. A dissenting assessment of his work can be found among practitioners of POSTCOLONIAL BIBLICAL INTERPRETATION, a leading spokesperson for which looks upon Schweitzer as an "active colonial agent" (Dube Shomanah; see *DBI*).

For the significance of Schweitzer's *Quest*, see James M. Robinson's "Introduction" to the 1968 paperback edition, published by the Macmillan Company. See QUEST OF THE HISTORICAL JESUS.

Scope   (fr. Gk.: *skopos*: target, aim) denotes the aim, intent, or central purpose of a text. Traditional Christian HERMENEUTICS held that knowledge of a text's scope is necessary for a correct understanding of its constituent elements and of its LITERAL SENSE. Significantly, many Christian interpreters before the modern era held that a given biblical passage should be interpreted not only in light of the scope of the book of which it was a part, but also (and more contentiously from the perspective of HISTORICAL-CRITICAL METHOD) in light of the scope of the canon as a whole. The term was an important part of patristic and Protestant interpretive theory (ca. 1550–1850) and remains current today in Orthodox theology and biblical interpretation.

For the Greek fathers of the church, the scope corresponds to the central theme of the canon that delimits the purpose or point of any part of scripture. For Athanasius in his dispute with Arius, the canon's scope was CHRIST in his humanity and deity. Matthew Flacius Illyrius (1520–1575), a pioneer of Lutheran hermeneutical theory, advised, "When you start to read a book, try so far as possible, from the beginning, to keep in mind first of all, the scope (*scopum*), purpose, or intention of the whole book/work which is, as it were, its head or face." The term gradually fell out of favor in the 19th cent. as biblical scholars increasingly embraced the view that "the most primitive meaning of the text is its only valid meaning, and the historical-critical method is the only key which can unlock it" (D. Steinmetz). More recently, however, some advocates of a canonical approach to the scripture have sought to retrieve the notion of scope, arguing that it usefully encapsulates the insight that correct interpretation of a text in its canonical context depends on a concurrent search for the central or unifying aim of the canon as a whole.

See G. T. Sheppard, "Between Reformation and Modern Commentary: the Perception of the Scope of the Biblical Books," in *A Commentary on Galatians, William Perkins*, ed. G. T. Sheppard (New York, 1989), xlviii–lxxvii. See CANONICAL CRITICISM; PRECRITICAL BIBLICAL INTERPRETATION; THEOLOGICAL INTERPRETATION.

Second Temple Period/Literature refers to the years between ca. 520 and 515 B.C.E. and the Third or Herod's Temple, started during King Herod's reign (37–4 B.C.E.), and to the literature produced during that time. The terms are increasingly substituted for "the intertestamental period/literature" in recognition of the importance of the Jewish history and literature encompassed by the terms. More important, the change in nomenclature is due to the growing conviction among some scholars that the HB is in important respects the product of the period of the Second Temple rather than that of the First or Solomon's Temple, making the term "intertestamental" misleading and inaccurate. See DEUTEROCANONICAL.

Sellin, Ernst (1867–1945). Professor of OT in Vienna, Rostock, Kiel, and, from 1921 until his retirement in 1935, in Berlin. Sellin's most influential work is his *Introduction to the OT* (Ger: 1910; Eng: 1923; rev. by Georg Fohrer [Nashville: Abingdon Press, 1968]), in which he took a mediating position between the RADICAL CRITICISM of the Wellhausen school on one hand and the traditional conservative position on the other.

Semantics (fr. Gk: *sema, semeron*: sign) is a term first employed by the French linguist Michel Breal (*Essai des semantique* [Paris: Hachette, 1897; Eng: *Semantics: Studies in the Science of Meaning*; New York: Dover Press, 1964]) to refer to the complex rules by which linguistic expressions are created and die and to how meaning changes and new expressions are chosen. Breal's interest lay in the historical (DIACHRONIC) development of the meaning of linguistic forms, an interest that in subsequent decades did not remain the central focus of semantics.

As a field of study today, semantics is so diverse and complicated that the term itself is ambiguous and, as the Polish linguist Adam Schaff has written, "needs to undergo semantic analysis" (Ger: *Einführung in die Semantik* [Berlin: 1966], Preface). In general usage the term may refer to (1) the study of the relationship between the meaning and content of words and phrases; (2) SEMASIOLOGY; (3) that aspect of language analysis that studies the relationship of linguistic units to the objects and processes described by them; and (4) the empirical investigation of the meaning (content) of linguistic signs and sign combinations, in brief, "the study of meaning" (see Th. Lewandowski, *Linguistisches Wörterbuch*, vol. 3 [Heidelberg: Quelle & Meyer, 1975], ad hoc).

Semasiology (fr. Gk: *sema, semeion*: sign) usually refers either to (1) the study of meaning and is equivalent to SEMANTICS or (2) that branch of LINGUISTICS that investigates the lexical meanings of words in terms of their SYNCHRONIC and DIACHRONIC aspects. According to Th. Schippan (*Einführung in die Semasiology* [Leipzig: Bibliographisches Institut, 1972]), semasiology is the heart of lexicology; it is the study of words and their origins, particularly the lexical division of a language and of the variations occurring within it. Semasiology investigates the structure of the "lexic" ("vocabulary"; cf. LEXICON), the meaning of its elements and lexical units and their semantic relationships; it describes the changes in a vocabulary and the causes and conditions lying behind them; and it investigates the connection between the development of a society and vocabulary adaptation and creation. The foundations of semasiology go back to the Latin studies of C. K. Reisig in Germany. (For this definition see Th. Lewandowski, *Linguistisches Wörterbuch*, vol. 3 [Heidelberg: Quelle & Meyer, 2nd rev. ed., 1976].)

Semeia is "an experimental journal devoted to the exploration of new and emergent areas and methods of BIBLICAL CRITICISM," published under the auspices of the SOCIETY OF BIBLICAL LITERATURE (SBL). It is perhaps the best source for understanding the development of theory in the area of biblical interpretation since the journal's founding in 1974.

Semiotics; Semiology (fr. Gk: *sema, semeion*: sign, signal) are technical terms, now used interchangeably, to denote studies toward a general theory of signs or sign systems. Semiotics is perhaps more a field of studies waiting to be unified into a single discipline than a single discipline unified

by a comprehensive semiotic model (U. Eco). The field of semiotics includes studies in a vast range of communicative processes (semiosis). It assumes that underlying each process is a *system of significations* (or "Code") that makes communication possible. Semiotic studies may concentrate on the production (encoding) or reception (decoding) of signs as each is an inherent part of every event of communication. Areas encompassed by contemporary research are zoosemiotics (animal sign systems); tactile communication; codes of taste; paralinguistics (voice sets, qualities, etc.); kinesics (gesturing); musical codes; formalized languages (e.g., algebra); written languages; natural languages; plot STRUCTURE; visual communication; text theory; cultural codes; mass communication; RHETORIC; etc. (In any single event of human communication a number of discrete systems [codes] is likely to be involved.)

In recent decades BIBLICAL CRITICISM has experienced the growing impact of semiotic studies. These include the general theoretical studies of Ferdinand de Saussure (*Course in General Linguistics* [New York: McGraw-Hill, 1959; Fr orig.; 1916]), Charles S. Peirce (*Collected Papers* [Cambridge: Harvard University Press, 1931–1958]), and Charles Morris (*Writings on the General Theory of Signs* [Approaches to Semiotics, 16, The Hague/Paris: Mouton, 1971]), and the more specialized investigations within the field of NARRATIVE or plot structure, e.g., Vladimir Propp (*Morphology of the Folktale* [The Hague: Mouton, 1958; 2nd ed. Austin, Tex. and London: University of Texas Press, 1968; Russian orig.: 1928]), and Roland Barthes (*Mythologies* [Paris: Seuil, 1957]). Semiotics has taken another turn in the structural SEMANTICS of A. J. Greimas (*Sémantique structurale* [Paris: Larousse, 1966]; with J. Courtés, *Semiotics and Language: An Analytical Dictionary* [Bloomington, Ind.: Indiana University Press, 1982]); and Greimas's own work has shifted in recent years from text to readers.

This diverse theoretical background has led to diverse approaches and results within the field of biblical studies, since semiotics is not a methodology; it has more appropriately been described as "a perspective which clarifies the nature, task, and goals of critical biblical studies and which, consequently, helps biblical scholars to perform their roles in a self-conscious, critical, and responsible way" (Patte). This means of course that the application of semiotic insights to biblical studies has led to highly idiosyncratic results, with no two theorists proceeding in precisely the same way, i.e., using different "codes" of interpretation. For a helpful study in noting the plausibility of divergent interpretations, see Mieke Bal, *Murder and Difference: Gender, Genre, and Scholarship on Sisera's Death* (Bloomington, Ind.: Indiana University Press, 1988) and *On Meaning-Making: Essays in Semiotics* (Sonoma, Calif.: Polebridge Press, 1994).

Two fields of interest within the domain of semiotics are semantics and pragmatics, the first dealing with the relationship of signs to the object to which they point, the latter referring to the relationship of signs to interpreters. Aspects of pragmatics are explored in G. R. O'Day, *Revelation in the Fourth Gospel: Narrative Mode and Theological Claim* (Philadelphia: Fortress Press, 1986).

For a listing of approximately 1900 books and articles relating semiotic theory to religious studies, see Alfred M. Johnson, Jr., *A Bibliography of Semiological and Structural Studies of Religion* (Pittsburgh: Clifford E. Harbour Library, Pittsburgh Theological Seminary, 1979). For a historical sketch of the changing focus of semiotic theory in more recent decades and a defense of its religious and ethical value for critical biblical study, see Daniel Patte, ed., *Thinking in Signs: Semiotics and Biblical Studies . . . Thirty Years After* (*Semeia* 81; Atlanta: Scholars Press, 1998). In brief, that change in focus has been from "signifying systems towards the singularity of texts, . . . from general

problems towards signifying practices, beginning with . . . reading" (Delorme). See INTERTEXTUALITY, READER-RESPONSE CRITICISM, STRUCTURE, STRUCTURALISM.

Semitism (also Semiticism). Broadly speaking, a Semitism is a word or IDIOM derived from a Semitic language; in biblical study it more specifically designates a feature of LXX or NT Greek that shows the influence of Semitic (Hebrew or Aramaic) style and terminology. Except for Daniel, the LXX contains only Hebraisms; the Hebraisms of the NT may point either to a quotation from the LXX or to an imitation of LXX style (Luke-Acts)—just as the style of the KJV is imitated today. Proven Aramaisms in the NT, however, are likely to go back either to Jesus or to early Palestinian Christianity; terms such as *Abba* ("Father," Mark 14:36), *Maranatha* ("Our Lord, come," 1 Cor 16:22), and *Talitha cumi* ("Little girl, arise," Mark 5:41) are examples. In general, Semitic style is characterized by a frequency of PARATAXIS (the sequential ordering of subjects and main verbs rather than using subordinate clauses—e.g., Mark 10:32); PARALLELISM (e.g., Luke 12:48); and *chiasmus* (Matt 9:17; 1 Cor 5:2–6, etc.), which, however, are also found, though to a far less degree, in Greek. The Semitic style of the *MAGNIFICAT* (Luke 1:46–55), the *BENEDICTUS* (1:68–79), and the *NUNC DIMITTIS* (2:29–32), plus other considerations, have led scholars to postulate their pre-Christian origin within the movement associated with John the Baptist. See Fred S. Heuman, *The Uses of Hebraisms in Recent Bible Translations* (New York: Philosophical Library, 1977). See LATINISM; SEPTUAGINTISM.

Sensus Literalis (Lat: literal sense). See **Literal Sense.**

Sensus Plenior designates "the deeper meaning, intended by God but not clearly intended by the human author, that is seen to exist in the words of Scripture when they are studied in the light of further revelation or of development in the understanding of revelation" (Brown). Coined by A. Fernández in 1925, the term *sensus plenior* was advocated chiefly by a number of Roman Catholic theologians during the mid-twentieth century (J. Coppens, P. Benoit, R. E. BROWN) who wished to recognize the limited scope of the literal (or historical) sense of biblical passages but still affirm the validity of THEOLOGICAL INTERPRETATIONS that extended beyond the LITERAL SENSE. Scholars often appealed to the *sensus plenior* in connection with the NT's use of OT texts, but also the patristic interpretation of the Bible more generally, e.g., Gen 3:15 applied to Mary's participation in CHRIST's victory over evil (the *PROTEVANGELIUM*). The term lost currency after 1970, but its intention has been at least partly taken up elsewhere, e.g., "excess of meaning," "INTERTEXTUALITY," "canonical criticism," etc. See RAYMOND E. BROWN, *The Sensus Plenior of Sacred Scripture* (Baltimore: St. Mary's University, 1955). See *FOURFOLD SENSE OF SCRIPTURE*; TYPOLOGY.

Sentences of Holy Law.   See *Sätze heiligen Rechtes.*

Septuagint   (Lat: seventy; *siglum:* LXX; sometimes called the Old Greek or Proto-LXX translation) is the name of the earliest Greek translation of the Hebrew TORAH; it later came to include the whole HB and the APOCRYPHA, as well as works not in the Apocrypha, viz., 3–4 Macc and Ps 151. According to tradition the PENTATEUCH was translated at the order of Ptolemy II (ca. 285–247 B.C.E.) in Alexandria, Egypt, by 70 (or 72) Hebrew elders, whence its name and symbol. In its expanded VERSION it became the favored translation of holy scriptures in the EARLY CHURCH and for this reason fell into disfavor among Jews. In OT text-critical discussions, the symbol LXX often denotes the Lucianic RECENSION of the LXX (Lucian d. 312 C.E.), hence terms such as "Old Greek" or "Proto-LXX" refer to the earliest forms of the text. Further, "Proto-Lucian" (2nd–1st cent. B.C.E.) denotes a

form of the Old Greek text revised in the direction of the Palestinian Hebrew text. Another early recension of the Old Greek is called the Proto-Theodotion or *KAIGE* RECENSION (1st cent. C.E. or earlier). By JEROME's day (ca. 400 C.E.) there were three editions of the LXX called the *Trifaria Varietas:* the HEXAPLARIC text of ORIGEN, another by Hesychius of Egypt, and Lucian's.

The International Organization for Septuagint and Cognate Studies maintains a series of publications under the auspices of the SOCIETY OF BIBLICAL LITERATURE (SBL). See AQUILA; THEODOTION; SYMMACHUS.

Septuagintism   ("belonging to the Septuagint"). Words or phrases that are peculiar to or especially characteristic of the Greek OT (the SEPTUAGINT) and are used by NT writers in imitation (conscious or otherwise) of its style and expression are called Septuagintisms. Luke in particular appears to have cast his history of the EARLY CHURCH (the book of Acts) in the style of the LXX. The expressions "lifted up his voice," "let this be known," and "give ear," all in Acts 2:14, are examples. The subsequent speech by Peter (Acts 2:15–39) and another in 3:12–26 are generally recognized as Lukan imitations of Septuagint Greek. A Septuagintism may be, but is not necessarily, also a SEMITISM. For example, Matthew's use of *parthenos* (virgin) in his quotation of Isa 7:14 (Matt 1:23) follows the LXX and may be termed a Septuagintism, since the Hebrew READING contains *ʿalmah* meaning "a young woman." The use of *parthenos* is peculiar to the LXX and has nothing to do with Hebrew (Semitic) terminology or expression. This is one of the reasons 1st–2nd cent. Judaism, in reaction to Christian EXEGESIS, rejected the LXX. See LATINISM.

Sermon on the Mount (The)   is the name given to Matt 5–7 in the NT, perhaps first by Augustine (4th–5th cent.) but not widely used until modern times. A number of parallel verses are found in Luke 6:17–49 and are often given the name "The Sermon on the Plain." See Hans Dieter Betz, *The Sermon on the Mount*, Hermeneia Commentary Series (Minneapolis: Fortress Press, 1995); Dale C. Allison, *The Sermon on the Mount: Inspiring the Moral Imagination* (New York: Crossroad, 1999).

Setting in Life. See *Sitz-im-Leben*.

Shema (Heb: hear) is the common name given to the three prayers offered daily by the pious Jews of the 1st cent. C.E., taken from Deut 6:4–9; 11:13–21; and Num 15:37–41; the term (*Shema*) itself is from the longest section of the second prayer beginning, "Hear, O Israel: The Lord our God, the Lord is One." In their brief form the prayers are (1) *Yoser*, "Blessed art thou, O Lord, Creator of the luminaries"; (2) *Ahabah*, "Blessed art thou, who hast chosen thy people in love" (the *Shema* follows here ending, "I am the Lord your God, who brought you out of the land of Egypt, to be your God; I am the Lord your God"); (3) *Geullah*, "Blessed art thou, O Lord, who redeemest Israel." In NT faith, cf. Mark 12:29; Rom 3:30; Gal 3:20; Jas 2:19; esp. 1 Cor 8:6; Phil 2:6–11.

Shemoneh Esreh (Heb: Eighteen) or "The Eighteen Benedictions." A Jewish daily prayer thought to have been in use since as early as the 1st cent. C.E. It is known to us today through two later recensions, a longer Babylonian one and a shorter Palestinian one. The prayer, beginning "O Lord, open thou my lips and my mouth shall show forth thy praise," contains eighteen benedictions concerning (1) the patriarchs, (2) making the dead live, (3) sanctification of the name, (4) understanding, (5) repentance, (6) forgiveness, (7) redemption, (8) healing, (9) the blessing of the year, (10) the gathering of the dispersed, (11) restoration of the judges, (12) against heresy, (13) the blessing of proselytes, (14) Jerusalem, (15) hearing prayer, (16) worship, (17) thanksgiving, and (18) peace.

Signs   Source This technical term derives from the source-critical analysis of the GOSPEL of John, specifically that section of the Gospel containing the seven miraculous "signs" of Jesus' divine power (chs. 2–11), which in whole or part is thought to have existed in written form prior to the compilation and redaction of the Gospel. This theory, first proposed by A. Fauré (1922), is generally accepted though debated in its details (content, setting-in-life, etc.). The word "sign" is a literal translation of the Greek *semeion*, which the author uses in place of the common word for miracle (see John 2:11, 18, 23; 3:2; 4:54; 6:2, 14, 26, 30, etc.). For a discussion, see Robert T. Fortna, *The Gospel of Signs: A Reconstruction of the Narrative Source Underlying the Fourth Gospel* (Cambridge: Cambridge University Press, 1970). See LITERARY CRITICISM.

Simile. See **Metaphor**.

Sitz-im-Leben (Ger: setting in life, or life situation) has become a technical term in FORM CRITICISM to refer to that sociological setting within the life of Israel or the EARLY CHURCH in which particular rhetorical forms (LEGENDS, SAYINGS, liturgical FORMULAS, PSALMS, prophecies, PARABLES, etc.) first took shape. (See Martin J. Buss, "The Idea of *Sitz-im-Leben*—History and Critique," *ZAW* 90 [1978]: 157–70.) More recently, form criticism's concern with *Sitz-im-Leben* has been taken up by sociological analysis and is expressed by terms such as social location and SOCIAL WORLD.

As first employed by HERMANN GUNKEL (1906), *Sitz-im-Leben* referred to the social setting of literary form in Israel (*Sitz-im-Volksleben Israels*). MARTIN DIBELIUS applied the concept to the NT, particularly to the GOSPEL materials because, unlike the NT Epistles, they had existed in oral form prior to being written down in the Gospels (*From Tradition to Gospel* [London: Ivor Nicholson & Watson, Ltd.; repr. James Clarke, 1971; New York: Charles Scribner's Sons, 1935; Ger: 1919]). Here the term functioned in the sense of "the setting in the life of the church" (*Sitz-im-Leben der Kirche*). According to Dibelius, it was the church's need for sermonic and didactic material that was the "life situation" that had either created or formatively shaped and determined the content of the traditions.

C. H. DODD (*The Parables of the Kingdom* [London: Nisbet & Co., 1935]) and Joachim Jeremias (*The Parables of Jesus* [New York: Charles Scribner's Sons, 1955; London: SCM Press, 1972; Ger: 1947; 1971[8]]) sought to go behind the sociological setting of the church to the "setting in the life of Jesus" (*Sitz-im-Leben Jesu*), which they defined in part as the impending crisis of divine judgment and Jesus' controversies with the Pharisees.

In NT REDACTION CRITICISM, however, the term, or rather a modification of it, refers not to a sociological but to a literary setting, viz., "the setting in the Gospel" (*Sitz-im-Evangelium*; i.e., in Matt, Mark, Luke, or John) that the various traditions (parables, miracle stories, sayings, etc.) have been given by the writers. Here it is recognized that linguistic forms have been adapted to the kerygmatic, CATECHETICAL, and apologetic purposes of the Gospel writers and that their meaning and function for the writer can in part be ascertained by the literary setting he gives them. See *KULTGESCHICHTLICHE SCHULE*; MOWINCKEL; TRADITION CRITICISM.

Social World Social world is a term derived from sociology of knowledge that denotes how the people of a given time and place perceive and construct the social reality in which they live. According to Peter L. Berger and Thomas Luckmann, two influential theorists of the sociology of knowledge, humans are constantly engaged in the construction and maintenance of social worlds that provide the institutions, structures, and patterns for everyday life. Although attempts to describe the social world of the Bible are well over a century old, recent decades have seen an explosion of interest among scholars in this approach to understanding biblical texts.

The renewed concern with social world reflects a dissatisfaction with readings of the NT that are perceived to be narrowly concerned with "theological ideas" at the expense of the ordinary people who held them and the families and communities in which they lived. Investigations of social world frequently try to describe the customs and institutions of Hellenistic society or 1st-cent. Jewish Palestine and how early Christians inhabited these worlds with their neighbors even as they created overlapping communities centered on new customs and institutions.

The importance of social world to contemporary biblical scholarship is illustrated by the M. Barth and H. Blanke COMMENTARY on *The Letter to Philemon* (Grand Rapids: Eerdmans, 2000). The bulk of its 561 pages is devoted to social background and especially the status and function of the slave in the Greco-Roman world. See Peter L. Berger and Thomas Luckmann, *The Social Construction of Reality: A Treatise in the Sociology of Knowledge* (Garden City, N.Y.: Doubleday, 1966). See SOCIAL-SCIENTIFIC CRITICISM; SOCIOLOGICAL INTERPRETATION; IDEOLOGY CRITICISM.

Social-Scientific Criticism is a delineable approach within the larger domain of SOCIOLOGICAL INTERPRETATION. In the field of BIBLICAL CRITICISM it has been defined as "that phase of the exegetical task which analyzes the social and cultural dimensions of the text and of its environmental context through the utilization of the perspectives, theory, models, and research of the social sciences" (Elliott). Under study is not only the text itself and the social factors influencing its form and content, but the sender and recipient(s) of the text within their social contexts, and the response that the text is intended to elicit. As a subdiscipline of EXEGESIS social-scientific criticism sees itself as a necessary component of HISTORICAL CRITICISM; at the same time it makes use of, and is a complement to, all other exegetical methodologies and approaches. The questions of historical criticism pertain mainly to "Who?" "Where?" "What?" and "When?" The questions of social-scientific criticism inquire into "How?" "Why?" and "What for?" By way of theoretical models social-scientific criticism investigates how societies are organized and operate; how values and beliefs are shaped by natural and social environments; how religious concepts and symbols develop into "universes of meaning" in which actions, lifestyles, and conditions are justified and given motivation; and so on. Its general objective has been stated as "the analysis, synthesis, and interpretation of the social as well as the literary and ideological (theological) dimensions of a text, the correlation of these textual features, and the manner in which it was designed as a persuasive vehicle of communication and social interaction, and thus an instrument of social as well as literary and theological consequence" (Elliott).

Social-scientific criticism distinguishes itself from traditional forms of sociological interpretation in its belief that the time has come within biblical criticism to go beyond social description to "social-scientific analysis." Its claim to being scientific rests on the application and testing of theories and models from the wide range of social sciences to the data, including texts, of the biblical world. The presuppositions guiding social-scientific criticism have been enumerated as (1) all knowledge is socially conditioned and perspectival in nature; (2) therefore the differing social locations of the interpreter (sic) and the authors and objects to be interpreted must be distinguished; (3) theories and models play an essential role in the clarification of the differences between ancient texts and modern readers as well as in the clarification of the properties and relations of ancient social and cultural systems; (4) the logic of social-scientific criticism moves from evidence to hypothesis and back again (a type of HERMENEUTICAL CIRCLE); (5) the texts of the

Bible must be set within their geographical, social, and cultural region, that is, within the circum-Mediterranean and ancient Near East; (6) texts are units of meaningful social DISCOURSE that (a) encode aspects of the social system of which they are a part and (b) whose meaning, intent, and impact cannot be understood apart from knowledge of the social systems and linguistic conventions of both the author and the audience/readers; further, (c) that texts have not only a cognitive and affective dimension but also an IDEOLOGICAL one through which the varied self-interests of the author (person, group, or class) are expressed, and (d) that an understanding of the author or the recipient cannot be achieved apart from identifying the social location of each; (7) social-scientific criticism so described is different from but complementary to the aims of strictly historical orientations, and (8) a study of biblical religion requires this study of social structures and relations.

Most characteristic of social-scientific criticism is the use of models as heuristic tools for the identification and organization of data (whether actually available or hypothetically desirable) for comparative analysis. Such data would include geographic, temporal, and social location. Social location itself would include data concerning economic activity (modes of ownership, production, management, labor, commerce, etc.); population structure; social systems (organization, roles and statuses, kinship, classes, etc.); political organization (legal and military); cultural systems (education, language, art, music, values, norms and sanctions, etc.); belief systems and ideologies, etc. Social-scientific criticism contends that when the data fits the model then "the hypothesis is confirmed and the study is added to the body of confirmed social-science theory" (Elliott).

Social-scientific criticism has been criticized for being "pretentiously scientific" and for applying to antiquity what is only properly applicable to contemporary societies where the testing of models and theories is truly possible. Although the former criticism is certainly illustratable, there are many notable exceptions. With regard to the latter, proponents defend their methodology by contending that hypothetical models developed for reconstructing the social contexts of ancient texts can be tested and proved valid or invalid. In any case, social-scientific criticism is still regarded as a nascent, increasingly recognized, undertaking—though not without its severe critics. It still accords legitimacy to HISTORICAL-CRITICAL METHODOLOGIES and assumptions, a position roundly rejected by almost all forms of postmodern criticisms.

A full explication of social-scientific criticism, from which this synopsis is taken, plus illustrative models of interpretation, an example of its application to 1 Peter, a glossary of technical terms and selected bibliography of the wider field is found in John H. Elliott's *What Is Social-Scientific Criticism?* Guides to Biblical Scholarship, ed. Dan O. Via (Minneapolis: Fortress Press, 1993).

Although social-scientific criticism is deeply and diversely rooted, some of the major early works in English include John G. Gager, *Kingdom and Community: The Social World of Early Christianity* (Englewood Cliffs, N.J.: Prentice-Hall, 1975); Gerd Theissen, *The Social World of Early Palestinian Christianity* (Philadelphia: Fortress Press, 1978; Ger: 1977); John H. Elliott, *I Peter: Estrangement and Community* (Chicago: Franciscan Herald, 1979); Norman K. Gottwald, *The Tribes of Yahweh: A Sociology of the Religion of Liberated Israel, 1250–1050 B.C.E.* (Maryknoll, N.Y.: Orbis Books, 1979); Fernando Belo, *A Materialist Reading of the Gospel of Mark* (Maryknoll, N.J.: Orbis Books, 1981); Bruce Malina, *The New Testament World: Insights from Cultural Anthropology* (Atlanta: John Knox Press, 1981); and Wayne Meeks, *The First Urban Christians: The Social World of the Apostle*

Paul (New Haven, Conn.: Yale University Press, 1983).

Society of Biblical Literature (SBL)

Founded by Protestant scholars in 1880 as the Society of Biblical Literature and Exegesis, SBL has become the principal professional organization in North America for the critical study of the BIBLE and cognate studies. It is increasingly ecumenical, international, and interfaith. Its stated purpose is "to stimulate the critical study of the Scriptures by presenting, discussing, and publishing original papers on Biblical topics." This is accomplished through its publications and through annual regional, national, and international conferences for its now more than 8,000 members. Its primary publication is the *Journal of Biblical Literature* (founded: 1881), but it also publishes the *SBL Monograph Series; Semeia; Semeia Supplements;* Dissertation Series; *Sources for Biblical Study;* Texts and Translation Series; *Septuagint and Cognate Studies,* and *Masoretic Studies*—inter alia. RELIGIOUS STUDIES NEWS is jointly published with the American Academy of Religion. The *SBL Handbook of Style* (Peabody, Mass.: Hendrickson Publishers, 1999) is the Society's authorized guide for preparing manuscripts for its publications and is of general value for authors and publishers alike. For a history of the Society, see E. W. Saunders, "A Century of Service to American Biblical Scholarship," *Bulletin of the Council on the Study of Religion* 11 (1980): 59–76.

Sociological Interpretation,

an umbrella term encompassing immense diversity, stresses that knowledge of the social milieu in which the texts of scripture arose is necessary for any adequate understanding of the texts themselves. Common, often overlapping but not exhaustive, classifications of sociological interpretation distinguish between (a) social description, (b) social history, and (c) social theory. Biblical scholars have in the main left social theory to academic social theorists, sociologists, and cultural anthropologists (Marx, Weber,

Durkheim, Mannheim, and more recently Lévi-Strauss, Berger, Douglas, et al.), applying their theories to the description and history of the sociocultural phenomena behind and within biblical texts. A recent, more exegetically oriented branch of sociological interpretation, known as SOCIAL-SCIENTIFIC CRITICISM, is discussed separately. What follows highlights only a few aspects of sociological interpretation as it was articulated in the early years of its general acceptance in the later decades of the 20th cent.

Following N. K. Gottwald, a leading early proponent, one can say that sociological interpretation seeks to understand typical patterns of human relations in their structure and function, both at a given time in history (SYNCHRONICS) and in their trajectories of change over a specified time span (DIACHRONICS). The hypothetically "typical" in collective human behavior is ascertained by comparative study of societies and expressed theoretically in "laws," "regularities," or "tendencies" that attempt to abstract structures and processes of a translocal and transtemporal character. As a method the sociological interpretation of scripture includes all the methods of inquiry proper to the social sciences (such as anthropology, sociology, political science, and economics), as well as those typical of the humanities (history, comparative religions, LITERARY CRITICISM, FORM CRITICISM, RHETORICAL CRITICISM, REDACTION CRITICISM, TRADITION HISTORY, etc.).

Its characteristic assumptions are (1) that humanistic and sociological methods are equally valuable and complementary methods for reconstructing the ancient past; (2) that religion is best understood as one part of a wider network of social relations in which it has intelligible functions to perform; (3) that changes in religious behavior and thought are best viewed as aspects of change in the wider network of social and economic relations; and (4) that religion is intelligible to the degree that it

exhibits lawful behavior and symbolic forms that can be predicted and retrodicted within limits set by the total matrix of changing social and economic relations (cf. Norman K. Gottwald, *The Tribes of Yahweh: A Sociology of the Religion of Liberated Israel, 1250–1050 B.C.E.* [Maryknoll, N.Y.: Orbis Books, 1979], Preface, xxiii; also "Sociological Method in the Study of Ancient Israel," in Martin J. Buss, ed., *Encounter with the Text: Form and History in the Hebrew Bible* [Missoula, Mont.: Scholars Press, 1979]).

From its earliest inception in the mid-19th cent. until 1970, the application of nascent sociological theory to ancient Israel and to Christian beginnings was relatively sparse and sporadic. Among the earliest practitioners in OT studies were W. Robertson Smith (*Lectures on the Religion of the Semites: The Fundamental Institutions* [London: A. & C. Black, 1901]); Max Weber (*Ancient Judaism* [Glencoe, Ill.: Free Press, 1952; Ger: 1923]); and JOHANNES PEDERSEN (*Israel, Its Life and Culture*, vols. 1–4 [London: Oxford University Press, 1926–40]). In the NT those usually cited are Shailer Mathews (*The Social Teaching of Jesus* [New York: Macmillan Co., 1906]); SHIRLEY JACKSON CASE (*The Social Origins of Christianity* [Chicago: University of Chicago Press, 1923]); and ADOLF DEISSMANN (*St. Paul: A Study in Social and Religious History* [London: Hodder & Stoughton, 1912]). However, other names in the fields of archaeology, *Religionsgeschichte*, and form and redaction criticism could be added as persons interested in describing aspects of the social history of the Bible.

In recent decades, in which sociological interpretation has experienced rapid development, studies combining sociological theory and methodology to biblical texts have demonstrated four different (though often overlapping) approaches and/or concerns: (1) *a description of social facts* related to the material culture: institutions, occupations, economics, food, etc., e.g., R. DE VAUX, *Ancient Israel: Its Life and Institutions* (New York: McGraw-Hill,

1961); Martin Hengel, *Judaism and Hellenism* (Philadelphia: Fortress Press, 1974); Joachim Jeremias, *Jerusalem in the Time of Jesus* (London: SCM Press, 1969); and Ronald F. Hock, *The Social Context of Paul's Ministry* (Philadelphia: Fortress Press, 1979); (2) the development of the *social history* of a movement integrating hard data with social and political history by means of a theoretical framework, e.g., G. E. Mendenhall, *Law and Covenant in Israel and the Ancient Near East* (Pittsburgh, Pa.: The Biblical Colloquium, 1955); Abraham Malherbe, *Social Aspects of Early Christianity* (Baton Rouge, La.: Louisiana State University Press, 1977); and Robert M. Grant, *Early Christianity and Society* (New York: Harper & Row, 1977); (3) an account of the *social organization* involved in a movement's origins and developments, e.g., N. K. Gottwald's work previously cited; Gerd Theissen, *Sociology of Early Palestinian Christianity* (Philadelphia: Fortress Press, 1978); and Leander Keck, *The New Testament Experience of Faith* (St. Louis: Bethany Press, 1976); (4) the reconstruction of the SOCIAL WORLD of a religious movement, attempting to suggest what it is like to live in a world structured by the symbols, rituals, and language used by the movement, e.g., Peter Berger, *The Sacred Canopy: Elements of a Sociological Theory of Religion* (Garden City, N.Y.: Doubleday & Co., 1967); Wayne Meeks, *The First Urban Christians: The Social World of the Apostle Paul* (New Haven, Conn.: Yale University Press, 1983); and Jerome Neyrey, ed., *The Social World of Luke-Acts: Models for Interpretation* (Peabody, Mass.: Hendrickson, 1991) For this synopsis, see James A. Wilde, "The Social World of Mark's Gospel: A Word about Method" in *SBL Seminar Papers*, vol. 2, ed. Paul J. Achtemeier (Missoula, Mont.: Scholars Press, 1978), 47–70; also Walter Brueggemann, "Trajectories in OT Literature and the Sociology of Ancient Israel," *JBL* 98 (1979): 161–85.

Since 1980 a greater interest has been shown in macro-social theory and, particularly, so far as the HEBREW BIBLE is concerned, in the role of techno-economic factors in the study of society (so J. F. Priest). But diversity and controversy typify the approaches and interests, not unanimity or uniformity. Like a kaleidoscope, the bits and pieces of social analysis, some large in scope, others quite narrowly specific, can be placed in infinitely varying patterns and rubrics, a task not undertaken here. *Note:* Social-scientific criticism, seeing itself as a necessary component of HISTORICAL CRITICISM, has sought to differentiate itself from sociological interpretation generally by its attention to critical methodology and its focus on the EXEGESIS of texts. See SOCIAL WORLD; TRADITIONISTS; RECEPTION THEORY.

Source Criticism   Considered the oldest of modern critical methods of analyzing scripture, source criticism first appeared in the 17th and 18th centuries when scholars began to read the Bible from a secular perspective. Close reading of the text revealed apparent contradictions, repetitions, doublets, and changes in literary style and vocabulary that seemed best explained by asserting the composite nature of the text itself, i.e., the presence of written sources lying behind, and therefore antedating, the text at hand. In Genesis, for example, it was noted that there were different names for God (YHWH, Elohim, El Elyon, El Shaddai, etc.), inconsistencies concerning when human beings were created (cf. Gen 1:26 with 2:5), the duration of the flood (40 days vs. 150 days), the number of the kinds of animals on the ark (cf. Gen 6:19 with 7:2), the age of Abraham when he left Ur (cf. Gen 12:4 with 11:32), etc. The identification of such discrepancies and differences and their attribution to discrete literary entities or "sources," coupled with the dating of these hypothetical sources to historical periods and geographic regions (preexilic/ postexilic; north/south, Israel/Judah) comprised the task of source criticism.

Its heyday was during the last quarter of the 19th cent., when a consensus began to form with regard to the sources of both the PENTATEUCH and the Synoptic Gospels. The sources of the former came to be known as J, E, D, and P, representing in turn the Yahwist, Elohist, Deuteronomist, and Priestly traditions. The ruling literary and historical reconstruction of these four sources was known by the names of its leading theorists, viz., the GRAF-WELL-HAUSEN HYPOTHESIS. Though widely debated and continually revised, this hypothesis remains at least the starting point of any discussion concerning the origins of the Pentateuch.

In NT scholarship the issue of sources revolved around explaining the verbal similarities between extensive portions of Matthew, Mark, and Luke. Two solutions, one an elaboration of the other, gained dominance, viz., the TWO SOURCE and the FOUR DOCUMENT (or SOURCE) HYPOTHESES. These sources are Mark, "Q", "M" or special material peculiar to Matthew, and "L" or special material peculiar to Luke. The use of sources in the book of Acts was made compelling by Luke's own words (1:1–4) and by the sudden appearance of the first person plural in the narrative (called the "WE-SECTIONS"). In the book of Revelation, the abundance of Aramaisms and Hebraisms also raised the question of sources.

The nature, extent, and date of sources used in the composition of the majority of books in the HB, as well as of the Gospels, Acts, and Revelation in the New Testament continue as debatable issues among biblical scholars. Increased interest in the *GOSPEL OF THOMAS* as a possible source for authentic sayings of Jesus and renewed interest in the Septuagint and its transmission and relationship to the HB help keep the issues alive.

SP Common abbreviation for the **Samaritan Pentateuch.**

Spät-Judentum (Ger: "late Judaism"). See **Late Judaism.**

Sprachereignis (Ger: "language event"). See **Language event.**

Stich, *stichos* (Gk: row, line, verse; fr. *steichein*, to go, walk). See **Colon.**

Strack-Billerbeck is the common call name of the *Kommentar zum Neuen Testament aus Talmud und Midrash*, vols. 1–4/2; edited by (Hermann L. Strack and) Paul Billerbeck (Munich: C. H. Beck Verlag, 1926–28), which is an indispensable tool for the comparative study of early Christianity and 1st–4th-cent. Judaism.

Strauss, David Friedrich (1808–1874). Born in Ludwigsburg (Württemberg), Germany, a student of F. C. BAUR in Blaubeuren (1821) and Tübingen (1825), and later influenced by his READING of Hegel and by F. D. E. SCHLEIERMACHER in Berlin (1831–32), Strauss became "infamously famous" (KARL BARTH) for his *Life of Jesus Critically Examined* (Ger: 1835–36 [reprint 1969]; Eng: 1846). Strauss's *Life* for the first time applied the category of "MYTH" to the NT and concluded that its miraculous reports, including those of the resurrection, were without historical foundation, being the products of the subjective conviction of the apostles and their primitive cultural context. The resulting controversy ended his academic career (with pension) in 1839 before it had really begun. In his subsequent writings, Strauss embraced atheism and later still Darwinism (he is said to have been the first theologian to do so); these changes hardened critical opinion toward him and he died embittered. His last works included *The Old Faith and the New* (Ger: 1872; Eng: 1873) and *Der Christus des Glaubens und der Jesus der Geschichte [The Christ of Faith and the Jesus of History]* (Ger: 1864; reprint 1971; Eng reprint: Philadelphia: Fortress Press, 1973).

Streeter, Burnett Hillman (1874–1937), a Fellow at Queen's College, Oxford, is noted in TEXTUAL CRITICISM particularly for his theory concerning the text FAMILY used by ORIGEN in Palestine, called the Caesarean text; and in source criticism for his FOUR DOCUMENT (or SOURCE) HYPOTHESIS, with which he proposed to replace the older TWO SOURCE HYPOTHESIS, through the establishment of two additional ancient documents known as "M" and "L," encompassing material peculiar to Matt and Luke respectively.

Streitgespräch   (Ger: "controversy dialogue"). In OT form-critical studies, *Streitgespräch* is a descriptive term used in reference to the book of Job; in NT studies it is a technical term employed by RUDOLF BULTMANN as a subcategory of APOPHTHEGMS; it includes, e.g., Mark 2:1–12, 15–17; 3:1–5; 7:1–23; 10:2–12, 17–30; 12:13–17, etc.

Strophe   (Gk: lit., turning). In the wider sense, a strophe is one of two or more series of lines possessing metrical regularity that form the divisions of a lyric poem. In Greek choral and lyric poetry, the term pertained to a metrical structure that was repeated in a following series of lines called the antistrophe. In the study of OT poetry, the applicability of the term is much disputed, since Hebrew poetry is characterized by parallelism of thought, not by rhyme or metrical regularity. When the term *strophe* is used in OT criticism, therefore, it is loosely applied and may mean simply a verse paragraph of indeterminate length uncontrolled by any formal artistic scheme (G. B. Gray, *Forms of Hebrew Poetry* [New York: KTAV Publishing House, 1970], 192), or, more closely defined, as a series of parallel figures (bicola or tricola) with a discernible beginning and ending, possessing identifiable unity in thought, structure, and style. Sometimes the strophes are opened with particular FORMULAS ("Behold," "Praise," "How Long?" "O Lord") or closed with a refrain (Pss 39; 42; 43; 46; 49; 56; 57; 59; 62; 67; 78; 80; 99; 107; 114; 136; 144; 145; cf. Amos 1; 2; 4; Isa 4; 5; 9; and 10), with alteration in length of line or METER. Strophic division is more frequently marked by the sense of the poem itself, since the structuring of thought patterns into parallel forms is the basic characteristic of Hebrew poetry. Occasionally, a poem is structured by ACROSTIC (Pss 9–10; 25; 34; 37; 111; 112; 119; 145; Lam 1–4; and Nah 1). See COLON; PARALLELISM.

Structuralism   refers to a family of theories that apply the methods of structural LINGUISTICS to a range of cultural phenomena, including literature, kinship relations, popular culture, and so on. Ferdinand de Saussure (1857–1913), the founder of structural linguistics, held that to understand a language, one must understand it not as the physical representation of words in sound or writing (for this is arbitrary), nor even as a catalog of actual uses of language (for this is potentially infinite), but rather as *a system of relations* (STRUCTURE) that distinguishes and interrelates the available stock of linguistic signs at a given point in time. According to Saussure, linguistic signs have no meaning in themselves apart from their place within the inclusive system of which they are a part. Other seminal theorists of structuralism include Claude Levi-Strauss (1908–), who applied Saussure's insights to the study of anthropology, and A. J. Greimas, who applied them to LITERARY CRITICISM and NARRATIVES. Whatever their domain, structuralists hold that cultural phenomena are rightly understood only when seen as distinguishable positions or "differences" in a structure or system of relations. Accordingly, structuralism focuses on cultural systems and expressions as they exist at a given point in time, not as they evolve or develop over time (see DIACHRONIC; SYNCHRONIC). In this respect, it differs markedly from historical-critical methodologies (classical literary criticism, FORM CRITICISM, REDACTION CRITICISM, et al.), which are chiefly interested in origins and development.

Biblical scholars have shown interest in structuralism since the 1960s and have used its methods to study a variety of phenomena, including biblical languages, dietary codes, genealogies, etc. An early and well-known application of structuralism to the Bible is Mary Douglas's *Purity and Danger: An Analysis of Concepts of Pollution and Taboo* (London: Routledge & Kegan Paul, 1966), in which Douglas argues that the animals listed in Lev 11 were prohibited because they were anomalies with respect to the classification of the world implied in Gen 1. Structuralism's major influence on biblical studies, however, has been in the area of literary analysis. A classic study is Roland Barthes's (1915–1980) application of Greimas's narratological categories to the story of Jacob and the angel in Gen 32:22–32 (see Roland Barthes et al., *Structural Analysis and Biblical Exegesis: Interpretational Essays*, trans. Alfred M. Johnson, Jr. (Pittsburgh Theological Monograph Series, 3; Pittsburgh: Pickwick Press, 1974).

Major concepts and terms in structural linguistics include the following:

1. A language (*la langue*), as a given system of conventions such as Spanish or Hebrew, is distinct from speaking (*le parole*), a given use of language. As a system of conventions, *la langue* is inherently social but has no architect and is not the product of human intent. *Le parole*, as an individual utterance, is typically intentional, but it is logically dependent on the existence of the underlying system of *la langue*. According to Saussure, only *la langue* constitutes the proper study of linguistics.
2. Every language is a system of signs, and signs are a combination of a *signifier* and a *signified*. A signifier is a material entity—a sound, pencil mark, image—with meaning. Its meaning is the signified associated with it. The relationship between the signifier and the signified is arbitrary, as the multitude of languages proves. The meaning of signs is determined solely through their differences with other signs.
3. Since the elements of language achieve meaning only in relationship, the structure of a linguistic system is basically one of combinations, contrasts, and oppositions (pre-/post-, love/hate, male/female, etc.). Signs can enter into either *syntagmatic* or *paradigmatic* relations. SYNTAGMATIC relations concern order and sequence, such as the relation of subject, verb, and direct object in a sentence: "Stan got the mail." Paradigmatic relations concern association between words in the same class or category, such as red, green, blue, yellow, etc.
4. Every language as a system of signs (the subject of SEMIOLOGY) operates on three distinct levels: (a) sounds (PHONEMES, the subject of phonology), (b) units of meaning (MORPHEMES, the subject of MORPHOLOGY) consisting of word stems (*lexemes*) and indicators such as prefixes and suffixes, and (c) sentences or phrases (*syntagma*), formed through the combination and opposition of units of meaning (the subject of grammar and SEMANTICS). Further levels can be distinguished depending on the field of study, e.g., *textemes*, literary units marked off by introductory and closing FORMULAS, *mythemes*, or elements of MYTH, etc. Sounds that do not conform to the phonetic rules of a linguistic system cease to function as components of verbal signs (see 1 Cor 14), just as verbal signs that do not conform to the rules of SYNTAX when combined fail to function as units of meaning.

Generally speaking, the aim of structuralism's technical vocabulary is to equip readers with new kinds of competence that permit them to identify and respond to structures of a text (or other cultural phenomena) that otherwise remain implicit (i.e., that affect us without our knowing it).

In recent decades, structuralism has come under attack on the grounds that its presuppositions are excessively formal and rationalistic. Saussure's thesis that signs are defined solely through their difference from other signs suggests that signs can function at all only within systems that are closed, delimited, discrete. Postmodern thought gets much of its intellectual energy from exposing the difficulties that this position creates. For example, if it could be shown that the full system of relations is indeterminable (see INTERTEXTUALITY), then it would seem, on the structuralist view, that the meaning of any sign must also be indeterminable. Conversely, it would seem that the effort to "force" meaning could be achieved only by arbitrarily drawing limits and hence by a willful act of exclusion.

See Daniel Patte, *The Gospel According to Matthew* (Philadelphia: Fortress Press, 1987), *Religious Dimensions in Biblical Texts: Greimas's Structural Semiotics and Biblical Exegesis* (Atlanta: Scholars Press, 1990), and his *Structural Exegesis for New Testament Critic*, Guides to Biblical Scholarship (Minneapolis: Fortress Press, 1990); also see D. Jobling, *The Sense of Biblical Narrative II: Structural Analysis in the Hebrew Bible*, 2 vols. (Sheffield: Sheffield Academic Press, 1986).

For additional bibliography, see SEMIOLOGY; STRUCTURE. Also see BIBLICAL CRITICISM; EXEGESIS; HERMENEUTICS; PARABLE.

Structure The term *structure* has a wide variety of applications. In nonstructuralist studies, *structure* often refers to a text's poetic, literary, or rhetorical composition and is described by terms such as metric pattern, PARALLELISM, anaphora, DIATRIBE, etc. From the perspective of STRUCTURALISM, the structures in question here are "surface" rather than "deep" in nature; that is, they can be identified and described by conventional methods of literary analysis.

In structuralist studies, whose basic units are usually complete texts, stories, MYTHS, etc., structure refers to the organization that gives a text its intelligibility. Structuralism holds that a meaningful text inevitably conforms to structures that are latent rather than explicit, that are "deep" rather than "surface" in nature. Just as a sentence must conform to implicit grammatical rules if it is to be coherent, so, it is argued, must NARRATIVES and myths. The constituent elements of narratives and

myths (called narrative syntagma and mythemes) must be ordered according to underlying "laws" or "constraints" in order to be intelligible. And just as grammatical rules can be said in a certain sense to create or generate the intelligibility of a sentence, so too the "laws" or "deep structures" of narratives and myths can be said to create the meaningfulness of the same. From this perspective, it is less accurate to say that a narrative or myth *has* a structure than that it conforms to a structure. Structuralism commonly sets itself the goal of expressing the logic of deep structures in a FORMULA or diagram, a task it undertakes on the basis of the study of a large number of texts, myths, stories, etc.

The question of the relationship of surface structures to deep structures, what constitutes a deep structure, and how it is to be modeled or diagrammed, are all moot points. For example, U. Eco writes that a structure "is a model built and *posited* in order to standardize diverse phenomena from a unified point of view" (*A Theory of Semiotics* [Bloomington/London: Indiana University Press, 1976], 46, n. 4). In this sense, the "structure" of a text is less an objective reality than an operational hypothesis. A concurring but qualifying caveat is offered by Jean Pouillon: "A model is not a structure. It is a simplification of reality, which is tested in order to make it undergo variations which will permit the structure to be more easily read. And the diagram, thanks to which the model appears, refers to the analysis and to its method, not to a particular reality whose representation it would be" ("Structuralism: A Definitional Essay," in *Structuralism and Biblical Hermeneutics*, ed. and trans. Alfred M. Johnson, Jr. [Pittsburgh: Pickwick Press, 1979], 42–43).

In point of fact, few structural models for narratives and myths exist, and none that has remained undisputed or unqualified. Although it is not possible here to explain structure or structural models in detail, the following illustration will suggest what is involved. Claude Lévi-Strauss, a structural anthropologist, suggests that the structure or myths can be expressed by the formula $F_x(a) : F_y(b) :: F_x(b) : F_{a-1}(y)$, in which opposing subjects (or states) a and b with functions (F) x and y are resolved by a transformation of states and an inversion of functions (Claude Lévi-Strauss, *Structural Anthropology* [New York/London: Basic Books, 1963], 228).

A. J. Greimas and proponents of his theories, working on the structural analysis of narratives, have attempted to deduce from large numbers of texts *actantial* and *functional* "constants" or "elements of structure" operative in all narratives. The functions of actants in narratives are said to be seven in number: (1) Arrival vs. Departure or Departure vs. Return, (2) Conjunction vs. Disjunction, (3) Mandating vs. Acceptance or vs. Refusal, (4) Confrontation, (5) Domination vs. Submission, (6) Communication vs. Reception, (7) Attribution vs. Deprivation. Actants or "spheres of action" (not to be confused with the various characters of the narrative) that are deemed constant structural elements in every narrative are expressed in the actantial model below.

For detailed explanations of these "structures," see Jean Calloud, *Structural Analysis of Narrative* (Missoula, Mont.: Scholars Press, 1976), and Daniel and Aline Patte, *Structural Exegesis: From Theory to Practice* (Philadelphia: Fortress Press, 1978).

A highly simplified but useful application of structuralist insights in the context of religious instruction is André Fossion's "Structural Readings of Scripture in Catechesis," in *Lumen Vitae* 33 (1978): 446–70. See also in Johnson, *Structuralism* (cited previously): "Appendix: Structural Readings: How to Do Them," 183–208. See SEMIOTICS.

Subpauline.   See **Deuteropauline.**

Sui ipsius interpres   (Lat: "itself its own interpreter") is a cardinal rule of scriptural interpretation in the Reformation traditions, which holds that Holy Scripture is its own interpreter (*sacra scriptura sui ipsius interpres*). The rule is commonly traced to Martin Luther's insistence that scripture not be interpreted according to the Councils and church fathers at the expense of its plain sense or at the expense of saving truth plainly taught in the BIBLE. In later Protestant tradition, theologians held that while all of the Bible is true, its truth is not equally clear everywhere. According to the rule *sui ipsius interpres*, the Bible's clearer passages are to be used to understand more doubtful or obscure passages. Thus scripture provides both text and COMMENTARY; it is an interlocking, self-glossing whole. The Roman Catholic rejoinder to the rule has long been that in practice it subordinates the Bible to each person's fancy and engenders spiritual anarchy. See HERMENEUTICS; INTERTEXTUALITY.

Surface Structure.   See **Structure.**

Symmachus   (abbrev.: Symm. or Σ). According to Eusebius, Symmachus was an Ebionite Christian who translated the OT freely into Greek during the second half of the 2nd cent. His translation, known by his name, made use of the LXX, AQUILA, and THEODOTION. Although of minor importance for OT TEXTUAL CRITICISM, it did influence JEROME's Latin translation, the VULGATE. It is extant primarily only in fragments of ORIGEN's *HEXAPLA*. See also SEPTUAGINT.

SENDER ⟶ OBJECT ⟶ RECEIVER
HELPER ⟶ SUBJECT ⟶ OPPONENT

Symploce (Gk: a weaving together) is the technical term for the rhetorical device of combining ANAPHORA (repetition of initial sounds) and EPIPHORA (repetition of final sounds) in the same STRUCTURE, as e.g., Ps 67.

Synchronic. See **Diachronic.**

Synecdoche (Gk: to receive together) in RHETORIC is a figure of speech by which (a) a part stands in the place of the whole ("the circumcised" for "the followers of the LAW," i.e., Jews; Gal 2:7–9); or (b) the whole for a part (John 3:16, either: world = humankind, or, as in [a] above, world = creation; cf. also Rom 8:22); or (c) the species for the genus (cross = self-sacrifices; Matt 10:38; 16:24 par.); or (d) the genus for the species (creature = humankind; Rom 1:25). See METONYMY.

Synonymous   Parallelism. See **Parallelism.**

Synopsis. In NT criticism, a synopsis is a book that presents Matt, Mark, and Luke (sometimes John) in parallel columns, arranged to show where the GOSPELS agree and disagree; also called a Gospel Parallel. The best known in Greek are Albert Huck's *Synopse der drei ersten Evangelien* (13th ed. by Heinrich Greeven [Tübingen: J. C. B. Mohr (Paul Siebeck), 1981]), and KURT ALAND's *Synopsis Quattuor Evangeliorum* (15th rev. ed. [Stuttgart: Deutsche Bibelgesellschaft, 1996/97]); and in English (following Huck's format): *Gospel Parallels*, ed. by Burton H. Throckmorton, Jr. (5th ed. [New York: Thomas Nelson & Sons, 1992]); Kurt Aland, *Synopsis of the Four Gospels: Greek-English Edition of the Synopsis Quattuor Evangeliorum with the Text of the Revised Standard Version* (New York: United Bible Societies, 1972), which omits material in the earlier Greek edition, such as EXTRACANONICAL parallels, Greek and Latin patristic quotations, and the GOSPEL OF THOMAS; and H. F. D. Sparks, *The Johannine Synopsis of the Gospels* (New York: Harper & Row, 1975). The color-coded *A Diagram of Synoptic Relationships* by Allan Barr (2nd ed. [Edinburgh: T. & T. Clark, 1995]), first published in 1938, was reedited with an introduction by James Barr and is visually quite helpful. *The Horizontal Line Synopsis of the Gospels in English* by Reuben L. Swanson, 2nd rev. ed. (Pasadena, Calif.: William Carey Library, 1984) provides a new format. James M. Robinson et al. have edited *The Critical Edition of Q: Including the Gospel of Matthew and Luke, Mark and Thomas* (Minneapolis: Fortress, 2000).

Akin to a synopsis of the Gospels is *Pauline Parallels* by Fred O. Francis an J. Paul Sampley, 2nd ed. (Philadelphia: Fortress Press, 1984); each of the ten chief LETTERS attributed to Paul is divided into thematic units with related passages placed in parallel lines.

Synoptic Parallel In NT criticism a synoptic parallel refers to a passage in Matt, Mark, or Luke that is parallel in content with one or both of the remaining Synoptic GOSPELS; in OT criticism the term is sometimes used in discussions of parallels between 1 Sam–2 Kgs and 1–2 Chr. A synoptic parallel is often referred to by the abbreviation "par(s)." or //.

Synoptic Problem (The) derives from the observation that the first three books of the NT (Matt, Mark, and Luke) contain a strikingly high degree of verbal agreement between them and, further, that the order of the material in each is in large measure the same. It is for this reason that the three books are called the "Synoptic GOSPELS" or simply the "Synoptics" (meaning, "with the [same] eye"). The synoptic problem, therefore, is to explain how this similarity came to be. What is the literary relationship of these Gospels? Who copied from whom? Luke explicitly states that others preceded him (1:14). To whom does he refer? The early church fathers (Papias, Clement of Alexandria, Augustine) do not agree in their explanation of the relationship of the Gospels.

The problem is best seen with the aid of a Greek or English SYNOPSIS, which places the texts of the Gospels in parallel lines. In lieu of a synopsis, compare the following passages in any standard translation: Matt 26:20–29 and Mark 14:17–25; Matt 26:36–46 and Mark 14:32–42; Mark 5:1–20 and Luke 8:26–39; Mark 9:37–40 and Luke 9:48–50; Luke 3:7–9 and Matt 3:7–10; Luke 4:1–13 and Matt 4:1–11; or Matt 12:1–8 and Mark 2:23–28 and Luke 6:1–5.

Theoretically, there are eighteen different solutions to the problem of literary dependence. (See William R. Farmer, *The Synoptic Problem* [New York: Macmillan Co., 1964], ch. 6.) Most of these are ruled out by the literary data itself. But variations on the viable alternatives, including the postulation of primitive sources (see UREVANGELIUM; LOGION; Q; "M"; "L"), intermediary documents (see URMARKUS; PROTO-LUKE), or divergent recensions of the existing Gospels, extend the number of alternatives almost indefinitely.

In spite of this, widely accepted solutions have been few in number: (1) the Augustinian Hypothesis (ca. 400) accepted the canonical order (Matt, Mark, Luke, John), stating that each Gospel depended on its predecessor; (2) the GRIESBACH HYPOTHESIS (1783) excluded John from consideration and made Mark an abridger of Matt and Luke; (3) the TWO SOURCE HYPOTHESIS (formally stated by H. J. Holtzmann, 1863) proposed a primitive collection of the SAYINGS of Jesus (subsequently called "*Quelle*" or "Q") and an earlier form of Mark (URMARKUS), both of which were used by Matt and Luke independent of each other; and, (4) the FOUR SOURCE HYPOTHESIS proposed by B. H. STREETER in 1924, which is but a modification of the Two Source theory.

W. R. Farmer (op. cit.) and others argued in defense of the Griesbach Hypothesis with a degree of success. The majority of scholars, however, accept some variation of the Two Source Hypothesis on which almost all modern Gospel criticism, esp. REDACTION CRITICISM, rests. See David Laird Dungan, *A History of the Synoptic Problem: The Canon, the Text, the Composition, and the Interpretation of the Gospels*, Anchor Bible Reference Library (New York: Doubleday, 1999).

Syntagm/Syntagmatic/Paradigmatic   *Syntagm* is a technical term in LINGUISTICS first used by Ferdinand de Saussure to refer to a word-chain or combination of words (such as "the good life," "towards us," "to go away," etc.) that, when constructed according to strict rules, forms a level of meaning within a language that falls between the word and the sentence; grammatically speaking, such word sequences or syntagms are equivalent to single words.

Syntagmatic and *paradigmatic* express two different kinds of relationships in which words can stand to one another. A syntagmatic relationship is a relationship of sequence, as is formed, for example, through the combination of noun, verb, and direct object in the sentence "Peter denied Jesus." A paradigmatic relationship is a relationship of category or kind, as obtains between the words yellow, blue, black, white, etc. Any utterance can be analyzed in syntagmatic and paradigmatic terms, i.e., in terms of its sequential structure and in terms of its specific selection of terms from the available stock of speech in each relevant category. See Lewandowski, ad hoc.

Syntax   (fr. Gk: *syntaxis*: arrangement, organization, etc.) most commonly refers to (1) the study of the rules (or simply the rules themselves) by which sentences are constructed in a given language; more technically, it may refer to (2) that subdivision of SEMIOTICS that deals with the arrangement and relationship of linguistic signs to each other (in distinction from two other subdivisions: SEMANTICS and pragmatics).

Synthetic Parallelism.   See **Parallelism.**

Tale   The term *tale* has several connotations, most of which are unrelated to

BIBLICAL CRITICISM; in its literary sense, however, it refers to any story or NARRATIVE, usually brief, told for its inherent interest. The term enters criticism as a technical translation of MARTIN DIBELIUS's form-critical category "Novelle" (From Tradition to Gospel [London: Ivor Nicholson & Watson, Ltd., 1934; repr. James Clarke, 1971; New York: Charles Scribner's Sons, 1935], ch. 4), which he distinguished from PARADIGMS on the one hand and LEGENDS on the other. Dibelius identified nine PERICOPES in Mark as "tales": 1:40–45 (the leper); 4:35–41 (the storm); 5:1–20 (the demons and the swine); 5:21–43 (Jairus's daughter and the woman with an issue of blood); 6:35–44 (the feeding of the five thousand); 6:45–52 (the walking on the sea); 7:32–37 (the deaf mute); 8:22–26 (the blind man); and 9:14–29 (the epileptic). In addition are five stories in John developed from tales: 2:1ff. (the marriage at Cana); 4:46ff. (the centurion's son); 5:1ff. (the lame man); 9:lff. (the man born blind); and 11:1ff. (Lazarus); also similar is Luke 7:11ff. (the raising of the widow's son). In more recent criticism, this category has been subsumed under the larger genre of miracle story or aretalogy. See ARETALOGY; FORM CRITICISM.

Talmud   (fr. Heb: lamad, "study," limmah, "instruction"). The word Talmud is the comprehensive term for the Mishnah and its accompanying commentary, called the Gemara (here meaning "teaching"). The Gemara contains a wide variety of material (proverbs, tales, customs, folklore, etc.) bearing directly or remotely on the subjects of the Mishnah, as well as strict exposition on the text in legal argumentation and exegesis. The structure of the Talmud is therefore that of the Mishnah, having six orders divided into sixty-three tractates, a form it had obtained by the 3rd cent. The Gemara, being the work of the rabbis known as Amoraim (expounders), developed primarily in two centers, Babylon and Palestine (Tiberias), from the 3rd through the 5th centuries.

The two editions of Talmud, though similar in form, differ greatly in content. The Babylonian Talmud, being 5,894 pages of standard pagination, is four times the length of the Palestinian, since the latter was in large part lost in antiquity. For this reason, the Babylonian Talmud has in past centuries been the authoritative document. According to some authorities, the halakic portions of the Palestinian Talmud are more irenic and temperate, and the haggadic portions purer and more rational, than the corresponding material in the Babylonian Talmud. Of the sixty-three tractates in the Babylonian Talmud, only thirty-six contain Gemara (commentary). See MISHNAH.

Tanakh   (also Tanach or Tanak) is a Hebrew abbreviation for the canon of Jewish scriptures derived from the initial letters of the names of its three divisions: TORAH (PENTATEUCH), NEBIIM (Early and Later PROPHETS), and KETUBIM (Writings or HAGIOGRAPHA). See HEBREW BIBLE; OLD TESTAMENT/NEW TESTAMENT.

Tannaim; Tannaitic Literature   (fr. Aram teni: to teach orally, learn). The term tanna (pl.: -im) generally "designates a teacher either mentioned in the MISHNAH or of Mishnaic times" (i.e., 20–200 C.E.; Enc Jud), whose teachings were compiled to form the Tannaitic literature. The Tannaim are credited with preserving Jewish tradition threatened by extinction after the Fall of Jerusalem (70 C.E.), the defeat of the Bar Kokhba revolt (135 C.E.), and the rise of Christianity. Tannaitic literature falls under two main headings: (a) Mishnah—succinct halakic formulations arranged under various legal categories or other mnemonic devices and (b) halakic Midrashim—arranged as extended exegetical commentaries to the books of the PENTATEUCH, such as the Tosefta, Mekilta, Mekilta of R. Simon, Sifre on Leviticus, Sifre on Deuteronomy, Sifre Zutta, and Sifre on Numbers. Also belonging to the Tannaitic literature is the Seder Olam Rabbah. Leading Tannaim of the 1st cent. included Hillel (20 B.C.E.–20 C.E.), Shammai (30 B.C.E.), Gamaliel I (20–50 C.E.), Simeon ben Gamaliel (d. 70 C.E.), and Johanan ben Zakkai (d. ca. 80 C.E.). Concerning the earliest period of the Tannaim, see Jacob Neusner, *The Rabbinic Traditions About the Pharisees Before 70*, vols. 1–3 (Leiden: E. J. Brill, 1971). See also his *The Memorized Torah: The Mnemonic System of the Mishnah* (Chico, Calif.: Scholars Press, 1985).

Target (or Receptor) Language is a term employed in translation theory to denote the receptor language of a translation, e.g., when translating an English text into the Korean language, Korean is referred to as the target language. Target language may also refer to a particular IDIOM within a given language, such as highly literate or moderately literate. The New Revised Standard Version targets its translation of the Bible for highly literate persons; its language is formal and its vocabulary large. The Good News Bible employs a language targeted at persons for whom English is a second language; its language is informal and its vocabulary purposely simplified.

Targum (Aram: translation, interpretation). In broad uses, the word *Targum* means "translation" or "interpretation"; as most frequently used, however, it refers specifically to Aramaic versions of the OT. In rabbinic literature the word may refer simply to the Aramaic portions, even single words, of the BIBLE, as found in Ezra, Nehemiah, and Daniel. The Targum arose out of the synagogal practice of accompanying the reading of the Hebrew text with an Aramaic translation (*Targum*) for the benefit of Aramaic-speaking Jews. The translation, however, was provided with interpretive additions, making the Targum an expanded PARAPHRASE of the original. No single Targum, therefore, existed; rather, numerous targumic traditions arose on the various books of the OT—except those listed previously. The most authoritative (esp. for Orthodox Jews) is *Targum Onkelos*,

a VERSION of the Palestinian Targum developed by Babylonian Jews. A reportedly Palestinian Targum of the PENTATEUCH containing a tradition going back possibly to the 1st cent. C.E. was discovered by A. Diez Macho in the Vatican Library in 1956, called *Neofiti I*. Pseudo-Jonathan is the name of another Babylonian version of the Palestinian Targum, also of the Pentateuch alone. An English translation of all the extant Targums, with introductory articles, has been published as *The Aramaic Bible* by Liturgical Press, Collegeville, Minn. See DAUGHTER TRANSLATION.

Tatian (ca. 120–173 C.E.). A Syrian convert to Christianity and pupil of Justin Martyr in Rome (ca. 160), Tatian is best known for his *Diatessaron*, a harmony of the life of CHRIST based on the four GOSPELS, and for *Oratio ad Graecos*, a bitter polemic against Greek culture. Tatian broke with Orthodox Christianity as interpreted in the West and returned to Syria to found an ascetic order known as Encratites. His views were in the main repudiated by the Western church.

Teaching of the Twelve Apostles. See **Didache.**

Tell Mardikh. See **Ebla.**

Tendenz Criticism (Ger: *Tendenzkritik*) refers to the analysis of the intention of an author or, more pointedly, to the particular bias with which the author treats his subject matter. The term is especially identified with the work of F. C. BAUR (1792–1860), who contended that the *Tendenz* of the author of the book of Acts was to minimize the differences between Peter and Paul in order to depict the EARLY CHURCH as unified and harmonious.

Terminus ad quem is a Latin term that means "a fixed date or point to which"; similarly, its counterpart, *terminus a quo* means "a fixed date or point from which," and together they set the terminal limits for the dating of an event or a document, e.g.,

27 C.E. and 33 C.E. mark the *terminus a quo* and the *terminus ad quem* respectively of the crucifixion of Jesus.

Terminus a quo. See **Terminus ad quem.**

Terminus technicus (abbrev.: t.t.). Latin for "technical term."

Tertium comparationis (Lat: point of comparison). See **Bildhälfte.**

Tetragrammaton (Gk: "having four letters") refers to the personal proper name of the God of Israel, YHWH, called the Tetragrammaton since the time of PHILO because it consists of four Hebrew consonants, *yod, he, waw, he.* The Tetragrammaton appears over 6,000 times in the HEBREW BIBLE and is strictly speaking its only personal proper name for God, other names being common nouns, appellations, or epithets (see T. N. D. Mettinger, *In Search of God* [Minneapolis: Fortress Press, 1987]). During the SECOND TEMPLE PERIOD, the licit pronunciation of the name was increasingly restricted to the Temple, and pious Jews used reverential PARAPHRASES in its place, a practice clearly evident in the NT (see Gustaf Dalman, *The Words of Jesus* [Edinburgh: T. & T. Clark, 1909]) and still current in Judaism today. In addition, several NT writings contain interpretive allusions to the Tetragrammaton, e.g., Phil 2:9–11; Rev 1:4, 8, etc. (see Sean M. McDonough, *YHWH at Patmos* [Tübingen: J. C. B. Mohr (Paul Siebeck), 1999]).

Because of the Tetragrammaton's sacred, singular character, scribes and translators have long accorded it exceptional treatment. The most ancient Greek VERSIONS of the Jewish scriptures write the Divine Name in Hebrew (or other special) characters in the Greek text, a precedent followed by ORIGEN in his *HEXAPLA.* Most ancient Christian copies of the LXX read *KYRIOS* in place of YHWH, but the Christian system of abbreviations known as the

NOMINA SACRA may nevertheless reflect a Christianized form of piety for the Name. In the MT of the HB, the Tetragrammaton is pointed with vowels of *Adonai* (Lord) to remind the reader to pronounce the surrogate instead of the Name (see KETHIB and QERE), a practice that gave rise in Christian circles to the erroneous reading Jehovah (ca. 1300). LORD in capital letters is used to designate the Tetragrammaton in most English translations of the HB (so KJV, RSV, NEB, NASV, NAB; but the JB transliterates as Yahweh; so similarly Luther's Bible and other European translations.

Yahweh is a scholarly reconstruction of the vocalized Tetragrammaton current chiefly among Christian academicians since the early 19th cent. Though still current in biblical scholarship, it has scant basis in Christian liturgical life and none at all in Jewish, and indeed is regarded as distasteful or offensive by many Jews. In recent years many writers (including the authors of this book) have discontinued its use in favor of the unvocalized form of the name, YHWH. For an overview of issues involved in rendering the divine name, see Christopher Seitz, "Handing Over the Name: Christian Reflection on the Divine Name YHWH," in *Trinity, Time, and Church,* ed. by Colin Gunton (Grand Rapids: Eerdmans, 2000). See KETHIB AND QERE; LORD.

Tetrateuch (Gk: four books) is a technical term derived from Greek for the first four books of the OT: Genesis, Exodus, Leviticus, and Numbers. See PENTATEUCH.

TEV. See **Today's English Version.**

Text Fragment refers to those texts in scripture, particularly in the OT, that are incomplete or "fragmentary" as they now read and that derive from earlier, complete but now otherwise lost texts or traditions. An example is found in the story of Noah's ark; here two flood stories are combined at the expense of one of the stories (or "texts"), fragments of which may be found in Gen 7:8–9, 13–15, 19–21; 8:1–5—although the precise identity of the "fragments" is disputed. Cf. also Gen 6:1–4 and in the NT, 2 Cor 6:14–7:1.

Textual Criticism   The function and purpose of textual criticism is of a dual nature: (1) to reconstruct the original wording of the biblical text; and (2) to establish the history of the transmission of the text through the centuries. The first of these two goals is in fact hypothetical and unattainable. In every instance the original copy (called the AUTOGRAPH) of the books of the BIBLE is lost, hence every reconstruction is a matter of conjecture. Textual criticism's task, therefore, is to compare existing MSS, no two of which are exactly alike, in order to develop a "CRITICAL TEXT" that lists VARIANT READINGS in footnotes, called a "CRITICAL APPARATUS." Modern translations of the Bible are, in the main, based on such critical texts (TEV, JB, NEB). (*Note:* The readings of the TEV are explained by Bruce M. Metzger, *A Textual Commentary on the Greek New Testament* [New York and London: United Bible Societies, 1971].) In this way, textual criticism not only provides an idea of how the original text may have read, it also provides knowledge of how in fact it did read, and in some respects how it was interpreted, at various centers of faith at various times in Christian history. For example, at some time after 300 C.E., and first in MSS of the Western church, there was added to John's GOSPEL the PERICOPE of the woman caught in adultery (John 7:53–8:11). This fact, attested by textual criticism, provides data for understanding the church of the 4th cent., the status of the canon, etc., irrespective of the authenticity of the passage itself. This is a dramatic illustration from the history of textual transmission, but scores of other examples could be adduced. The student unfamiliar with Hebrew, Aramaic, and Greek, the languages in which the Bible was originally written, can nevertheless gain some idea of the results of tex-

tual criticism by comparing modern standard English translations with the KJV. The latter, written in 1611 prior to the discovery of all the major VELLUM and PAPYRUS MANUSCRIPTS of the Bible, was prepared from MSS less ancient than and notably inferior to those available today. The DEAD SEA SCROLLS of the OT, found 1947–54, are an example.

In antiquity and until the invention of the printing press, MSS were copied by hand; none, therefore, is free of error, each inevitably carrying within it the errors of the MS from which the new copy was made. *Variations* between MSS arose from a variety of causes: (a) physical damage, by accident and decay, leaving holes (LACUNAE) in the text; (b) accidental omission by slip of the copyist's eye (see DITTOGRAPHY; HAPLOGRAPHY; HOMOIOTELEUTON, HOMOIOARCHTON); (c) aural mistakes (as in English dictation one might confuse "their" with "they're," so ancient scribes misheard the reader of the text); (d) exegetical misjudgment (placing the wrong vowels on the Hebrew consonants, or misdividing Greek letters into words, since the original Hebrew OT texts appear with consonants only [see MASORETIC TEXT], and the original Greek NT texts possessed neither word division nor punctuation); and (e) deliberate alteration of the text for purposes of clarification, correction, and apologetic (see GLOSS; CONFLATION; ASSIMILATION).

The *sources of OT* textual criticism are vastly fewer in number than for NT: (a) the Greek OT, known in its various ancient editions (some of which are preserved only fragmentarily, as in quotations of the church fathers and in marginal notations of the LXX): AQUILA; *KAIGE* RECENSION; Lucianic; Old Greek (LXX); SYMMACHUS; and THEODOTION; (b) the Dead Sea Scrolls, which antedate by nearly 1,000 years all previously known MSS of the Hebrew OT; (c) the Masoretic Text (MT) of the Hebrew OT, dating from the 11th cent. C.E.; (d) ancient VERSIONS of the LXX (called

"DAUGHTER TRANSLATIONS"): Old Latin, Coptic, Ethiopic, Syro-Hexaplar, et al.; (e) ancient versions of the Hebrew OT: TARGUMS, the PESHITTA, and the Latin VULGATE; and (f) the SAMARITAN PENTATEUCH. (*Note:* The dearth of Hebrew examplars of the OT is due in no small measure to the destruction of Jewish antiquities by Christians and others.)

The *sources of NT* textual criticism present a different picture, with MSS numbering over 5,000. MSS are categorized according to a system initiated by J. J. Wettstein (1751) and since expanded to include (1) papyrus MSS, the oldest extant NT MSS and the most recently discovered being the Chester Beatty and Bodmer papyri in the 1930s; (2) UNCIALS, or MSS written in capital letters, such as CODEX SINAITICUS; (3) MINUSCULES, or MSS written in cursive letters, dating from the 9th cent.; (4) ancient versions, such as Syriac, Coptic, Ethiopic, Old Latin, etc.; (5) quotations from the church fathers; and, (6) ancient LECTIONARIES (quotations from scripture used in public worship and private devotion). Of little but historical interest are OSTRACA and talismans inscribed with scripture as memory exercises and charms. (See chart on p. 191.)

The principles of textual criticism are little more than rules of thumb, or "codified common sense" as someone has suggested, or "common sense and use of reason" (A. E. Housman). These include the following:

1. *External Criteria.* Because every MS of a given text is theoretically related to all other MSS of that text, it is possible to treat MSS genealogically, as subfamilies within one large FAMILY. These subfamilies are called text types, or in some instances simply "families." Text types are divided, more or less accurately, into the geographical area of their origin, such as Alexandrian (Egypt), Western, Byzantine. The nomenclature and the categories are themselves debated by textual criticism.

Text types vary in value. An MS from an inferior family, though ancient, may be of less value than a more recent MS of a superior type. It is the evaluation of given MSS and of the theories of text types that occupies much of textual criticism today.

2. *Internal Criteria.* The following are the traditional formulations: (a) The more difficult reading is often preferred (*lectio difficilior potior*). (b) Which reading would be more likely to have given rise to the other? (c) The shorter reading is generally preferred. (d) The reading characteristic of the author is generally preferable. That these "rules" are considered by some scholars as circumlocutions for the truism *melior lectio potior* ("the better reading is to be preferred") indicates that textual criticism is not an objective science and shares in some of the subjectivism ascribed to so-called "Higher Criticism" (see LOWER CRITICISM).

The history of textual criticism cannot be sketched here. It is the oldest of the critical approaches to scripture, dating back at least to ORIGEN (ca. 185–254 C.E.). As a critical methodology, however, it began in the 17th and 18th cents. with the work of John S. Mill (1645–1707) and others in England and J. A. Bengel (1687–1752), J. J. Wettstein (1693–1754), J. S. Semler (1725–1791), and J. J. GRIESBACH (1745–1812) on the Continent. (See F. M. Cross and S. Talmon, eds., *Qumran and the History of the Biblical Text* [Cambridge and London: Harvard University Press, 1975]; P. Kyle McCarter, *Textual Criticism: Recovering the Text of the Hebrew Bible*, Guides to Biblical Scholarship: Old Testament Series, ed. Gene M. Tucker [Minneapolis: Fortress Press, 1986]; Emanuel Tov, *Textual Criticism of the Hebrew Bible*, 2nd ed. [Minneapolis: Fortress Press, 2001]).

See also Bruce Metzger, *The Text of the New Testament: Its Transmission, Corruption and Restoration*, 3rd enl. ed. (New York: Oxford University Press, 1992) and *The Text of the New Testament in Contemporary*

THE DEVELOPMENT OF OLD TESTAMENT TEXTS

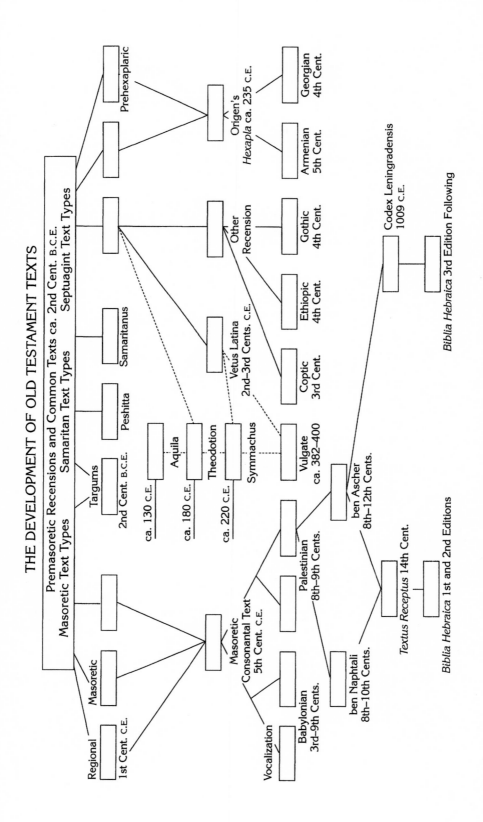

Research: Essays on the Status Quaestionis, ed. by Bart D. Ehrman and Michael W. Holmes (Grand Rapids: Wm. B. Eerdmans, 1995).

A significant new cache of ancient Greek MSS, uncials and minuscules, plus other MSS in Arabic, Armenian, Coptic, Ethiopic, Georgian, Karshuni, Latin, Slavic, Syria Estrangela, and Syriac was discovered at St. Catherine's Monastery on Mt. Sinai in May, 1975. They are expected to shed much light on the history of the Greek text of the Bible, on Byzantine art and Greek calligraphy, particularly for the "period of great silence"—7th–9th cents. Both canonical and EXTRACANONICAL writings (*Testament of the Twelve Patriarchs*) were found, including Homer's *Iliad* and certain "lost" books of Christian tradition. See *Biblical Archaeologist* 43 (Jan.–Feb., 1980): 26–34.

In addition to terms and names above, see BIBLICAL CRITICISM; CODEX ALEXANDRINUS et al.; ERASMUS; NESTLE TEXT; PALIMPSEST; RECENSION; OLD LATIN MSS; *TEXTUS RECEPTUS*; TISCHENDORF; WESTCOTT; HORT.

Textus Receptus (Lat for "Received Text"). *Textus Receptus* is the name given in Britain to the 1550 edition of the Greek NT published by Robert Stephanus in Paris, which essentially reproduced ERASMUS's text of 1535. On the Continent, the accepted or "received (Greek) text" was the 1633 edition of Elzevir (or Elsevir), a Dutch printing house. Until the 19th cent., the *Textus Receptus* was the authoritative text of the NT. Its modern equivalent is published in two editions, identical except in their CRITICAL APPARATUSES: the *Greek New Testament,* 4th rev. ed. of *Greek NT* (1993) and the 27th rev. ed. of *Novum Testamentum Graece* (1993), both edited by K. ALAND et al. See AMERICAN STANDARD VERSION; CRITICAL TEXT; KING JAMES VERSION; REVISED STANDARD VERSION; TEXTUAL CRITICISM.

In OT textual criticism, the term *Textus Receptus* denotes the Second Rabbinic Bible of Jacob ben Chaim (also Chayyim), which was published in Venice in 1524–25 by Daniel Bomberg (hence it is also called Bombergiana). In addition to the Hebrew text the *Textus Receptus* includes the Aramaic translation and commentaries by the most influential of the Rabbis (Rashi, Ibn Ezra, etc.). It was used as the basis for the first two editions of R. KITTEL's *Biblia Hebraica,* then replaced in the third edition by CODEX Leningradensis. See "L"; MASORETIC TEXT.

Theios Aner in Greek means "Divine Man" and was particularly applied to spiritual leaders with purportedly miraculous powers. See ARETALOGY.

Theodotion (abbrev.: Theod.). The traditional name of a Greek VERSION of the OT that may be a revision of the LXX in the direction of the Hebrew text or a more literal translation of the Hebrew. It has been argued that Theodotion was based on a still earlier revision called Proto-Theodotion, but this theory has been questioned by some scholars. The Theodotionic RECENSION was widely used by the church fathers of the 3rd and 4th cents. C.E.; it came to supplant the LXX text of much of Job and Jeremiah. It formed the sixth column in ORIGEN's *HEXAPLA* and was used by him to fill LACUNAE in the LXX text at his disposal. Little is known of Theodotion himself; it is thought that he lived during the second half of the 2nd cent. and was a convert to Judaism. So-called "Theodotion" of Daniel, citations of which appear in the NT, replaced the LXX of Daniel in all LXX MSS except two (88 and 967 in Rahlf's list). "Theodotion-Daniel," to be dated in the 1st cent. B.C.E., is not in the same textual tradition as Theodotion. See AQUILA; SYMMACHUS; TEXTUAL CRITICISM.

Theodotion Daniel. See *Kaige Recension.*

Theological Interpretation refers to any approach to understanding the Bible whose central concern is knowledge of and communion with God. Like other interpretive approaches, theological interpretation is characterized by distinctive presuppositions and aims. In the Jewish and Christian traditions, the distinguishing presupposition of theological interpretation is that the Bible is sacred scripture, that is, that it has its origin, subject matter, and purpose in God, and that as such it is both a source of and a norm for the community's life with and knowledge of God. The key aim of theological interpretation is to understand sacred scripture *as* sacred scripture, that is, in a manner that is attentive to its origin and subject matter in God. It seeks critically to advance knowledge of and communion with God, both in the interpreter and in the wider community of interpretation.

Christians and Jews interpreted the Bible theologically as a matter of course during the first centuries of the C.E., the formative period when both communities gave lasting shape to their CANONS of sacred scripture and to the hermeneutical practices that they would use to read those canons for generations to come. Of course, both canon and hermeneutical practices differed between the two communities in fundamental and lasting ways. Jews read the TANAKH through the lens of the MISHNAH and Gemara, while Christians read the OLD TESTAMENT through the lens of the NT's witness to JESUS CHRIST. Yet despite these differences, Jews and Christians shared certain theological convictions that shaped their practice of theological interpretation in common ways. For example, both Christians and Jews (1) approached the scriptures as an inexhaustible source of divine truth, given by God through inspired figures of the past for the purpose of forming the community's practice and belief in the present; (2) read the scriptures as a unity, interpreting passages from widely different contexts in light of each other; (3) gave priority to the literal or plain sense of scripture, at least in certain contexts, while simultaneously holding that scripture's plain sense did not exhaust its valid meaning (see FOURFOLD SENSE OF SCRIPTURE); (4) regarded valid interpretation in the present as compatible with and indeed dependent on reliance on prior tradition; and finally, (5) held that to read scripture well a person needed to cultivate spiritual disciplines, such as prayer, humility, and readiness to learn. These characteristic features of theological interpretation remained relatively constant for many centuries even as they permitted wide latitude in their application.

The story of theological interpretation in recent times is tied up with the emergence of HISTORICAL CRITICISM and the related methods that constitute modern BIBLICAL CRITICISM (c. 1750–). Historical criticism originated in part as an extension of theological interpretation's own interest in the LITERAL SENSE of scripture. However, historical criticism also transformed this interest in the literal sense and gradually came to define itself over against theological interpretation. The hard-fought rise of historical criticism as an independent discipline challenged the traditional practice of theological interpretation in three important ways.

1. *Premises and goals.* Briefly, historical criticism's goal has been to determine the most primitive meaning of a biblical passage in its original historical context, using criteria of judgment that are as neutral and nontheological in character as possible. According to the new PARADIGM, the fact that certain communities regard the Bible as scripture ought to have no bearing at all on its interpretation. The interpreter who happens to be a member of such a community must seek to approach the Bible as free as possible from the ways of reading that are characteristic of that community as such, i.e., free from any prior commitment to the scripture's rootedness in God, its inexhaustible truthfulness, its relevance to contemporary life, etc. Only in this way can the Bible be set free to "speak for itself," rather than being made to say what corresponds to the interpreter's prior dogmatic commitments.

2. *Results.* Historical criticism produced results that irrevocably changed the way many people understand the historical origins and literary diversity of the Bible. The relatively simple picture of the Bible's origins from the hands of a few inspired authors was replaced by a vastly more complex and ambiguous picture of the variegated development of biblical literatures over long stretches of time in the context of similar cultures of the ancient Near East. The new picture created an overwhelming impression of diversity that put enormous stress on traditional notions of the unity of the Bible and cast doubt on the viability of reading passages from widely different context in light of each other. The new approach insisted that each discrete unit of biblical literature be allowed to speak on its own terms, without trying to "harmonize" it with other passages according to dogmatic preconceptions.

3. *Disciplines.* Finally, the rise of historical criticism contributed to the drawing and enforcement of new divisions between concerns that had been previously interwoven in theological interpretation, such as biblical learning, theology, praxis, and spirituality. These areas became specialized disciplines in their own right, and proficiency in one field was not thought to be necessary for proficiency in another. For example, the job of the biblical scholar became to determine what the text *meant*, while the question of what it *means* for the life of faith today is a separate one that has no place in the task of exegesis itself.

Theological interpretation has responded to the challenge of historical criticism in a variety of ways. Different approaches have been developed by pietism, Protestant liberalism, fundamentalism, mid-twentieth-century "Word of God" theologies (R. BULTMANN, K. BARTH, etc.), the tradition of dialogical HERMENEUTICS (W. DILTHEY, P. Ricoeur, etc.), feminist theologies, liberation theologies, etc. Moreover, it is important to note that in some respects, the relation between older forms

of theological interpretation and modern biblical criticism has proven to be a stalemate, with traditional theological interpretation persisting (with various degrees of vitality) in worshiping communities, and modern biblical criticism restricted largely to the academy. Bearing in mind the diversity of approaches, however, one can identify three important models that together delineate the range within which much contemporary discussion of theological interpretation takes place.

1. *A conservative model* reasserts the Bible's character as scripture and on that basis seeks to *deny the validity* of modern historical criticism's findings and methods. Conservative theological interpretation typically locates the authority of scripture in its *origin* in God's inspiration of the biblical writers (e.g., Moses of the PENTATEUCH), and in the intrinsic veracity of the writings themselves that is presumed to flow from this. (Indeed, modern conservative interpretation often has doctrines of VERBAL INSPIRATION and inerrancy that are far more extensive and prominent than those of premodern interpretation.) Conservative theological interpretation also rejects historical criticism's findings regarding the diversity of the biblical writings. It reasserts the unity of the Bible and the validity of traditional forms of reading such as typology on the basis of the harmonious and noncontradictory agreement of its writings. Finally, conservative interpretation rejects historical criticism's methods, especially its insistence that the Bible be read like any other piece of ancient literature. According to conservative interpretation, a prior commitment to scripture's authority is necessary in order to understand it properly. If the reader subjects the Bible to scrutiny and testing according to ordinary reason and experience, he or she will only miss its message because that message transcends ordinary reason and experience.

2. *A liberal model* adopts historical criticism's approach to the Bible as a diverse collec-

tion of ancient religious literature and on that basis proposes a radically revised understanding of the Bible's significance for today. According to liberal theological interpretation, contemporary religious communities are justified in using the Bible as a *historical source* of the community's memory, symbols, language, etc. However, they are not justified in appealing to the Bible as a *theological norm* of contemporary belief and action. Typically, liberal interpretation locates the norm of theological understanding independently of the biblical text, in a divine principle or purpose to which the modern reader is presumed to have independent access, such as justice, liberation, human flourishing, etc. Liberal theological interpretation shows little interest in precritical methods that presuppose the Bible's unity and authority and tends to be suspicious of efforts to rehabilitate them. Rather, it emphasizes the relativizing and pluralizing impact of historical criticism and the corresponding need to distinguish between biblical traditions that can enhance the community's life and those that are destructive of it. On this view, biblical text and modern interpreter stand in principle on the same level and the relation between them is one of dialogue, or, more realistically, struggle. The reader should take the biblical text seriously and be open to its influence, especially insofar as it inspires the contemporary community to transcend itself toward greater justice, human flourishing, etc. On the other hand, in view of the long history of the Bible's ideological misuse, readers must approach biblical texts with suspicion and must be prepared to reject the claims of the biblical texts whenever they legitimate oppressive interests. (See ADVOCACY CRITICISM; FEMINIST BIBLICAL INTERPRETATION; IDEOLOGICAL CRITICISM; MUJERISTA BIBLICAL INTERPRETATION; WOMANIST BIBLICAL INTERPRETATION.)

3. *A postcritical model* grants the validity and limited usefulness of a historical-critical approach to the Bible but not its claim to enjoy exclusive validity or priority with respect to other approaches. It insists on the independent integrity of a specifically theological approach to biblical interpretation that regards the Bible *as scripture,* i.e., as a source of and a norm for the worshiping community's knowledge of and communion with God. Postcritical theological interpretation rejects the idea that the Bible "speaks for itself" only when its character as scripture is ignored. It agrees with conservative interpretation that such a view actually gives unwarranted normativity to the presuppositions of the modern interpreter. Unlike conservative interpretation, however, postcritical theological interpretation does not conceive the authority of scripture chiefly in terms of its *origins* but rather in terms of its *subject matter* or SCOPE (e.g., God's identity and purposes) and in terms of its proper use in community (e.g., building up the community in love of God and neighbor). This shift allows postcritical interpretation to combine interest in precritical methods with a modern acknowledgment of the historical diversity of the biblical witnesses. Similarly, postcritical theological interpretation agrees with liberal interpretation that the Bible is subject to ideological distortion. However, it holds that the most reliable and efficacious criterion for judging such distortion is ultimately found in the Bible's own witness to God, rather than in the reader's independent conceptions of justice, human flourishing, etc. Finally, postcritical interpretation seeks to resist the fragmentation of biblical study into self-sufficient disciplines and to reintegrate biblical learning, theology, praxis, and spirituality. (See KARL BARTH, SACHEXEGESE, POSTCRITICAL BIBLICAL INTERPRETATION.)

Of course, it is important to remember that these three models represent ideal types and are not a complete inventory of actual approaches to theological interpretation.

See Stephen E. Fowl, *Engaging Scripture* (Malden, Mass.: Blackwell, 1998); Stephen E. Fowl, ed., *The Theological Interpretation of Scripture: Classic and Contemporary Readings* (Cambridge: Blackwell, 1997); Charles M.

Wood, "Hermeneutics and the Authority of Scripture," in *Scriptural Authority and Narrative Interpretation,* ed. by Garrett Green (Philadelphia: Fortress Press, 1987); Charles M. Wood, *The Formation of Christian Understanding: An Essay in Theological Hermeneutics* (Philadelphia: Westminster Press, 1981); Edward Farley, *Theologia: The Fragmentation and Unity of Theological Education* (Philadelphia: Fortress Press, 1983); Elisabeth Schüssler Fiorenza, *Bread Not Stone: The Challenge of Feminist Biblical Interpretation* (Boston: Beacon Press, 1984).

Theologumenon (Gk: pl: *theologumenona.;* pres. pass. ptc., neuter, of *theologein:* to speak of God). Broadly, any proposition, idea, or concept pertaining to God or belonging to a system of religious belief. In Roman Catholic tradition a *theologumenon* is defined more specifically as "a proposition expressing a theological statement which cannot be directly regarded as official teaching of the Church, as dogma binding in faith, but which is the outcome and expression of an endeavour to understand the faith by establishing connections between binding doctrines of faith . . . " (K. Rahner, *Sacramentum Mundi* 6, ad hoc). In recent BIBLICAL CRITICISM (Protestant and Catholic), *theologumenon* has also been defined as "the historicizing of what was originally a theological statement" (R. BROWN). So defined, the genealogy of Jesus and perhaps his virginal conception may be understood as *theologumena,* that is, as the "historization" of the theological assertions that Jesus was "Son of David" and "Son of God" respectively. What constitutes a *theologumenon,* what is historical, and what is presented as history are debated.

Theophany (Gk: a manifestation of God or the divine). Theophany refers generally to a manifestation of the divine, especially one that is powerful and perceptible by ordinary means, e.g., hearing, seeing, touching, etc. So defined, theophany is an important element in many religions and can occur in conjunction with natural objects (stones, trees, animals), natural events (thunder and lightning, the conjunction of planets), miraculous events (possession, miraculous healing), or the fate of nations and persons (the exodus, calling of a prophet) (cf. Mircea Eliade, *Images and Symbols: Studies in Religious Symbolism* [London: Harvill Press, 1961]).

In the HB, theophany occurs at decisive points in the history of Israel: the promises to the patriarchs (Gen 17; 18; 28; 1 Kgs 19), the call of Moses (Exod 3), the exodus-Sinai tradition (Exod 13; 16; 24; 40), the accession to the Promised Land (Josh 5), and the call of PROPHETS (Isa 6; Ezek 1). The HB's greatest theophany is surely YHWH's address to all of the people at Sinai (Exod 19–20). These theophanies are in the main auditory, God's self-manifestation through his word. Even in theophany YHWH does not become directly visible, but instead his presence is concealed by smoke and cloud. Moses himself sees God's back, not his face (Exod 33:18–23). Thus theophany both reveals and conceals the divine presence. According to Samuel Terrien, the Elijah stories mark a dramatic turning point in the mode of YHWH's presence in Israel, bringing an end to the era of theophany and introducing the era of prophetic vision, "where miracles of nature become miracles of character." Yet APOCALYPTIC writers regard Mt. Zion as the site at which theophany would one day become an everyday reality.

In the NT, theophany reappears (Mark 1:9ff.: Jesus' baptism; Mark 9:22ff.: the transfiguration) alongside CHRISTOPHANY (Mark 6:45ff. and John 6:16–21: walking on the sea; the resurrection appearances; Acts 9:4–16: Paul's conversion) and pneumatophany (Acts 2: the Spirit of Pentecost). The dialectic of disclosure and concealment takes the form *inter alia* of the tension between the manifestation of God's will in CHRIST (John 1; Phil 2:5–10; Col 1:15–20, etc.) and the Spirit on the one hand, and anticipation of the eschatological theophany (the PAROUSIA) on the other (Rev 6; 12:3 [9]; 13:1).

Samuel Terrien treated theophany as the heart of biblical theology in *The Elusive Presence* (San Francisco: Harper & Row, 1978). See also Jon Levenson, *Sinai and Zion: An Entry into the Jewish Bible* (Minneapolis: Winston Press, 1985).

Third Quest, The. See **Quest of the Historical Jesus.**

Tischendorf, Constantin (1815–1874). Professor of NT at Leipzig, Germany, beginning as a *Privatdozent* in 1839. An ardent traveler throughout Europe and the Near East, Tischendorf discovered a number of important and ancient UNCIAL manuscripts of the BIBLE, most notably CODEX SINAITICUS, CODEX VATICANUS, and CODEX Claromontanus, and succeeded in deciphering the difficult PALIMPSEST Codex Ephraemi. He published editions of the Greek NT and the Greek OT; his last CRITICAL TEXT of the NT, known as the *Editio Octava Critica Maior* (1869/72), was, until the age of the computer, a standard tool of NT TEXTUAL CRITICISM.

Today's English Version A translation of the BIBLE published by the American Bible Society (NT, 1966; OT 1976), commonly abbreviated as TEV. The NT, better known as *Good News for Modern Man,* was translated by Robert G. Bratcher; the OT by a number of OT scholars under Bratcher's chairmanship. The translation places emphasis on clarity of meaning rather than on literary form. It employs a standard of English common to all who speak the language, whether of a high or low level of education. Since it avoids technical, traditional language (e.g., synagogue, scribe, etc.), it is not as useful a study Bible as the NRSV, RSV, JB, or NEB. It is however a faithful, highly readable VERSION. It has now been replaced by the United Bible Societies' CONTEMPORARY ENGLISH VERSION. See AMERICAN STANDARD VERSION; DOUAY; JERUSALEM BIBLE; LIVING BIBLE (PARA-PHRASED); NEW AMERICAN BIBLE; NEW ENGLISH BIBLE; NEW INTERNATIONAL VERSION; NEW JEWISH VERSION; KING JAMES VERSION; PARAPHRASE; REVISED STANDARD VERSION.

Topos; *Toposforschung; Topik* Topos (pl.: topoi; fr. Gk: place) is a technical term from ancient Greek RHETORIC whose ancient meaning is discussed under the Latin equivalent: *LOCUS.* The term *topos* was introduced into modern LITERARY CRITICISM with a change in meaning and spelling (*Topik:* topics) by Ernst R. Curtius (*European Literature and the Latin Middle Ages* [Princeton: Princeton University Press, 1953; Ger: 1948) and the school of *Toposforschung* (topos research) after him. The term refers to a general concept that through cultural and literary tradition has become the common possession of at least a certain strata of society and is used by an author in a delimited and conventional way in the treatment of the subject. A topos is therefore often, but one-sidedly, understood as merely "something handed down in literature and taken over as a stereotype, i.e., defined as a traditional FORMULA, inherited motif or thought schemata" (see Edgar Mertner, "Topos and Commonplace," in *Strena Angelica,* Festschrift für Otto Richter, ed. by G. Dietrich and F. W. Schulze [Halle: M. Niemeyer, 1956]). So defined, works such as the G. KITTEL-Friedrich *Theological Dictionary of the New Testament,* or the Botterweck-Ringgren *Theological Dictionary of the Old Testament* can be termed examples of *Toposforschung* in that they attempt to illumine history or literature on the basis of the smallest elements of the tradition (viz., single words).

Recent topos research, however, recognizes the ancient and primary role of topoi in the discovery (*inventio*) of arguments for use in a given rhetorical situation. Such analysis begins by postulating the general topoi (*loci communes* or "commonplaces") through which the argument of a given text received its STRUCTURE. The topos has been likened to a vessel sometimes filled with water, sometimes with wine, i.e., a form possessing different functions at different times depending on what is deemed appropriate to the rhetorical situation. The reader, who because of ignorance of the topos considers a specific formulation of an author to be a completely original creation of the moment, overestimates its meaning and errs just as the reader who, filled with knowledge of the topos, considers the passage nothing but a semantically empty filler (cf. Lausberg, p. 39). For example, in 1 Cor 1:20–21, 26–30; 2:6–7, Paul contrasts the wisdom of the world with the wisdom of God. This theme does not originate with the apostle Paul but is a topos of Hellenistic Jewish (-Christian) missionaries in competition with the miracle workers and magicians of the Gentile world (so K. Berger). Yet Paul gives the topos a new and transformed sense by bringing it to focus in the crucifixion of Jesus of Nazareth. See Dan 2:27–28; *Jos. Ant.* 2.286; 10.203; Hippolytus, *Dan* 2:3, 27; Justin, *Apol.* 60:11; *Syr. Apoc. of Dan* (*Pseudo-Daniel*) 1:16. Similarly, a central paraenetic topos is that of not being ashamed under adversity, e.g., Rom 1:16; 2 Tim 1:8, 12, 16; 2:15; Ign., *Eph* 2:2. See RHETORICAL ANALYSIS.

Torah   Although commonly and correctly translated as "LAW," Torah has a wider semantic range than the English word and can also mean "instruction," "teaching," and "guidance." Strictly speaking, Torah refers to the PENTATEUCH, the first five books of the HB: Genesis, Exodus, Leviticus, Numbers, and Deuteronomy. More broadly, it may refer to the whole HB, and more widely still, to the body of teaching that according to Jewish tradition was revealed by God to Moses at Mt. Sinai, that is, to the Written Torah (the HB) and the Oral Torah (the MISHNAH and Germara). In its most comprehensive sense, Torah is virtually synonymous with divine Wisdom (cf. Sir 19:20; 24:23), and in

this sense bears on the character and STRUCTURE of the whole created order.

Tractate   (Lat: to treat). A treatise or essay on a specific subject.

Tradition Criticism,   also **Tradition History** or **Tradition-Historical Criticism,** are all acceptable translations for the German technical term *Traditionsgeschichte* and are increasingly used as translations of the word *Überlieferungsgeschichte* (lit., "the history of transmission") even though in Germany the latter has been used in contradistinction to *Traditionsgeschichte*. For *Überlieferungsgeschichte* some scholars prefer the longer but more accurate "history of the transmission of tradition," but this is deemed unnecessarily redundant. In English the word *tradition* denotes both the process of transmission (Latin: *traditio*) and that which is transmitted (*traditum*), as does the word *Überlieferung*.

   Broadly stated, tradition-historical criticism is the study of the history of ORAL TRADITIONS during the period of their transmission. In this sense it is usually distinguished from source criticism, FORM CRITICISM, TEXTUAL CRITICISM, LITERARY CRITICISM, and REDACTION CRITICISM. But since the scope and methods of these disciplines are not rigid, particularly source and form criticism, it is not surprising that tradition-historical criticism is variously represented (1) as the same as form criticism (VON RAD) or as an extension of it (Klaus Koch), (2) as reliant on the observations of source criticism (NOTH) or as basically antithetical to them (Engnell), (3) as distinct from the other methodologies (Wolfgang Richter) or (4) as a special amalgam of them all (Magne Saebø).What constitutes the focus of tradition-historical criticism is defined in an equally varied manner. In the main, however, it is the history of oral traditions that is in view. Sometimes this excludes compositional stages, but more often it includes the reconstruction of the whole history of a literary unit from its hypothetical origin and development in its oral stage to its composition and final redaction in literary form. So-called "streams of tradition" also come under investigation, that is, the socioreligious milieu of the TRADITIONISTS (e.g., prophetic and priestly circles) that gave shape and significance to certain bodies of tradition, such as the festival rites accompanying Israel's annual renewal of the divine covenant. Considerable conjecture has also been given to the geographical site of origin for these various traditions, such as Shechem, Jerusalem, Bethel, etc. Other tradition historians focus not on specific units of scripture or on particular oral forms but on certain ideas, themes, or motifs, and their development.

Traditionsgeschichte, as employed by Swedish OT scholar Ivan Engnell (1906–1964), applied almost completely to the final stage of the tradition. Denying the possibility of discerning the original wording of the tradition or the stages of its transmission, he analyzed instead the end product with reference to compositional techniques, patterns, motifs, and purposes as well as the smaller units of the tradition in relationship to their context within the text. At the same time, he called for the use of all other relevant data: literary, ideological, psychological, sociological, archaeological, and cultural. However, Engnell's emphasis on the final stage of the tradition has met with criticism and has led to the suggestion that his use of this term was inappropriate, motif criticism being suggested in its place.

Interest in the oral stages of the biblical traditions prior to their literary formulation dates back to the 18th cent. and before; it remained essentially dormant throughout the 19th cent., finally to be revived by HERMANN GUNKEL, Hugo Gressmann, et al. at the turn of the cent. Tradition-historical criticism, however, is especially identified with Gerhard von Rad (1901–1971) and Martin Noth (1902–1968) in Germany, and SIGMUND MOWINCKEL (1884–1965) and Ivan Engnell in Scandinavia. Tradition critics have tended to concentrate on specific forms, such as NARRATIVE, law, PROPHECY, wisdom, etc., and

their variation and application through time. For a historical overview of tradition-historical-critical methodologies and their assessment, see Douglas A. Knight, *Rediscovering the Traditions of Israel* (Missoula, Mont.: Society of Biblical Literature, 1973); see also M. Fishbane, *Biblical Interpretation in Ancient Israel* (Oxford: Oxford University Press, 1987) and J. W. Groves, *Actualization and Interpretation in the Old Testament* (Atlanta: Scholars Press, 1987).

In NT studies, tradition criticism is concerned with the development of tradition in the PRE-PAULINE period, ca. 30–50 C.E. It has dealt especially with the oldest liturgical fragments, HYMNS, juridical FORMULAS (see *SÄTZE HEILIGEN RECHTES*), etc., within the context of baptism, the EUCHARIST, catechesis, proclamation, etc. In the GOSPELS, the classic study is RUDOLF BULTMANN's *History of the Synoptic Tradition* (New York: Harper & Row, 1963); for the Gospel of John, see Louis J. Martyn, *The Gospel of John in Christian History* (New York: Paulist Press, 1978). Studies in the developmental stages of Q and the logia of the *GOSPEL OF THOMAS* represent the most recent examples of tradition history research in NT scholarship. See INTERTEXTUALITY; QUEST OF THE HISTORICAL JESUS; TYPOS.

Traditionist(s); *Tradent; Trägerkreis*

A person, or group of persons (Ger: *Kreis*: circle; cf. *Schule*: school), who preserve and transmit (Ger: *Träger;* lit.: one who bears) traditional material, whether written or oral. (Also used is the Latin *Tradent*: "a person who delivers or hands over any property to another," OED.) Recent interest in the social history of Judaism and early Christianity, quickened by studies in the sociology of knowledge, liberation theology, and both Old and New Testament *TRADITIONSGESCHICHTE* has focused attention on the sociotheological perspectives of the Traditionists. The questions being asked are, Who is responsible for preserving and transmitting the traditions (canonical or extracanonical)? What sociotheological perspectives are present in the traditions? How do these views fit into the sociotheological matrix of ancient society? (For bibliography, see SOCIOLOGICAL INTERPRETATION.) Michael Fishbane makes wide use of these terms in his reflection on inner-biblical EXEGESIS; see *Biblical Interpretation in Ancient Israel* (Oxford: Clarendon Press, 1985).

Traditionsgeschichte (Ger: the history of the tradition; tradition history). See **Tradition Criticism.**

Translation. See **Version.**

Transliteration is the act or process by which the words, letters, or characters of one language are written in the letters or characters of another, or the result thereof.

Biblical languages and the languages of the Bible's environment, are often transliterated into Roman script. Unfortunately, there is no single system in common use for transliterating Hebrew, although greater uniformity is to be hoped for since the publication of the SOCIETY OF BIBLICAL LITERATURE's handbook of style (see pp. 201–2). Normally, such systems as are employed attempt to transliterate Hebrew so that both letters (mainly consonants) and vowels will be perfectly or nearly perfectly represented. These systems require the adaptation of diacritical marks to the Roman alphabet.

Treaty Form The form-critical study of ancient Near Eastern treaties, particularly from the archives of the HITTITE empire, reveals a sixfold STRUCTURE, parallels of which scholars have sought in the OT. The classic form, not always present in every part or in order, contains six members: (1) preamble introducing the speaker (cf. Deut

1:1); (2) historical prologue describing previous relations (cf. Deut 1:3–4); (3) stipulations detailing the obligations of the vassal state (cf. Deut 24:7); (4) document clause providing for the safekeeping and regular public reading of the agreement (cf. Deut 27:8); (5) the gods who are witnesses to the treaty (cf. Deut 32:1; Isa 1:2, Ezek 17:12–21); (6) curse and blessing FORMULA (cf. Deut 28). See, e.g., Dennis J. McCarthy, *Treaty and Covenant*, rev. ed. (Rome: Pontifical Biblical Institute, 1978). See LAW.

Tricolon (pl.: tricola). See **Colon.**

Triple Tradition refers to material common to Matt, Mark, and Luke; the term is used to avoid implying the nature of the source or the direction of dependency, if any, between the three GOSPELS. See DOUBLE TRADITION; Q; SYNOPSIS; SYNOPTIC PROBLEM; TWO SOURCE HYPOTHESIS.

Trito-Isaiah. See **Deutero-Isaiah.**

Trope (Gk: a turn). A figure of speech; the use of a word in a sense other than its normal meaning. The four basic kinds of tropes are METAPHOR, METONYMY, SYNECDOCHE, and IRONY.

Tropology. See *Fourfold Sense of Scripture, The.*

"Tu es Petrus" pericope (Lat: "You are Peter"; PERICOPE: Gk: passage). The Latin name for Matt 16:18–19, which has played an important role in the Roman Catholic doctrine of the church.

Tugendkatalog (Ger: catalog of virtues). See *Lasterkatalog.*

Two Source Hypothesis (The) proposes a solution to the SYNOPTIC PROBLEM by

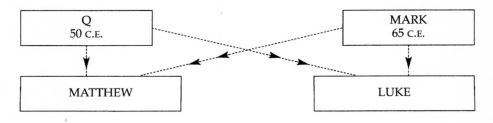

Listed below are three systems of current and historical interest:

Hebrew Consonants	Name (SBL: 1999)	RGG^3	JBL: 1971	Academic Style SBL: 1999
א	'ālep	'	'	'
בּ	bet	b	b	b
ב			(b̠)*	
גּ	gîmel	g	g	g
ג			(g)	
דּ	dālet	d	d	d
ד		d̠		
ה	hê	h	h	h
ו	wāw	w	w	w
ז	zayin	z	z	z
ח	ḥêt	ḥ	ḥ	ḥ
ט	ṭêt	ṭ	ṭ	ṭ
י	yôd	y	j	y
כּ ךּ	kāp	k	k	k
כ ך		k̠		
ל	lāmed	l	l	l
מ ם	mêm	m	m	m
נ ן	nûn	n	n	n
ס	sāmek	s	s	s
ע	'ayin	'	'	'
פּ ףּ	pê	p	p	p
פ ף		p̠		
צ ץ	ṣādê	ṣ	ṣ	ṣ
קּ ק	qôp	ḳ	q	q
ר	rêš	r	r	r
שׂ	śîn	ś	ś	ś
שׁ	šîn	š	š	š
תּ	tāw	t	t	t
ת		t̠		

Hebrew Vowels

ָ	qāmeṣ ḥāṭûp/qāmeṣ	å or a	o or ā	o
ַ	pataḥ	ă	a	a
ֶ	sĕgōl	ae	e̜	e
ֵ	ṣērē	e	ē	ē
ִ	long/short ḥîreq	i	ī** or i	ī or i
ֹ	ḥōlem	o	ō	ō
ֻ	long/short qibbûs	u	ū** or u	ū or u

*The spirant form of b, g, d, k, p, and t is normally not indicated; when absolutely needed, the underlined letter (here in parenthesis) is used.

**defectively written long vowel.

Hebrew Vowels	Name (SBL: 1999)	*RGG³*	*JBL:* 1971	*SBL:* 1999
(ֹ)ָ	*3d masc. sg. suf.*	â(w)	ā (y) w	āyw
ֶי	*sĕgōl yōd*	âe	ẹ(y)	ê (ֶי =êy)
ֵי	*sērē yōd*	ê	ê	ê (ֵי =êy)
ִי	*ḥîreq yod*	î	î	î (ִי =îy)
וֹ	*full ḥōlem*	ô	ô	ô
וּ	*šûrek*	û	û	û
ָ:	*ḥāṭēp qāmeṣ*	ă	o	ŏ
ֲ	*ḥāṭēp pataḥ*	a	a	ă
ֱ :	*ḥāṭēp sĕqōl*	ae	e	ĕ
ֱ	*vocal šĕwă'*	e	e	ĕ
ְ	*furtive pataḥ*	a	a	a
הָ	*final qāmeṣ hê*	ā	āh	â
הֱ		āe	eh	
הֵ		ē	ẹh	
הֹ		ō	ōh	

RGG³ Die Religion in Geschichte und Gegenwart, 3. Aufl.; Heraus. Kurt Galling (Tübingen: J. C. B. Mohr [Paul Siebeck], 1957–1965), 1, xxx.

JBL Journal of Biblical Literature 90 (December 1971): 513.

The SBL Handbook of Style: For Ancient Near Eastern, Biblical, and Early Christian Studies, ed. Patrick H. Alexander et al. (Peabody, Mass.: Hendrickson Publishers, 1999), 26, 29.

Greek is normally transliterated as follows:

A	α	a	Ξ	ξ	x
B	β	b	O	o	o
Γ	γ	g*	Π	π	p
Δ	δ	d	P	ρ	r
E	ε	e	Σ	σ(ς)	s
Z	ζ	z	T	τ	t
H	η	ē	Υ	υ	y or u***
Θ	θ	th	Φ	φ	ph
I	ι**	i	X	χ	ch
K	κ	k	Ψ	ψ	ps
Λ	λ	l	Ω	ω	ō
M	μ	m		ʿ ****	h
N	ν	n			

*(n before γ, κ, ξ, χ).

**iota subscript is often omitted or represented by a cedilla under the vowel concerned.

***used in dipthongs (e.g., au, eu, ui).

****rough breathing mark.

postulating independent use by Matt and Luke of two distinct sources in the writing of their GOSPELS: (1) *Q(uelle)*, a no longer extant collection of SAYINGS (except as recoverable from Matt and Luke) and (2) Mark's Gospel. (See figure bottom of p. 200.) This solution replaced the GRIESBACH HYPOTHESIS. See FOUR DOCUMENT HYPOTHESIS; HOLTZMANN; LACHMANN; Q; STREETER; SYNOPTIC PROBLEM; *UREVANGELIUM*.

Typology (fr. Gk *typos*: pattern, archetype). Typology refers to the interpretation of persons, events, and institutions in light of their resemblance or correspondence to other persons, events, and institutions, within a common framework of sacred history. Typology in this sense is characteristic of both biblical literature itself and of the Jewish and Christian traditions of biblical interpretation. For a study of typology in the HB, see Michael Fishbane, *Biblical Interpretation in Ancient Israel* (Oxford: Clarendon Press, 1985). In the Christian tradition, typology ordinarily expounds persons, events, or, things of the OT in light of their correspondences to JESUS CHRIST and the church, and vice versa. Christian typology "establishes a connection between two events or persons, the first of which signifies not only itself but also the second, while the second encompasses or fulfills the first" (Auerbach). The roots of Christian typology are visible in the NT; for example, in 1 Cor 10:1–6, Paul interprets the exodus as a type of baptism and as an event ordained to instruct his own generation (v. 11); in Rom 5:14, Adam is declared a "type" of the one who was to come, viz., Jesus; in Heb 7, the author patterns the priestly office of Jesus after the OT priest Melchizedek, etc. The classic study of NT typology is Leonhard Goppelt, *Typos: The Typological Interpretation of the Old Testament in the New* (Grand Rapids: Eerdmans, 1982 [orig. pub. 1939]).

Since as early as the 4th cent. C.E., Christians have often sought to draw a distinction between typology and ALLEGORY (see ALEXANDRIA, SCHOOL OF). Allegory is said to move between two qualitatively different planes of reality (physical/spiritual, outward/inward, earthly/heavenly), whereas in typology "the two poles of the figure are separate in time, but both, being real events or figures, are within time, within the stream of historical life" (Auerbach). The distinction is useful but easily overdrawn: typology is a "not easily specifiably yet definite bridge between allegorical and literal READING" (HANS FREI).

According to Reformation theory and practice, typological interpretation supplements rather than competes with scripture's literal or historical sense. In contrast, modern historical criticism has typically viewed both typological and allegorical interpretation as incompatible with respect for the LITERAL SENSE of scripture. Despite (or perhaps because of) this, the 20th cent. witnessed numerous efforts on the part of theologians and biblical scholars to reclaim the possibilities of typology for the interpretation of the BIBLE. See Erich Auerbach, "Figura," in *Scenes from the Drama of European Literature* (Gloucester, Mass: Peter Smith, 1973); James S. Preus, *From Shadow to Promise: Old Testament Interpretation from Augustine to the Young Luther* (Cambridge, Mass.: Harvard University Press, 1969). See HERMENEUTICS; INTERTEXTUALITY.

Überlieferungsgeschichte (Ger: history of transmission). See **Tradition Criticism.**

Ugarit, Ugaritic Texts. See **Ras Shamra Texts.**

Uncial is a technical term for 3rd- to 10th-cent. codices of the BIBLE written in majuscule or capital letters on parchment or VELLUM. Technically, PAPYRUS MANUSCRIPTS are also uncials (written in capital letters) but are designated instead by the material on which they are written (*siglum:*

P). The uncial style of writing was ordinarily reserved for formal and literary documents; the autographs of Paul's LETTERS were likely written in cursive. The most important uncials of the NT and certain EXTRACANONICAL writings (in whole or part) are: B (Vaticanus); or S (Sinaiticus); D (Bezae); L (regius); θ (Koridethi); A (Alexandrinus); C (Ephraemi); and W (Washingtonianus or Freer).

Urevangelium (Ger: original or primal GOSPEL) is the name given by G. E. LESSING in 1778 to a Hebrew or Aramaic document that he believed lay behind and thus explained the relationship of the first three Gospels, a shorter VERSION of which was used by Mark; a theory supplanted by the TWO SOURCE and FOUR DOCUMENT HYPOTHESES. See *URMARKUS*.

Urgemeinde, **Urkirche** (Ger: *ur*: primitive, primal, original, ancient, early. *Gemeinde*: congregation, community. *Kirche*: church). See **Early Church (The).**

Urmarkus (Ger: primitive, original or primal Mark) is the name given by H. J. HOLTZMANN in 1863 to a hypothetical source document behind, and abbreviated (Holtzmann), or expanded (Hermann von Soden [1905], Paul Wendland [1908], Hugo Gressmann [1925–31], et al.) by Mark. The existence of DOUBLETS (e.g., the feeding of the five thousand and its sequel in 6:30–7:37 and the feeding of the four thousand and its sequel in 8:1–26), the collections of logia (4:21–25; 8:34–9:1; 9:42–50; and 13:1–37), and the apparent absence of 6:45–8:26 in Luke (called the "Great Omission") have led to the common conviction that Mark used sources in the writing of his GOSPEL. Whether these sources formed a *Urmarkus* prior to its redaction by Mark, or were added to a *Urmarkus* at various stages by a REDACTOR(S) is debated. What could constitute a *Urmarkus* is also not clear; e.g., RUDOLF BULTMANN has written, "It is . . . probable that the text of Mark which the two other EVANGELISTS used lay before them in an older form than that in which we have it today. This *Urmarcus* (as it is usually called) was altered and enlarged at certain points; but it can scarcely be distinguished from the present text of Mark in any important way" (*Form Criticism*, ed. F. C. Grant [New York: Harper & Row, 1962], 13–14). See SYNOPTIC PROBLEM; TWO SOURCE HYPOTHESIS.

Urrolle (Ger: *Ur*: earliest, original. *Rolle*: scroll) is occasionally employed as a technical term (German) for the *earliest* form of a document presumably written on a *scroll*, that is, as originally composed prior to any additions or redactions—as are found for example in the book of Jeremiah in the OT. The term Ur-*text* is similar, referring to the text itself rather than to the form of the material on which it was written.

Variant Reading In TEXTUAL CRITICISM, variant reading refers to a variation in the wording of a passage of scripture (whether parts of words, words, or sentences) as found in the comparison of two or more MSS of the text in hand. All the variant READINGS in all the MSS of the NT, added together, would number over 500,000, mostly minor variations in spelling and word order. The difference between Mark 1:2 in the KJV and the RSV is due in part to MS variation.

Vaticinium ex eventu (pl.: vaticinia) is a Latin phrase meaning "a prophecy from an outcome." In NT criticism it is used to designate a passage in the Gospels that foretells an event that was in fact first known to and experienced by the early church and then placed back as prophecy on the lips of Jesus. The extent of the phenomenon in the NT is a matter of debate. For example, R. Bultmann regarded Jesus' prophecy of the destruction of Jerusalem (Luke 14:42–44) as a *vaticinium ex eventu*, but his view has been sharply challenged by N. T. Wright, *Jesus and the Victory of God* (Minneapolis: Fortress Press, 1996).

Vaux, Roland Guérin de   (1903–1971), born in Paris, studied at the Sorbonne and at the Seminary of St. Sulpice, entering the Dominican Order of the Roman Catholic Church in 1929. In 1933 he went to the École Biblique et Archéologique de St. Étienne in Jerusalem, where he served in various capacities, including professor of biblical history (1935–70), of biblical archaeology and Israelite institutions (1935–70), and as director (1945–65). As chairman of the board of the Palestine Archaeological Museum, he was intimately involved in the purchase and publication (as editor-in-chief) of the DEAD SEA SCROLLS (see DJD) and was director of the excavation of KHIRBET QUMRAN (1953–58). His major works include *Ancient Israel: Its Life and Institutions*, trans. John McHugh (New York: McGraw-Hill, 1961); *Archaeology and the Dead Sea Scrolls* (The Schweich Lectures of the British Academy for 1959; Oxford: Oxford University Press, 1973); and *The Early History of Israel*, trans. David Smith (Philadelphia: Westminster Press, 1978); he also translated Genesis, 1 & 2 Samuel, and 1 & 2 Kings for the *Bible de Jérusalem*. He received nine honorary degrees from universities in Europe, Great Britain, and the United States.

Vellum   (Lat: *pellis vitulina*) in the proper sense refers to calfskin processed for writing; the skins of all other animals when used for writing are technically known as parchment. In current usage, however, this distinction is no longer observed and the term *vellum* can denote the skin of any animal prepared as writing material. While dating from about the 2nd cent. B.C.E., vellum came into dominance ca. 4th cent. C.E. Second Tim 4:13 refers to such parchments with the Latin loan word *membrana*; the author (Paul?) may be speaking of OT scriptures. The word *parchment* is derived from Pergamum, the city in Asia Minor most noted for producing it. See PAPYRUS; TEXTUAL CRITICISM; UNCIAL.

Verbal Inspiration   (also known as "mechanical inspiration" or the "dictation theory of inspiration," implying that every word [*litera*] is of God or is filled with his Spirit; hence, also "literal inspiration").

In reaction to the rise of HISTORICAL CRITICISM in the 18th and 19th cents., which, by discovering errors in biblical fact and reason, threatened scripture as the authoritative word of God, there developed a theory of biblical inspiration in which every word was defended as directly coming from God. Verbal inspiration usually but not always implied absolute inerrancy, e.g., "God employed men in writing. But these men were so controlled by Him, that He is the Author of the writing; and so [completely] the Author, that any charge of inaccuracy against the record, or Scripture, as originally given, must be preferred against Him" (Kennedy, *The Doctrine of Inspiration*, 1878, p. 6; quoted by Marcus Dods, "Inspiration," in *A Dictionary of Christ and the Gospels*, ed. James Hastings [New York: Charles Scribner's Sons, 1906], I, 833). Other views of verbal inspiration, based on passages such as Matt 10:20; Exod 4:11–12; Jer 1:9; Ezek 3:27, conceded the possibility of defects but not apart from God's permission or as being inconsistent with his purpose. See John Robson, *The Bible: Its Revelation, Inspiration, and Evidence* (London: Hodder & Stoughton, 1883). See HERMENEUTICS.

Version   In TEXTUAL CRITICISM the term *version* denotes an early translation of the NT from Greek into another language; these early versions of the NT are in Latin, Coptic, Syriac, Armenian, Arabic, Ethiopic, Persian, Gothic, Georgian, and Slavonic. In the field of BIBLE translation, however, the word *version* (e.g., KJV, RSV, TEV) denotes an edition of the Bible that incorporates something of the language and style of a previous translation or version in the same language; a "translation" on the other hand, in contradistinction to a version, proceeds directly from the

Hebrew, Aramaic, or Greek text without the conscious influence of an earlier version: *The Complete Bible,* translated by J. M. Powis Smith, Edgar J. Goodspeed, et al. (Chicago: University of Chicago Press, 1935), is an example of a translation. In OT criticism, the term "DAUGHTER TRANSLATION" is sometimes used of translations of the LXX into Latin, Coptic, Ethiopic, etc., because they are not translations of the original Hebrew (and Aramaic) scriptures but of a prior (Greek) translation. See PARAPHRASE.

Volksspruch *(pl.: Volkssprüche;* Ger: popular, or folk, saying). In OT FORM CRITICISM a distinction is sometimes made between proverbial SAYINGS of the common people, called *Volksspruch,* and those arising first with the sages, called , *Kunstspruch* (an artistic saying or aphorism). So defined, the book of Proverbs in the OT is classified as *Kunstspruch.* Examples of the folk sayings are 1 Sam 10:11; 19:24: "Is Saul also among the prophets?" and Jer 31:29; Ezek 18:2: "The parents have eaten sour grapes, and the children's teeth are set on edge"; cf. Jer 23:28; 1 Sam 24:13; 1 Kgs 20:11. The origin of proverbs is a matter of conjecture and hence the distinction is disputed. It is clear that proverbs first arose with the awareness of "common" sense.

Vorlage (pl.: Vorlagen; Ger: copy, model, text; lit., "that which lies before") is a technical term borrowed from German scholarship to denote a particular copy of a document used as a source; e.g., to refer to "Luke's Markan *Vorlage*" is to draw attention to the fact that Luke's copy of Mark may have differed in important ways from the RECENSION of Mark as it comes to us in the major MSS or from the copy used by Matt.

Vulgate (Lat: common, popular) is the name given to that VERSION of the Latin BIBLE recognized by the medieval church and later by the Council of Trent (1546) to be the *vetus et vulgata editio* (the "old and popular edition"). The Council decreed that it was to be the official Bible of the Roman Church. Most of the books of this version stem from JEROME (ca. 340–420), who undertook the translation of the Bible at the behest of Pope Damasus (382) in order to end the proliferation of inferior (Old Latin) versions. Jerome's translations, completed in 405, circulated separately until bound in a single volume in the mid-6th cent. These bound editions, however, later known as the Vulgate, included translations not attributable to Jerome. Although all the OT is from Jerome, of the APOCRYPHA only Tobit and Judith, and of the NT only the GOSPELS can be ascribed to Jerome with certainty. The remainder are older Latin versions. The textual history of the Vulgate is, however, a matter of debate. See *DIVINO AFFLANTE SPIRITU;* OLD LATIN MSS.

Weiss, Bernhard (1827–1918). Born in Königsberg, Germany, Weiss taught NT studies at Königsberg (1852–63), Kiel (1863–76), and Berlin (1877–1908). He published a number of commentaries (in the H. A. W. Meyer series) and theological works which used HISTORICAL-CRITICAL METHODS to achieve generally conservative results. English translations include *Biblical Theology of the NT* (Edinburgh: T. & T. Clark, 1882–83) and *The Life of Christ* (T. & T. Clark, 1883).

Weiss, Johannes (1863–1914). Born in Kiel, the son of Bernhard Weiss and the son-in-law of the famed theologian, Albrecht Ritschl, Weiss taught in the field of NT at Göttingen (1888–95), Marburg (1895–1908), and Heidelberg (1908–14). An advocate of the methodology of comparative religions (*RELIGIONSGESCHICHTLICHE SCHULE*), his major contribution to subsequent NT EXEGESIS and theology was the discovery of the eschatological nature of Jesus' proclamation of the kingdom of God (*Jesus' Proclamation of the Kingdom of God* [Ger: 1892; Eng: London:

SCM Press, 1971; Philadelphia: Fortress Press, 1971]). Ironically, Weiss himself (in keeping with the ethical optimism of his time) believed that Jesus' eschatological expectation was utterly foreign to the modern mind and could possess no relevance for contemporary faith. In fact, ESCHATOLOGY became a dominant theme of Christian theology in the 20th cent. and promises to remain so in the 21st.

Wellhausen, Julius (1844–1918). Born the son of a Lutheran pastor in Hameln, Germany, Wellhausen studied under the famed OT scholar Heinrich Ewald in Göttingen, and became professor of OT on the theological faculty in Greifswald in 1872, a position from which he resigned because of ecclesiastical opposition to his radically historical approach to OT studies, most notably to his theories concerning the formation of the PENTATEUCH. Subsequently, he became professor of Semitic languages in Halle (1882), Marburg (1885), and Göttingen (1892). Accomplished in NT and Islamic studies as well as the OT, Wellhausen's great influence on BIBLICAL CRITICISM nevertheless derived largely from his classic work *Prolegomena to the History of Ancient Israel* (1878, 1883²; reprint: Gloucester, Mass.: Peter Smith, 1973). See GRAF-WELLHAUSEN HYPOTHESIS; LITERARY CRITICISM.

We-sections is a term of convenience referring to those passages in the book of Acts in which the autobiographical first-person plural ("we") appears instead of the biographical third person (Acts 16:10–17; 20:5–15; 21:1–18; 27:1–28:16; CODEX BEZAE adds 11:28). Though generally thought to be from Luke's own "travel diary," it is possibly a convention of Hellenistic NARRATIVE style.

Westcott, Brooke Foss (1825–1901). Educated in Birmingham and at Trinity College, Cambridge, England; taught at Harrow (1852–69); Regius Professor of Theology at Cambridge (1870–90); Bishop of Durham (1890–1901). An author of numerous studies on NT theology and history, Westcott is most widely noted for his critical edition of the Greek NT (1881), prepared with F. J. A. HORT. See CRITICAL TEXT; TEXTUAL CRITICISM.

Westermann, Claus (1909–2000). Born in Berlin, Westermann rose to prominence as OT professor at the University of Heidelberg starting in 1958, after beginning his teaching career at the Kirchliche Hochschule in Berlin. A prolific scholar, Westermann's major contributions centered on the PSALMS, the book of Genesis, and Isaiah 40–66. In each arena his studies marked a starting point for all subsequent interpretation, particularly for those interested in FORM CRITICISM. A pastor during the early years of the German church crisis, Westermann retained throughout his life a concern for the church and for the THEOLOGICAL INTERPRETATION of scripture. To the reigning emphasis on salvation in history as the central thesis of Israel's faith, so prominently articulated by his older colleague G. VON RAD, Westermann added Genesis's vision of creation as the domain of universal blessing, one not limited to Israel. Most notable of his many publications in English translation are *Isaiah 40–66* (1969); *Genesis: A Commentary*, 3 vols. (Minneapolis: Augsburg, 1984–86); *Praise and Lament in the Psalms* (Atlanta: John Knox Press, 1981); *Theological Lexicon of the OT*, 3 vols. (Peabody, Mass.: Hendrickson, 1997); and *Blessing in the Bible and in the Life of the Church* (Philadelphia: Fortress Press, 1978).

Western Text, The In NT TEXTUAL CRITICISM, the Western text is one of the geographical place names given to MSS of the NT bearing similar textual characteristics. Western Texts are in the main the bilingual Greco-Latin MSS, Old Latin MSS, and quotations from the Latin Fathers, all associated with Italy, Gaul, and Africa. The term is only partly accurate (since some Old Syriac and Coptic MSS show the same textual characteristics) and is replaced by some scholars with the designation "Delta," after its central witness, CODEX BEZAE CANTABRIGIENSIS (D or D^{ea}). According to E. J. Epp, the Western text is one of only two distinct early text types and can be traced from P^5 and P^{29} through P^{48}, P^{38}, P^{37} and 0171 to D and thereafter to more recent centuries, to F and G (9th cent.) and to MSS 614 and 383 (13th cent.). (See Epp, *JBL* 93 [1974]: 386–414.) It is suggested that by the 5th cent., the Western text and the Neutral (Alexandrian) text had been melded together to form the BYZANTINE TEXT, the dominant text type of subsequent centuries. See ALEXANDRIAN TEXT.

Wie es eigentlich gewesen ist   is a German phrase meaning "as it really was." It is sometimes quoted as a catchphrase to characterize the assumption prevalent among some 19th- (and 20th-) cent. historiographers that the past could be reconstructed "wie. . . ." This was the formulated intention of the distinguished German historian Leopold von Ranke (1795–1886), who made the phrase famous in this connection. Though the goal of presenting the past as it happened is a perennial goal of HISTORIOGRAPHY (note, e.g., the opprobrium rightly directed against deniers of the Holocaust), the phrase is often used in a cautionary fashion to denote methodological perspectives that are insufficiently attentive to the limitations of historical method, e.g., dimensions of past reality that elude historical method, the provisionality of historical judgment, and the historically conditioned character of the interpreter. See HISTORICAL-CRITICAL METHOD; PSYCHOLOGICAL RECONSTRUCTION; QUEST OF THE HISTORICAL JESUS.

Wirkungsgeschichte   (Adj.: *Wirkungsgeschictlich*; Ger: lit.: "history of [a text's] effect or impact.")

Wisdom Literature   broadly defined, is the name given to those ancient writings that deal primarily with humanity's acquisition of knowledge about and mastery of life; its explanations appeal to reason, experience, and human initiative rather than to revelation and to divine initiative; in Jewish tradition, wisdom literature, narrowly defined, is made up of Job, Proverbs, Ecclesiastes (also called *Qoheleth* or *Koheleth*), Ecclesiasticus (also called the Wisdom of Jesus ben Sira or Sirach), and the Wisdom of Solomon; to these is sometimes added the didactic poem in Baruch 3:9–4:4. The last three appear only in the Greek canon of the OT.

James L. Crenshaw suggests that, on the basis of these texts, wisdom literature can be divided into four kinds: (1) juridical, (2) natural, (3) practical, and (4) theological. He further distinguishes between "(1) family/clan wisdom, the goal of which is the mastery of life, the stance hortatory and the style proverbial; (2) court wisdom, with the goal of education for a select group, the stance secular, and method didactic; and (3) scribal wisdom, with the aim of providing education for everyone, a stance that is dogmatico-religious, and a dialogico-admonitory method." Crenshaw also notes eight categories in which wisdom literature appears: (a) proverbs (see the book of Proverbs), (b) riddle (Judg 14:10–18), (c) fable (Judg 9:8–15; Num 22:21–35; Gen 37:5–11, etc.) and ALLEGORY (Prov 5:15–23; Eccles 12:1–6), (d) HYMN (e.g., Prov 1:20–33; 8; Job 28; Sir 24:1–22; Wis 6:12–20; 7:22–8:21; Pss 1; 32; 34; 37; 49; 112; 128) and prayer (e.g., Sir 22:27–23:6; 36:1–17; 51:1–12; Wis 9:1–18), (e) dialogue (the book of Job), (f) confession or autobiographical NARRATIVE (e.g., Prov 4:3–9; 24:30–34; Eccles 1:12–2:26; 8:9–9:1; Sir 33:16–18; 51:23–30; Wis 7–9), (g) lists or ONOMASTICA (e.g., Job 38; Sir 43), and (h) didactic poetry (e.g., Pss 37; 49; 73; 139) and didactic narrative (e.g., Prov 7:6–23; Sir 44–50; Wis 10–19). (See *Old Testament Form Criticism*, ed. John H. Hayes [San Antonio: Trinity University Press, 1974], 227ff.)

In contemporary scholarship the nature and limits of wisdom are widely debated; some scholars include practically all non-revelatory speech in this category, such as the narratives of primeval history (Gen 1–11), the Joseph cycle (Gen 37–50), etc. A mediating position is found in GERHARD VON RAD's *Wisdom in Israel* (Ger: 1970; Eng: London: SCM Press, 1972). (See James L. Crenshaw, ed., *Studies in Ancient Israelite Wisdom* [New York: KTAV, 1976].) Since von Rad's work an "enormous explosion" (Brueggemann) of literature dealing with wisdom has appeared, summarized by Roland E. Murphy, *The Tree of Life: An Exploration of Biblical Wisdom Literature* (Garden City, N.Y.: Doubleday, 1990). At issue is the relation of wisdom to OLD TESTAMENT theology generally, and specifically to the doctrines of creation and redemption. Also at issue is the social setting of wisdom literature, including a social profile of the "sage." Feminist scriptural interpretation has found the personification of wisdom as a feminine force (e.g., Job 28; Prov 1, 8, 9; Bar 3:9–4:4; Sir 24, etc.) a fruitful starting point of theological reflection (see esp. Elisabeth Schüssler Fiorenza, ed., *Searching the Scriptures: A Feminist Commentary*, 2 vols. (New York: Crossroad, 1998). In NT studies, the figure of the wandering cynic or sage, as one who utters brief, pithy wisdom SAYINGS as found in Q, has served as a model for the historical Jesus (see literature under QUEST OF THE HISTORICAL JESUS).

Woe-Oracle   See **Oracle.**

Womanist Biblical Interpretation appeared shortly after the Black theology movement, which began in the 1960s and '70s in America, as an enterprise of African American women who wanted to differentiate themselves both within the renascent feminist movement and within male-dominated Black liberation theology.

According to one scholar, womanist biblical interpretation operates on three assumptions: (1) that the BIBLE, being the church's book, is central to the life of the African American Christian community and to its understanding of God and is a plumb line for the community's life and practices; (2) that womanist interpreters must nevertheless acknowledge the pervasively androcentric and patriarchal character of biblical texts, which consequently must be critiqued from the perspective of a HERMENEUTICS of suspicion, one that properly assesses texts in terms of their socio-historical and ideological contexts; and (3) that the multiply interlocking systems of ideology, both within the Bible and within the dominantly Eurocentric exegetical theories and practices by which it has traditionally been interpreted, must be identified and demystified.

Although the tasks of womanist interpretation are varied and multifaceted, four have been identified by the noted womanist scholar C. J. Martin. The first is to recover the history of women in the Bible, using traditional methodologies to expand on earlier feminist interests, acknowledging the methodological complexities, and keeping in view the needs of the various audiences for whom these reconstructions are made. Second is to reclaim from centuries of neglect and misinterpretation the presence and function of Black peoples within the biblical traditions, including their varied roles in the dramas of salvation, both in ancient Israel and in the early Christian movement (cf. Gen 16:1–15; 21:8–21; 1 Kgs 10:1–10; Acts 8:26–40, et al.). The third task is to challenge both theologians and biblical interpreters on the subject of race, which, when coupled with issues of gender, ethnicity, and class, constitutes an interpretive domain of consequent historical and sociopolitical effects. The fourth is to archive and analyze the history of the interpretation of the HEBREW BIBLE and Christian scriptures in Western culture in terms of its effects on peoples of African descent, both positively (as in the abolitionist movement) and negatively (as in the scriptural justification of slavery).

For this synopsis, see C. J. Martin, "Womanist Biblical Interpretation," in John H. Hayes, ed., DICTIONARY OF BIBLICAL INTERPRETATION (Nashville: Abingdon Press, 1999). For the term *womanist*, see Alice Walker, *In Search of Our Mothers' Gardens: Womanist Prose* (San Diego: Harcourt Brace Jovanovich, 1983). Also see C. H. Felder, ed., *Stony the Road We Trod: African American Biblical Interpretation* (Minneapolis: Fortress Press, 1991); J. Grant, *White Woman's Christ and Black Woman's Jesus: Feminist Christology and Womanist Response* (Atlanta: Scholars Press, 1989). See AFROCENTRIC BIBLICAL INTERPRETATION; FEMINIST BIBLICAL INTERPRETATION; MUJERISTA BIBLICAL INTERPRETATION.

Wortgeschehen (Ger: word event) is a technical term in the hermeneutical theory of Gerhard Ebeling. See LANGUAGE EVENT.

Wrede, William (1859–1906). Pastor (1887–89), later *Privatdozent* (lecturer) in NT studies at Göttingen, Germany; assoc. prof. (1893) and prof. (1895–1900) at Breslau. Noted primarily for his book, *Das Messiasgeheimnis in den Evangelien* (Göttingen: Vandenhoeck & Ruprecht, 1901; see MESSIANIC SECRET), which revealed the theological STRUCTURE of Mark's GOSPEL, ending the current view that it contained an essentially objective and historically accurate account of Jesus' ministry on which a "Life of Jesus" could be based. Wrede strenuously insisted that the work of the NT scholar was purely historical and descriptive in nature and that theological concerns could only threaten the interests of NT studies. He wrote of his own approach, "One might say that this account of New Testament theology entirely surrenders its specifically theological character. It is no longer treated any differently from any other branch of history in general or the history of religion

in particular. This is correct." ("On the Task and Methods of 'New Testament Theology,'" in *The Nature of New Testament Theology*, ed. Robert Morgan (Naperville Ill.: Alec R. Allenson, 1973). See BIBLICAL THEOLOGY; REDACTION CRITICISM; THEOLOGICAL INTERPRETATION.

Writings, The. See **Hagiographa.**

Yahwist. See **J (Yahwist).**

Zadokite Document (or Fragments), The. See **Dead Sea Scrolls.**

Zimmerli, Walther (1907–1983) was born in Schiers, Switzerland, the son of the director of a Protestant academy; he studied theology in Zurich, Berlin, and Göttingen. While serving pastorates in Aarburg, Switzerland (1933–35) and Zurich (1935–50), he pursued his interest in the HB, publishing studies on Genesis and Trito-Isaiah. He was called to Göttingen in 1950, where he remained until his death, having retired in 1975. Zimmerli viewed the self-revelation of the divine name at the time of the exodus as the beginning of God's covenant with Israel and as the center of any reformulation of the theology of the OLD TESTAMENT and any sketch of Israel's religious history. In the themes of word and act, of promise and fulfillment, Zimmerli found continuity between the Testaments. With G. VON RAD and MARTIN NOTH, et al., Zimmerli founded the *Biblischer Kommentar*. He was intensely interested in the founding of the state of Israel and early called for Jewish-Christian dialogue. Major works available in English translation are his two-volume magnum opus on Ezekiel (Hermeneia series, 1979–83), *The Law and the Prophets: A Study of the Meaning of the Old Testament* (New York: Harper Torchbooks, 1963), and *Old Testament Theology in Outline* (Atlanta: John Knox Press, 1978).

Zweiquellentheorie (Ger: two-source theory). See **Two Source Hypothesis.**

ABBREVIATIONS IN TEXTUAL CRITICISM

(Plus Common Latin Words and Phrases)

A:	Codex Alexandrinus	C., cum:	with
a.: ante:	before	ca.:	about
ab origine:	from the origin	cet., cett.:	another, others
ab ovo:	from the beginning	cf.:	compare
ad:	at, to	cj.:	conjecture
add., addit:	add(s)	cod., codd.:	codex, codices
addendum:	something to be added	col.:	column(s)
ad infinitum:	to infinity	comm.:	commentary
ad loc.:	at the passage discussed	comma:	phrase
		cont.:	continued
a fortiori:	with stronger reason	cor., corr.:	corrector, corrected
Agnus Dei:	Lamb of God	*cum grano salis:*	with a grain of salt
al.:	other(s)	D:	Codex Bezae
aliq.:	other form		Cantabrigiensis; D^P:
al. omn.:	all others		Codex Claromontanus
al. pc.:	a few others		
al. pb.:	very many others	def.:	is lacking; *also:*
alt.:	the other (alternate)		definition
ante:	before	de facto:	in reality
ap., apud:	with, according to	del.:	effaced
a posteriori:	to argue from effect to cause	de novo:	anew
		de profundis:	out of the depths
app.:	apparatus	desideratum:	a thing desired
append.:	appendix	deus ex	
a priori:	to argue from cause to effect	machina:	a god out of a machine
		E:	Codex Basiliensis; E^a:
argumentum e silentio:	an argument from silence		Codex Laudianus
		e:	the Gospels
aut:	or	e, ex:	from
B:	Codex Vaticanus	ead.:	likewise
bis:	twice	ed., eds.:	edition/editor(s)
C:	Codex Ephraemi Rescriptus	editio princeps:	first edition
		e.g.:	for example

ergo:	therefore	novum:	a new thing
err.:	error	numerus:	number
et, etiam:	also	*obeliscus:*	obelisk
et al.:	and others	*occidentalis:*	Western
evl.:	Gospel	om.:	omit
exc.:	except	omn.:	all
fere:	almost	Opt.:	the best
fin.:	the end	P.:	papyrus
fluct.:	varies	p.:	post (after) *or* page
fol., foll.:	leaf, leaves	par(s).:	parallel(s) *or*
fort., fortasse:	perhaps, probably		paragraph(s)
frg. (frgg.):	fragment(s)	*pari passu:*	side by side
hab.:	has	partim:	in part, some
hapaxl.:	hapaxlegomenon	passim:	everywhere
hiat.:	is lacking	patr.:	the church fathers
hoc:	this	pauc., pc.:	few
ibid., id., idem:	the same	permulti:	very many
i.e.:	that is, in other words	petitio principii:	to beg the question
infra:	below	pl., pler.:	very many
in limine:	at the threshold	plur.:	plurality
in ovo:	in the inception	plus:	more
int., interp.:	interpretation	pon.:	put, place
inter alia:	among others	post:	after
in toto:	entirely	pr.:	first occurrence
in vacuo:	in empty space	praem.:	precede(s)
ipsissima mens:	the very mind	punct.:	punctuation
ipsissima verba:	the very words	q.v.:	which see (that is,
ipsissima vox:	the very voice		see the preceding
ipso facto:	obvious from the facts		item)
item:	thus	recto:	right-hand page
κτλ:	and so forth	redivivus:	returned to life
l:	Lectionary	*regula fidei:*	rule of faith
leg.:	it reads	ret., rell.:	remaining
loc.:	place	S:	Codex Sinaiticus
LXX:	Septuagint	saec.:	century
magnum opus:	a great work	schol.:	scholion
mal:	badly	scil.:	that is to say, to wit
matres lectionis:	consonants used to rep-	sec.:	second occurrence
	resent vowel sounds	sec., secundum:	according to
metri causa:	for the sake of meter	sed:	but
mg.:	margin	sem.:	only one
MS (MSS):	manuscript(s)	seq.:	the next
MT *or* Mas.:	Masoretic Text	sic:	thus, note
mu., mutt.:	many	*siglum (a):*	sign(s)
mutatis	with necessary changes	sim.:	similar
mutandis:	being made (not	sine:	without
	normally	sine qua non:	without which not
	abbreviated)		(an indispensable
non:	not		condition)
nonnul.:	some	sive . . . sive:	either . . . or

solum:	alone	ut:	as
sq., sqq.:	the next verse(s)	V. *or* vide:	see
sui generis:	of its own kind	v. *or* vs. (vv. *or* vss.):	verse(s)
supp., suppl.:	supply		
supra:	above	vacat:	absent
s. v.: *sub voce, sub verbo:*	under the entry	var.:	variant reading
		vers.:	version
tant., tantum:	this alone	verso:	left-hand page
tert.:	third	vid.:	apparently
tertium non datur:	a third does not exist	vide:	see
		v. l.:	variant reading
tertium quid:	a third something	vol.	volume
tot.:	all	VT:	Old Testament
t.t.: *terminus technicus:*	technical term	W:	Codex Washingtonianus or Freer Gospels (q.v.)
unice:	alone, solely		
usque:	as far as		

ABBREVIATIONS
OF SELECTED WORKS

Commonly cited in biblical studies according to the standard adopted by *The SBL Handbook of Style: For Ancient Near Eastern, Biblical, and Early Christian Studies,* ed. Patrick H. Alexander et al. (Peabody, Mass.: Hendrickson, 1999).

Scriptures: Canonical, Deutero- and Extracanonical Texts

Hebrew Bible/Old Testament

Gen	Genesis	Eccl (or Qoh)	Ecclesiastes (or Qoheleth)
Exod	Exodus	Song or (Cant)	Song of Songs (Song of Solomon, or Canticles)
Lev	Leviticus	Isa	Isaiah
Num	Numbers	Jer	Jeremiah
Deut	Deuteronomy	Lam	Lamentations
Josh	Joshua	Ezek	Ezekiel
Judg	Judges	Dan	Daniel
Ruth	Ruth	Hos	Hosea
1–2 Sam	1–2 Samuel	Joel	Joel
1–2 Kgdms	1–2 Kingdoms (LXX)	Amos	Amos
		Obad	Obadiah
1–2 Kgs	1–2 Kings	Jonah	Jonah
3–4 Kgdms	3–4 Kingdoms (LXX)	Mic	Micah
		Nah	Nahum
1–2 Chr	1–2 Chronicles	Hab	Habakkuk
Ezra	Ezra	Job	Job
Neh	Nehemiah	Ps/Pss	Psalms
Esth	Esther	Prov	Proverbs

Zeph	Zephaniah	Zech	Zechariah
Hag	Haggai	Mal	Malachi

New Testament

Matt	Matthew	1–2 Thess	1–2 Thessalonians
Mark	Mark	1–2 Tim	1–2 Timothy
Luke	Luke	Titus	Titus
John	John	Phlm	Philemon
Acts	Acts	Heb	Hebrews
Rom	Romans	Jas	James
1–2 Cor	1–2 Corinthians	1–2 Pet	1–2 Peter
Gal	Galatians	1–2–3 John	1–2–3 John
Eph	Ephesians	Jude	Jude
Phil	Philippians	Rev	Revelation
Col	Colossians		

Apocrypha/Deuterocanonical Books and Septuagint(*)

Bar	Baruch	Jdt	Judith
Add Dan	Additions to Daniel	1–2 Macc	1–2 Maccabees
		3–4 Macc	3–4 Maccabees(*)
Pr Azar	Prayer of Azariah	Pr Man	Prayer of Manasseh
Bel	Bel and the Dragon	Ps 151	Psalm 151(*)
		Sir	Sirach/Ecclesiasticus
Sg Three	Song of the Three Young Men	Tob	Tobit
		Wis	Wisdom of Solomon
Sus	Susanna		
1–2 Esd	1–2 Esdras		
Add Esth	Additions to Esther		
Ep Jer	Epistle of Jeremiah		

Selected Dead Sea Scrolls

CD	*Damascus Document* (Cairo Genizah copy)
1Qap Genar	*Genesis Apocryphon*
1QH	*Thanksgiving Hymns*
1QIs^a	Isaiah (pub. by ASOR)
1QIs^b	Isaiah (pub. by Hebrew University, Jerusalem)
1QM	*War Scroll*
1QpHab	*Pesher Habakkuk*
1QS	*Rule of the Community (Manual of Discipline)*
1QSa	*Rule of the Congregation* (Appendix a to 1QS)
1QSb	*Rule of the Blessings* (Appendix b to 1QS)

3Q15	*Copper Scroll*
4QBeat	*Beatitudes*
4QFlor	*Florilegium (Midrash on Eschatology*[a]*)*
4QPrNab ar	*Prayer of Nabonidus*
11QPs[a]	*Psalm Scroll*[a]
11QMelch	*Melchizedek*
11QtgJob	*Targum of Job*
11QTa	*Temple Scroll*

Apostolic Fathers

Barn.	*Barnabas*
1–2 Clem.	*1–2 Clement*
Did.	*Didache*
Diogn.	*Diognetus*
Herm. *Mand.*	Shepherd of Hermas, *Mandate*
Herm. *Sim.*	Shepherd of Hermas, *Similitude*
Herm. *Vis.*	Shepherd of Hermas, *Vision*
Ign. *Eph.*	Ignatius, *To the Ephesians*
Ign. *Magn.*	Ignatius, *To the Magnesians*
Ign. *Smyrn.*	Ignatius, *To the Smyrnaeans*
Ign. *Phld.*	Ignatius, *To the Philadelphians*
Ign. *Rom.*	Ignatius, *To the Romans*
Ign. *Pol.*	Ignatius, *To Polycarp*
Ign. *Trall.*	Ignatius, *To the Trallians*
Mart. *Pol.*	*Martydom of Polycarp*
Pol. *Phil.*	Polycarp, *To the Philippians*

New Testament Apocrypha (Apocryphal NT) and Pseudepigrapha

Acts Andr.	*Acts of Andrew*
Acts Andr. Mth.	*Acts of Andrew and Matthias*
Acts Andr. Paul	*Acts of Andrew and Paul*
Acts Barn.	*Acts of Barnabas*
Acts Jas.	*Acts of James the Great*
Acts John	*Acts of John*
Acts John Pro.	*Acts of John (by Prochorus)*
Acts Paul	*Acts of Paul*
Acts Peter	*Acts of Peter*
Acts Pet. (Slav.)	*Acts of Peter (Slavonic)*
Acts Pet. Andr.	*Acts of Peter and Andrew*
Acts Pet. Paul	*Acts of Peter and Paul*
Acts Phil	*Acts of Philip*
Acts Phil. (Syr.)	*Acts of Philip (Syriac)*
Acts Pil.	*Acts of Pilate*
Acts Thad.	*Acts of Thaddaeus*
Acts Thom.	*Acts of Thomas*

Apoc. Pet.	*Apocalypse of Peter*
Ap. John	*Apocryphon of John*
Apoc. Dosith.	*Apocalypse of Dositheus*
Apoc. Messos	*Apocalypse of Messos*
Apoc. Thom.	*Apocalypse of Thomas*
Apoc. Vir.	*Apocalypse of the Virgin*
(Apocr.) Ep. Tit.	*Apocryphal Epistle of Titus*
(Apocr.) Gos. John	*Apocryphal Gospel of John*
Apos. Con.	*Apostolic Constitutions and Canons*
Ps.-Abd.	*Apostolic History of Pseudo-Abdias*
(Arab.) Gos. Inf.	*Arabic Gospel of the Infancy*
(Arm.) Gos. Inf	*Armenian Gospel of the Infancy*
Asc. Jas.	*Ascent of James*
Assum. Vir.	*Assumption of the Virgin*
Bk. Bart.	*Book of the Resurrection of Christ by Bartholomew the Apostle*
Bk. Elch.	*Book Elchasai*
Cerinthus	*Cerinthus*
3 Cor.	*3 Corinthians*
Ep. Alex.	*Epistle to the Alexandrians*
Ep. Apos.	*Epistle of the Apostles*
Ep. Chr. Abg.	*Epistles of Christ and Abgar*
Ep. Chr. Heav.	*Epistle of Christ from Heaven*
Ep. Lao.	*Epistle to the Laodiceans*
Ep. Lent.	*Epistle of Lentulus*
Ep. Paul Sen.	*Epistles of Paul and Seneca*
Gos. Barn.	*Gospel of Barnabas*
Gos. Bart.	*Gospel of Bartholomew*
Gos. Bas.	*Gospel of Basilides*
Gos. Bir. Mary	*Gospel of the Birth of Mary*
Gos. Eb.	*Gospel of the Ebionites*
Gos. Eg.	*Gospel of the Egyptians*
Gos. Eve	*Gospel of Eve*
Gos. Gam.	*Gospel of Gamaliel*
Gos. Heb.	*Gospel According to the Hebrews*
Gos. Marcion	*Gospel of Marcion*
Gos. Mary	*Gospel of Mary*
Gos. Naass.	*Gospel of the Naassenes*
Gos. Naz.	*Gospel of the Nazarenes*
Gos. Nic.	*Gospel of Nicodemus*
Gos. Pet.	*Gospel of Peter*
Ps.-Mt.	*Gospel of Pseudo-Matthew*
Gos. Thom.	*Gospel of Thomas*
Gos. Trad. Mth.	*Gospel and Traditions of Matthias*
Hist. Jos. Carp.	*History of Joseph the Carpenter*
Hymn Dance	*Hymn of the Dance*
Hymn Pearl	*Hymn of the Pearl*
Inf. Gos. Thom.	*Infancy Gospel of Thomas*
Inf. Gos.	*Infancy Gospels*
Mart. Bart.	*Martyrdom of Bartholomew*

Mart. Mt.	Martyrdom of Matthew
Mart. Paul	Martyrdom of Paul
Mart. Pet.	Martyrdom of Peter
Mart. Pet. Paul	Martyrdom of Peter and Paul
Mart. Phil.	Martyrdom of Philip
Melkon	Melkon
Mem. Apos.	Memoria of Apostles
Pre. Pet.	Preaching of Peter
Prot. Jas.	Protevangelium of James
Ps.-Clem.	Pseudo-Clementines
Rev. Steph.	Revelation of Stephen
Sec. Gos. Mk.	Secret Gospel of Mark
Vis. Paul	Vision of Paul

Orders and Tractates in the Mishnah and Related Literature

ABBREV. (SBL)	NAME (SBL ACADEMIC TRANSLITERATION)	COMMON ALTERNATE SPELLING	SBL GENERAL PURPOSE TRANSLITERATION
ʿAbod. Zar.	ʿAboda Zarah	Abodah Zarah	Avodah Zarah
ʾAbot	ʾAbot	Aboth	Avot
ʿArak.	ʿArakin	Arakhin	Arakhin
B. Bat.	Baba Batra	Baba Bathra	Bava Batra
B. Meṣiʿa	Baba Meṣiʿa	Baba Mezia	Bava Metziʾa
B. Qam.	Baba Qamma	Baba Kamma	Bava Qamma
Bek.	Bekorot	Bekoroth	Bekhorot
Ber.	Berakot	Berakoth	Berakhot
Beṣah	Beṣah (= Yom Ṭob)	Bezah	Betzah (= Yom Tov)
Bik.	Bikkurim	Bikkurim	Bikkurim
Demai	Demai	Demai	Demai
ʿErub.	ʿErubin	Erubin	Eruvin
ʿEd.	ʿEduyyot	Eduyyoth	Eduyyot
Giṭ.	Giṭṭin	Gittin	Gittin
Ḥag.	Ḥagigah	Hagigah	Hagigah
Ḥal.	Ḥallah	Hallah	Hallah
Hor.	Horayot	Horayoth	Horayot
Ḥul.	Ḥullin	Hullin	Hullin
Kelim	Kelim	Kelim	Kelim
Ker.	Kerithot	Kerithoth	Keritot
Ketub.	Ketubbot	Kethuboth	Ketubbot
Kil.	Kilʾayim	Kilayim	Kilʾayim
Maʿaś.	Maʿaśerot	Maaseroth	Maʾaserot
Maʿaś. Š.	Maʿaśer Šeni	Masseroth Seni	Maʾaser Sheni
Mak.	Makkot	Makkoth	Makkot
Makš.	Makširin	Makshirin	Makhshirin
Meg.	Megillah	Megillah	Megillah

Meʿil	Meʿilah	Meilah	Me'ilah
Menaḥ.	Menahot	Menahoth	Menahot
Mid.	Middot	Middoth	Middot
Miqw.	Miqwaʾot	Mikwaoth	Mikwa'ot
Moʾed	Moʾed	Moed	Mo'ed
Moʾed Qaṭ.	Moʾed Qaṭan	Moed Katan	Mo'ed Qatan
Naš.	Našim	Nashim	Nashim
Naz.	Nazir	Nazir	Nazir
Ned.	Nedarim	Nedarim	Nedarim
Neg.	Negaʿim	Negaim	Nega'im
Nez.	Neziqin	Nezikin	Neziqin
Nid.	Niddah	Niddah	Niddah
ʾOhal.	ʾOhalot	Ohaloth	Ohalot
ʿOr.	ʿOrlah	Orlah	Orlah
Parah	Parah	Parah	Parah
Peʾah	Peʾah	Peah	Pe'ah
Pesaḥ.	Pesahim	Pesahim	Pesahim
Qinnim	Qinnim	Kinnim	Qinnim
Qidd.	Qiddušin	Kiddushin	Qiddushin
Qod.	Qodašim	Kodashim	Qodashim
Roš Haš.	Roš Haššanah	Rosh Hashanah	Rosh HaShanah
Sanh.	Sanhedrin	Sanhedrin	Sanhedrin
Šabb.	Šabbat	Shabbath	Shabbat
Šeb.	Šebiʿit	Shebi'ith	Shevi'it
Šebu.	Šebuʿot	Shebuoth	Shevu'ot
Seder	Seder	Seder	Seder
Šeqal.	Šeqalim	Shekalim	Sheqalim
Soṭah	Soṭah	Sota	Sotah
Sukkah	Sukkha	Sukkah	Sukkah
Taʿan.	Taʿanit	Taanith	Ta'anit
Tamid	Tamid	Tamid	Tamid
Tem.	Temurah	Temurah	Temurah
Ter.	Terumot	Terumoth	Terumot
Ṭehar.	Ṭeharot	Teharoth	Teharot
Ṭ. Yom	Ṭebul Yom	Tebul Yom	Tevul Yom
ʿUq.	ʿUqṣin	Ukzin	Uqtzin
Yad.	Yadayim	Yadayim	Yadayim
Yebam.	Yebamot	Yebamoth	Yevamot
Yoma	Yoma (= Kippurim)	Yoma	Yoma
Zabim	Zabim	Zabim	Zavim
Zebaḥ.	Zebahim	Zebahim	Zevahim
Zera.	Zeraʿim	Zeraim	Zera'im

Note: Since these names are also used for tractates in the Tosepta (Tosefta), Babylonian Talmud, and the Jerusalem Talmud, they are often preceded by abbreviations designating these works, such as Mish., M., or m. for Mishnah; Tos., T., or t. for Tosepta; Bab. Talm., Bab., B.T., or b. for Babylonian Talmud; and, Jer Talm., Jer, or y. for Jerusalem Talmud.

PERIODICALS, REFERENCE WORKS,
SERIALS, AND SELECTED BOOKS

A *or* Aq.	Aquila
AAA	Annals of Archaeology and Anthropology
AARDS	American Academy of Religion Dissertation Series
AASOR	Annual of the American Schools of Oriental Research
AB	Anchor Bible
ABD	*Anchor Bible Dictionary*
ABQ	*American Baptist Quarterly*
ABR	*Australian Biblical Review*
ABW	*Archaeology in the Biblical World*
ACCS	Ancient Christian Commentary on Scripture
ACNT	Augsburg Commentaries on the New Testament
ACW	Ancient Christian Writers. 1946–
Adv haer	Irenaeus, *Adversus haereses*
AEL	*Ancient Egyptian Literature*
AevTh	*Abhandlungen zur evangelischen Theologie*
AfO	*Archiv für Orientforschung*
AGSU / AGJU	Arbeiten zur Geschichte des (Spätjudentums) antiken Judentums und des Urchristentums
AJA	*American Journal of Archaeology*
AJBI	*Annual of the Japanese Biblical Institute*
AJSL	*American Journal of Semitic Languages and Literature*
AJSR	*Association for Jewish Studies Review*
AJT	*American Journal of Theology*
AJT	*Asian Journal of Theology*
AnBib	Analecta Biblica
ANEP	*The Ancient Near East in Pictures* (ed. Pritchard, 3rd ed., 1969)
ANET	*Ancient Near Eastern Texts* (ed. Pritchard, 3rd ed., 1969)
ANF	*Ante-Nicene Fathers*
AnOr	Analecta Orientalia
ANQ	*Andover Newton Quarterly*
Ant	Josephus, *Antiquities*
ANTC	Abingdon New Testament Commentaries
AO	*Der Alte Orient*
AOT	*The Apocryphal Old Testament* (ed. Sparks, 1984)
Apoc.	Apocrypha
APOT	*The Apocrypha and Pseudepigrapha of the Old Testament* (ed. R. H. Charles, 1913)
ARE	*Ancient Records of Egypt* (ed. Breasted, 1905–7)
ASNU	Acta seminarii neotestamentici upsaliensis
ASOR	American Schools of Oriental Research
ASTI	*Annual of the Swedish Theological Institute*
ASV	American Standard Version
ATA	Alttestamentliche Abhandlungen
ATD	Das Alte Testament Deutsch
AThR	*Anglican Theological Review*
AV	Authorized Version (King James Version)

B&R	*Books and Religion*
BA	*Biblical Archaeologist*
BAGD	Bauer, W., W. F. Arndt, F. W. Gingrich, and F. W. Danker, *Greek-English Lexicon of the New Testament and Other Early Christian Literature*. 2nd ed., 1979
BAR	*Biblical Archaeology Review*
BASOR	*Bulletin of the American Schools of Oriental Research*
BBB	Bonner biblische Beiträge
BDAG	Bauer, W., F. W. Danker, W. F. Arndt, and F. W. Gingrich, *Greek-English Lexicon of the New Testament and Other Early Christian Literature*. 3rd ed., 1999
BDB	Brown-Driver-Briggs, *A Hebrew and English Lexicon of the Old Testament*. 1907
BDF	Blass-Debrunner-Funk, *A Greek Grammar of the New Testament and Other Early Christian Literature*. 1961
BEvT	Beiträge zur evangelischen Theologie
BGBE	Beiträge zur Geschichte der Biblischen Exegese
BGBH	Beiträge zur Geschichte der Biblischen Hermeneutik
BH (S) or (K)	*Biblia Hebraica (Stuttgartensia)* or (R. Kittel)
BHT	Beiträge zur historischen Theologie
Bib	*Biblica*
Bib. Ant.	Ps Philo, *Biblical Antiquities*
BibS (F or N)	Biblische Studien (Freiburg, 1895–; Neukirchen, 1951–)
BiLeb	*Bibel und Leben*
BiT	*The Bible Translator*
BJRL	*Bulletin of the John Rylands University Library of Manchester*
BK	*Bibel und Kirche*
BKAT	Biblischer Kommentar: Altes Testament
BNTC	Black's New Testament Commentaries
BO	*Bibliotheca Orientalis*
BPCI	Biblical Perspectives on Current Issues
BR	*Biblical Research*
BRL	*Biblisches Reallexikon*
BRev	*Bible Review*
BSac	Bibliotheca Sacra
BSMS	*Bulletin of the Society of Mesopotamian Studies*
BSNA	Biblical Scholarship in North America
BSOAS	*Bulletin of the School of Oriental (and African) Studies*
BT	Babylonian Talmud
BT	*The Bible Translator*
BTB	*Biblical Theology Bulletin*
BU	Biblische Untersuchungen
BWA(N)T	Beiträge zur Wissenschaft vom Alten (und Neuen) Testament
BZ	*Biblische Zeitschrift*
BZAW	Beihefte zur Zeitschrift für die alttestamentliche Wissenschaft
BZNW	Beihefte zur Zeitschrift für die neutestamentliche Wissenschaft
CAH	Cambridge Ancient History
CAT	Commentaire de L'Ancien Testament
CBC	Cambridge Bible Commentary

CBQ (MS)	*Catholic Biblical Quarterly* (Monograph Series)
CBW	*Cities of the Biblical World*
CDC (or CD)	Zadokite Document (Cairo Genizah Document), Damascus Document
CEV	Contemporary English Version
CG	Coptic Gnostic Library
CGTC	Cambridge Greek Testament Commentary
CHB	*Cambridge History of the Bible* (ed. Ackroydt et al., 1967–70)
Chr.Cent.	*Christian Century*
ClassBul	*Classical Bulletin*
CNT	Commentaire du Nouveau Testament
Comm	*Communio*
CP	*Classical Philology*
CPT	Cambridge Patristic Texts
CRBR	*Critical Review of Books in Religion*
CR:BS	Currents in Research: Biblical Studies
CRINT	Compendia rerum iudaicarum ad Novum Testamentum
D	Deuteronomic Source
Di	*Dialog*
Did.	*Didache*
DJD	Discoveries in the Judean Desert
DSS	Dead Sea Scrolls
E	Elohist Source
EBib	*Etudes bibliques*
EDNT	*Exegetical Dictionary of the New Testament* (ed. H. Baltz et al., 1990–93).
EEC	*Encyclopedia of Early Christianity* (ed. Ferguson, 2nd ed., 1990)
EHAT	Exegetisches Handbuch zum Alten Testament
EKKNT	Evangelisch-katholischer Kommentar zum Neuen Testament
EKL	*Evangelisches Kirchenlexikon* (ed. Fahlbusch et al., 3rd ed., 1985–96)
Elenchus	*Elenchus bibliographicus biblicus of Biblica*
Enc	*Encounter*
EnchBib	*Enchiridion biblicum*
EncJud	*Encyclopaedia Judaica*
Ep. Arist.	*Epistle of Aristeas*
ErIsr	*Eretz-Israel: Archaeological, Historical, and Geographical Studies*
ExpTim	*Expository Times*
Euseb.	Eusebius
EvK	Evangelische Kommentare
EvT	*Evangelische Theologie*
EWNT	*Exegetisches Wörterbuch zum Neuen Testament*
ExpB	Expositor's Bible
ExpTim	*Expository Times*
FAT	Forschungen zum Alten Testament
FB	Forschung zur Bibel
FFNT	Foundations and Facets: New Testament
FOTL	Forms of the Old Testament Literature
FRLANT	Forschungen zur Religion und Literatur des Alten und Neuen Testaments

GAT	Grundrisse zum Alten Testament
GBS	Guides to Biblical Scholarship
GKB	Gesenius-Kautzsch-Bergsträsser, *Hebräische Grammatik*
GKC	*Gesenius' Hebrew Grammar*, ed. E. Kautzsch, trans. A. E. Cowley
GNB	Good News Bible
GNT	Grundrisse zum Neuen Testament
GOODSPEED	*The Complete Bible: An American Translation*, E. J. Goodspeed
GTT	*Gereformeerd theologisch Tijdschrift*
HAT	Handbuch zum Alten Testament
HBC	*HarperCollins Bible Commentary* (ed. Mays et al., 1988)
HBD	*Harper's Bible Dictionary* (ed. Achtemeier et al., 2nd ed. 1996)
HBK	Herders Bibelkommentar
HB/OT	*Hebrew Bible, Old Testament: The History of Its Interpretation* (ed. Saebø, 1996)
HBT	*Horizons in Biblical Theology*
HDB	Hastings' *Dictionary of the Bible* (1898–1904)
HDR	Harvard Dissertations in Religion
Herm. (Man., Sim., Vis.)	*The Shepherd of Hermas* (Mandates; Similitudes; Visions)
Hev	Nahal Hever caves or texts
HHMBI	*Historical Handbook of Major Biblical Interpreters*
HJTM	Harvard Judaic Texts and Monographs
HKAT	Handkommentar zum Alten Testament
HKNT	Handkommentar zum Neuen Testament
HNT	Handbuch zum Neuen Testament
HNTC	Harper's New Testament Commentaries
HNTR	*History of New Testament Research*
HR	*History of Religions*
HS	*Hebrew Studies*
HSM	Harvard Semitic Monographs
HSS	Harvard Semitic Studies
HTC	Herder's Theological Commentary on the New Testament
HTKNT	Herders theologischer Kommentar zum Neuen Testament
HTIBS	Historic Texts and Interpreters in Biblical Scholarship
HTR	*Harvard Theological Review*
HTS	Harvard Theological Studies
HUCA	*Hebrew Union College Annual*
IB	*Interpreter's Bible* (ed. Buttrick et al., 1951–57)
IBC	Interpretation: A Bible Commentary for Teaching and Preaching
ICC	International Critical Commentary
IDBSup	*The Interpreter's Dictionary of the Bible: Supplementary Volume*
IEJ	*Israel Exploration Journal*
Int	*Interpretation*
ISBE	*International Standard Bible Encyclopedia*
ISBL	Indiana Studies in Biblical Literature
ITQ	*Irish Theological Quarterly*
JAAR	*Journal of the American Academy of Religion*
JAOS	*Journal of the American Oriental Society*

Jerusalem Bible
Jerome Biblical Commentary
Journal of Biblical Literature
Jewish Bible Quarterly
Journal of Bible and Religion
Jerusalem Biblical Studies
Journal of Cuneiform Studies
Judean Desert Series
The Jewish Encyclopedia (ed. Singer, 1925)
Journal of Egyptian Archaeology
Journal of Ecumenical Studies
Journal of the Economic and Social History of the Orient
Journal of Feminist Studies in Religion
Johns Hopkins Near Eastern Studies
Journal of Near Eastern Studies
Journal of Northwest Semitic Languages
Josephus
Journal of Translation and Textlinguistics
Journal of Palestine Oriental Society
Jewish Publication Society
Jewish Quarterly Review
Journal of Religion
*Journal for the Study of Judaism in the Persian, Hellenistic, and
    Roman Periods*
Journal for the Study of the New Testament
Journal of the Society of Oriental Research (1917–32)
Journal for the Study of the Old Testament
Journal for the Study of the Pseudepigrapha
Jewish Studies Quarterly
Journal of Semitic Studies
Journal for the Scientific Study of Religion
Journal for Theology and the Church
Journal of Theological Studies
Judaica
Judaism
Kommentar zum Alten Testament
Kommentare und Beiträge zum Alten und Neuen Testament
Koehler-Baumgartner Hebrew Lexicon (2nd ed., 1958)
Kerygma und Dogma
Kritisch-exegetischer Kommentar über das Neue Testament
King James Version
Linguistica Biblica
Living Bible
Library of Biblical Studies
Library of Christian Classics
Loeb Classical Library
Library of Early Christianity
Lives of Jesus Series
Liddell-Scott-Jones, *A Greek-English Lexicon* (9th ed., 1996)

LTK	*Lexicon für Theologie und Kirche*
MLB	Modern Language Bible
MNTC	Moffatt New Testament Commentary
MOFFATT	*The New Testament: A New Translation,* James Moffatt
MTZ	*Münchener theologische Zeitschrift*
Mur	Wadi Murabba'ât caves or texts
NAB	New American Bible
NASB	New American Standard Bible
NAV	New American Version
NCB	New Century Bible
NCE	*New Catholic Encyclopedia*
NEAEHL	*The New Encyclopedia of Archaeological Excavations in the Holy Land*
NEB	New English Bible
Neot	*Neotestamentica*
NF	Neue Folge ("New Series")
NHC	Nag Hammadi Codices
NHS	Nag Hammadi Studies
NIB	*The New Interpreter's Bible*
NIBCNT	New International Biblical Commentary on the New Testament
NIBCOT	New International Biblical Commentary on the Old Testament
NIDB	*New International Dictionary of the Bible* (ed. Douglas and Tenney, 1987)
NIDNTT	*New International Dictionary of New Testament Theology*
NIGTC	New International Greek Testament Commentary
NIV	New International Version
NJB	New Jerusalem Bible
NJBC	*The New Jerome Biblical Commentary*
NJPS	*Tanakh: The Holy Scriptures: The New JPS Translation according to the Traditional Hebrew Text*
NKJV	New King James Version
NLT	New Living Translation
NovT (Sup)	*Novum Testamentum (Supplements)*
NPNF	*Nicene and Post-Nicene Fathers*
NRSV	New Revised Standard Version
NTA	*New Testament Abstracts*
NTAbh	Neutestamentliche Abhandlungen
NTD	Das Neue Testament Deutsch
NTG	New Testament Guides
NTL	New Testament Library
NTS	*New Testament Studies*
NTT	*Nieuw theologisch Tijdschrift*
NTTS	New Testament Tools and Studies
OBT	Overtures to Biblical Theology
ODCC	*The Oxford Dictionary of the Christian Church*
OECS	Oxford Early Christian Studies
OECT	Oxford Early Christian Texts
OED	Oxford English Dictionary
OLZ	*Orientalistische Literaturzeitung*

Or	*Orientalia*
OTA	*Old Testament Abstracts*
OTE	*Old Testament Essays*
OTG	Old Testament Guides
OTL	Old Testament Library
OTP	*Old Testament Pseudepigrapha* (ed. Charlesworth, 1983)
OTS	*Old Testament Studies*
PEQ	*Palestine Exploration Quarterly*
PG	Patrologia graeca (ed. J.-P. Migne, 1857–86)
PHILLIPS	*The New Testament in Modern English*, J. B. Phillips
PL	Patrologia latina (ed. J.-P. Migne, 1844–64)
PNTC	Pelican New Testament Commentaries
Pseudep.	Pseudepigrapha
PW (*RKA*)	Pauly-Wissowa, *Realenzyklopädie der classischen Altertumswissenschaft* (new edition, 1980)
Q	Quelle (Source) (q.v.) or Qumran
RAC	*Reallexikon für Antike und Christentum* (ed. Klauser et al., 1950–)
RB	*Revue biblique*
REB	Revised English Bible
RelSRev	*Religious Studies Review*
RelStTh	*Religious Studies and Theology*
RevExp	*Review and Expositor*
RevQ	*Revue de Qumran*
RevScRel	*Revue des sciences religieuses*
RGG[1–3]	*Religion in Geschichte und Gegenwart* (1st–3rd ed.)
RHR	*Revue de l'histoire des religions*
RinL	*Religion in Life*
RNT	Regensburger Neues Testament
RR	*Review of Religion*
RSV	Revised Standard Version
RV	Revised Version
SAC	Studies in Antiquity and Christianity
SANT	Studien zum Alten und Neuen Testaments
SBA	Studies in Biblical Archaeology
SBL	Society of Biblical Literature
SBLABS	SBL Archaeology and Biblical Studies
SBLAS	SBL Aramaic Studies
SBLASP	SBL Abstracts and Seminar Papers
SBLBAC	SBL The Bible in American Culture
SBLBMI	SBL The Bible and Its Modern Interpreters
SBLBSNA	SBL Biblical Scholarship in North America
SBLDS	SBL Dissertation Series
SBLEJL	SBL Early Judaism and Its Literature
SBLMas	SBL Masoretic Studies
SBLMS	SBL Monograph Series
SBLNTGF	SBL The New Testament in the Greek Fathers
SBLRBS	SBL Resources for Biblical Study
SBLSBS	SBL Sources for Biblical Study
SBLSCS	SBL Septuagint and Cognate Studies

SBLSP	*SBL Seminar Papers*
SBLSS	SBL Semeia Studies
SBLTT	SBL Texts and Translations
SBLWAW	SBL Writings of the Ancient World
SBS	Stuttgarter Bibelstudien
SBT	Studies in Biblical Theology
SE	*Studia evangelica*
Sem	*Semitica*
Semeia	*Semeia*
SHANE	Studies in the History and Culture of the Ancient Near East
SJ	Studia judaica
SJCA	Studies in Judaism and Christianity in Antiquity
SJOT	*Scandinavian Journal of the Old Testament*
SJT	*Scottish Journal of Theology*
SNT	Studium zum Neuen Testament
SNTSMS	Society for New Testament Studies Monograph Series
SNTSU	Studien zum Neuen Testament and seiner Umwelt
SOTI	Studies in Old Testament Interpretation
SOTSMS	Society for Old Testament Studies Monograph Series
SP	Sacra pagina
SPhilo	*Studia philonica*
SPIB	Scripta Pontificii Instituti Biblici
SSEJC	*Studies in Early Judaism and Christianity*
SSS	Semitic Study Series
SStLL	Studies in Semitic Language and Linguistics
StABH	Studies in American Biblical Hermeneutics
STDJ	*Studies on the Texts of the Desert of Judah*
SThZ	*Schweizerische theologische Zeitschrift*
StPatr	Studia patristica
StPB	Studia post-biblica
Str-B	Strack-Billerbeck, *Kommentar zum Neuen Testament aus Talmud und Midrash*
StudBib	Studia Biblica
StudNeot	Studia neotestamentica
StZ	Stimmen der Zeit
SUNT	Studien zur Umwelt des Neuen Testament
SVTP	Studia in Veteris Testamenti pseudepigraphica
SWBA	Social World of Biblical Antiquity
SWR	Studies in Women and Religion
Symm.	Symmachus (q.v.)
StZ	Stimmen der Zeit
T&K	Texte und Kontexte
TANZ	Texte und Arbeiten zum neutestamentlichen Zeitalter
TAzB	Texte und Arbeiten zur Bibel
TB	Theologische Bücherei
TBC	Torch Bible Commentaries
TBT	*The Bible Today*
TD	*Theology Digest*

TDNT	*Theological Dictionary of the New Testament* (ed. G. Kittel and Friedrich; trans. Bromiley, 1964–76)
TDOT	*Theological Dictionary of the Old Testament* (ed. Botterwick and Ringgren; trans. Willis et al., 1974–)
TEV	Today's English Version (= *Good News for Modern Man*)
Text	*Textus*
Theo	*Theologika*
Theod.	Theodotion
THKNT	Theologischer Handkommentar zum Neuen Testament
ThSt	*Theologische Studien*
ThT	*Theologisch Tijdschrift*
ThTo	*Theology Today*
TLNT	*Theological Lexicon of the New Testament* (ed. Spicq; trans. Ernest, 1994)
TLOT	*Theological Lexicon of the Old Testament* (ed. Jenni; trans. Biddle, 1997)
TLZ	*Theologische Literaturzeitung*
TNTC	Tyndale New Testament Commentaries
TQ	*Theologische Quartalschrift*
TRev	*Theologische Revue*
TRu	*Theologische Rundschau*
TS	*Theological Studies*
TS	Texts and Studies
TSK	*Theologische Studien und Kritiken*
TU	Texte und Untersuchungen zur Geschichte der altchristlichen Literatur
TUMSR	Trinity University Monograph Series in Religion
THWAT	*Theologisches Wörterbuch zum Alten Testament* (ed. Harris and Archer, 1980)
TWNT	*Theologisches Wörterbuch zum Neuen Testament* (ed. G. Kittel and Friedrich, 1932–79)
TZ	*Theologische Zeitschrift*
UF	*Ugarit-Forschungen*
UNT	Untersuchungen zum Neuen Testament
USQR	*Union Seminary Quarterly Review*
VC	*Vigiliae christianae*
VCaro	*Verbum caro*
VD	*Verbum domini*
VF	*Verkündigung und Forschung*
VS	*Verbum Salutie*
VT	*Vetus Testamentum*
VTSup	Supplements to Vetus Testamentum
Vulg. *or* Vg	Vulgate
WDB	*Westminster Dictionary of the Bible*
WEYMOUTH	*The New Testament in Modern Speech*, R. F. Weymouth
WHAB	*Westminster Historical Atlas of the Bible*
WMANT	Wissenschaftliche Monographien zum Alten und Neuen Testament

WO	*Die Welt des Orients*
YCS	Yale Classical Studies
YOSR	Yale Oriental Series, Researches
ZABR	*Zeitschrift für altorientalische und biblische Rechtgeschichte*
ZAC	*Zeitschrift für Antikes Christentum*
ZAH	*Zeitschrift für Althebräistik*
ZAW	*Zeitschrift für die alttestamentliche Wissenschaft*
ZDPV	*Zeitschrift des deutschen Palästina-Vereins*
ZB	Züricher Bibel
ZKG	*Zeitschrift für Kirchengeschichte*
ZNW	*Zeitschrift für neutestamentliche Wissenschaft*
ZS	*Zeitschrift für Semitistik und verwandte Giebete*
ZST	*Zeitschrift für systematische Theologie*
ZTK	*Zeitschrift für Theologie und Kirche*

MAJOR REFERENCE
WORKS CONSULTED

Anchor Bible Dictionary. 6 vols. Ed. by David Noel Freedman. New York: Doubleday, 1992. Abbrev.: *ABD.*

Berger, Klaus. *Exegese des Neuen Testaments.* Heidelberg: Quelle & Meyer, 1977.

Dictionary of Biblical Interpretation. 2 vols. Ed. by John H. Hayes. Nashville: Abingdon Press, 1999. Abbrev.: *DBI.*

Encyclopaedia Judaica, vols. 1–16. Jerusalem: Keter Publishing House, 1972.

Fokkema, D. W., and Elrud Künne-Ibsch. *Theories of Literature in the Twentieth Century: Structuralism, Marxism, Aesthetics of Reception, Semiotics.* London: C. Hurst & Co., 1977.

Garvin, Paul, ed. *A Prague School Reader on Esthetics, Literary Structure, and Style.* Washington: Georgetown University Press, 1969.

Lausberg, H. *Handbuch der literarischen Rhetorik.* Munich: Huebner Verlag, 1923^b.

Lewandowski, Theodor. *Linguistisches Wörterbuch.* Heidelberg: Quelle & Meyer, vol. 1, 1973; vols. 2 & 3, 1975.

Lexikon für Theologie und Kirche. 2nd ed. 11 vols. Ed. by Josef Höer and Karl Rahner. Freiburg: Herder Verlag, 1957–1967. Abbrev.: *LTK.*

The Oxford Dictionary of the Christian Church. 3rd ed. Ed. by F. L. Cross and E. A. Livingstone. London: Oxford University Press, 1997. Abbrev.: *ODCC.*

Reallexikon für Antike und Christentum. 8 vols. Ed. by Theodor Klauser et al. Stuttgart: Hiersemann Verlag, 1950–1972. Abbrev.: *RAC.*

Die Religion in Geschichte und Gegenwart. 2nd ed., 5 vols. Ed. by Hermann Gunkel and Leopold Zscharnack. Tübingn: J. C. B. Mohr (Paul Siebeck), 1927–1931. Abbrev.: *RGG*^{2}.

Ibid. 3rd ed. 6 vols. Ed. by Kurt Galling. Tübingen: J. C. B. Mohr (Paul Siebeck), 1957–1965. Abbrev.: *RGG*^{3}.

Routledge Encyclopedia of Philosophy. 10 vols. Ed. by Edward Craig. New York: Routledge & Kegan Paul, 1998.

The SBL Handbook of Style: For Ancient Near Eastern, Biblical, and Early Christian Studies. Ed. by Patrick H. Alexander et al. Peabody, Mass.: Hendrickson Publishers, 1999.

Theologische Realenzyklopädie. 28 vols. Ed. by Gerhard Krause and Gerhard Müller. New York: Walter de Gruyter, 1977–. Abbrev.: *TRE.*

DIAGRAM OF BIBLICAL INTERPRETATION

The diagram that follows provides a visual overview of the terms, methodologies, and interpretive approaches in the *Handbook*. It consists of horizontal rows (A-B-C) and vertical columns (1-2-3). The focus of row A is the biblical text itself as a center of a typical event of communication between an author or "sender" (who may make use of traditional materials, written or oral) and a receiver (the original receiver or subsequent interpreters). Rows B and C consists of selected terms, methodologies, and interpretive approaches organized in columns according to the aspect(s) of the text with which they are most concerned.

The chart is not perfect. Methods and approaches are complex and fluid, at times even antithetical, and they cannot be displayed with complete accuracy by a diagram. Nevertheless, the diagram offers an initial point of reference for study and reflection. Its advantages and shortcomings will become clearer as the methods themselves are more fully understood.

Columns: Three Questions and Three "Worlds"

The diagram's vertical columns depict (from left to right) three basic questions that have been addressed to the biblical text and their corresponding "worlds" of investigation.

1. *Whence? The World Behind the Text.* A first question inquires into the *historical origins* of a biblical text. Here the primary object of concern is the text's history of development, the person or persons who created it, and the communities and cultures in which they lived. The column is subdivided into "Sources" and "Historical Author or Sender" since virtually all biblical texts as we now have them incorporate earlier traditions, whether written or oral.

2. *What/What About? The World of the Text.* A second pair of questions inquires into the *content* of a biblical text, to *what the text says* and *what it means.* Here the primary object of study is the text itself as a grammatical, literary, and rhetorical unity.

3. *Whither? The World in Front of the Text.* A third question inquires into the *destination* of the text, to those who received and receive the text and seek to hear and understand it. Here the central concern is the interaction between text and the community of interpretation. The column is subdivided into "Historical Receiver" and "Interpreter" in order to distinguish between a text's first or original audience and its subsequent history of interpretation.

Rows: Examples and Methods

The diagram's horizontal rows provide (from top to bottom) illustrations and examples pertinent to each of the three "worlds" of the text and a list of methods and interpretive approaches.

A. *Event of Communication and Examples.* The diagram, we hope, mostly self-explanatory, though a few clarifications are called for. The symbols joining the Sender to the Text (>), and the Text to the Receiver (<) serve as reminders of the multifaceted connections (literary, cultural, social, political, religious, theological, etc.) that link biblical texts to their world of origin and to the world of their interpretation and use. The symbols also serve as reminders that a text always contains both more than (>) and less than (<) a speaker intends by his or her choice of words and than a hearer grasps on any single occasion. For further discussion, see INTERTEXTUALITY.

The circles marked "Implied Author" and "Implied Receiver" refer to literary perspectives intrinsic to the world of the text that can be distinguished from the historical sender and receiver. For further discussion, see RECEPTION THEORY and NARRATIVE CRITICISM.

B. *Methods and Interpretive Approaches.* The methods and interpretive approaches are arranged in chronological order according to their chief area(s) of interest. Dates indicate *approximate* times of origin, and (when more than one date appears) periods of major definition or renewal. Each method is placed in the "world" that best corresponds to its central area of concern, and shaded bars indicate the range of its interests.

C. *So What?* The last row addresses two comprehensive approaches to the Bible, HERMENEUTICS and THEOLOGICAL INTERPRETATIONS. These approaches are comprehensive in the sense that they are at least potentially interested in all three "worlds" of the text and because they can in principle make use of any or all of the other methods and approaches. They are also comprehensive because they are concerned with ultimate or final questions.

So, for example, the phrase, "The 'Whence' in God" indicates that theological interpretation is concerned with a text's *ultimate origin,* e.g., God's spirit or inspiration as the ultimate horizon and impetus of the text's human production. The phrase "The 'What/What About?' in God" indicates that theological interpretation is concerned with a text's *ultimate subject matter or concern,* e.g., God's identity, nature, and purposes for humankind and creation. Finally, the phrase "The 'Whither' in God" indicates that theological interpretation is concerned with the text's *ultimate destination,* e.g., the ever-renewed hearing of the text in God's spirit for the increase of faith and obedience and for the greater glory of God.